On Basque Politics
Conversations with Pete Cenarrusa

European Research Institute
Basque Politics Series, No. 1

On Basque Politics

Conversations
with
Pete Cenarrusa

Xabier Irujo Ametzaga
Pete T. Cenarrusa

European Research Institute
EURI

European Research Institute
Minority Politics Series, No. 1
Series Editor: Xabier Irujo

Cenarrusa Foundation for Basque Culture
712 Warm Springs Ave.
Boise, Idaho 83712 USA
http://cenarrusa.org/

First edition printed in Europe.
Second edition printed in the United States of America.

Cover and Series design © 2012 by EURI
Originally published as On Basque Politics: Conversations with Pete Cenarrusa © 2009 by EURI

First edition ISBN-13: 978-84-613-3965-5
Second edition ISBN-13: 978-0-9846900-1-5
Second edition ISBN-10: 0984690018

Table of Contents

Preface   13

To Be Basque in Idaho   15
On the People who Had Laws before They Had Kings   85
On the Rising of the First Basque Political Nationalism   117
Gernika, April 26, 1937   141
On the Cooperation between the Basque Secret Services
and the U.S. Office of Strategic Services   197
On the Long Spanish Dictatorship   213
The Basque Country, a Nation Politically Divided into
Two States   223
On Political Violence   243
On Ideologies and Political Formulas. Political Parties in
the Basque Country Today   295
On the Elections of March 1, 2009   327
On Language Policies   339
On Anti-terror Policies and their Collateral Damage   355
On the *Egunkaria* and *Batasuna* Cases   373
On Independence. The Basque Republic   387
Basque Nationalism and Europeism   423

Documental Appendix   439

Senate Joint Memorial No. 115. Boise, April 6, 1972
House Joint Memorial No. 14. Boise, March 13, 2002
House Joint Memorial No. 26. Boise, April 12, 2006
Senate Joint Memorial No. 14. Boise, March 26, 2012
Answer by 180 scholars to the article written by Keith
Johnson in the Wall Street Journal in November 2007

Selected Readings (in English)   463

"The Basque problem" has existed for those who have ruled the Iberian Peninsula since the days before Spain was a nation. Often described as the oldest homogeneous racial group in Europe, the Basques are closely knit and have resisted amalgamation since the first Roman legions descended upon them. They waited until the 11th century to embrace the "foreign" influence of Christianity, but when they did, they produced such illustrious Christians as St. Francis Xavier and St. Ignatius of Loyola.

(Dickson, Paul A., "Oppression in Spain", *Washington Post*, August 3, 1969. In, Church, Frank, "The Brave Spirit of the Basques and the Tyranny of their Persecutors." In, *Congressional Records. Proceedings and Debates of the 91st Congress, First Session*, Vol. 115, N° 135, Washington, Friday, August 8, 1969).

Pete T. Cenarrusa has served for fifty-two years, four months and eight days in the State of Idaho, nine two-year terms at the House of Representatives (1950-1967), in 1963, 1965 and 1967 as Speaker of the House, and nine four-year terms as Secretary of State (1967-2003) for the Republican Party. Cenarrusa has served longer than any elected official in Idaho. Source: Cenarrusa archive.

Preface

When, in the summer of 2005 I came to Idaho to head the Program for Basque studies at Boise State University, I found that the lack of books written in English on Basque issues posed one of the most serious challenges that a Basque professor at an American university had to face. This is a general problem, typical of virtually all areas of knowledge related to the history and culture of the Basque Country, but it is particularly acute in certain important fields, such as politics. The reader may find dozens of tasty Basque recipes translated into English or numerous articles and a wide range of books on violence in the Basque Country, but it is certainly difficult to find anything written in English on, say, the Basque elections, the side effects of anti-terrorism, and the various ideologies that currently collide in the lands of the Basques.

Speaking on this subject with Teresa Boucher, Chair of the Department of Modern Languages, she suggested that I should write a book for our students in the course on Contemporary Basque Politics. I should add that this conversation took place (as I have carefully noted in my agenda) on November 23, at six o'clock in the afternoon, while our Thanksgiving turkeys rested unattended in the fridge.

But covering a new area aimed at a student who has not been exposed to the daily ravages of the Basque politics of recent years or who does not have a knowledge of the history of this nation over the last 222 painful and grim years is not an easy task. However, shortly after our conversation an event occurred which gave me a good opportunity to shape the project that Teresa had proposed. The same day my fifth son Belatz was born, rumors started flowing about the impending announcement by ETA of a ceasefire and the subsequent start of a period of negotiation in which all Basques had placed our hopes for peace. The truce took effect on March 24, 2006, the sixth anniversary of my firstborn Enekoitz.

I knew at the time that the Idaho House of Representatives intended to adopt a new Memorial to back the peace process, calling for peace, democracy, and freedom for the Basque people in their struggle for independence. On April 12th of that year the state of Idaho extended its encouragement and support to the Spanish, French and Basque governments in their ongoing efforts to establish a process to bring a lasting peace, as well as to enhance an appropriate degree of governmental autonomy for the Basque peoples.

A few days after the approval of that third Memorial, I met with Mr. Cenarrusa to write an article about it. In autumn 2006 the article was finished and I remember that when I informed Mr. Cenarrusa, he asked me if the article was limited to a certain length. I said no, and that article has become a book.

This book is therefore an analysis of the key aspects of contemporary Basque politics from the perspective of a Basque American who has dedicated his life to politics in the state of Idaho and has been involved for at least the last forty years in the most critical events of Basque politics. The book is interesting for the American reader as it is written from the perspective that an Idahoan politician has on European events and for the European reader because distance has allowed Mr. Cenarrusa on numerous occasions to make an original approach to the constituent elements of the Basque political conflict.

The book has been written from the transcript of long hours of recorded conversation that took place at the Frank Church room in the library of Boise State University and at "Cenarrusa Country" in Carey, Idaho.

In July 2008 I went to Brussels at the invitation of a group of former members of the European Parliament who had undertaken the difficult task of creating a Foundation named EURI, European Research Institute, who took over the first edition of the work. I thank them for their effort.

To be Basque in Idaho

Xabier Irujo. Claude G. Bowers, U.S. Ambassador to the Spanish Republic, wrote in his memoires:

> There is no finer, nobler race than these. Their origin is lost in mists of history, but they have stoutly lived from time immemorial in the shadow of the Pyrenees, and scholars have called them "the oldest race in Europe." Robust, courageous, fiercely independent, passionately devoted to their liberties, intensely individualistic, and deeply religious, they have changed but little in character through the centuries. (...) The Basques are the most energetic and progressive, and have the most initiative of the Spaniards. Nature has blessed them with great deposits of iron and coal, and has given them a coastline from Bilbao to Fuenterrabia rich in natural harbors. With the coming of the industrial age, Bilbao became the Pittsburgh of Spain, the fourth city in population. The Basques harnessed the mountain torrents and made them turn the wheels of industry. Paper mills sprang up beside the mountain streams. Thousands of miners produced iron ore and coal to feed the furnaces of factories. The harbor of Bilbao teemed with shipping from every quarter of the globe. Fishermen, seamen, artisans, peasants, manufacturers, merchants, bankers— all the Basques prospered. High-minded, clean living, deeply religious, it is commonly agreed that in no other region is Catholicism more sensitive or profound. The people profited from better teaching. The Basque priests, usually of healthy peasant stock themselves, have a sympathetic understanding of their people, entering intimately into their lives as counselors and friends, sharing their instincts and fidelities, entering enthusiastically into their pleasures, competing with them on the pelota court.[1]

Pete Cenarrusa. This is so true about the Basque people and the Basque character and certainly their origin is lost in the myths of

---

[1] Bowers, Claude G., *My Mission to Spain*, Simon and Schuster, New York, 1954. Pp. 338-339.

history. They have lived from time immemorial in the shadow of the Pyrenees and scholars still call them "the oldest race in Europe." The Basques created mills beside their streams, and thousands of miners produced iron ore and the coal that heated the furnaces of their factories. However, the country is not so rich in natural elements or resources, so the Basques became great manufacturers. With the coming of the industrial age, Bilbao became the Pittsburgh of Southern Europe, the capital of shipbuilding, the first city in population of the Bay of Biscay that is named after her. On my trip to see Bilbao in 1971 it really was the Pittsburgh of the Bay of Bizkaia. You couldn't see three blocks ahead because of the smog, but now it is very clean, and you can see for miles.

Bilbao, 'the Pittsburgh of the Bay of Bizkaia'. Source: Basque Archive of the Univeristy of Nevada, Reno.

I would like to remark that if so many Basques have done it right in America, it has been in part due to their individualism, work ethic and sense of community. I've also talked about how the Basque go ahead because they don't go behind. They don't feel discriminated against. They blend right into society and that is why so many people here like the Basques, because they have been in society and they go about learning about society and going ahead. They are highly competitive, like most of the sheepherders who worked for my father or for me. I told them more than once, "You don't have anything to do today, why don't you take a day off and go to town?" They ended up not going to town and, instead, they filled sacks with sand to see who could lift the most.

XI. You are an Idahoan, born in Carey (Idaho).[2] I read,

> *Mr. Cenarrusa's father Jose Maria Zenarruzabeitia was born in Munitibar and his mother Ramona Gardoqui was born in Gernika. Jose immigrated to America in 1907 at the age of 17. His mother came as an immigrant from Gernika to Idaho in 1914 at the age of 23. They met one another in Shoshone, Idaho and were married in 1915. They raised a family of five children here in Idaho. All of the children learned the Basque language first, and then mastered the English language after entering the school system.*[3]

PC. Yes, I am the son of Basque immigrants. My parents are Joseph Zenarruzabeitia and Ramona Gardoki. They came from two villages of Urdaibai in Bizkaia; my father from Munitibar and my mother from Gernika. My father, Joe, came to Boise in 1907 at the age of seventeen. He left Munitibar with two friends to Bordeaux

---

[2]   The intent of this interview is not to give a biography; there are many interesting articles on Pete Cenarrusa's life,

- Weatherly Sharp, Nancy; Sharp, James Roger; Petonito, Gina; Atwater, Kevin G., *American Legislative Leaders in the West (1911-1994)*, Greenwood Publishing Group, 1997. P. 80.
- Etulain, Richard W.; Echeverria, Jeronima, *Portraits of Basques in the New World*, University of Nevada Press, Reno, 1999. Pp. 172-191.
- Totoricaguena, Gloria P., *Boise Basques: Dreamers and Doers*, University of Nevada Press, Reno, 2004.
- Bieter, John; Bieter, Mark, *An Enduring Legacy. The Story of the Basques in Idaho*, Nevada University Press, Reno, 2004.
- Merrill D. Beal; Wells, Merle W., *History of Idaho* (three vols.), Lewis Historical Publishing, New York, 1959.
- Clements, Louis J. (Ed.), *Fred T. Dubois. The Making of a State*, Eastern Idaho Publishing, Rexburg, 1971.

[3]   Letter by Miren Artiach to Andoni Ganboa, Boise, October 8, 1993. Boise State University Library, Pete Cenarrusa Collection, MSS 240, Box 13, Fol. 23.

where they boarded a ship towards the United States. Only after spending eight days on board they arrived in New York. As all Basques before them, they went to Valentin Agirre's boarding house. Valentin told them where to catch the train to Boise and how to face their trip to Idaho without speaking a word of English. Joe got his first job at the Barber Lumber mill a few miles east of Boise and then he went to work at the Rawson's Ranch, north of Carey.

In 1908 Joe had started working with prominent central Idaho sheepman Thomas C. Stanford in Carey (Idaho) and within a year, Joe called for his brother Pete, who came to work for Stanford too. Stanford wrote his old friend Senator William Borah in these terms:

> *For five years he worked for me, and his brother worked for me for four. During the time that Joe Cenarrusa was in my employ, I found him to be an exceptional foreigner, both in intelligence and character, so much that he was received by my family as one of them.*[4]

That is how my father Joe and uncle Pete got U.S. citizenship. They took their saved earnings and bought sheep, which they had operated successfully since their arrival.

The sheep business was cyclical. The ewes had their lambs in the winter in lambing sheds, wool was shorn in the spring and lambs and mutton harvested in the summer and fall. Then the breeding ewes were doubled up as two bands and they were put together for the fall breeding season.

That left months of downtime, especially through the winter. Many Basque immigrants spent that time in the boarding houses throughout southern Idaho, Nevada, eastern Oregon and California, keeping language and traditions alive.[5] They enjoyed themselves. Basques in the American West used to call other Basques "Gure Modukoak", that is, "[Basques] like us." During one of these lazy winters, Joe met Ramona in Shoshone and they were married there in 1915.

---

[4]   Thomas C. Stanford, letter to Idaho Senator William Borah. Cenarrusa archive.

[5]   Kenyon, Quane, *Bizkaia to Boise. The Memoirs of Pete Cenarrusa*, Center for Basque Studies, University of Nevada, Reno, Reno, 2009. P. 30.

XI. So, your father and mother were born back in the Basque Country ten miles from each other, but they met for the first time here, in Idaho?

PC. As did many other Basques, they met in a Basque Boarding House, at Soloaga's, in Shoshone in 1914 and married a year later. A long time ago Jeronima Echeverria, Provost and Vice President of Academic Affairs of California State University, Fresno, gave a talk here on the boarding houses. She had written a good book about the topic. When she gave that talk, we were listening to her and I was thinking, "you know, I wouldn't be here had it not been for the boarding house." Just like you.

Ramona Gardoki, second from the left, with a group of friends and relatives in Gernika before departing to the Americas. Source: Cenarrusa archive.

XI. Right. My parents met in a Basque Center, in Caracas, where they lived in exile until the end of the Francoist dictatorship. I was born there. So were two of my three brothers. The fourth one is the first member of the family in five generations who has not known exile, yet. There are no boarding houses in South America but Basques organized themselves in Basque Centers there and, as here, also in South America the Basque Centers were the places to meet, dance, sing and get married. Many of us, sons of exile, are born from parents who met in Basque Centers or Boarding Houses in America. But, what about you, how many brothers and sisters do you have?

PC. My parents had five children. My sister Nieves was the first one born in 1916 and then me, in the winter of 1917. I was born in the old Harris ranch house near the junction of U.S. highways 26 and 93. And the house is still there. In 1919 my brother Luis was born, my sister Juanita was born the next year on June 24, Saint John's Day, and then another sister, Lucia, was born in 1922 in Picabo. Like most of the Basques my parents were Catholic. My mother was so devoted as a Catholic that she knew when she died where she was going and thus felt comfortable. All of us were baptized and grew up as Catholics. They talked about how the Basques were devout and hard workers. That way they could achieve anything. They are not afraid to do any kind of labor.

XI. And the Cenarrusa brothers formed their own sheep business in 1912 in Picabo, the Cenarrusa Brothers Sheep Co.

PC. Right, it was a tough period. 1917 was a hard winter. My parents were preparing to lamb the ewes about six miles south of Carey. However the heavy snow forced them to take the sheep to a more suitable place south, about seventy-five miles to Paul, Idaho. It was not the first time that something like that happened, and would not be the last either. In fact by February 25, 1917 the snow had come down so heavily, beginning on February 17 that a town 35 miles north of Carey at the North Star Mine was devastated by a snow slide, or avalanche, where seventeen miners were killed when their bunk house was destroyed.

My father had sensed the hard winter, which prompted him to move the sheep south to Paul where there was substantial, good quality hay available, and corn for supplement was transported in from Nebraska by Union Pacific railroad. (I was born December 16, 1917 in Carey. The first-born daughter, Nieves, was one year and four months older than I.) My father experienced a good lambing season, producing a 135% lamb crop - 35% more lambs than the number of ewes. It was a good move for my father. The lambing took place in February and early March. By early April the snow had melted off and the lush green grass came up in abundance so that the grazing across the desert from Paul back to Carey produced prime-weight lambs for marketing. The prices for lamb had increased greatly so it made it a very good year to be in the range sheep business.

My mother told me that she rode and lived in a Karrokanpo (or sheep camp) crossing that spring the desert area between Paul and Carey along with her first-born daughter, Nieves, who was eight months old. She also told me that she and my father had to be very resourceful in order to battle the elements. It was necessary to retrieve cooking and drinking water from the 'playas', or snow/rain water ponds, strain it through cloth, then boil it for drinking and cooking.

The livestock drank water from the same playas. There was no piped-in water. It was pioneering all the way. My mother was telling me that during those early days living conditions were not easy.

My parents had to move their sheep by railroad from Tikura to Paul, about 75 miles south, where they acquired lambing quarters. They loaded the sheep on the train at Tikura, about eight miles south of Carey. Tikura was one of those little water replacement stations that steam trains needed about every fifty miles along the railroad. These old trains that hardly reached a speed of 70 miles per hour needed to be refilled with water every fifty miles, and resupplied with coal every one hundred miles.

As anyone can read in an article for the Longman's Magazine, only two men lived in Tikura, and one shot the other, so there was only one left, the telegraph operator. Tikura, consisted of the telegraph-office and railway-station (a small wooden hut), and a canvas dwelling, euphemistically described as a saloon and store, inhabited by the victim, 'Major' Cunningham, and his wife. Needless to say that the latter was the cause of the shooting. The major, suspecting the telegraph operator of paying too much attention to the lady, went for him with a Winchester rifle, but his aim being defective, the other man found his opportunity, and returned the fire with damaging effect.[6]

---

[6]   Palmer, Greville, "Snow bucking in the Rocky Mountains", Longman's Magazine, 5, 1885, pp. 423-424.

Basque Girl. The Basque society is considered to be a matriarchy by anthropologists, a social system in which the "etxandre" or lady of the house shares duties with the "etxekojaun" or lord of the house. Source: *Euzko Deya*, Buenos Aires, January 30, 1941.

But the way to Paul was shorter through the desert so, after loading the sheep on the train, the two karrokanpos were horse drawn along with the supply wagon down to Paul by crossing the Pagari bridge between Carey and Richfield which crossed the Little Wood river. I have been all over that desert. There is a point they call Wild Horse, northeast of Laidlaw Butte. From there they went southwest to Paul, about forty miles of desert road travel. The draft horses had no problem going through the snow-covered terrain and the snow was lighter going toward Paul but it took them about two long days and two short nights to reach Paul.

By 1924 the Cenarrusa brothers, Joe and Pete (known as Pete Zarra or Old Pete) became entrepreneurs of their own sheep companies. My father started his business with 1,000 head and in ten years he increased it to two bands totaling 2,500 head of ewes, and my uncle Pete with 1,250 head of lambing ewes. My uncle acquired his lambing quarters in Richfield, and my father obtained quarters about six miles south of Carey.

XI. The winter of 1948-1949 was a tough one too. The U.S. Air Force was forced to deploy its pilots and cargo planes for Operation Haylift, to drop tons of alfalfa for the cattle herds in the north of Nevada. Do you remember any of that?

PC. Yes. I recall that on 5th of December 1948 my father had trailed his sheep into the Carey feed yard/lambing quarters from the Laidlaw Park Bureau of Land Management (BLM) grazing allotment. He seemed to have a natural instinct of the oncoming of serious snow storms. He happened to be right because the snow storm started in serious proportions on December 3rd. He had instructed his herders to start for the winter headquarters without delay. The 2,500 head of pregnant ewes arrived in Carey on the afternoon of December 5th, 1948.

As I visited with my father on that evening he said, "I wonder if my brother Pete has arrived at his wintering quarters in Richfield." Pete Zarra's sheep were near Wildhorse Butte, which would take all of three days to trail into Richfield under the best of conditions.

I telephoned my uncle Pete's home in Richfield and learned from his wife, Claudia, that he had not arrived. Therefore, on the morning of December 6th I warmed up my airplane, a

P.T.26, a Royal Canadian Air Force training aircraft that I had purchased the previous September as a war surplus aircraft, and had it converted to a U.S. Civilian aircraft status. I took off toward the Wildhorse Butte area. Not only did I locate the marooned, snowbound sheep, sheep camps, pickup trucks, but also sheep herders (all looking at the sky). I had with me a large piece of cardboard and a marker pen on which to write instructions to drop out to the men. There were also four other sheep companies within three miles of each other looking for help. They were all happy to see an airplane, and still happier to see the cardboard with instructions that I threw out of the plane. I wrote each of them to stay put, but if they were able to move at all, they should move toward the Wood River, which was east toward Richfield.

Sheepherder and his wagon near the band of sheep he has guarded throughout the snowstorms and bitter cold. Sheep wagons were called *Karrokanpo* or *Ardikanpo* in Basque. The first sheep wagon was built in Wyoming in 1884. Schulte Hardware Company of Casper Wyoming was the first producer of sheep wagons until the beginning of the 20th century. Source: Special Collections Department, University of Nevada, Reno Library.

Arriving back in Carey I contacted people with snow dozers, the County Road and Bridge crew. Every dozer and piece of snow removal equipment was busy clearing roads. I received the same reply from the State of Idaho road crews. The BLM headquarters had no extra equipment available. In desperation, I contacted a local farmer, Oliver Payne, who had a T.D-9 about the size of a small D-4 dozer. He assured me he could immediately cross the Wood River, between Carey and Richfield, and head for the Wildhorse Butte. He arrived there at about 1:00 am and located Pete Zarra's camp, sheep and men. On the way to the rescue, he had cleared the road for travel, but the viscous winds had filled in the cleared road worse than it was before.

The next day I made another flight to contact each of the marooned sheep outfits, Tom Gooding, Charlie Browning, and two others to tell them that help was on the way and to attempt to move toward the north eastern area of Wildhorse Butte. Browning had already moved toward Kimama, a tough four miles the wrong way, but he adjusted after receiving my instructions. On the second day after Oliver Payne had located the outfits, the small TD-9 could be seen approaching the river and the Carey-Richfield highway with all the outfits trailing behind like companies of soldiers. All four outfits managed to get to the Pagari bridge, to safety.

The BLM had a trailer near the bridge with food and hot coffee, they had learned about the near disaster from a newspaper article in the Twin Falls Times News, which I had informed them about, along with Tommy Gooding and his foreman. Gooding had managed to acquire a D-7 dozer to go out to the stranded sheep, but by the time it reached the river, it was not needed as all the sheep were approaching the river.

The second day I flew out to the sheep outfits, I dropped out some supplies - such as wood, coal and "a bottle of Old Crow" for one of uncle Pete's sheepherders who was an Anglo and liked his booze. He told me he could see that package dropping from the plane — "there was only one rock protruding from the snow as far as the eye could see, and that carefully-wrapped package made a direct hit!" It was obliterated, otherwise everything ended up all right and all the sheep made it safely to their winter headquarters.

XI. And in 1924 you moved to Bellevue, Idaho.

PC. Right. When I was five years of age my parents moved to Bellevue, about twenty-three miles north of Carey. I learned English at the territorial school in Bellevue. In Bellevue we were like one big family. I remember the days I played football for the Bellevue Bulldogs when we beat the Hailey Wolverines 53-7. They were a real rival because we always felt they had stolen the county seat of Alturas County. I received my early education there and graduated from high school in 1936. I then attended the University of Idaho where I majored in agriculture and received my Bachelor of Science degree in 1940. While there I was a member of the university's first boxing team to win the intercollegiate championship.

I went to summer school in 1940 for additional course work in Fort Collins, Colorado, and gained further academic learning during a summer session spent at the Colorado State University (CSU). I needed one more course so that I could teach agriculture. While at CSU I wrote a thesis for my studies on the main aspects of the Basque culture. This was my first academic approach to Basque culture and politics.

While over there, I wanted to find out more about the Basques so I spent hours at the library and that is when I really started to find things out, pointing out what was going on. I researched several sources and read a lot. I especially remember the articles by Dorothy Thompson during the late 1930s on the bombing of Gernika; her description was very good.

And then I took my first job teaching agriculture, science, and mathematics at Cambridge High School and coaching in the town of Cambridge (Idaho). A year later (1941-1942) I moved to Carey (Idaho) in my second year of teaching to be near my family who had moved there. I worked as a teacher of agriculture and mathematics and I also added football to my teaching schedule. This was the first time since 1929 that football had been coached at Carey High. And I also conducted an after-hours boxing class.

XI. I read from Pat Bieter's biography:

> *Pete went to the neighboring town of Twin Falls to enlist in the Army Air Corps on a Sunday shortly after the bombing of Pearl*

Harbor. The army office was closed and would reopen Monday -a teaching day for Pete; he would not be there. He was informed that the navy recruiter was in Twin Falls and that he was available on Sundays. Pete volunteered to be a naval aviator, and after finishing the 1941-1942 school year he left Carey for naval air training in Corpus Christi.[7]

PC. Pat, he was a good man, and a great friend. Yes, I chose to be a Marine Naval Aviator because it was a challenge. My first and primary training began at Seattle (Washington) where I signed up for the naval cadet flight training program. I was there for about two weeks and the war effort was coming so fast that they built more airplanes and needed more pilots.

They opened up a new base in Pasco (Washington). I did my primary flight training and moved there after two or three weeks, about the first of August in 1942. That is where I first learned to fly and that was my first ride in an airplane. I passed my primary A, B and C stages there and then we went to Corpus Christi (Texas) in December 1942 to take the basic and advanced training.

XI. President George Bush Sr. also got his wings of gold at Corpus Christi.

PC. Yes, Bush also got his wings there and graduated and became a naval aviator in Corpus Christi at the same place that I did. John Glenn, the first American astronaut to orbit the Earth, also attended flight training there, three weeks before I did. I had the yearbook of naval aviation with pictures of those classes and he signed his name there, John Glenn. When President George Bush Sr. came to Idaho and the State Officials were all lined up and he was shaking hands with everybody, he came to me and I said, "Mr. President, I have a little gift for you here." It was the airplane that he used to fly, a tie-clasp; it was an Avenger Torpedo Bomber. He said, "Oh, thank you very much." He noticed I had an F4U Corsair marine fighter plane tie-clasp and told me that he took his

---

7   Etulain, Richard W.; Echeverria, Jeronima, *Portraits of Basques in the New World*, University of Nevada Press, Reno, 1999. For a short biography see Chapter 10 on Pete Cenarrusa. Pp. 176-177.

advanced training in Beeville, Texas. I took mine in Kingsville, Texas. Those were different places and different phases of aviation –(the patrol bombers and torpedo bombers and fighters and dive bombers). I was in fighters and dive bombers in Kingsville about 40 miles south of Beeville. That night he talked about Republicans, as it was Lincoln-Day festivities and he mentioned meeting me and how we both went through flight training in Corpus Christi.

I joined the U.S. Marines. In May 1942, I got orders to report to the Sand Point Naval Air Station in Seattle. I swore in as a seaman second class, classified as V-5 Naval Aviation with twenty-one dollars pay. I had orders to the Pacific Fleet in an F4U Corsair Fighter Squadron 462 (VMF-462) from the El Toro Marine base near Santa Ana, California. On 28 April 1943 I got my Navy Wings of Gold in Corpus Christi and I was commissioned as a Second lieutenant in the Marine Corps. Due to my experience as an instructor at Cambridge and Carey, I served at Corpus Christi as a naval aviation instructor from 1943 to 1944 for close air support pilots. After eighteen months of instruction at Corpus Christi, I received orders to the Jacksonville Naval Air Station in Florida for operational flight training in F4U Corsairs. I was named head of the education department of the training squadron by April 28, 1943.

On 18 April 1945 my orders were changed from Pacific theater sea duty to a Marine dive-bomber squadron stationed at Cherry Point in North Carolina. I tried to get my orders changed but I had to report to Cherry Point. Years later I learned that the sudden change was because the military command planned to invade the mainland of Japan, and that the invasion troops needed the most accurate close-air support to protect them during the invasion. The forward air controller would inform the dive-bombers of the most accurate position of the enemy firepower that needed knocking out, such as tanks, machine gun nests and enemy troops. Accuracy was essential so that friendly troupes would not be bombed. But the dropping of the atomic bombs at Hiroshima and Nagasaki ended the war abruptly.

Pete Cenarrusa during World War Two. Source: Cenarrusa archive.

The original SB2C-1 Curtis Helldiver was not liked by the pilots who flew them. They were slow and under-powered and not dependable as a top notch dive bomber. The SB2C-4 was a more powerful and desirable dive-bomber in order to knock out the enemy forces. It was equipped with perforated dive brakes and more power and speed was desirable. We generally rolled over and started the vertical dive from 18,000 feet elevation. The speed brakes were immediately activated to stabilize the descent at 280 knots with the bombsight accurately sighted to hit the target, such as a tank or machine gun nest, or a bridge. I had no problem with the SB2C-4. The trigger was activated at 2500 feet above ground. Recovery from the vertical dive at 280 knots was suddenly accomplished by retracting the dive brakes and flying evasive tactics at a much greater speed for a rendezvous with the squadron.

Pete Cenarrusa flying a Corsair from coast to coast. Photograph taken by Lt. Bill Albert. Source: Cenarrusa archive.

My log book shows that I flew an SBD Dauntless on May 9, 1945 for the first time at Cherry Point. Then, on May 11 I flew it from Cherry Point to Clinton, Oklahoma for moth-balling.

The SBD was totally replaced by the SB2C-4 Helldivers. The Helldivers had much more horsepower and bomb carrying capacity and was superior to the SBD Dauntless, even though the SBD Dauntless was a good dive-bomber. Indeed, the SBD Dauntless dive-bomber was largely successful in destroying the Japanese fleet during the battle of Midway in the Pacific. However, my log book shows that I flew the SB2C-4 for an additional sixty-two hours even after the surrender of the Japanese aboard the Battle Ship Missouri. We practiced to do a fly-over with thirty-six dive-bombers at the Miami Orange Bowl game in January 1946, but it got cancelled.

Pete Cenarrusa in a Corsair. Source: Cenarrusa archive.

In 1946 the separation from active duty brought me back to Carey on the end of March 1946 and I went into sheep ranching. However, I remained a member of the VMF 216 Marine Ready Reserve Squadron and continued flying Navy and Marine aircraft one weekend per month and participated in annual maneuvers in F4U Corsair, F7F Tiger Cat, F8F Grumman Bearcat, F9F-2 Panther and F9F-6 Cougar Navy jet fighter planes. I retired in July of 1963 with the rank of Major, but continued civilian flying for another thirty-four years. I have been a pilot for fifty-five years and have flown over a million miles and logged over 15,000 hours of flight time without an accident. I also earned the Marine Jet Flying "OMIAS" card while training in jet bail-out practice.

XI. I have read that Ben Ysursa, your long-time deputy who succeeded you as secretary of state in 2003, never thought twice about flying with you. "The most dangerous thing about flying with Pete was the drive to and from the Boise airport," he said once.[8]

PC. True. By 1950 I knew every family in Blaine County because I visited all the farms as an institutional trainer, teaching war veterans how to manage farms after World War II. While teaching a group of young people to fly, in Carey, a young woman came to have classes in 1947. Her name was Freda Coates, and we got married soon after and had a son, Joe.

XI. I learned from Pat Bieter's biography that the hamlet of Carey, which in the 1940s and 1950s had a population of about five hundred, had, under your direction, built a small airport.

PC. Yes. The Idaho State Department of Aeronautics director Chet Moulton came to Carey and told me he wanted to build an airstrip in one day. As my son Joe pointed out in an article that he wrote in 1971 for the Idaho Satesman, since Moulton's appointment in 1946, Idaho became number one in airports and aircraft per capita in the U.S. We owe Moulton the fortune of having an airport at nearly every town, large or small, in the state.

---

[8]   Kenyon, Quane, *Bizkaia to Boise. The Memoirs of Pete Cenarrusa*, Center for Basque Studies, University of Nevada, Reno, Reno, 2009. P. 88.

Pilots are now able to travel about in a town served by an airport with the aid of a state-furnished courtesy car. Moulton's idea was to come into a community and have the community involved in the construction of the airstrip; Carey was the first one in a list of villages to come. The state would furnish all the fuel but the local farmers would furnish the equipment, the graders and the farm equipment, tractors, scrapers and things like that. At that time we were landing in an alfalfa field and another field about six miles out of Carey where the County Commissioners had cleared from sagebrush. But Moulton wanted to get air strips right close to town so people could come and do their business and that is why they built this one right next to Main Street, on the West side. It was one of the first airstrips ever built in a single day. We leveled it all off so that airplanes could land there. Now we have another one with better direction on the other side of Main Street, on the East side.

XI. And you invited President Harry S. Truman to Carey to inaugurate the new airstrip.

PC. Right. Harry Truman was running against the Governor of New York, Thomas Dewey, and he was in Sun Valley (Idaho) on a whistle stop tour on the rail car and stopping in towns and having political rallies. He came to Sun Valley and he stayed there in the Harriman cottage. Freda's uncle came to me and told me that Harry Truman was up there in Sun Valley. He said, "maybe you can go up there tonight and see him." The newspaper had that he was coming through Carey that next morning and going to Idaho Falls and then to Butte (Montana) in a caravan –(a car caravan, not the railway). "Maybe we can get him in for a stop and dedicate that airstrip in honor of a sixteen year old girl who got killed in an aircraft accident down there." And I said, "Sure, I'll go up there and see if we can do that." I went up to Ketchum, to the Tram Club that was owned by two Basques. It was a nice club. I then met with the Chairman of the National Committee of the Democratic Party, he was a good one to talk to, a sheep man. I told him what I was trying to get done: get President Truman to come to Carey and stop and dedicate that airstrip. He said, "No way we can do that, just forget it." Then I walked to the editor of the newspaper. He had been up to the entertainment session with the President's tour people and the President's reception at Sun Valley. And I told him the same thing. He was my friend, Con Gillespie was his name. He said, "Well, I just came from there so let's go back up to the reception and we'll get it done." So we went right to Sun Valley and contacted Charlie Ross, the President's press secretary. He was a tall, good-looking fellow and he had a drink in his hand, feeling pretty good; we didn't see the President but I put the question to Charlie Ross: "We'd like to have the President stop momentarily when you come through Carey on Main Street. There is a Mormon Church and right beyond it there is an airstrip; we'd like to have it dedicated in honor of this girl that got killed in an aircraft accident in Carey."

President Harry Truman in Carey (ID) to dedicate the air-strip that was built in a day. Source: Cenarrusa archive.

XI. That girl was Wilma Coates, Freda's cousin?

PC. Yes, she was a pretty little girl who crashed in 1947 with her boyfriend when he was "buzzing" her home.

Ross said, "That sounds good; we'll do it. We will get it done." I then thought "Well, nobody will know about it when the President comes at nine in the morning so we better get back to Carey and tell the people." We went to Carey and Gillespie and his wife were with me. I went through the town honking the horn, you know. Because of all of that noise Blaine County deputy sheriff Frank Inama was just going into his home and came up out of his car and stopped me. He said, "I am going to put you under arrest." I replied, "Well the people have to be alerted that the President of the U.S. is coming to Carey in the morning and we wanted everybody to be here."

He didn't believe it. Gillespie said, "Here is the badge. We just came from the President's recreation meeting and I was there. We were both there and he is coming. This is a guarantee. The President is coming." But he didn't believe it and added, "If you don't shut up you will get a ticket too for disturbing the peace." Sure enough, we got on the telephone then and called one family and that family called one family... and pretty soon everybody in town went out and the Secret Service people came to town. They gave the information on what it was all about. So then the President came and started speaking from the rumble seat of his Cadillac. He said, "We'll dedicate the air-strip in honor of a serviceman who got killed in the war." This girl's mother was there and she said, "No, no, Mr. President, that was my daughter." And he replied, "Well, it is an honor. She died in honor of our country and for our servicemen." But she insisted, "No, no, she was not in the service. She was from right here." And he said, "She died in honor of her country." That was making her mad and Time Magazine published the story. That was an awkward position.

Anyhow, after that, I had to go to the judge, for the ticket. Bill Briggs was his name, a real good guy. He emigrated from England and was a real gentleman. I knew his whole family. He just said, "Well, Pete, it isn't every day that the President of the U.S. comes to our little town of Carey, case dismissed."

XI. At that time the Basque Secret Services and the U.S. Office of Strategic Services were cooperating and in 1947 President Truman barred the Drumbeat report which suggested for the first time the idea of installing U.S. military bases in the Spanish state in exchange for the international recognition of the Spanish regime. But we will go into that later on.

So in 1950 you were elected to the Idaho House of Representatives as a Republican from Blaine County.

PC. Yes. I was then thirty-two. I served in that capacity for seventeen years, including six as speaker of the house for the 1963, 1965 and 1967 sessions. I became the first Basque to be a Speaker of the House.

In May 1967, I was appointed Secretary of State by Governor Don Samuelson to fill a vacancy caused by the death of Edson H. Deal. I was elected to a full term for the first time in 1970 and then I was reelected seven consecutive times in 1974, 1978, 1982, 1986, 1990, 1994 and 1998. I did not run for reelection in 2002, instead I supported my Chief Deputy Ben Ysursa who got 297,189 votes, 77.5 percent. He was reelected in November 2006 by 364,871 votes.

I have been an active politician for fifty-two years. My last term of office ended on 6 January 2003, when I was more than eighty years old.

XI. You never lost an election, did you?

PC. No. I won them all. When I started in 1970 I got 60 percent of the popular vote. Then I jumped to 64 percent in 1974 and in the next four elections in 1978, 1982, 1986 and 1990 I was unopposed by any candidate. In 1982 I got 262,357 votes and in 1990 I got 247,908 votes. In the elections on 8 November 1994 I was most successful and I won in all forty-four Idaho counties against the Democrat candidate Edith M. Stanger, 267,039 votes (67 percent) against 131,475 (33 percent). In 1998 I ran for the last time against Democrat candidate Jerry Seiffert and Liberal T. J. Angstman. I won in forty-three of the forty-four counties and achieved 256,594 votes, 68.89 percent.

XI. I have heard the mermaids singing that the Constitution of the State of Idaho says that to be Basque is a prerequisite to become Secretary of State. Is that right?

PC. [Laughing] Yes, right.

XI. How did you get involved in politics for the first time?

PC. In 1949, representatives of the Republican Party approached me to run for elected office. Every family in the county knew my

[36]

father and also me personally because we had visited all of their ranches and farms, and so I was elected to the Idaho House of Representatives in 1950. I was a Basque Catholic running in a Mormon district, and I beat Mormon Bishop Buford Kirkland for the seat. A year later I became the president of the Idaho Flying Legislators.

Following the elections, I was selected as the Chair of the House of Representatives' Agriculture Committee because my expertise in that matter. I was re-elected from my district to the House of Representatives for nine consecutive terms, totaling seventeen years of service. During this time, I was elected as Chairman of the first Idaho Legislative Council of 1963 and as the Speaker of the House beginning in 1963, for three two-year terms.[9]

XI. According to Quane Kanyon the Capitol in 1965 was a crucible for legislation that would chart the course of Idaho for generations. Major decisions were made on taxation, natural resource management, education, health care, and government administration.[10]

PC. Right. The thirty-eighth regular session of the legislature in 1965 was one of the best legislatures ever in Idaho. The legislature established Idaho's first permanent sales tax, set at 3 percent. The Legislature had already passed the so called "sin taxes" on cigarettes and alcohol and also the property tax and the income tax but I was in favor of the sales tax so we have a good three legged stool on which to seat the expenses of the State. And we did. The legislature also created the Idaho Water Resources Board and Department of Water Resources and the Department of Parks and Recreation and its board, to manage existing parks and develop new ones. The legislature also passed the creation of community mental health centers and state community colleges and the position of executive director for the state Board of Education to coordinate all higher education activities in Idaho. We also created

---

9   "Pete Cenarusa, Carey Rancher, Was Unanimous Choice as Speaker of House", Magic Valley Portrait, *Twin Falls Times-News*, Sunday, January 27, 1963. P. 21.
10   Kenyon, Quane, *Bizkaia to Boise. The Memoirs of Pete Cenarrusa*, Center for Basque Studies, University of Nevada, Reno, Reno, 2009. Pp. 99-112.

a merit system for state employees and took the first steps to draft the Uniform Commercial Code. No legislative session has been more influential than the "watershed session" of 1965.

XI. Two years later Governor Bob Smylie was defeated by Don Samuelson who appointed you Secretary of State.

PC. Yes. After completing the remaining three years and eight months I was elected Secretary of State for the first time in 1970. As Secretary of State, I had a seat on the State Board of Land Commissioners which rules on many agriculture-related issues. The agriculture sector is the most important in the state of Idaho. Water rights, public land use, endangered species, agricultural research and animal husbandry are all a part of the job.

Term	Period	Governor	Party
22	January 6, 1947 January 1, 1951	C. A. Robins	Republican
23	January 1, 1951 January 3, 1955	Leonard B. Jordan	Republican
24	January 3, 1955 January 2, 1967	Robert E. Smylie	Republican
25	January 2, 1967 January 4, 1971	Don Samuelson	Republican
26	January 4, 1971 January 24, 1977	Cecil D. Andrus	Democratic
27	January 24, 1977 January 5, 1987	John V. Evans	Democratic
28	January 5, 1987 January 2, 1995	Cecil D. Andrus	Democratic
29	January 2, 1995 January 4, 1999	Phil Batt	Republican
30	January 4, 1999 May 26, 2006	Dirk Kempthorne	Republican

Governors of the State of Idaho during the period in which Pete Cenarrusa served as member of the House of Representatives and Secretary of State, from 1950 to 2003. After fifty-two years on duty, Cenarrusa is the longest serving elected official in the history of Idaho and the longest serving Secretary of State presently living in the United States.

When Idaho became a state, U.S. Congress granted by an Act dated July 3rd, 1890, about three million acres (12,140 km²) of public lands, including Section 16 and 36 within every township of the state, amounting to more than 200,000 acres (809 km²), for the support of public schools and in aid of various public institutions. Where Section 16 or 36 or any part thereof had been sold or otherwise disposed of by or under the authority of any act of Congress, the State of Idaho kept the right to select other lands equivalent in lieu of those. Congress also granted lands to the University of Idaho which became a land grant institution. The Idaho Board of Land Commissioners managed these lands and decided which would be available for agricultural purposes.

When I was a member of the Idaho Board of Land Commissioners we applied for 22,000 acres (89 km²) in lieu lands that were lost to the Federal Government when the U.S. Forest Service was established. Cecil Andrus was U.S. Secretary of the Interior and he communicated back to the Land Board and to Governor John Evans that if we kept the request under 10,000 acres he could get it for us. But the Board did not want less than 22,000 acres and so voted four to one to reject Andrus' proposal. And one of the four was a Democrat, State Controller Joe Williams. Governor Evans was the only one to vote for the Andrus deal. Andrus left the U.S. Secretary of the Interior office when Ronald Reagan won elections against Jimmy Carter.

Then, four of us went to Washington D.C. and met with the new Secretary of the Interior James Watt and explained to him our situation and he said that he could make that happen. And few months after the State of Idaho received 22,000 acres of land.

Cecil Andrus spent fourteen years on the Land Board with me. He served as Governor of Idaho from 1971 to 1977 and from 1987 to 1995 and, as U.S. Secretary of the Interior from 1977 to 1981, under Jimmy Carter. While we had strong respect for one another we clashed occasionally. I was president of the Carey Chamber of Commerce and a member of the Idaho Government Reorganization Committee, the Blaine County Woolgrowers Association and the Blaine County Livestock Marketing Association. Once Andrus said that I was a sheepherder at heart, and added: "Cenarrusa even wears wool underwear...!"

Pete Cenarrusa and his wife Freda Coates in front of the Capitol Building in Boise, Idaho. C. 1963. Source: Cenarrusa archive.

The Bureau of Land Management lands were public lands. The state sold or leased some of these lands and the revenues were used for the benefit of various public institutions such as the school of the deaf and the blind in Gooding and the penitentiary and the insane asylum.

Some teachers' colleges also benefited by the revenues coming from public lands. One of them was called Lewiston Normal Teachers' College that was closed and in the risk of not being reinstated. At that time Governor Robert E. Smylie wanted to run for governor in 1959 but the Constitution of Idaho would not allow him to run for two consecutive terms.

Thus, Smylie needed to pass a constitutional amendment with two thirds majority in both Houses. And for that he needed the support of the Democrats. He proposed to reinstate Lewiston College as Lewis & Clark College with revenues from the public lands in exchange for the Democrats voting in favor of the constitutional amendment permitting candidates for governor to run unlimited terms.

Democrat senator Holger Albrethsen of Blaine County did not want to go along with changing the Constitution of Idaho which seemed to be a trade off and, expressed in the Senate that Smylie "didn't have the guts to veto the bill" even if the Democrats did not vote in favor of the constitutional amendment.

However, although Holger's protests, that is how the Legislature appropriated $200,000 to reopen Lewiston College and the Idaho Constitution was changed with the support of the Democrats on 25 February 1955. Smylie got to be reelected in 1959 and was governor for two more terms from 1959 to 1967. Beverly Weston, journal clerk at the Senate, wrote a poem about this story:

> *Here lies Holger the lion hearted, the fighting senator from Blaine,*
> *Who went to the Idaho State Senate to make himself a name,*
> *When things got going rough, he said, 'come on men, let's call his bluff.*
> *He ain't got the guts, I tell you men, to strike that bill with a veto pen,*
> *It's up to the Senate to make it right, so that Lewiston College will see the light.'*

XI. The Secretary of State administers executive orders of the Governor and is also in charge of all the elections held in Idaho.

PC. Yes. People in Idaho get to vote for so many different positions each election year and one of the most important responsibilities is as chief elections officer of the state. The Secretary of the State office certifies all of the ballot counting and all elections results for Primary and General, State and National elections. The Secretary of State registers all corporations and all of the elections candidates and interest groups and anyone making campaign donations and, files all of the bills and finalized laws passed by the legislature for the State archives.

XI. You also served as a member of the Republican Party.

PC. Yes, I served as Idaho Chairman to draft Governor Ronald Reagan of California for President in 1968. I was a delegate to the Republican National Convention in 1976 and again in 1984. I was State co-chairman of "Reagan for President" in 1980.

XI. In addition, you were appointed to first Idaho Human Rights Commission by Governor Cecil Andrus, chaired the Idaho Legislative Council and were elected delegate to the Council of State Governments. And you also were made Governor for one day.

You have the unprecedented honor of being inducted into seven Halls of Fame: Agriculture, Athletic, GOP (Republican Party), Basque and Idaho. You were listed in the Honor Society of Agriculture (Gamma Sigma Delta) of the University of Idaho 1978 and were also listed in Who's Who in America and Who's Who in the American West. The State of Idaho's largest government building was named in your honor by Governor Phil Batt in 1998. You are a recipient of the University of Idaho President's Medallion and, in 2001 you were also awarded the honor of "Basque of the World" by the Sabino Arana Foundation in the Basque Country and, in 2010 the Government of Bizkaia conceded the Gold Medal of Bizkaia to you.

No other Idaho elected official has ever served the State as long as you. And you have written two manuscripts.[11]

PC. Right. I have served in the House of Representatives for nine two-year terms from 1950 to 1967, the last three terms as a speaker of the House. Then, Governor Donald Samuelson appointed me Secretary of State on first of May 1967, forty-five years ago, until January the 6th 2003.

---

[11]   Cenarrusa, Peter Thomas, *Cost of Production of Range Sheep*, University of Idaho, Moscow, 1940. And, Cenarrusa, Peter Thomas, *Corporation Laws of the State of Idaho, 1979: A Compilation of the Business, Nonprofit and Professional Corporation Laws with Amendments through the 1979 Legislative Session*, Secretary of State, Boise, 1979.

The Oinkari Basque Dancers of Boise (Idaho) is a Basque-American group created in 1960 to promote Basque culture in the United States. Source: Urrutia archive.

I have served for fifty-two years and eight months as an elected state official. I have served longer than any other state elected official in Idaho and I have served as Secretary of State longer than any other person in the United States who is still living. There is one person who served longer than me. He died in 1993 and served for fifty-two as Secretary of State of North Carolina. His name was Thaddeus A. Eure.

My belief is that it is important to be able to get along with a person's colleagues and to be able to understand their problems. No matter where I was, I was always ready and willing to listen to the "other side" and weigh the facts that were presented to me before making any stand or decision. Once made, one has to have the courage of his convictions, and proceed to carry them out in a diplomatic manner. I learned that from my parents. My father was really a good man and a very stable person. He was very well liked. Everybody who met him liked him for he was helpful to a lot of people. I remember the bankers telling him, "Whatever you need Joe, it is right here. Just sign your name. That is all." He died in an automobile accident. Fellow woolgrower Roy Ross told me, "Blaine County has lost its best man."

XI. Well, I know that Idaho Representative Max Black said to the *Idaho Statesman* on first of April that the 2012 Idaho legislature's proudest moment was "when the whole body stood to show their respect and support for the Basque peace resolution sponsored by Pete Cenarrusa. Pete was given a standing ovation for his long service to the state. The former secretary of state is the longest-serving elected officeholder in Idaho's history. Neither the age nor cancer seems to be able to retire you from public life.

PC. Yes. The day after the Memorial passed the House Dan Popkey, journalist for the Idaho Statesman, asked me if I was planning to live one hundred years. I told him, "I am shooting for one hundred." In 2011 Dr. Szentes from St. Lukes Hospital diagnosed me with lung and liver cancer. We also consulted with Dr. Gamboa of Basque ancestry. They told me that there was no cure but that they were treatable. Now both have disappeared. In March 2012 Dr. Norman Zuckerman told me "Pete, we thought that these types of cancer were not curable. You are a miracle!" I suppose that this may be because I have always exercised and I am still exercising. I have several exercising machines at home and I use them all. I used to do a lot of rope skipping from the time I was on the boxing team at the University of Idaho. Currently I do from 500 to 2,000 jumps in my elastic trampoline with the polka music.

It was in 1951 when I presented the first Memorial of the Basques in the legislature. From this over sixty years have passed. I think it's hard for me to stop now. It is not in my hands to say how much I can continue working for the future of these people, but I'm sure I can say that it will be until the end of my days. Our Foundation has a good group of people working every day in Idaho and this guarantees the generational change of the Basques in Idaho. The Basques of Boise have a Basque center, a cultural center, a museum, an Ikastola and several restaurants from which the cultural, social, and economic future of this society is constantly being promoted and developed. There are thousands the Basques who regularly participate in celebrations, conferences, sport events and other daily activities in our state and also in Nevada, California, Oregon, Arizona, New Mexico, Colorado, Wyoming and New York, among other states. In February 2012 the state of Idaho sealed an agreement of cooperation with the Basque government, which suggests that there are future projects and that, in fact, the Basque society in Idaho and, overall, throughout the United States is a dynamic and strong one, capable of facing the challenges the future will interpose to them.

XI. Was it special for you to return to the legislature in March 2012, after years of retirement?

PC. Yes, it was very special. Many things came to my mind. I was looking at the podium where the speaker of the House stands and where he uses the gavel and operates the session. The speaker runs the show. I was the Speaker of the House for three terms. In 1958 Governor Bob Smiley appointed the 2% Sales Tax Committee to study the possibility of implementing a sales tax in Idaho. When finally the committee read the report Smiley backed out and did not support its proposal in favor of the implementation of a sales tax for he was running for governor and he was afraid of a backlash from the voters. That angered Robert Doolittle, speaker of the House and one of the members of the Sales Tax Committee that, when the report was read to the House members to be placed in the Journal of the legislature and, he brought the gavel down so strong that he broke the handle off. Later, in 1963, I was speaker of the House and the House passed the sales tax but it was killed in the senate because of the scathing editorial at the Idaho Statesman by the editor Jim Brown. However, in 1964 I had a meeting at Lieutenant Governor Jack Murphy's home in Shoshone (Idaho) with Governor Smylie to make sure that the governor was going to back the report of the committee in favor of the sales taxes which incomes were going to be dedicated to education and other appropriations. The problem in my opinion was that we had a system that resembled a two legged stool supported by the property taxes and the income taxes, but we needed the third leg of the stool, the sales tax. Finally, in the 38th session of the legislature in 1965 both Houses supported the 3% sales tax. As a speaker of the House I made sure that I did not need to break the gavel as Doolittle did!

XI. You received a standing ovation from the members of the senate and the 2012 Joint Memorial was passed unanimously. Is it usual that all representatives vote together in favor of an initiative, or was it an exception?

PC. Yes, it is usual that all representatives vote together by voice vote unless the members request a recorded vote. The members of the senate gave a special treatment to Joint Memorial No. 14 in my honor and in the memory of all the Basques who as my parents came as sheepherders to Idaho and worked so hard in this country.
        The Joint Memorial No. 14 that was approved unanimously by voice vote, by acclamation, in both Houses is an expression of this recognition. After the Memorial was presented by Carlos Bilbao and passed in the House of Representatives, the Senate State Affairs Committee was bypassed by the chairman of the committee. That is called "buck slip". It may take two or three days to get the committee to meet so they decided to skip the first and second readings and went immediately to the third reading. Then, the chairman of the committee asked the majority leader of the senate Bart Davis what time did he want to have the Memorial read on the floor and Davis just answered "whatever time Pete would be in the gallery". And so they waited for me and, after I

knew that I had killed the cancer, I arrived in the senate on Monday, March 26 at 10:30.

Sixty-first Idaho Legislature passed House Joint Memorial No. 14 on March 22, 2012. Pete Cenarrusa, in the gallery, receiving a standing ovation from the members of the Idaho House of Representatives. Source: Cenarrusa archive.

Senator Patti Anne Lodge read in behalf of the Senate several excerpts from my political memoirs published by the Center for Basque Studies at the University of Nevada, Reno under the title *Bizkaia to Boise*. After the reading, Lt. Governor Brad Little, breaking the protocol, called for the House Memorial to be passed by acclamation. Little said "all those in favor say aye, all opposed nay" and then he slammed the gavel and announced "the ayes have it" without giving any time for a nay vote. That is what we call a quick gavel [laughing]. All senators rose from their seats and gave a standing ovation and, I expressed from the gallery my thanks on behalf of the Basque people who always have believed in peace and deserve a place among equals in the international community of nations.

[47]

Tree carving made by a Basque sheepherder in Borel creek, Treasure Mountain Road (Tahoe National Forest, Nevada). It reads *Euskadi* (Basque Country). The drawing represents a Lauburu (Four heads), an ancient Basque symbol. Source: Irujo Ametzaga archive.

The Basques are highly regarded all over the Americas and it was not easy for them to earn this recognition, it is the fruit of several generations of hard work and honesty. This explains why John Adams, one of the principal drafters of the constitution of this country decided to visit the Basque Country and study the Basque laws, specifically the Code of Laws of Bizkaia of 1526 before the U.S. constitution was drafted in 1788. He included a chapter on the Basques in his book *In Defense of the Constitutions of Government of the United States* (1787). I am a descendant of Diego Gardoki who during the war of independence provided the patriots of this nation with 215 bronze cannons, 30,000 muskets, 30,000 bayonets, 51,314 musket balls, 300,000 pounds of gunpowder, 12,868 grenades, 30,000 uniforms and 4,000 tents. It was Gardoki who sent warm clothing and boots to General Washington at Valley Forge. I am also the son of a Basque shepherd who settled and helped create the state of Idaho, a person to whom bankers trusted money without written guarantees. There are countless cases of Basques who helped shape this country with their honesty and hard work, values that they learned and transmitted from generation to generation and that explains why Idaho has recognized the Basques in parliament.

Sheep grazing in a typical Nevadan landscape. Source: Cenarrusa archive.

My parents were part of that first massive wave of Basque immigrants into Idaho at the beginning of the 20th century. But the Basques had inhabited the West long before, since the end of the 18th century. They knew this land very well. Many of the Governors of New Mexico between 1598 and 1788 were Basque like Juan de Oñate (1598-1608), Cristóbal de Oñate (1608-1609), Juan Eulate (1618-1625), Bernardo Lopez Mendizabal (1659-1661), Antonio de Otermin (1677-1683), Gervasio Cruzat y Gongora (1731-1736), Henrique de Olavide y Michelena (1736-1739), Pedro Fermin Mendinueta (1767-1778) or Juan Bautista Anza (1778-1788). During the period 1792 to 1847 many Governors of California were also Basque like Matias Armona (1769-1771), Jose Joaquin Arrilaga (1792-1794 and 1800-1814), Jose Maria Echeandia (1825-1831 and 1832-1833) and Manuel Micheltorena (1842-1845). They were political leaders as well as rich California businessmen.

The first two Basques to come to Nevada brought 3,000 head of cattle from Texas, to establish their business in Nevada.[12] A Basque landowner gave the name of his ranch to a state of the Union, Arizona, "the good oak" in Basque.[13] And both the first emissary of the Castilian Empire to the United States (Diego Gardoqui) and the first Consul General of the Spanish government at San Francisco (Joaquin M. Satrustegui) were Basque.

The first sheep were brought to the American West in the mid-1800s. The first Basque sheep men came here from Argentina when the gold gave out, they branched out into the cattle business and the meat business. The Gold Rush stimulated the sheep industry to feed miners after the discovery of silver in the western Utah Territory (Nevada) in 1858. Between 1880 and 1890 about 750,000 sheep were driven across Nevada to the east.

XI. According to the data at the exhibit Sheep Herding in Northern Nevada of the University of Nevada Reno's Special Collections, Scottish sheep grower John G. Taylor became one of the largest sheep growers in Nevada, owning over 250,000 acres (1,011 km²) and leasing a half a million acres (2,023 km²). There are many Basques among these first sheep barons. The Saval brothers, John and Joe, who started working for Taylor, created the Saval Ranch 40 miles north of Elko (Nevada) of 49,105 acres (198 km²) and, the Altube brothers from Oñati, Bernardo and Pedro, also built their own sheep empire at the end of the nineteenth century in Independence Valley, near Elko, with 400,000 acres (1,618 km²) of land.

PC. Right. These Basque sheep growers and ranchers got sheepherders from the Basque Country to come help them, mostly family members and friends from the same towns or valleys back in Europe. Just like the Saval brothers or the Altube brothers, my father and his brother created the Cenarrusa Sheep Company in Idaho. They came to work in the sheep business and didn't get fooled into it. These Basques found all this open country of public domain known as vacant land. Whoever got there first had the

---

12 Power, Camille B., "Basque Culture", manuscrit. In, Boise State University Library, Camille B. Power Collection, MSS 61, Box 3, Fol. 3.
13 From "Haritz" or "Ariz" (oak) and "Ona" (good).

right to graze it first, had priority; a doctrine of prior use: *first in time, first in right.*

In 1790 the United States contained nearly 569,000,000 acres of land, but as a result of the Louisiana Purchase in 1803, the Spanish cession of Florida and eastern Louisiana in 1819, the annexation of Texas in 1845, the Oregon Compromise of 1846 and, the Mexican Cession in 1848, the amount of land had incremented dramatically. The population grew from 3.9 million in 1790 to 31.4 million in 1860, being an increase of seven hundred per cent. The Republican Party favored the distribution of free land in the West and adopted this idea for its platform in 1860. On the contrary the Southern states were opposed because of its implications regarding slavery.

The Homestead Act of 20 May 1862 was enacted by President Abraham Lincoln on 20 May 1862, during the Civil War. The law provided that any head of a family or adult citizen, or anyone who had filed his or her declaration intention to become a citizen and, who had never borne arms against the U.S. government, could enter one quarter section or a less quantity of unappropriated public lands and, on payment of ten dollars, claim 160 acres (0.647 km^2) of undeveloped government land west of the Mississippi River. No individual was permitted to acquire title to more than one quarter section (160 acres) under the provision of the Act. The applications had to be made for the applicant's exclusive use and benefit and for the purpose of actual settlement and cultivation, and not either directly or indirectly for the use or benefit of any other person. After having resided upon or cultivated the land for the term of five years, the land called "homestead" became property of the claimant. The homestead could also be acquired after six months of residence at $1.25 an acre. Fifteen years later, on 3 March 1877, the Desert Land Act was enacted at the U.S. Congress. This new Act provided that any married couple who settled and irrigated 640 acres (2.6 km^2) of vacant uncultivated dryland within three years was entitled to hold it. 320 acres if it was given to a single person. The claimants had to pay 25 cents per acre and an additional fee of one dollar per acre after the irrigation work had been done.

Also, the grazers paid no charges or fees. And agriculture moved west. Can you imagine? The Basques coming over to this country found that all the vacant land was free and open and that they could even take as many animals there as they wanted as long as they raised them on certain lands, particularly from Boise on to Jordan Valley and into Oregon and Nevada. All that range in there was sheep and cattle range and everything was open. Well, that led to a lot of problems and also tragedies. There were so many Basques who had so much competitive spirit; they went ahead and got this vacant land in this country and thus were termed as the "tramp sheepherders," "itinerant sheepherders" and "coyotes."

The early 1930s were bad years. Black Tuesday, 29 October 1929, had left so many men out of work for so long. Many cattlemen with hay producing ranches who owned a base for their operations were gradually going to bankruptcy while roving sheep men passed by. Cowmen claimed that the sheepherders – contemptuously known as "coyotes"- over-grazed the land down to the roots, leaving local operators without feed and out of business. It was common belief that sheep spoiled lush pastures by moving across the range and that the fluid secreted by sheep from a gland between their toes stopped cattle from entering these pastures.

Consequently, cattlemen's Code of the West was severe on the woolgrowers. "Sheep dead-lines" were proclaimed all over the West by cattlemen and caused more deaths among the flocks than the bluetongue. In July 1902 several gunmen killed 2,000 sheep and one sheepherder at Green River Valley in Wyoming. One August evening in 1905 at Shell Creek in Big Horn County, Wyoming, a group of riders stormed in Louis Gantz's camp and killed 4,000 head, shot horses and burned the wagons and the sheepdogs alive. Some other times sheep were stampeded over a cliff, a method of killing sheep known as rimrocking. On April 2, 1909, one of the last armed conflicts between cattlemen and sheep growers occurred in Nowood Valley at Spring Creek, Wyoming. Several armed men rode into Joe Allemand's sheep camp, killed the dogs and sheep, shot Allemand to death and burnt his two nephews Joe Lazier and Jules Emge in their sheep wagon.

However, the sheep industry grew fast. By the end of the nineteenth century sheep growers had bought vast extensions of land from cattlemen and forest permits. This way the sheepherder had a base from where they could trail during the spring to fall season.

Basque sheep ranch in Nevada. Source: Cenarrusa archive.

XI. But vacant grazing land was disappearing. The National Forest Preserve began measuring and controlling federal lands in 1906 and, the government started to charge five to eight cents per head of sheep to graze them seasonally on federal land. Farmers were occupying lands which formerly were dedicated to grazing sheep and, on 19 February 1909 the U.S. Congress passed the Enlarged Homestead Act that doubled the 160 acres of land deeded to each homesteader by virtue of the 1862 Homestead Act to 320 acres. The law required that 1/8 of the land be continuously cultivated for agricultural crops other than native grasses. The Stock-Raising Homestead Act of 1916 doubled homesteads again, providing settlers 640 acres of land for ranching purposes. From 1862 to 1920 homesteaders and ranchers had occupied 3.9 million acres (15,783 km²) of land in Wyoming and thus the number of sheep had been reduced by 40 percent.

Finally, by virtue of the 1931 Range Act of Nevada, sheep grazing on public land was restricted in Nevada and, finally, the Taylor Grazing Act of 1934 seriously limited the itinerant sheep industry in the Western United States.

PC. Yes. Congressman from Colorado Edward T. Taylor introduced the Taylor Grazing Act of 28 June 1934. According to the law, in order to promote the highest use of the public lands pending its final disposal, the Secretary of the Interior is authorized, in his discretion, by order to establish grazing districts or additions thereto and/or to modify the boundaries thereof, of vacant, un-appropriated, and unreserved lands from any part of the public domain of the United States. This way eighty million acres (323,750 km²) of previously unreserved public lands of the United States were placed into grazing districts to be administered by the Department of the Interior. The law was intended to stop injury to the public grazing lands by preventing overgrazing and soil deterioration; to provide for their orderly use, improvement, and development; and to stabilize the livestock industry dependent upon the public range.[14]

Section 3 of the Taylor Grazing Act regulated grazing permits issued on public lands within the grazing districts established under the law. It gave leasing preference in the issuance of grazing permits to those within or near a district who were landowners engaged in the livestock business, bona fide occupants or settlers, or owners of water or water rights, as might be necessary to permit the proper use of lands. Grazing permits were to be issued only to citizens of the United States or to those who have filed the necessary declarations of intention to become such, and to groups, associations, or corporations authorized to conduct business under the laws of the State in which the grazing district was located. Permits were issued for a period of not more than ten years, subject to the preference right of the permittees to renewal in the discretion of the Secretary of the Interior, who had to specify from time to time numbers of stock and seasons of use. By June 1935, over sixty-five million acres had been placed in grazing districts.

XI. Today, Linda Dufurrena's photographs of sheep men in the American West decorate several halls of John Ascuaga's Nugget Casino and Orozko restaurant in Reno.

Also, the National Monument to the Basque Sheepherder was erected at Rancho San Rafael park in Reno (Nevada), on 27 August 1989, with funds donated by Basque and American institutions and family members who wanted to honor their fathers or grandfathers' and have their names inscribed on a stone wall next to the statue. A memorial to the past.

---

14   *Administration and use of public lands, Parts 14-17*, U.S. Government Printing Office, Washington D.C., 1946. P. 4435.

The Monument was opened in 1987, fruit of the hard work done by the members of the Basque National Monument Committee, among them, Carmelo Urza, Robert Laxalt and William Douglass. However, it was dedicated two years later, on 29 August 1989. To realize this project, a non-profit commission was formed for the purpose of acquiring a monument site, selecting a sculpture through competition and financing its renders. The project was conceived in 1984 by Jose Ramon Cengotitabengoa, President of the Society of Basque Studies in America of New York. Basque artist Nestor Basterretxea designed the 22-foot bronze statue representing a Basque sheepherder under the disc of the moon. Even though, in a recent conversation with Nestor Basterretxea in Bermeo, I told him that the sun in Nevada is much heavier than the moon. He answered that I have his permission for seeing the sun instead of the moon every time I visit the Monument. That way I become Basterretxea's metaphysical eclipse when I go to San Rafael.

The commission, which was under the auspices of the Society of Basque Studies in America, was comprised of Basque and other interested persons from several parts of the United States and the Basque homeland. The Honorary Chairmen of the Committee were President of the Basque Country Jose Antonio Ardanza, former Senator of Nevada Paul Laxalt, Nevada Governor Richard Bryan, California Governor George Deukmejian and, Idaho Governor Cecil Andrus.

In the opening ceremony the Basque National Monument Committee spokesman said:

> *Today, with far fewer bands of sheep on the open ranges, the Basque sheepherder is disappearing. With the passage of time, his existence may be quickly forgotten and his contribution to western history lost along with him. To avoid such neglect we propose to erect an enduring national monument, memorializing Basque contributions to the United States. In many ways, the monument recognized immigrants of all nationalities who came to the United States in search of opportunity and new horizons.*[15].

---

15   National Monument to the Basque Sheepherder of the American West. In, Boise State University Library, Camille B. Power, MSS 61, Box 3, Fol. 22.

PC. The first Basques came to Idaho in the mid-1800s, but the first massive wave of Basque sheepherders came after the 1900s. To become a sheepherder was a good deal for them because they didn't need to know English to herd sheep. I once read a good article in the *News Tribune* of Caldwell (Idaho) that we may well quote,

> *Contrary to what is widely believed, scrubby Idaho desert did not remind Basques of their homeland. As one Basque noted, Idaho is "the farthest from it." The Portland area does remind him of Euzkadi, he said. The real drawing card of the United States was the opportunity to be free and independent, a right denied to the Basques in Spain. Husbandry and agriculture were not the occupations of many of the Basques before they migrated here. Those from the coastal regions were fishermen, shipbuilders, carpenters and masons. Nevertheless, they took naturally to the job of sheepherding and were soon in demand. Those who enjoyed the new life they found wrote to their relatives and friends in Euzkadi and won those people on their way. Jordan Valley, Oregon, became one of the most typical Basque colonies in the West, with more than half the population Basque from about 1910 to 1950. The first Basques arrived there in 1897. They were Antone Azcuenaga and Joe Navarro, who started out as sheepherders and eventually built a small financial empire. Other Basques like them worked hard at sheepherding or other ranch work living frugally and saving their money for the chance to buy a piece of land of their own. As Basques settled in the communities, boarding houses and hotels sprang up where they could gather and speak their own language. Boise had several such establishments. Through the years, the sheep business dwindled in importance and Basques gradually diffused into every other occupation. Many remained in ranching, however, and in this area today names like Basel Aldecoa, George Goiri and Dick Gabica, are prominent in the business. Others have gone into the professions, commerce and politics, with the name of Pete Cenarrusa, Idaho's Secretary of State, the most well known in the latter category.[16]*

---

[16]   Miller, Barbara R., "Idaho's Basques Proud to Retain Own Heritage", *News Tribune*, Caldwell, May 1970.

Robert and Paul Laxalt. Robert Laxalt (1923-2001) was a Basque-American writer from Nevada. His most renowned novels are *Sweet Promise Land* (1957), *In a Hundred Graves: A Basque Portrait* (1972), *A Cup of Tea in Pamplona* (1985. Nominated for a Pulitzer Prize in fiction), *Basque Hotel* (1989. Also nominated for the Pulitzer) and *The Governor's Mansion* (1994). *Sweet Promise Land* is based on the story of his father Dominique who returned to the Basque Country after forty-seven years working as a sheepherder in Nevada. Paul Laxalt (1922-2010), the "son of a Basque sheepherder," was Lieutenant Governor of Nevada (1963-67), Governor of Nevada (1967-71) and U.S. Senator (1974-87). Close friend to President Reagan, when the last was elected President in 1980, the press referred to Laxalt as "The First Friend."

I am convinced that Senator Pat McCarran considered that there were not more trustworthy people than the Basques to fulfill the job of a sheepherder. It may be considered a cliché, but the truth is that from the high mountains in northern Idaho to the Pampa in Argentina, the Basques are considered hard workers and noble people.

I like a poem by C. C. Wright from the book on the American Basques entitled *Americanuak. Basques in the New World* by John Bilbao and William Douglass, *Luck a la "Basquo"*,

> *Some "Basquos" came from Spain last week*
> *And all went out to herding sheep;*
> *They passed some loafers on the way,*
> *Who had some unkind things to say*
> *About the country -how it's run-*
> *To what dire end it's bound to come,*
> *And how the poor man stands no show-*
> *He might as well to Hazen go.*
> *And so they sat and chewed the rag,*
> *And went o'er and o'er that time-worn gag*
> *About dividing up the wealth,*
> *When each could travel for his health.*
> *And as their cigarettes they smoked*
> *They all about sheepherding joked,*
> *And wished, meantime, some easy gink*
> *Would come along and buy a drink.*
> *Five years the Basque will follow sheep,*
> *And every cent he gets he'll keep,*
> *Except what little goes for clothes.*
> *And then the first thing someone knows*
> *He's jumped his job and bought a band*
> *And taken up some vacant land;*
> *And then the fellows who still prate*
> *About hard luck and unkind fate,*
> *And wail because they have no pull,*
> *May help the "Basquo" clip his wool.*[17]

---

[17]   Douglass, William A.; Bilbao, Jon, *Amerikanuak: Basques in the New World*, University of Nevada Press, Reno, 2005. Pp. 247-248.

That may well be my parents' own story, the Basque sheepherders who ended up owning the Cenarrusa Sheep Co. in Idaho.

National Monument to the Basque Sheepherder in Reno, Nevada. Source: Irujo Ametzaga archive.

XI. You also established a sheep ranch near Carey.

PC. Yes. I kept on working in the operation of my family's sheep business in Carey after I was elected a member of the Legislature in 1950 because the Idaho Legislature, which meets in Boise, three hours trip from Carey, does not function as a full-time assembly. Also, as I have already mentioned, I became an institutional trainer, teaching war veterans how to manage farms after World War Two. Therefore, by 1950 I got to know the lamb business quite well.

Freda and I started making our living in the sheep business in 1953 when we bought 1,200 head of Wyoming ewes. We were not rookies but that was a tough business. The first year we went to buy the sheep and realized that the owner had taken them to graze for the day and to drink at night since the sheep were bought by the pound. Those sheep seemed balloons, swollen from drinking so much.

[59]

That first year we wintered them in Carey and pastured them in the fall in Richfield, twenty-three miles south of Carey. In 1954 we partnered with my brother-in-law, Frank Somsen, to buy 1,250 three-year-old ewes from Rawlins Feeders in Wyoming, and another 600 from Bud Purdy of Picabo. We leased as much as 3,800 acres (15 km²) around Hailey to graze the sheep in the summertime and pioneered the system of transporting the sheep 767 miles south to Blythe in California, for better winter range feed and better lambing conditions.

By taking the sheep to California for the lambing season in the winter we got them to fatten up on lush vegetation provided by moist seasons on the southwest desert. We learned that from the Basque sheep operators in California who used to summer in the high country and winter in the low country. It minimized a lot of work because the sheep took care of the mowing machine; the sheep harvested the alfalfa with their teeth and all we had to do was to turn the fields to them. That way we did not have to mow the hay, bale it in 100-150 pounds bales, take them out of the fields into a dry quarter and stack it into stacks nine bales high, four bales wide and, from 70 to 120 bales long. We saved money but also much work and we did not need the sheds anymore like we did in the snow country. You see the difference in work and cost; we eliminated all of that. Also, since it was a warmer country the sheep did not grow that much wool and went fatter and, thus, we produced more meat per lamb and made a better income.

John Peavey, a rancher and Democratic politician from Carey, took the idea from us and started wintering in California too. At that time he had seventeen Basque sheepherders working for him. This has remained a common practice for Idaho sheep producers into the twenty-first century. We also collaborated with the United States Sheep Experiment Station at Dubois to test melatonin, a hormone taken to increase ovulation in ewes in order to produce early-season twin lambs.

XI. That was the time when the U.S. Congress provided special immigrant quotas for Basque sheepherders.

PC. Right. In the postwar period, workforce shortage led to recruit alien workers. In the 1950s about a million and a half quota immigrants were authorized but only one million actually entered the United States while one million and a half nonquota immigrants got to enter the country.

Eat sheep, wear wool. As Freda recalls, "The baker at Albertson's made a mistake for it should have read 'Eat lamb, wear wool'...!" In the photo, Freda Coates Cenarrusa (on the left) and Phyllis Laird campaigning for sheep companies in 1963. The photo was taken in the Caucus room of the House of Representatives, in the Idaho state capitol. Source: Cenarrusa archive.

Sheepherders were recruited to provide relief for the sheep-raising industry by making special quota immigration visas available to a specific number of alien sheepherders.

On 30 June 1950 Senator Pat McCarran of Nevada sponsored the first of these measures in Congress. It was Public Law 587 [S. 1165] that made 250 special quota immigration visas available to alien sheepherders within the period of one year after the effective date of the Act.

XI. President Harry S. Truman appointed Democratic Senator from Rhode Island J. Howard McGrath Attorney General of the United States on 24 August 1949 and he occupied that duty until April 3, 1952. McGrath suspected that the Basques might constitute a danger to national security.

PC. Yes, so I passed the first of a series of Memorials on the Basques. In short, a Memorial or Joint Memorial is a declaration adopted by both houses and used to make a request of or to express an opinion to Congress, the President of the United States, or both.

In January 1951 I passed a Joint Memorial to allow Basque sheepherders to come work in the United States urging Congress to take necessary action to activate Public Law 587 previously passed to allow the importation to the United States of 250 skilled sheepherders for the purpose of assisting the wool-growing industry of the West.

I explained that the sheepherders needed were being kept from entry to the United States by a ruling of Atty. Gen. McGrath and that they were aliens of political leanings which might endanger the security of the United States. There was no valid reason for the action taken by the Attorney General. He had made his ruling under the Anticommunist Internal Security Act passed by the Congress in 1950. The Security Act of 1950, sponsored by Nevada Senator Pat McCarran, Chair of the Judiciary Committee, was one of the most relevant laws passed during the Cold War.[18] I tried to explain that because of McGrath's action the wool industry of the West had suffered with the result that the price of both wool and

---

[18] Schrecker, Ellen, *The Age of McCarthyism: A Brief History with Documents*, Macmillan, London, 2002. P. 217.

lamb had increased considerably to the consumer and, as a consequence, there was a wool shortage in the United States to supply the needs of our armed forces and our citizens. McGrath apparently made his ruling because Basques by law under Dictator Franco were forced to attend official schools and thereby could become indoctrinated with fascism.[19] But that was far from being true, as history has shown all of us thereafter.

XI. The Memorial proved to be successful. Also, the California Range Association later known as the Western Range Association (WRA) was organized in 1951 to alleviate the critical shortage of labor in the sheep raising industry. The WRA lobbied on behalf of ranch owners throughout the American West to pass bills that allowed ranchers to sponsor herders from the Basque Country. The WRA directly negotiated with the Spanish government and established a recruiting office in Bilbao.

As a consequence, on 9 April 1952, the U.S. Congress enacted Public Law 307 [S. 2549] according to which the U.S. Attorney General, under the authority of the Immigration Act of 1917, granted permission for the importation of no more than five hundred skilled sheepherders into the United States for a period of one year. Public Law 307 provided that the employment offered to such skilled sheepherder had to be permanent and that a special immigration visa might be issued to an alien sheepherder if no immigration quota number of the country of which such alien sheepherder was a national was then available. The Act also provided that such alien sheepherder was admissible into the United States for permanent residence. The Attorney General had to certify to the Secretary of State the name and address of every skilled sheepherder for which an application for importation under the fourth proviso to section 3 of the Immigration Act of 1917 was approved. If a quota number was not then available for such alien sheepherder, the proper consular officer might issue a special quota immigration visa to him. According to Section 3.a of the law, no more than five hundred special quota immigration visas could be made under this Act.

---

[19]   "Congress Urged to Activate Law Allowing Basques' Importation"

And soon after the Immigration and Nationality Act of 1952 [S. 2550] was enacted on 27 June 1952. Known as the McCarran-Walter Omnibus Immigration Bill, the Immigration and Nationality Act was supposed to codify within a single body of text the amalgam of United States immigration laws. The Act restricted immigration into the U.S. and established a system of preference determining which ethnic groups were desirable immigrants. The Act defined three types of immigrants, namely, immigrants with special skills or relatives of U.S. citizens; average immigrants whose numbers were not supposed to exceed 270,000 per year and, refugees. Western Hemisphere immigration continued to be quota-free and quota preferences were established for relatives and skilled aliens. President Truman tried to veto the Act because he regarded the bill as un-American and discriminatory due to the fact that limited the entrance of Eastern European or Asian citizens escaping from Communist countries. In McCarran own words:

> *I believe that this nation is the last hope of Western civilization and if this oasis of the world shall be overrun, perverted, contaminated or destroyed, then the last flickering light of humanity will be extinguished.*[20]

PC. This measure did not affect Basque sheepherders that were considered average Western European immigrants.

XI. Right. Two years later, on 3 September 1954 Public Law 770 [S. 2862] was passed at Congress to provide relief for the sheep-raising industry by making special nonquota immigrant visas available to certain skilled alien sheepherders. In any case in which the Attorney General, under the authority of section 204 of the Immigration and Nationality Act, granted permission for the importation of a skilled alien sheepherder into the United States and the investigation of the application for such importation disclosed that the employment offered such skilled alien sheepherder was permanent and that no immigration quota number of the quota to which such skilled alien sheepherder was chargeable under section 202 of the Immigration and Nationality

---

[20]   Shanks, Cheryl L., *Immigration and the politics of American sovereignty, 1890 to 1990*, University of Michigan, Ann Arbor, 1994. P. 229.

Act was then available, a special nonquota immigrant visa might be issued to such skilled alien sheepherder under the immigration laws. As in the previous years the Attorney General had to certify to the Secretary of State the name and address of every skilled alien sheepherder for which an application for importation under section 204 was approved. No more than three hundred and eighty-five special nonquota immigrant visas were to be passed under Public Law 770.

On 31 August 1954 Private Law 936 [S. 2074] was passed for the relief of certain Basque sheepherders. The U.S. Congress authorized and directed Attorney General to discontinue any deportation proceedings and to cancel any outstanding orders and warrants of deportation, warrants of arrests, and bonds which might have been issued in the cases of forty-four Basque sheepherders. By this Act, these forty-four alien sheepherders should not again be subject to deportation by reason of the same facts upon which such deportation proceedings were commenced or any such warrants and orders had been issued and, their residence was legalized. And on 28 July 1955 a new Act [S. 633] for the relief of six Basque sheepherders was enacted in Congress and thus, these Basque alien citizens were lawfully admitted to the United States for permanent residence as of the date of the enactment of the Act, upon payment of the required visa fees.

According to the data at the exhibit Sheep Herding in Northern Nevada of the University of Nevada Reno's Special Collections, by 1956, 893 Basque sheepherders had entered the United States under the above mentioned immigration programs. By 1966, 1,283 herders were under contract to the WRA. Contract wages were $230 per month in Nevada for a herder's first year, with $10 increases per year during the next two years of the contract. By 1970, 1,500 herders were under contract to the WRA and 90 percent were Basque but in 1976, 742 herders were under contract to the WRA and only 106 were Basque (14.3 percent).[21]

PC. The improvement of social and economic conditions in the Basque Country in the mid-1960s made it difficult to recruit Basque herders. Thus, the WRA redirected its recruiting efforts to Mexico and Peru. Currently, most of the sheepherders working for

---

[21]   http://knowledgecenter.unr.edu/sheepherders/default.htm

us are Peruvian. And the foreman is a Peruvian citizen also. [Laughing] His name is Pedro Loiola Etxeberria.

XI. One of the last cases of massive Basque immigration happened in the late sixties, when Senator Frank Church introduced legislation to allow fifty-five Basque sheepherders permanent residence in the United States on 2 August 1968. Church said on that occasion:

> *The Basques are threatened with deportation unless Congress grants them permanent residence in this country. You have on numerous occasions heard me speak of the Basques of Idaho and the high regard in which we hold them, Church told the Senate. Theirs is an important contribution to Idaho and these men specifically to the sheep industry. This is a contribution that we cannot afford to lose.*[22]

PC. This was in 1968. At the end of the 1930s most of the Basques in Idaho (like my parents) were sheep men and owners of boarding houses and bars, to accommodate the herders, when they came to town. But slowly they started becoming owners of their own ranches and in the 1940s we have the first generation of professionals, lawyers, politicians, professors and so on. Now the descendants of those immigrants are found in all of Idaho's businesses and professions. Most of the ancient Basque boarding houses have disappeared in Idaho, such as the old Delamar Hotel, the Oñate and Valencia Restaurants or The Star Rooming House that was converted into offices.[23]

In 1968 a news release from Frank Church reported that generational shift:

> *The days of the lonely Basque sheepherder are past. Today's Basque is found in offices, classrooms, factories and department stores. He is a second or third generation Basque who probably knows little of the native language. One of his parents may be of Irish or German descent, or one of the other "melting pot" nationalities. His home is*

---

[22] News release from Frank Church, Washington, August 2, 1968. In, Boise State University Library, Frank Church Collection, MSS 56, Box 43, Fol. 15.

[23] Power, Camille B., "Basque Culture", manuscript. In, Boise State University Library, Camille B. Power Collection, MSS 61, Box 3, Fol. 3.

typical American, except for the occasional "txorizuak" or other Basque dish which may be prepared for special events. If it weren't for his name, and possibly for his dark coloring, he would be indistinguishable from a Smith or a Jones whose ancestors emigrated from other parts of Europe. He is an American. (…) Eiguren, who is an aide at the Nampa office of the State Department of Employment, said he felt his generation tended to lose contact with the Basque culture in their efforts to "fit in." Young people today, however, are recognizing the value of the old language and customs. "Basques are beginning to realize they can adapt and still retain their own heritage," he said.[24]

A century after the first Basque sheepherders came to Idaho the Basque community here proudly celebrates its cultural heritage. As Charles Herrington, from the Office of the Governor of Idaho, put it, the Basque Center at 601 Grove Street in downtown Boise is a focal point of Basque community life and we may say that also of the Idahoan society; the Basque Museum venerates Basque history, and Basque choirs and dance groups exalt the Basque language and arts. The Basques also have a preschool, Boiseko Ikastola, and every week about 200 kids gather at the Basque Block in Grove Street.

We have lunch and dinners at our taverns and restaurants such as the Gernika and Leku Ona. The Basque community holds many celebrations throughout the year such as the Mass for the Basques who have passed away during the year or the Sheepherder Ball, held each December in the Basque Center. The proceeds have been donated to charity every year since the inception of the event in 1928. Another special event is the St. Ignatius Day picnic, held the last day of July or the first of August at the Boise Municipal Park. Once every five years it becomes an international event and Basques from all over the world come to gather with us in a seven-day non-stop celebration.

---

[24]   Miller, Barbara R., "Idaho's Basques Proud to Retain Own Heritage", *News Tribune*, Caldwell, May 1970. In, *Congressional Records. Proceedings and Debates of the 91st Congress, Second Session*, Vol. 116, N° 91, Washington, Thursday, June 4, 1970.

WESTERN BASQUE FESTIVAL

RENO & SPARKS, NEVADA

JUNE 6-7 1959

ZAZPIAK-BAT

OPENING DAY Parties at Basque Hotels
MAMMOTH SUNDAY BARBECUE and
PICNIC at Dick Graves' **NUGGET**-Sparks

Costumed Dancing Contests
MUS Card Game Contest-Tests of Strength and Skill
Basque Orchestra and La Jota Dancing

TICKETS TO BARBECUE FESTIVAL
$3.50 Per Person
(Children-Half Price)

FOR TICKET RESERVATIONS	FOR ROOM RESERVATIONS
Write to:	*Write to:*
WESTERN BASQUE FESTIVAL	RENO CHAMBER OF COMMERCE
650 Cardinal Way • Reno, Nevada	P.O. Box 2109 • Reno, Nevada
Information About Festival Sent Upon Request	SPARKS CHAMBER OF COMMERCE
	859 B Street • Sparks, Nevada

The Coat of Arms of the Basque Country at the top, with the motto *Zazpiak Bat* (The seven are one). Poster for the Western Basque Festival celebrated in Reno (Nevada). Source: Irujo Ametzaga archive.

These celebrations are the product of an intense cultural, political and also economic communication between the Basque Country and the state of Idaho and that is why three presidents of the Basque Country have visited Idaho between 1988 and 2011:

> *Idaho imports wine, cheese, and other products from the Basque country, but our ties are more political than economic. Spain is our 17th largest export market. The European Commonwealth as a whole is our third largest regional market (following Asia and North America). Basque immigration has enriched Idaho's culture. Our citizens are familiar with Basque music from listening to Basque choirs. We have learned about Basque dancing from numerous Basque dance groups. We can savor delicious Basque food in Boise. The Basque Museum and the Basque Cultural Center teach Basque history and the Basque language to our citizens. I now wish I had attended those language classes!*[25]

Many returned home with a sizable fortune to go into business. As noted by Camille Power "one bar in Bilbao is named the 'Boise Bar', and I saw another in Guernica with the same name. In Durango, we visited a very elegant bar patterned after a bar of the 40's in Ketchum, Idaho, built with the money two brothers earned on the Cenarrusa Ranch near Carey."[26] As Senator Frank Church, a good man and a good friend, stated at the U.S. Congress on the occasion of a visit by a Basque dance troupe:

> *Idaho is justly proud of its Basque people, the descendants of a hardy and fierce race, the origins of which are shrouded in the mist of antiquity. Through the centuries they have amassed a fascinating and colorful history. It was through the Pyrenean mountain passes that the battle between Charlemagne and the Saracen invaders flowed back and forth; the Basques proudly identify themselves as the mountaineers who cut off the rear guard of Charlemagne's army and brought on its destruction. The adventurous spirit of the Basques is*

---

[25]   Briefing Memorandum by Charles Herrington, Office of the Governor of Idaho, to Cecil D. Andrus, Governor of the State of Idaho, Boise, April 23, 1992. In, Boise State University Library, Cecil D. Andrus Collection, MSS 141, Box 374, Fol. 6.

[26]   Power, Camille B., "Basque Culture", manuscrit. In, Boise State University Library, Camille B. Power Collection, MSS 61, Box 3, Fol. 3.

typified by two famous mariners: Lakotza was the navigator who led Columbus to the New World, and Elkano who assumed command from Magellan after the latter's death, and became the first seaman to circumnavigate the earth. The Basque language, too, is shrouded in mystery. It is one of the most difficult languages to be found anywhere and has not been related to any other language family in the world. (...) The Basques are known for their honesty, energy, and fidelity, for their agility in dancing and their fine voices. Close borne ties and strong filial devotion have produced this exemplary group of young dancers whom we welcome here this week. Dancing has always played an important role in the life of the Basques in their homeland and it is no less important here.[27]

'Welcome Basques'. Photograph taken in 1959, during the celebration of the Western Basque Festival of June 1959. Source: Basque Archive of the University of Nevada Reno.

XI. I remember my parents speaking to me about how grateful they were to America, the land that had welcomed and fed them

---

[27]   Church, Frank, "The Basque Dancers." In, *Congressional Records. Proceedings and Debates of the 90th Congress, Second Session*, Vol. 114, Nº 113, Washington, Monday, July 1, 1968.

when a dictator had exiled them from their homes. In this sense, what does it mean to you to be American?

PC. To be an American is really a great thing. As Joe Eiguren expressed in his book *Kashpar*, I grew up American and also Basque. To be an American is similar to me to being Basque. As the Basques once had, we also had a great statesman who left England and came to this country to find a new country, a land ruled under a new Constitution, similar to the Basque laws and the Basque feelings, and the Basque make-up. The Basque laws were conceived for protecting the individual people, for people were supreme, not the government. Likewise, here in Idaho the government is not supreme. It is the people who are supreme. I feel comfortable in this country, being Basque, because we think similarly and the law provides similar feelings to the Basque people and the American people. It is very easy for Basques like myself to blend in to American society.

XI. So you think that, for instance, individualism, the idea of democracy and politics and the way of organizing work are similar in both cultures?

PC. Yes. Maybe it is why so many Basque groups are successful here in the West, because they blend in. They commit. And that explains why Americans, Idahoans included, have strong feelings about the Basques and like them, because of their nature and how they have grown and developed.

XI. And then, what does it mean to you to be Basque?

PC. I may answer with pride but without vanity, "We are the Basques. Who are the rest of you?"
 I have often read of the Basques that they are devout, independent, simple, physically splendid and, in the words of Spanish philosopher José Ortega y Gasset, "with souls beautiful and strong." The Basque people have lived in the Pyrenees since long before any of the surrounding peoples appeared in Europe. As I once read, "To wring simple but wholesome livelihoods from their high, four and five acre (15,000 to 20,000 m²) farms, to enjoy their lightning swift dances, the game of pilota or jai-alai which they

play from childhood to old age, to follow the Catholic faith in their own manner, and to be let alone, is all they ever have asked. For that they have fought successfully through ages until now."

Iconic Louis Basque Corner Basque restaurant in central Reno, Nevada. Louis and Lorraine Erreguibel opened Louis Basque Corner in 1967. Today, Chris Shanks and Brian Elcano own the Home of the famous Picon Punch and, in their own words, traditional dishes such as sweetbreads, oxtail, tongue and tripe can still be found in the menu and are served family-style in long tables covered with red-&-white tablecloth. The homemade food is expertly prepared, the picon punches flow freely, and the conversation is never lacking. "To us, you're one of the family." Source: Irujo Ametzaga archive.

Strong family life, religion and language have kept us together. One of the strongest Basque traditions is that of family unity and inheritance. Traditionally the family homestead was not divided at death but went intact to one of the descendants. So strong is still this attachment that most of the Basque surnames are names of houses for the house gave its name to the family.

After a century some of the Basques who rest at the Boise cemetery where no longer registered, like the "unknown Basque sheepherder" who died in 1904. The Basque Museum organized a research team and erected a tombstone to honor the memories of all Basques who passed away in Boise. Source: Irujo Ametzaga archive.

XI. What could you underline about the Basque language?

PC. I have always felt that Basques are clear speaking. They say straight what they feel, and that can generate problems from time to time, you know, because of a lack of diplomacy and an excess of forthrightness. I am very fortunate having been born to Basque parents. At the time that I was born, all the children, my whole family, we all learned the Basque language first. We learned it at home with our parents. My mother, she always talked Basque and my father who was working and meeting with and conversing with businessmen, he learned the English language very well without any accent. Later on in life, it was customary with us that we talked English with my father and always Basque with my mother. I always felt better speaking Basque with my mother. She didn't learn the English language as well as my father did.

I remember how the Basque Studies Program of the University of Nevada sponsored a summer school of Basque Studies in Uztaritze from June 15 to August 18, 1970. The students received instruction for six weeks in the Basque language, Basque culture and Basque literature. Our son Joe went to the Basque Country in that occasion. At his arrival he went to visit my parents and when my mother opened the door he just said to her "Zer moduz?" (How are you?). She hugged him, and cried.

The Basque language is the core of the Basque culture and the Basque way of life. In Basque we call ourselves "Euskaldunak" which means "Basque Speakers." So, anyone speaking Basque is considered Basque. There is a legend saying that no Basque can go to hell,

> *No Basque can go to hell. It seems the Devil spent seven years in the Basque country trying to master the language. After diligent study he had learned only "bai" and "ez" – "yes" and "no." As he was fleeing the country in a terrible thunderstorm he fell, hitting his head and knocking the two words he had learned from his memory. Since then Devil knows nothing of the language, he cannot tempt the Basques, thus none can go to hell. So says Ramona Garro, my receptionist.*[28]

---

[28]   Church, Frank, "The Basque Dancers." In, *Congressional Records. Proceedings and Debates of the 90th Congress, Second Session*, Vol. 114, N° 113,

Professor Nils Collet Vogt at the University of Oslo (1864-1923) described, Euskara, the Basque language, as the only surviving European language that predates the arrival of the Indo-European languages, and may be dated 25,000 to 30,000 BC. Its preservation is providential. It is the best contribution that the Basques could make to the study of European, not to say world civilization. The ancient law of Gipuzkoa of 1720 states in its first article that,

> *Strangers never governed these parts of Iberia, as they did in other regions, and the natural language of the first settlers of these lands has been gloriously preserved, and their descendants are in possession of the land left to them by inheritance until our times, and not the Egyptians, Chaldeans, Jews, Greeks, Carthaginians, Romans, Alans, Suevi, Vandals, Goths or Arabs, who dominated almost entirely in the other parts of the Kingdom, and introduced their national languages, were ever able to dominate us in our land, Gipuzkoa.*

Both ethnographers and linguists have been interested in the Basque language for many years. With greater or smaller rigor, many scientists have proposed their own theories to unravel the enigma of origins of Basque. Some swear by the Caucasian theory; others by the Iberian. Some others even look for its origins in North Africa or even in the legendary Atlantis. In the end it will turn out quite complicated to choose among them. However, regardless of its roots, looking to the future, Euskara is a language that has surpassed freezing periods, migrations, conquests and the worst political times of repression and censorship, which is why it seems that it will not disappear.

XI. A study recently published in "Scientific American" maintains that linguistically and genetically there is a common pre Indo-European kinship.[29] The two basic lines of the investigation -the

---

Washington, Monday, July 1, 1968.

[29]   Hamel, Elisabeth; Venneman, Theo; Forster, Peter, "La lengua originaria de los europeos prehistóricos", *Investigación y Ciencia*, 316, Barcelona, 2003. Pp. 62-71.

genetic and the linguistic one- come to the same conclusion: there is a common European substrate related to the Basque people. Many of the names of cities, rivers, mountains, valleys and landscapes in Europe have their origin in pre Indo-European languages, concretely in Proto-Basque. Elisabeth Hamell and Theo Vennemann, professors at the University of Munich, confirmed that peoples related to the Basques lived, in other times, almost all over Europe, whereas, on the other hand, Peter Forster, University of Cambridge, published a genetic study ensuring that virtually three quarters of the genes of Western Europeans come from the primitive Basques. According to Forster the present Basques are not, absolutely, a singular and marginal type, without any relation to the rest of the Europeans. Quite to the contrary, its genotype is set, in a surprising degree, on the whole Western European population.

PC. So, we do not exaggerate if we affirm that Western Europeans are partly Basque?

XI. Not according to Mr. Forster.

Without entering later details, the most widely accepted view among scientists is that the Homo Sapiens originated in the African savanna around 200,000 years ago (Mitochondrial Era) and that about 40,000 years ago started colonizing Eurasia (during the Würm cold period oscillations) displacing the Homo Neanderthalensis. After the arrival of the Cromagnon, the earliest prototype of European Homo Sapiens (c. 40,000 BC in Eastern Europe and c. 25,000 BC in Western Europe), not other human migration of such a magnitude, colonized the territory during such an expanded period of time.

During the climatically warm periods known as Paudorf, Bolling and Allerod oscillations of the glacial stage Würm (33,000-8,000 BC), the survivors of the cold periods hunted for refuge in the climatically more benign areas of Eurasia: the plains of the Eastern Europe (a partially coincident area with present Ukraine) and the Pyrenean southwest, the area between the Pyrenees and the Garonne river (centuries after called by the Romans Novempopulania or Aquitania). This last zone was climatically protected by southern and southwestern dry wind streams, warmed up by the Foehn or Föhn effect, making winters more bearable.

Dolmen of Aizkomendi in Egilaz of the late Neolitic. The dolmen consists of ten stones that form a burial chamber and an entrance hall. The original stone covering it weighs over ten tons. The mound that was about 60 meters in diameter and about 4 meters high, covered the entire chamber. Source: Irujo Ametzaga archive.

From here, after the 8,000 BC (post glacial period), the survivors of the Würm glacial stage were progressively repopulating the continent at the end of the Upper Paleolithic (last Magdalenian) and the beginnings of the Mesolithic.

These ideas gave rise to the "Solutrean hypothesis" that was first proposed in 1998 according to which Solutrean people who occupied Western Europe from roughly 21,000 to 17,000 years ago crossed the Atlantic for the first time during the last glacial maximum and arrived in the Americas where they developed the Clovis culture that consequently shares common characteristics with the Solutrean culture. Based on archaeological research, paleoclimatic analysis and genetic studies, archaeologists Dennis J. Stanford and Bruce A. Bradley have developed the Solutrean hypothesis in their book "Across Atlantic Ice: The Origin of America's Clovis Culture" (University of California Press, 2012).

Summarizing, the first Homo Sapiens entered Europe very slowly from the East displacing the Homo Neanderthalensis that disappeared following the direction of the advance of the Sapiens (from East to West) and during the same chronological framework (most probably due to the clash between these two species). Once established, these primitive Homo Sapiens developed a culture in the warmest areas of Western Europe for thousands of years during which the continent was practically isolated from the rest of the world (ices at the east end and ocean at the west). And this gave rise to the Proto-Basque culture and the mentioned gene pool in the territory that currently we call Western Europe. Obviously, after nearly 20,000 years of inhabiting the same territory and generating a genuine genetic pool, we must conclude that these peoples lived and worked together, communicated and even understood each other. Consequently, we may conclude that Proto-Basque was originated in Western Europe during this historical period. The Celts, peoples inhabiting the most occidental part of Asia, brought their language into Europe thousands of years later, during the Early European Bronze Age (c. 1,800 BC).

The linguistic investigations by Elisabeth Hamel and Theo Venneman reinforce this theory built around the great mystery of Basque as a non Indo-European language. These linguists have found a great number of toponyms all over Europe using Basque roots or Basque prefixes and suffixes and they defend the idea that these geographic denominations are the oldest linguistic traces of the continent, the earliest signs of civilization in Europe. Indeed, there are many toponyms related to water sharing the same lexical root all over Europe. It is frequent to find names that begin with the Basque prefixes "al-/alm-" like "Allery" or "Alm". Another very common variant is the group of names beginning with "var-/ver-", such as "Were". Names starting with "is-/eis-", and mainly "ur-/aur-" ("Ur" means "water" in Basque) like "Urach", "Urals", "Urola" or "Urwis" are also quite abundant. There are also many toponyms begining with "ibar-" and "am-" (from the Basque "Aran" which means "valley"), the same in the Pyrenees as in the Alps ("Aharenself", in Alsace or "Valle de Arán" in Catalonia). There exists a great correlation, in all the mentioned cases, between the toponyms, their meaning, and the geographical reality as it was 20,000 years ago (and, in many cases, as it is nowadays).

Proto-Basques did not only leave geographic names. According to researchers, the Basque substrate is also detected in the way of counting. The Indo-European brought the decimal system, but the Basques of our day continue counting by base twenty: twenty and ten ("hogeita hamar" meaning "thirty"), twice twenty ("berrogei" meaning "forty"), twice twenty and ten ("berrogeita hamar" meaning "fifty") and so on. The Celts would have taken from the Basques the vigesimal system that was conserved in old French. Even now, some relics like "quatre-vingts" (four times twenty) or "quatre-vingt-dix" (ninety) last in French.

The researchers point out that the Proto-Basque language was extended through Western Europe (they review examples from Germany to Portugal).

PC. And the genetic advances based on the DNA tests have come to complete this theory with a new slant.

XI. Yes. Twenty years ago, the genetic scientist Allan Wilsson was able to reconstruct the phylogenetic tree of the Homo Sapiens contributing new features to the theory about the origin of the European population. The most important result of the most recent genetic studies has been to reach the conclusion that at least three quarters of the present Western European genetic base come directly by matrilineal route (mother branch) from the prehistoric Homo Sapiens who came to live in Western Europe from the Near East before the apogee of the last freezing, more or less 30,000 years ago.

This investigation points out that the peoples who arrived from the East thousands of years later to Western Europe (mainly the Celts) did not contribute much (in genetic terms) to the pre existing European population.

As described by Brian Sykes in his book *The Seven Daughters of Eve*,[30] most Europeans descend from only seven mitochondrial DNA lineages or haplogroups, two of them located in the Basque region. As we have said its expansion began after the cold periods of the Würm glacial era. The first group is Haplogroup H "Helena"

---

30   Sykes, Brian, *The seven daughters of Eve*, W W Norton & Co Inc, Scranton (Pennsylvania), 2002.

("light" in Greek). This group is, by difference, the most extended haplogroup in Western Europe. It was originated approximately 20,000 years ago in Aquitania, between the valleys of Dordogne and the Pyrenees. 47 percent of the Europeans belong to it and, even if this lineage is extended all over Europe, its higher frequency is detected among the Basques (89 percent) suggesting that it was originated in the Basque lands.

Painting of a horse at Santimamiñe cave dating from the the Magdalenian period, in the Upper Paleolithic (14,000 to 9,000 years BC). It may be considered one of the first words written in proto-Basque. Source: Basque Archive of the University of Nevada Reno.

The second haplogroup is called Haplogroup V "Velda" by Sykes and it originated approximately 17,000 years ago in the Cantabrian region. Five percent of Europeans belong to it and it is not as common among the Basques (10 percent) as it is among the Cantabrians (21.6 percent).

PC. Yes, indeed. More recently, in 2006, Stephen Oppenheimer, a medical geneticist at Oxford University, has expressed that Celts, Angles, Jutes, Saxons, Vikings, Normans and others are all minorities in the modern British gene pool compared with the first unnamed pioneers from the Basque Country who, 15,000 to 13,000 years ago (at the end of the coldest period of Würm II, during the Bolling oscillation, 12.000-11.000 BC) ventured into the empty, chilly lands, so recently vacated by the great ice sheets.[31] In his own words:

> *Our subsequent separation from Europe has preserved a genetic time capsule of southwestern Europe during the Ice Age, which we share most closely with the former ice-age refuge in the Basque country. Overall, three quarters of our modern gene pool (two thirds in England) derives from this early source. The first settlers were unlikely to have spoken a Celtic language but possibly a tongue related to the unique Basque language. There were many later immigrations and invasions, and each left a genetic signal, but no subsequent immigrant event contributed much more than a 10th of our modern genetic mix. (...) Barry Cunliffe, professor of archaeology at Oxford, suggests that Celtic language developed along the Atlantic fringe of western Europe during the first four millennia of maritime trade, and was carried north into Ireland and Wales by metal prospectors from 4,400 years ago. New linguistic estimates give the age of the Celtic branch at around 6,000 years, consistent with Cambridge archaeologist Colin Renfrew's view of the Neolithic spread of Indo-European languages. My study found good evidence for Neolithic gene flow from the Mediterranean, around Spain to the British Isles, including at least one sizable genetic colonisation event in Abergele, North Wales, which matches the archaeological evidence of an early copper mining colony there around 3,700 years ago. This flow provided a third of modern male genes in that part of North Wales, but less than 10 percent in the rest of Britain, with the highest impact on the English South Coast (10 percent) and least in Ireland (four percent). Clearly the dominance of the "Celts" in Britain has been hugely exaggerated.[32]*

XI. We are going to speak about politics. What would you say to someone who is now ready to start reading this book?

---

[31]   Oppenheimer, Stephen, *The Origins of the British: A Genetic Detective Story. The Surprising Roots of The English, Irish, Scottish and Welsh*, Carroll & Graf, New York, 2006.

[32]   Oppenheimer, Stephen, "What does being British mean? Ask the Spanish", *The Telegraph*, October 10, 2006.

PC. I would start by explaining some arithmetic. Journalist Richard Mowrer once wrote in *The Star* that if we go to the Basque Country we may see scrawled on walls the equation: 4+3=1. In Basque we may say that *Lau gehi hiru dira zazpi*. Spelled out in Basque this comes to be correct, meaning that the four Basque territories within the Spanish state (Araba, Bizkaia, Gipuzkoa and Navarre) plus the three Basque territories within the French state (Behe Nafarroa, Lapurdi and Zuberoa) equal one united Basque nation; a nation that will become an independent European Republic.

Euskal Herria
Basque Country

As Camille B. Power, from Boise, put it after a trip to the Basque Country in 1970,

> *Professor Bilbao tells us that the Basques are not a part of the French Nation or the Spanish Nation. The difference between the notion of a State and a Nation is fundamental in understanding the development of Basque nationalism. The Basques form a Nation without having a State of their own. Spain is a State with several Nations living within her borders: Basques, Catalans, and*

Galicians. The same is true of France, which includes within her borders the Basque, Breton, and Occitan Nations. The more a Nation is persecuted, the stronger the Nationalist feeling becomes. As the Spanish government tries to combat the Basque Country by increasing the police force and occupying the Country militarily; the Basques increase their terrorist activities even more. The two main terrorist activities have been the killing of the Chief of Police of Guipuzcoa in 1968 whose aftermath, the Burgos Trials, were related so vividly by Margaret Shedd, in her recent novel "A Silence in Bilbao"; and the killing of the Spanish Premier last December.[33]

The Basque Country is a nation without a state aiming to become an independent republic and a free land.

---

[33]   Power, Camille B., "Basque Culture", manuscript. In, Boise State University Library, Camille B. Power Collection, MSS 61, Box 3, Fol. 3.

On the people who had laws before they had kings

Xabier Irujo. I read in Manuel Irujo's book, *Instituciones Jurídicas Vascas*, that when a new king was crowned in Navarre he was told: "Lord, remember that each one of us is as good as you, and that all of us together are worth more than you." Writing on the ancient Basque democracy, Manuel Sota recorded the following:

> *When they [the Basques] first appeared in history they were already a free people organized as a democracy. And in marked contrast with the other European countries they did not have to acquire their rights as free men through any revolutionary process. They did not have to struggle for them with any king; on the contrary whoever wished to be "Jauna"[34] of the Basques had first to bow to their democratic laws. As the Navarrese —(perhaps the most essentially Basque of all the Basques) said to King Philip V of Spain on November 21, 1706, "the people had laws before they had kings." As early as the IX century they had already made a pact in the peaks of the Pyrenees with Eneko Aritza (meaning the Oak), whom they had chosen as their leader. Thus the Pyrenean Monarchy was given a constitutional form at birth through this pact. And the Basques were governed by this monarchy for 410 years.[35]*

Pete Cenarrusa. In the digest of the laws of Zuberoa, written in 1520, we read that the law is "custom respected and observed since the most remote of ancient times." And it adds in chapter one, on the rights of the people, that the citizens of Zuberoa are free, exempt and under bondage to nobody:

> *By custom observed and obeyed ever since, all natives and residents of the land [of Zuberoa] are free and emancipated, under no blemished*

---

34   "Jaun" is the Basque word for "Lord".
35   Sota, Manuel de la, "The Antiquity of the Basque Democracy", *Basques. Bulletin of the Basque Delegation in the U.S.A.*, New York, 1942.

servitude. No person can raise people or troops in this land. No person may require rights over the persons or bodies of the said citizens or residents [of Zuberoa] or over any among them.[36]

XI. The text is certainly unambiguous, and has been written by people who felt free living in a land of freedom. We are going to speak about contemporary Basque politics, however, do you think that the Basque aim for freedom, for independence, finds its roots in the ancient Basque codes or in the ancient Basque theory of law?

PC. Yes. The Basques considered themselves free men and women since at least a millennium, when the first laws were written. The first code of laws of the Kingdom of Navarre was passed in the 13th century, in 1234; the assembly of freemen of Bizkaia passed the first Book of Laws in 1342; Gipuzkoa passed his book of laws in 1397, Lapurdi in 1400, Araba in 1458, Behe Nafarroa in 1611, Zuberoa in 1520. The oldest Basque ancient legal codes were written as early as the 11th century, such as the ordinances of 1076 of the city of Lizarra that was then named *Stella*, the city of the star.

XI. For instance, in the Seigniory of Bizkaia, one of the seven Basque states, the king had to kneel before the assembly and, beneath the holy oak of Gernika, recognize the ancient laws, which had preceded and should prevail over his rule. During the ceremony, the king had to promise that he would not rule without the consent of the assembly of the free men of Bizkaia,

> *He had to take the oath (…) and the said Lord and King, as Lord of Bizkaia, could not take them away from them nor add to them nor give them any new ones unless he should do so in Bizkaia, beneath the Tree of Gernika, in General Assembly and with the consent of the said Bizkaians. To avoid falling into the errors and wrongs and injuries into which they had fallen before, it was well to write down and enumerate all the freedoms and exemptions and customs and*

---

[36] *Et Premierement Deus Drets & De L'estat De Las Persones. Per la Costume de toute ancienetat observade & goardade, touts los natius & habitans en la terre son francs & de franque condition, sens tache de servitut. Et degun no a ne ne pot prener aucune suite de gens demoran en ladite terre, ne exiger aucun dret a cause de la persone & deu corsadge deusdits manans & habitans, ne de aucun de eds.* In, Grosclaude, Michel, *La Coutume de la Soule*, Izpegi, Baigorri, 1993. P. 9.

usages and alvedríos[37] and privileges that the said Villas[38] and Tierra Llana[39] had, but not in writing, at which time the said King and Lord should come to swear to safeguard them and to confirm them and give them as fuero.[40]

PC. As far back as the battle of Orreaga, in 778, when the Basques faced and defeated the largest army in Europe led by Charlemagne, King of the Franks, the Basques, or, as they call themselves, the *Euskaldunak*, have crushed each attempt to assimilate them into conquering kingdoms or even empires. Kings were not acknowledged as more than Lords in the Basque states, and always the Lord was reminded that he was under the laws of the people gathered in assembly. Moreover, to obtain even that limited recognition, the King or the Emperor had to go to the Basque parliaments, kneel and swear a sacred oath to perpetuate the laws, customs and rights of the Basques.

XI. We may affirm then that indeed, it is "a custom as ancient as the memory of man." Do you consider the Basque ancient law a constituent element of the Basque culture?

PC. Custom became law in the Basque Country; we may say that tradition was law and the spirit of freedom, the sense of equality and the essence of democracy conforms one of the main pillars of the Basque culture, of the Basque identity. No man has been born for servitude and all men are equal: that is a lesson of natural law written in the old Basque legal rolls for all times. We may say that indeed, democracy, understood as it is in the Basque ancient law, is a constituent element of the Basque culture.

XI. Equality, the law of laws, is one of the main political principles of the old laws. The oldest codes stand for equality before law; the Code of Laws of Lizarra confirms in 1076 (and also in the edition

---

37   Particular or unusual laws or ordinances.
38   Cities of the Seigniory of Bizkaia.
39   Valleys and small towns of Bizkaia.
40   "Fuero" means "law", specially the oldest ones, passed and compiled in the first codes. Ancient Law of Bizkaia of 1452. In, Monreal Zia, Gregorio, *The old law of Bizkaia (1452)*, Center for Basque Studies - University of Nevada, Reno, 2005. P. 166.

of 1164) that all the citizens of the city are free, acquitted of any bad laws and authorized not to perform any service that has not been approved by good will and agreed to by the citizens of the city in assembly.[41] Six hundred years later, on Chapter 2 of the Book of laws of Gipuzkoa of 1674, we read:

> *Of all the types of Nobility, the one that really and truly corresponds to the people of the province of Gipuzkoa is the Natural and Secondary that is commonly called "nobleness of blood" because this nobility is inherited by lineage and also because it is an honor due by law and justice, as inherited from the original parents of mankind. There are some authors that based on certain facts settle that all classes of nobleness originate from the gracious concession of Kings and gentlemen; yet, this statement does not follow the true origin of the Nobility of the peoples of Gipuzkoa as it will be seen, for this Gipuzkoan nobility is universal and uniform, and corresponds to each one of the descendants of this land, and has not been granted by any of the Kings of Spain, as it is attested by the fact that there is no record of it; and has not been acquired by the means provided by law, or transferred by some of the many foreign nations that dominated the Kingdom (for there would be some reference to it) but [Gipuzkoan nobility] was kept continuously and passed from parents to children, inviolably, from the first inhabitants of the Province until the present time, as is verified by the statements that follow.[42]*

---

41   *Hoc suprascriptum forum vel donativum dono vobis, et concedo et confirmo omnibus hominibus de Estella, tam maioribus quam minoribus, tam futuris quam presentibus, et filiis ac filiabus vestris, sive vestre generationis, et omni vestre posteritati, vel vestris sucesoribus, qui in Estella populavetint, quod habeatis illum salvum et ingenuum, liberum et francum per infinita secula seculorum. Amen.* I give, grant and confirm the aforesaid law and privilege, to you, to all the inhabitants of Estella, old and young, coming and present, and to your sons and daughters, of your generation and of forthcoming generations, and to your successors who will live in Estella, to keep it safe and dignified, free and frank for ever and ever. Amen. In, Lacarra, José María; Martín Duque, Ángel J., *Fueros derivados de Jaca. Estella-San Sebastián*, Institución Príncipe de Viana, Iruñea/Pamplona, 1969. P. 148.

42   "On the nobility and blood nobleness of the citizens of this Province", Chapter 2 of the *Book of laws of Gipuzkoa of 1674*. In, *Nueva recopilación de los fueros, privilegios, buenos usos y costumbres y leyes y órdenes de la M.N. y M. L. provincia de Guipúzcoa*, Diputación de Gipuzkoa, Donostia/San Sebastián, 1919. P. 18.

PC. This books of laws, some of them written many centuries before the American and the French Revolutions, reflect how important it was -and still is- for the Basques to be considered noblemen by their Kings and Lords, and, moreover, it illustrates that it was essential for them to declare that they were all equal before the law, that every one of them was a citizen with equal rights and duties, paying equal taxes and living in the same territory for centuries. This is a basic political principle of democracy and a basic element of Basque culture.

XI. And also, they made their kings declare that they had to be considered noblemen, for all intents and purposes, within the limits of their territory or even out of their republics. Like the rest of the Kings and Lords of the Basque states, Philip the Third, Lord of Gipuzkoa, wrote in 1610 that:

> *Their ancestors were founders and residents of the province of Gipuzkoa and they and their descendants were hijosdalgo[43] by blood, descendants of well-known places and houses, and so we and the Lords and Kings before us, our predecessors, and all nations of the world, shall affirm that whenever some noblemen have come to live outside the Province [of Gipuzkoa] to this Kingdom of Castile and have proved the independence of their houses, have been in our Audiencias[44] and Cancillerías[45] declared as being such hijosdalgo.[46]*

PC. Instead of eradicating nobility as the French revolutionary assembly did in 1789, the Basques declared nobility universal in their countries, and by doing that they granted equality within their territories and obtained for their citizens all the rights and privileges that the condition of noblemen gave to them abroad. It was a purely practical question.

---

43   Noblemen.

44   Royal Audiences or courts of justice.

45   Foreign ministries or secretariats, also courts of justice.

46   "On the nobility and blood nobleness of the citizens of this Province", Chapter 2 of the *Book of laws of Gipuzkoa of 1674*. In, *Nueva recopilación de los fueros, privilegios, buenos usos y costumbres y leyes y órdenes de la M.N. y M. L. provincia de Guipúzcoa*, Diputación de Gipuzkoa, Donostia/San Sebastián, 1919. P. 19.

Ceremony of Coronation of the King of Navarre at the Hall of the Parliament in the Cathedral of Iruñea/Pamplona. Seated the three branches of the legislative, the Noblemen (on the right), the Peoples (in front) and the Clergy (on the left). Source: Irujo Ametzaga archive.

XI. Free people need Parliaments. What could you say about it?

PC. The *Cortes* of the Old Kingdom of Navarre, the most ancient Basque parliament, was the base for the British parliament. Simon de Montfort, sixth Earl of Leicester, organized the first English representative parliament in 1265. He was sent to the Kingdom of Navarre in order to study the Navarrese legal system and to adjust it to the English one. De Monfort's democratic reformation did not gain royal approval so a riot against the king took place. The royal army was finally defeated at the battle of Lewes on May 14, 1264, Prince Edward was captured, and a treaty was signed one year later, in 1265. According to the new agreement, the king accepted the constitution formulated by De Monfort, a parliamentary system that shaped the first English parliament at which both knights and burgesses were present as in the *Cortes* of Navarre. On August 8, 1265, when, Simon de Montfort was defeated and killed in the battle of Evesham and his family persecuted by Henry III of England, Montfort's son, Richard and

Richard's wife Eleanor, sister of the king of England, were protected by the king of Navarre Theobald II.

XI. We still can walk through the "Precious Door", carved in 1350, at the Cathedral of Saint Mary in Iruñea/Pamplona, where the *Cortes* used to meet for centuries. Its name derives from the psalm that the canons sang when they passed through it to access the old dormitory: "Pretiosa in conspectu Domini mors sanctorum eius."[47] Some of these ancient Basque parliaments, made of stone -austere, unadorned, unpretentious as the field of Zaraobe-, are still there, open for us to visit, as old temples of ancient liberties.

Parliament of the Valley of Aiala, at Zaraobe. Source: Irujo Ametzaga archive.

PC. Each town, each valley and every one of the Basque states had its own parliament (legislative), its own courts of justice (judicial) and also its own government and militia (executive). Following the Baron of Montesquieu's concept of the division of powers (*De*

---

[47]   *Liber Psalmorum* 115:15. Precious in the sight of the Lord is the death of His Saints.

l'esprit des lois, 1748), we may argue that this is one of the bases of the ancient Basque political systems. He wrote:

> *In every government there are three sorts of power: the legislative; the executive in respect to things dependent on the law of nations; and the executive in regard to matters that depend on the civil law. (...) In order to have this liberty, it is requisite the government be so constituted as one man need not be afraid of another. When the legislative and executive powers are united in the same person, or in the same body of magistrates, there can be no liberty; because apprehensions may arise, lest the same monarch or senate should enact tyrannical laws, to execute them in a tyrannical manner. Again, there is no liberty, if the judiciary power be not separated from the legislative and executive. Were it joined with the legislative, the life and liberty of the subject would be exposed to arbitrary control; for the judge would be then the legislator. Were it joined to the executive power, the judge might behave with violence and oppression.*[48]

However, the origin of the codes was the almighty legislative assembly that were known as *Cortes* in Navarre; *États Généraux* in Behe Nafarroa; *Biltzar* or *Juntas Generales* in Araba, Bizkaia and Lapurdi; and *Cour d'Ordre* (*Silviet*) in Zuberoa. The Books of Laws, the legal codes, could only be modified by the citizens of each of the states gathered in assembly. The codes could only be printed with the permission of the assemblies. These parliaments reserved all powers, meanwhile they were deliberating, once a year or once every few years.

XI. The right of assembly is then one of the most important principles included in each one of the Basque legal codes. In this sense, we may read in the digest of the laws of Zuberoa of 1520 that:

---

[48]   Montesquieu, Baron de, *The Spirit of the Law*, Book XI. Of the Laws Which Establish Political Liberty, with Regard to the Constitution, The Colonial Press, London/New York, 1900. Pp. 151-152.

> *The parishioners of each parish, valley and town of the state [of Zuberoa] can assemble whenever necessary to address their common affairs and the ones of their parishes, vics and degairies.*[49] *They can adopt their particular regulations on maintenance and care of forests, and of vacant lands and livestock and in general to take care of all the legal affairs in their common interest and in the interest of their parishes, valleys and towns.*[50]

We may read the same principle in the Book of Laws of the state of Lapurdi of 1514:

> *The parishioners of each parish in this country of Lapurdi may assemble, whenever necessary, and settle their common needs and those of their parishes, and may pass and enforce among them individual statutes and ordinances to conserve and save their forests and rangelands, according to the law popularly known as San Benito, and also to discuss their legal business for their common interest and the particular interest of their parishes.*[51]

PC. And we may add that each village, town, city, valley and state elected their representatives democratically in their different ways and according to their different books of ordinances. It was very common for the representatives to be elected by drawing lots and always for a period of time, usually one year.

XI. The first chapter of the Ordinances of the Republic of Baztan establishes that,

---

[49]   "Vics" and "degairies" are territorial and administrative subdivisions of the estate of Zuberoa.

[50]   *Los parropians de cascune parropie deu dit pays, & degaeries de Sole, se poden assemblar per tractar de lors besognes communes, & de lors parropies, vics e degaeries, a cascune vegade, qui besonh los fey. Et poden far & ordenar entre eds statuts & ordenances particulars, per entretenir & goardar los boscadges, herems & bestiars, & autrement procurar lors negocis loisibles, au profieit commun d'entre eds, & de lorsdites parropies, vics & degaeries.* In, Grosclaude, Michel, *La Coutume de la Soule,* Izpegi, Baigorri, 1993. Pp. 10-11.

[51]   Title 20, Article 4, On the franchises and rights of the country and persons of Lapurdi. In, Haristoy, Abbé, *Nobleza y fueros vascos: Laburdi,* Auñamendi, Donostia/San Sebastián, 1959. P. 237-238.

According to the old custom observed and kept in this Valley and University of Baztan, there must be a jury in each one of the fourteen villages of the valley elected by the neighbors of each village, by acclamation in open assembly and, those that were thus named (…) have to present themselves in the General Assembly that juries and deputies will hold on the third day of Easter.[52]

All the representatives of the Republic were always chosen by universal suffrage:

When the delegates are gathered in the General Assemblies, all the neighbors of the valley are understood to have the free faculty of arriving (…) to give their votes (…) in the years in which it is necessary to elect the mayor or captain (war commander) *of this valley and that the votes for it have to be given by such neighbors who are present in the assembly.*[53]

PC. This people of Baztan put their laws in writing for the first time in 1560. That is, two hundred years before Jean Jacques Rousseau wrote *On the Social Contract* (1762), two hundred and sixteen years before Thomas Paine challenged the authority of the British monarchy in *Common Sense* (1776). Just like the free men of Baztan, we Americans also wanted our representative be freely elected at Congress. They were humble men, farmers or ranchers, they were owners of little pieces of land, big enough to feed their families but small enough not to allow them to become much richer than their neighbors.

XI. They went to court against the King's attempt to make them pay certain new taxes for using their lands to feed the cattle. The Navarrese court failed on their side on April 15, 1440. The document expresses that:

The land of Baztan and its inhabitants and the residents living in it since ancient times were conquerors of lands, as they were always called in the ancient laws, and those who populated these lands were noblemen, free, acquitted of any bad laws and unbound to any

---

[52]   Law 1 of the Book of Ordinances of the Valley of Baztan, 1696.
[53]   Law 1 of the Book of Ordinances of Baztan, 1696.

*servitude, attached and under the protection of the General Law of
Navarre, and each has a plot of his own, and it is their own, and not
attached to the services of the King, and their ancestors in their time
and the current inhabitants now have built and have made to build in
this land churches, palaces, houses, cattle huts, threshing floors, mills,
farmlands, fields of apple trees, gardens, orchards, fortresses of stone
and wood, and many other buildings, and have enjoyed and benefited
from their lands after they first came here, sowing and planting and
plowing where they wanted in this land, and also have taken, received
and depleted, distributing, enjoying and taking advantage of the fruits
that God, openly and freely, has given to them and gives to them,
without being forced to pay a tribute for it.*[54]

PC. They considered themselves noblemen, not because they were
born noble, but because they worked hard for it. The person who
wrote this verdict is telling the King that the people of the Valley of
Baztan have their rights on their land and do not owe any tax
because they have been working in them for centuries. He is telling
us that it is work what makes people noble.

XI. In this sense, do you think that there is some similarity between
American democracy and the ancient Basque way of understanding
equality?

PC. There is not any historical bond. Both theories of democracy
have different historical, social and political backgrounds, however,

---

[54]   *La dicha tierra de Baztan et los habitantes, et moradores en ella
antiguamente con otros esemble fueron conquistadores de las tierras, como algunament
face mencion en los Fueros; et (1) los que poblaron la dicha tierra fueron fidalgos,
infanzones, francos, ingenuos et libres de toda servitud aforados al Fuero General de
Navarra, et (2) han todos un termino suyo propio, et (3) solariego, et no realengo, et
(4) los antepasados en su tiempo, et los presentes en el suyo, han edificado, et fecho
edificar; et facer sen el dicho término, iglesias, palacios, casas, bordas, truillares,
molinos, piezas, manzanedos, huertos, vergeres, fortalezas de piedra et fusta, et otros
muchos edificios, et (5) han gozado e aprovechado después de la primera fundación, ata
de sembrar e plantar, o de rozar, doquieren, e por bien en el dicho término, e tomar,
recibir esquilmar, espleitar, gozar, et aprovechar de los frutos que Dios ha dado et da de
presente, franca y quitament, sin (6) que sean tenidos a la señoría pecha.* In,
Ezeizabarrena, Xabier, "Las Ordenanzas del Valle de Baztan", *Ekarpenak*,
2006.

the spirit beneath both systems is essentially the same. The first American settlers were also farmers and they soon learned that they did not have to pay taxes for their work, certainly not to a foreign king.

Indeed, John Adams cited the Ancient Basque laws, the Foruak, in the Letter IV of his book *A Defence of the Constitutions of Government of the United States of America* (October 4, 1776):

> *While their neighbours have long since resigned all their pretensions into the hands of kings and priests, this extraordinary people have preserved their ancient language, genius, laws, government, and manners, without innovation, longer than any other nation of Europe* -and added- *It is a republic; and one of the privileges they have most insisted on, is not to have a king: another was, that every new lord, at his accession, should come into the country in person, with one of his legs bare, and take an oath to preserve the privileges of the lordship.*[55]

The Basque political systems were considered European proto-democracies by Adams since both the *Batzar* (town, city or valley assemblies) and the *Biltzar* (General Assemblies) were open parliaments composed by free representatives elected directly by the people for a term.

XI. Except for the Lord or the King and his more direct executive assistants, all the political representatives and officials of the state were elected by the people represented in assemblies and for a certain period of time. In the case of the General Assembly of Gipuzkoa and according to the Book of Laws of 1674, we may say that,

1. The duty of the members of the assemblies was constrained in time to the meeting of the assembly that could not last for more than eleven days.
2. Every issue was decided by a majority of votes and each representative had a vote.

---

[55] Adams, John, *A Defence of the Constitutions of Government of the United States of America*, London, 1787.

3. No issue was beyond the power of decision of the assembly.
4. Every act passed at the assembly had to be observed and executed under penalty of death.
5. The members of the assembly were elected in each town, city or valley per term by the citizens and none could be elected on two consecutive occasions.
6. The assembly had to review the work done by the officials of the executive branch and these officials could be subject of trial at the end of their term.

In general, the same principles ruled in Araba, Bizkaia and Lapurdi.

PC. It must be said that priests and lawyers could not attend the assemblies. There were various reasons to exclude the priests. The primary reason was to make a clear distinction between ecclesiastical and civil matters, but also because the canon law, Roman or Latin in origin, was so different from the Basque civil law. Lawyers were not admitted for the same very reasons. Educated at the universities abroad, their philosophy of law clashed with the good sense and the way of self-governing of those humble peasants. The General Assembly of Gipuzkoa even banned the lawyers from residing near the town where the assembly was taking place. But, above all, a fundamental reason for denying lawyers entry to the assemblies was that it was unnecessary. The Basque laws were customary codes, laws that had their origin in the customs and traditions of the nation so every citizen knew them; so it was not necessary to have specialists in legal issues in the assemblies. The customary law was an essential part of the social and cultural life of the inhabitants of the Basque countries; these laws were part of their lifestyle.

XI. Consuetudinary laws are based on culture, expression of the life of a nation. When culture becomes law, can we say that freedom or democracy understood as it is in the Basque codes is one of the constituent elements of the Basque culture? In other words, is freedom as shaped in the ancient Basque codes one of the elements of Basque identity, one of the cultural essentials for being or feeling Basque?

Palace in Urreztieta where the ten representatives of the towns in the valley of Enkarterriak (Encartaciones) once held their assemblies. Source: Irujo Ametzaga archive.

PC. When a people have been ruled for more than a millennium under the same laws, we have to accept that they are an important part of their identity. We may add that by reading these ancient codes we may found many of the constituent elements of the Basque identity. Even today consuetudinary civil law has legal force in the Basque Country. Custom is considered a valid source law in Navarre, just as court precedents in the United States. To understand what it once meant to be Basque the ancient laws are as essential as the Declaration of Independence or the Gettysburg Address is for us to understand what it means to be or to feel American.

XI. What, in your opinion, are the principles beyond these customary laws?

PC. Some of the main principles beyond the ancient Basque laws are the peculiar institutions of the Basque family structure, the role of women, the way of conceiving collective property and cooperativism, the respect for human rights, federalism and the refusal of conquest.

XI. You have mentioned the family structure as the basis of the political system. Indeed, the nuclear family and not the person was the subject of rights and duties, therefore, the vote was not generally particular but "fogueral,"[56] that is to say, each family (each house or each "fire") had a vote in the open assemblies.

PC. And here we may find another link to the American or English law, the *non-proportional representativeness*. Each house or each family had a vote in the Basque *Batzarrak* or municipal assemblies and, each city had one vote or one seat at the Basque parliaments. This is also the origin of the English political system, a system that has an echo in the U.S. Senate non-proportional territorial representation. So we have, two senators per state at the U.S. Congress, no matter how many inhabitants the state has.

XI. Dealing with family structure, you also have mentioned the role of women as a key social, cultural and political element of the Basque identity.

PC. We should also add that it is an important factor of the Basque economy. The Basque woman has played a relevant role in the Basque economy. The Basque political systems reserved many rights for women since the very 11th century, such as the right of owning, inheriting and giving property in inheritance, the right to choose husband and the right to divorce among others.

XI. After marriage women acquired absolute right on all the goods of the couple, whether previously owned or later obtained. Property, though, was universal and completely shared within the marriage, *although [previously to the marriage] the husband had much and the wife nothing or the wife had much and the husband nothing*. And this is a principle that we can track in all the Basque codes.[57] That is how it was written in the Book of Laws of Lapurdi in 1514:

---

56   Relative to the "fire" around which each family comes together at home.

57   For instance, in the Title 20, Law 1 of the Book of Laws of

Article 5. Husband and wife together by common agreement may dispose of their acquired assets and give them to each other as they please as long as there is equality in the things that they give to each other; [and they have to] leave for their children of the purchased property what they consider appropriate, no matter how little it may be.

Article 6. The husband may not make any sale or disposition of the assets of the marriage if the wife does not consent, nor the wife without her husband's consent.[58]

PC. Both husband "Etxekojaun" and wife "Etxekoandre" were and still are considered lords of the Basque house. Women had the right of giving or receiving property in inheritance, that is, the right of making use of the property in equal conditions and, therefore, the right to buy and to sell real estate and to have titles on such properties.

XI. A widower owned all property according to the Basque laws. As written in the Code of Laws of Lizarra of 1076 (written in 1164):

If a woman becomes a widow and she does not marry again, while a widow, she owns all assets and properties that the marriage had, while the children remain at home. If any of them claims his or her part at puberty, he or she will share the legacy of his father. If the husband makes donation of what belongs to his wife without permission from the latter, it has no validity, and if his wife is present, but she does not authorize or denies, the husband is unable to dispose of the assets of his wife.[59]

Bizkaia (1526); Rubrica 25, Article 2 of the Book of Laws of Behe Nafarroa (1611); Title 9, Article 1 of the Book of Laws of Lapurdi (1514); Title 24, Articles 1 & 5 of the Book of Laws of Zuberoa (1520).

[58]   Title 9, Articles 5 & 6 of the Book of Laws of Lapurdi of 1514.

[59]   *Et si maritus facit donatium sine consensu mulieris de hoc quod pertinet mulieri, non ualebit; sed si facit donatium de hoc quod sibi pertinet, ualebit. Et si mulier audit facere donatiuum, et est in illo loco et tacet se, si non auctorizat, donatiuum non ualebit. Et si mulier niuit et maritus moritur quamuis sint ibi filii, quantum mulier uoluerit stare in viduitate, erit domina et potentissima tocius hereditatis; sed ratione viduitatis non tenebit mobile, sed dibidat mobile cum filiis uel*

Except for the military exemptions, women were obliged to comply with all duties and taxes as the rest of the citizens of the city. The Book of Laws of the Northern Kingdom of Navarre (1611), granted free marriage to women: *Parents or grandparents won't force their son or daughters or their grandsons or granddaughters to marry against their will.*[60] The same Book of Laws grants women the right to get the marriage annulment in equal conditions.[61]

PC. It is not common to find such legal rights for women in European medieval law. The involvement of women in political events has not been infrequent in the Basque Country. Throughout all 17th and 18th centuries (1669, 1697, 1709, 1773…) the royal attempts to introduce new taxes on the tobacco and the salt in Lapurdi caused frequent riots many of which were carried out by women. On October 3, 1784 the news that a tax was going to be established arrived at Hazparne and a civil insurrection burst out. Monsieur of Neville, *Intendent* of Guyena, accompanied by the Marques of Caupenne, Lieutenant of the King in Baiona, brought one hundred and fifty grenadiers into Lapurdi who were faced by more than 2,000 women in Hazparne. The revolt finished without incidents and the taxes were not collected.

---

filiabus suius, aut cum priuignis, uel cum omnibus mobile de iure debet diuidere. In, Lacarra, José María; Martín Duque, Ángel J., *Fueros de Navarra I. Fueros derivados de Jaca I. Estella - San Sebastián,* Institución Príncipe de Viana, Iruñea/Pamplona, 1969. P. 102.

60   Rubrica 24, Article 7 of the Book of Laws of the Northern Kingdom of Navarre (1611). The original text reads as follow: *Los pays & mays, pay grands & may granes, no constreigneran lors filhs filhas, refilhs & refilhas se maridâ contre lór volontat.* In, *Los Fors et Costumas deu Royaume de Navarre Deca-Ports,* Consejo de Estudios de Derecho Navarro, Iruñea/Pamplona, 1968. P. 68.

61   Rubrica 25, Article 16 of the Book of Laws of the Northern Kingdom of Navarre (1611). The original texts reads as follow: *Si ló Matrimony se separe per colpa deu marit, luy sera tengut entretenir la Molhè de vita & aliments, & si la colpa es en la Molhè, & qui sera heretera, sera tenguda de son hereditat entretenir ló Marit si luy no had'aillors deque se entretenir.* In, *Los Fors et Costumas deu Royaume de Navarre Deca-Ports,* Consejo de Estudios de Derecho Navarro, Iruñea/Pamplona, 1968. P. 77.

The principle of the inviolability of the dwelling is one of the personal rights and freedoms present in the legal codes of all the Basque states. Typical Basque house of the 16th century. Baraibar, Larraun (Navarre). Source: Irujo Ametzaga archive.

XI. We may take into account that the Basque woman (together with Japanese women) is one of the most long-lived human groups in the world (84 years on average) and her life expectancy is increasing four months a year. If we consider that property passes from husband to wife or from wife to husband and that Basque women live four years more than men on average, we shall conclude that property in the Basque Country is, up to a point, in the hands of women.

PC. And in the hands of the towns. Collective property is indeed another of the main pillars of the ancient Basque political systems. The Basque republics guaranteed private property and trade liberties and, at the end of the 18th century in some places such as the Valley of Baztan in Navarre, the proportion of public land was up to the 80 percent of the total land of the valley.

In this context public land does not mean state land. This is land owned by the towns, not by the state, and only the town or the valley's open assembly has rights over it. The products of the land (wood, water, grass, fruits...) were and still are equally shared house by house. This is in essence the origin of the "auzolan" or common work: all houses or families have to participate in the common effort and so enjoy the common wealth.

XI. From this perspective "auzolan" means common responsibility: cooperation among proprietors in virtue of the common wealth. "Auzolan" also means individual, familiar and social liability. The common work of the town is not an individual project, it is projected to forthcoming generations. In this sense, and keeping in mind that today cooperatives produce around 10 percent of the Basque Gross Domestic Product, which do you think are the basic elements of the Basque cooperativism?

PC. I can think now on three key elements of the Basque way of production:

1. The first aim of work is not solely to increase the capital, but the increasing of the living standards, the social transformation of the community, therefore, a good part of the capital has an important instrumental use and it is always reinvested.
2. Participation & commitment in the management, the democratic organization of the work is a second important element.
3. Solidarity and wealth distribution: equal lots shared by all owners. This is another important element of the cooperatives.

XI. You have also mentioned the respect for human rights as one of the basic elements of the ancient Basque legal codes. What were you making reference to?

PC. We should mention the Habeas Corpus, granted by the Basque laws as early as in 1452 and 1526 in Bizkaia, two centuries before the Habeas Corpus Act was passed in England in 1679. The Earl of Carnarvon, after a journey through the Basque country, wrote in 1836 that,

The house of the Biscayan is his castle in the most emphatic sense of the word. No magistrate can violate that sanctuary; nor can exertion be put on him, nor can his arms or his horse be seized; he cannot be arrested for debt, or subjected to imprisonment upon any pretext whatever, without a previous summons to appear under the old Tree of Gernika, where he is made acquainted with the offense imputed to him, and called upon for his defense; he is then discharged on the spot, or bailed, or committed, according to the nature of the crime and the evidence adduced against him. This, the most glorious privilege that free men can possess, this the most effectual safeguard against the wanton abuse of power, this a custom more determinately in favour of the subject than even our own cherished Habeas Corpus was enjoyed by the Biscayans for centuries before the far-famed guarantee of British liberty had an existence in our islands.[62]

XI. Following Manuel Sota we may add that certainly in Section 7 of the New Book of the Laws of Bizkaia (1526) the procedure to be followed in order to take a person to court was carefully outlined. It states that no person may be persecuted nor arrested for any crime whatsoever, no matter how grave, unless he has previously been handed a judicial notice and summons to appear for judgment within a period of thirty days, beneath the Tree of Gernika, where he is granted the privilege of choosing which public jail he prefers. This summons had to be incorporated in an edict, to be read publicly beneath the Tree of Gernika, every ten days, certifying that this requirement be carried out by a scrivener and also that an authentic copy of the edict be delivered to the person making the denunciation of the supposed criminal. If after this procedure was carried out the accused still did not present himself, then and only then was he declared to be in rebellion, in the words of the Fuero "acatado y encartado,"[63] and as the author of a criminal act might be detained or arrested by any citizen.[64]

---

[62]   Herbert, Henry J. G. Earl of Carnavon, *Portugal and Galicia with a Review of the Social and Political State of the Basque Provinces*, John Murray, London, 1848.

[63]   Cut off and outlawed.

[64]   Sota, Manuel, "The Basque Habeas Corpus", *Basques. Bulletin of the Basque Delegation in the U.S.A.*, New York, 1942.

Idahoan delegation at the Parliament of Bizkaia in Gernika when the City of the Tree (Gernika) and the City of Trees (Boise) became sister cities in 1993. From left to right: Roy L. Eiguren, Wayne Meulman, Susan Garro Meulman, Adelia Garro Simplot, Mayor of Gernika Eduardo Vallejo, Secretary of State of Idaho Pete Cenarrusa, Joanne Uberuaga, Ted Garro Simplot, Jesus Alcelay and President of Euzkaldunak Basque Center Michelle Alzola Zelaieta. Source: Cenarrusa archive.

Law 26, Title 11 of the New Book of the Laws of Bizkaia of 1526 reads as follows: *Let no prestamero,*[65] *merino,*[66] *nor executor of any kind dare to arrest any person without a writ from a competent judge except in the case of flagrante delicto.*[67] If a person had already been thus apprehended and a competent judge ordered his freedom he must

---

[65]   Holder of certain properties and benefits from the Church.

[66]   Royal judge and superintendent of sheep walks.

[67]   The original text reads as follows: *Que ninguno sea preso sin mandamiento de Juez y que los que él mandare soltar, no sean detenidos por las costas. Otrosí, dixeron: Que havian de Fuero, y establecian por Ley, que ningun Prestamero, ni Merino, ni Executor alguno, sea ossado de prender a persona alguna en la Tierra-Llana, sin mandamiento de Juez competente: Eceto en aquellos casos que el Derecho permite assi como infragante delito.* In, *Fuero Nuevo de Vizcaya,* Leopoldo Zugaza, Durango, 1976. P. 43.

immediately be set at liberty no matter what the cause or debt for which he had been taken prisoner. Also, torture was prohibited. The legal code was very clear on this point:

> *And they also said [in assembly] that it was their law, and custom, and privilege and liberty that for any offense or any fault, be it public or private, be it serious or minor, or be it of any quality and seriousness, that comes to the Judge's Office, no citizen of Bizkaia can be tortured or be threatened of being tortured, directly or indirectly, in Bizkaia, or outside Bizkaia in any other part.*[68]

The same principle is settled at Law 9, Title 9 of the same Book of Laws of 1526.

PC. Unlike other dispositions on the same matter in other parts of the world, the Basque law of 1526 refers to any person whatsoever, not only to certain Lords or noblemen, but to any citizen of Bizkaia. Indeed, the law of Bizkaia did not make any differences at all between citizens and secured the following procedural rights:

- Right of not being tortured
- Right to elect the judges
- Right to be judged by a legally elected judge
- Right not to be judged but for crimes and offenses typified in the laws passed at the assembly
- Right to know the charges
- Right to have time (30 days) to present oneself at court and so to prepare the defense
- Right to have a lawyer

---

[68] Law 12, Title 1 of the Book of Laws of Bizkaia of 1526. The original text: *Ley XII. Tormento, ni amenaza, no se puede dar a Vizcayno. Otrosi dixeron: Que havian de Fuero, e costumbre, e Franqueza, e Libertad, que sobre delito, ni maleficio alguno, publico, ni privado, grande, ni libiano, e de qualquier calidad, y gravedad que sea, agora sea tal, que el Juez de Oficio pueda proceder, agora no; que a Vizcayno alguno no se de tormento alguno, ni amenaza de Tormento, directe, ni indirecte, en Vizcaya, ni fuera de ella en parte alguna.* In, *Fuero Nuevo de Vizcaya,* Leopoldo Zugaza, Durango, 1976. P. 10.

- Right to be sentenced according to the law and not to be charged but with the punishments defined in the laws
- Right to appeal against the sentence

And these are principles that we found in the rest of the Basque legal Systems, such as in the one of Lapurdi of 1514, in which we read:

> *Nor at the request of the Attorney General of the King, neither at the request of the Procurador[69] or any other avenging person, should anyone be charged in court for any crime or offense without being previously reported on such crimes that should be previously decreed.[70]*

XI. You have also mentioned federalism as another element of the ancient Basque political systems.

PC. Yes. Each one of the Basque states was a confederation of families, towns, cities and valleys. Every valley was a confederation of towns, and every town was a little confederation of houses or families. The common property was owned by the town assembly and not by the state. Therefore, the state had no responsibility on the public land of valleys and towns. The right of property was and still is tied to the right of making use of the common land. We can mention John Adams again who, writing on the Biscayan democracy, stated:

> *Although the government is called a democracy, we cannot here find all authority collected into one center; there are, on the contrary, as many distinct governments as there are cities and merindades.[71] The general government has two orders at least; the Lord or Governor, and the biennial Parliament. Each of the thirteen subordinate divisions has its organized government, with its Chief Magistrate at the head of it. We may judge of the form of all of them by that of the metropolis, which calls itself, in all its laws, the noble and illustrious republic of Bilbao. This city has*

---

69   Attorney or town clerk.

70   Title 19, Article 1, *On the criminals and their punishments*, of the Book of Laws of Lapurdi of 1514.

71   Administrative and territorial units.

its Alcalde,[72] who is both Governor and Chief Justice, its twelve Regidores or Counsellors, Attorney-General, &c. and by all these, assembled in the consistorial palace under the titles of Consejo, Justicia, y Regimiento, the laws are made in the name of the Lord of Biscay, and confirmed by him.[73]

XI. The right of self-determination is a constitutive element of federalism. Do you think the Basque states included that political principle in their systems?

PC. Each one of the towns, cities and valleys had the right to determine their own political and economic future. And they did make use of that right. There are many examples of it; in use of that right the citizens of the city of Salinas de Añana decided by acclamation to become part of the Brotherhood of Araba in 1460; the valley of Aramaio decided in assembly to become part of the Brotherhood of Aiala in 1489; in 1491 Pedro Goirizelaia, solicitor of the Brotherhood of Laudio and in the name of the assembly of the valley, asked the inclusion of Laudio in the valley of Aiala; Orozko became a member of the parliament of Gernika in 1785; also the city of Oñati resolved to integrate into the province of Gipuzkoa in 1840. Gipuzkoa as a whole decided at the beginning of the 13th century to segregate from the Kingdom of Navarre and to incorporate into the one of Castile.

The Basque states were very complex political structures where every valley, city and town had the right of self-determination. The seven Basque states were, in origin, a political confederation of families, towns and valleys with the right of secession, that is to say, with the right to elect their political identity.

XI. Finally, you have mentioned the refusal of conquest as another of the constituent elements of the Basque political systems. Could you explain?

PC. War was regulated by law and the system of conscription and calling to war is almost identical in all the Basque states.

---

[72]   Mayor.

[73]   Adams, John, *A Defence of the Constitutions of Government of the United States of America*, London, 1787.

The city council of the Republic of Sara, in Lapurdi. As the commemorative plaque reads, Louis XIV of France, Lord of Lapurdi, was there in 1693. Source: Irujo Ametzaga archive.

First we have to underline that the military call up was forbidden out of the General Assembly, that is, the Lord could not declare war or peace without the resolution of the assemblies or the Cortes in Navarre. If the enemy attacked any of the territories, every house had to send a man (or pay for one) and provide for him while the enemy was within the limits of the republic. After the enemy was defeated, the soldiers had the duty to go on fighting abroad for three days out of the country on their own (paying for their provisions, clothes and weaponry). After three days each citizen had the right of being paid as a nobleman or to freely go back home. After nine days each citizen enrolled was completely free to return home, even if he had been paid. Many towns, cities and valleys, such as the ones of Baztan or Erronkari in Navarre, had the right to fight under the command of a member of their place of origin. The geographical limits for conscription were generally trees, such as the Malato tree in Lujaondo (Bizkaia) that once marked the limit of Bizkaia. Indeed, we can still visit today the cross that has been placed in the exact place where the Malato tree once stood.

XI. As it was an important law, it was always incorporated within the first articles of the ancient Basque Books of Laws. The Navarrese code of the 13th century establishes it in the first section that, *no King shall have the power to administer justice without the advice of the twelve native Councilors*[74] *of this Kingdom, neither peace nor war with another king or queen, or truce, nor any other important act, such as an embargo of lands within the Kingdom, can be carried out without the council of the twelve elderly advisors of the country.*[75] And it continues:

> *If an enemy army enters into the land of the king of Navarre and if this army crosses the river Ebro or the river Aragón against Navarre, after the royal call to arms has been touted throughout the Kingdom, all the knights and Infanzones of Navarra must leave by law and come to their king and pay for their supplies for three days. However, if the king crosses the river Ebro or the river Aragón, they can request to their king to pay for their provision and if the king does not wish to pay for the supplies for themselves and their men and theirs beasts (if he is a nobleman, as befits a nobleman; if he is an Infanzón, as befits an Infanzón; and if he is a farmer as it befits a farmer), after these three days they can return to their homes and they shall have no complaint of the king. If the king pays them for their food, they must stay with him for other nine days and after nine days, they are free to return to their homes and the king can have no quarrel with them.*[76]

---

[74]   The council of the twelve wise men is the antecedent of the Navarrese Cortes or parliament.

[75]   The original text states: *Que rey ninguno tenga poder de administrar justicia sin consejo de los ricos hombres naturales del Reino, ni guerra ni paz con otro rey o reina, ni tregua, ni ningún otro hecho granado o embargo de Reino sin consejo de los doce ricos hombres o doce de los más sabios ancianos de la tierra.* Book 1, Title 1, Chapter 1 of the Book of Laws of the Kingdom of Navarre (1234/1253).

[76]   The original text reads: *Si ejército enemigo le entrare al rey de Navarra en su tierra y si dicho ejército pasare el río Ebro o el río Aragón contra Navarra, si el llamamiento real fuese pregonado por todo el Reino, deben salir los caballeros e infanzones de Navarra por fuero y acudir junto al rey y costearse sus provisiones durante tres días. No obstante, si el rey cruzare el río Ebro o el río Aragón, al tercer día le pueden solicitar la provisión de víveres al rey y si el rey no les quisiere dar provisiones como conviene a caballeros, para sí mismos y para sus hombres y para sus bestias, y si fuere escudero como conviene a escudero y si fuese infanzón labrador como conviene a infanzón labrador, pasados esos tres días pueden regresar a sus casas y no*

When in 1160 Sancho VI the Wise of Navarre recovered the territories of the Errioxa and Bureba on the south, which had been occupied by troops of Alfonso VII of Castile in 1134, the king, upon arrival at Atapuerca nailed his sword to a tree and said "this is the limit of the kingdom of Navarre." Beyond that limit the troops did not have to fight. This norm was also incorporated into the law of Lizarra in 1076, so we may state that its origin reaches back to the Middle Ages.

PC. It is remarkable that the law of Navarra only mentions the rivers Ebro and Aragón, which are the borders with the kingdoms of Castile and Aragón, but did not mention the borders with the Seigniories of Bizkaia and Gipuzkoa, or the boundaries that the kingdom had with the Basques republics on the north. War always came from the south.

By virtue of the Book of Laws of Gipuzkoa, nobody was required to go to war beyond the limits of the Province except voluntarily and on payment: *their salaries shall be paid for the time they voluntarily serve outside their homeland under the order of the [assembly of the] Province*.[77] The citizens of the Basque states could not have their weaponry confiscated and the General Assembly of Gipuzkoa had the exclusive authority to appoint the leader of the army, even without the confirmation of the king, which otherwise was not necessary either to organize the troops or to call to war.[78]

This set of laws common to all the Basque republics clearly characterizes a cardinal point of the Basque law of war: the republic could only call to arms in defense of its territory, a war of

---

tendrán por ello querella del rey. Si el rey les costea su alimentación, deberán permanecer con él durante nueve días y pasados los nueve días, son libres de regresar a sus casa y el rey no podrá querellarse contra ellos. Book 1, Title 1, Chapter 4 of the Book of Laws of the Kingdom of Navarre (1234/1253).

[77] Chapter 1, Title 24, of the Book of Laws of Gipuzkoa (1674). In, *Nueva recopilación de los fueros, privilegios, buenos usos y costumbres, leyes y órdenes de la M.N. y M. L. provincia de Guipúzcoa*, La Gran Enciclopedia Vasca, Bilbao, 1975. P. 274.

[78] Chapter 11, Title 2, of the Book of Laws of Gipuzkoa (1674). In, *Nueva recopilación de los fueros, privilegios, buenos usos y costumbres y leyes y órdenes de la M.N. y M. L. provincia de Guipúzcoa*, Diputación de Gipuzkoa, Donostia/San Sebastián, 1919. Pp. 72-77.

aggression on behalf of the state was simply illegal. In fact, it never took place; no Basque army was led out of their territories to conquer another country. This implies a renunciation to the Basques' right of conquest at the international level, for it was indeed too expensive to maintain an army outside of the boundaries of the territories for nine days and, after that, there was no way of keeping soldiers attached to such an army.

XI. Many years after the ancient Basque codes were partially abolished by the Spanish and French governments, Basques remained reluctant to serve in the Spanish or French armies. Some figures illustrate this fact. During World War One a large number of young Basques fled before joining the French army and escaped to Gipuzkoa or Navarra.

The imposition of conscription in the Spanish state, beginning in 1981, generated a resistance to military service which would lead to an open political and social confrontation with the central government. The number of young people who refused to serve in the military exponentially multiplied between 1978 and 1981. In 1984 the opposition to the military service in the Basque Country reached 98.5 percent of the Basque youth (ages 18 to 21). In 1990 the number of evaders in the whole state was 2,450, 130 of whom were in prison. In Navarre 3.32 percent of the young people of military age in 1990 declared themselves in contempt. The figures are equally high in Araba (2.82 percent), Bizkaia (1.2 percent) and Gipuzkoa (2.04 percent), well above the state average which stood at 0.22 percent. Almost half of the evaders of the entire Spanish state in 1990 were Basque. That led to a policy of harsher sentences by the central government and, consequently, in 1991 the first sentences of 2 years, 4 months and 1 day on evaders were enforced. In 1992 107 trials were held, a large part of them, of Basque youngsters. In 2001 only 5,000 of the 91,000 people "drawn" to do the military service fulfilled the military service (5.4 percent of the total). At the beginning of the new millennium, more than 90 percent of the Basques of age to perform the military service did not do it. Social pressure led the Spanish government to opt for the professionalization of the army on December 31, 2001. Compulsory military service was consequently abolished.

The cross stands today in the place where the Malato tree once stood. Source: Irujo Ametzaga archive.

PC. People are in part what they were in the past, and these laws, even if no longer in force, still are part of the Basque culture as signs of this people's identity. Only that can explain the resistance of the Basque men to join the French or Spanish army. Moreover, some Basques escaped from their country not to serve in the army and then, once in America, they joined the U.S. army and fought in WWII. Some of them lived and died here, in Idaho.

XI. So you think then that liberty also has languages? That liberty and freedom are part of the cultural background of a nation?

PC. Yes, I do. And I also think that there are universal elements for what we call freedom, or liberty, self-determination or political independence. But let me answer to your question by reading *De l'esprit des lois* (1748) by Montesquieu on the different significations of the word "liberty":

> *There is no word that admits of more various significations, and has made more varied impressions on the human mind, than that of liberty. Some have taken it as a means of deposing a person on whom*

[113]

they had conferred a tyrannical authority; others for the power of choosing a superior whom they are obliged to obey; others for the right of bearing arms, and of being thereby enabled to use violence; others, in fine, for the privilege of being governed by a native of their own country, or by their own laws.[79]

XI. Which would be then, from your point of view, the basic elements of a Basque "definition" of freedom?

PC. Equality, the law of laws, would be one of the first elements of any definition of liberty. Also in the case of the Basques. The meaning of the universal nobility that has such a presence in the Basque ancient codes is the sharing of equal liberties for every citizen. And also the idea of a unique citizenship so all the citizens of the nation have the benefit of the same civil and political rights. Together with these principles, there are some rights that have a persistent and unambiguous appearance in all the Basque Codes through the history of the Basque law:

- Almighty popular assemblies
- The compulsory oath of the Lord and the King in front of the assembly and their promise of maintaining, defending and improving the laws
- Federalism
- The division of powers
- Right to vote in open assemblies
- Right to be elected per term for any public responsibility
- Right to elect all the officials of the Republic per term
- Right not to pay any tax that has not been passed and contracted in assembly
- Free trade
- Right to detent and make use of the common land in hands of the assemblies
- Habeas Corpus and other procedural rights

---

[79]   Book XI. Of the Laws Which Establish Political Liberty, with Regard to the Constitution. In, Montesquieu, Baron de, *The Spirit of the Law*, The Colonial Press, London/New York, 1900. P. 149.

[114]

- Inviolability of the dwelling, even with a judicial order
- Right not to serve in the army but in defense of the Republic
- Tenancy by the entirety
- Freedom of making one's will

Santa María de Najera, pantheon of the kings of Navarre, in Errioxa. According to the chronicles, the motto *Pro libertate Patria Gens Libera State* was carved in one of the bells of this church. Source: Irujo Ametzaga archive.

XI. Would you mention among them the *Pase Foral* or *Derecho de sobrecarta?*

PC. Yes of course. It is the key institution to protect the Assembly from the King. By virtue of the *Pase Foral* any law had to be sanctioned by the assembly or by the Council designated by the Assembly, so no law could be passed by the sole desire of the King. The formula, at the same time polite but firm and austere, used by the Assemblies to stop the King's will was the following, "the decrees against freedom shall be obeyed but not executed": *and they also said that they have the right, law, privilege and freedom, that any Royal letter or provision that the Lord of Bizkaia gives, or orders to give or provides,*

[115]

which is or may be contrary to the Laws and Rights of Bizkaia, directly or indirectly, to be obeyed and not fulfilled.[80]

XI. According to the legend –(because after a millennium of history of the Basque law, culture, politics, tradition and folklore harmonize) the following inscription was engraved by the Kings of Navarre on the bells of the church of Najera: *Pro libertate patria gens libera state.* That is, the citizens have to be free for the state to be free. Or, if you prefer, *Free Men for a Free Country.*

PC. "Free people in a free land"; carved indeed nearly 800 years ago, when the liberty bell of the Basques could be heard from all the corners of the country,

> *The Basques always preserved their independence, their autonomy, as we now say, making use of a Greek word. A long time before the Swiss they had already formed their confederation Iruracbat; long before the English had won for themselves their Magna Carta; long before the North Americans and the French had proclaimed their declarations of the rights of man and the citizen; they had organised a representative government, and their representatives met beneath the tree of Guernica. Thus they had government for the people, by the people, they had self government. And still today they protest against absorbent, suffocating, deadening centralization. The Basques, the Euskaros, had thus solved the political problem.*[81]

---

80   The original text at the Book of Laws of Bizkaia reads: Ley XI. *Que las Cartas contra la Libertad, sean obedecidas, y no cumplidas. Otrosí, dixeron: Que havian por Fuero, e Ley, e Franqueza, e Libertad, que qualquiera carta, ó Provission Real, que el dicho Señor de Vizcaya diere, o mandare dar, ó proveer, que sea, ó ser pueda, contra las Leyes, ó Fueros de Vizcaya, directe, o indirecte, que sea obedecida, y no cumplida.* In, *Fuero Nuevo de Vizcaya*, Leopoldo Zugaza, Durango, 1976. P. 10.

81   Peyret, Alejo, *Euskal Erria. Revista Vascongada*, Donostia/San Sebastián, 1880. Vol. 1, p. 292.

On the rising of the first Basque political nationalism

Xabier Irujo. From 1512-1521 (the war for the conquest of the Kingdom of Navarre), to 1789 (the French Revolution) the Basque states had known only three major bloody episodes, all of them with patent political connotations: the mutiny against the taxation of the salt in Bizkaia (1631-1634), the mutiny or "matxinada" against the royal attempt to abrogate the customs of the Basque states in 1718 and the mutiny of 1766 for the increasing of the prices and taxes on staple products. All of them had partly political motivations and while bloody, no more than a few hundred people died.

From 1789 on, that is, from the time the first attempts of abrogating the ancient Basque laws happened, one after the other, the French Revolution (1789-1799), the Convention's War (1793-1795), the Napoleonic Wars (1804-1815), the riot known as "Zamacolada" (1804), the Liberal insurrection (1820-1823), the First Carlist War (1833-1839) and the Second Carlist War (1872-1876) were fought in the Basque Country. Also, during the 20th century, the Basques suffered the dictatorship of King Alfonso XIII (1923-1931), the War of 1936 (1936-1937) and the dictatorship of Generalissimo Franco (1936-1975). After almost three hundred years of peaceful coexistence (1521-1789), the following two hundred and twenty two years have been marked by wars, rebellions, dictatorships and exile. And, as a direct consequence of these conflicts, hundred thousands of Basques have been killed, imprisoned or exiled. Do you think there is some link between the suppression of the ancient laws and the subsequent creation of the French and the Spanish states and the current Basque political conflict?

Pete Cenarrusa. No doubt about that. The Basque people's ways of life were taken away from them… What nation on earth would not react to that? What people on earth would pass through the abrogation of their laws, under which they had prosperously lived for at least eight hundred years, and remain silent? There are two key political consequences of the abolition of the laws of the Basques:

1. The Basques states lost their independence as a consequence of the unilateral rupture of a political pact of coexistence that had been established between the Kingdoms of France and Castile with the seven Basque states for so many centuries.
2. The abolition of the ancient laws set off a still unsolved political conflict.

The Enlightenment brought freedom to America. Jefferson, Adams or Paine gave origin to a democratic state based on the ideas of equality, freedom and liberty. And General Washington who had led the Revolutionary army to victory presented himself for election as a civilian, as a citizen, and became the first elected president of a new born republic in the western world.

XI. In Europe, by contrast, the French Revolution led to tyranny and tyranny to war. And in order to gain freedom and independence, many nations lost their ancient political rights during this difficult historic period. This is the case of Scotland that lost its independence in 1707, Catalonia that lost its independence in 1716 and the Basque states that lost their independence in 1789 (Lapurdi, Northern Navarre and Zuberoa) and 1876 (Araba, Bizkaia, Gipuzkoa and Southern Navarre).

While Washington led people to the polls and to a new life Napoleon led people to fight and die in battle. It is remarkable that one of the last battles to defeat Napoleon, the battle of the Victory, to which both Tchaikovsky and Beethoven dedicated their *Overtures*, was fought in 1812 in the Basque Country, in the fields at the south of the city of Vitoria/Gasteiz. Just before the battle Basques at both armies decided to desert to go watch a pilota match that was about to be played. It was not their war.

PC. General Bonaparte spread all over Europe the idea of a new political order based partially on the same enlightened political principles, but his *Grande Armée* was incompatible with democratic equality, freedom and civil liberties. In his hands the volumes by Rousseau, Voltaire, Montesquieu or Beccaria became nothing. And he turned out to be an Emperor. And any self-proclaimed emperor, declared to be chosen by the mercy of God as His representative on earth, is a tyrant.

On Sunday, July 15, 1804, Napoleon appeared for the first time before the Parisians surrounded by all the pomp of royalty. The members of the *Legion of Honor*, then in Paris, took the oath prescribed by the new Constitution:

> *Commanders, officers, legionaries, citizens, soldiers; swear upon your honour to devote yourselves to the service of the Empire, to the preservation of the integrity of the French territory, to the defence of the Emperor, of the laws of the Republic, and of the property which they have made sacred, to combat by all the means which justice, reason, and the laws authorise every attempt to reestablish the feudal system; in short, swear to concur with all your might in maintaining liberty and equality, which are the bases of all our institutions. Do you swear?[82]*

XI. The soldiers were requested to devote themselves to the service of an empire and the defense of an emperor in the name of liberty and equality.

PC. They did not swear indeed; they just cried what any disciplined soldier would: "Vive l'Empereur!." Quoting the Emperor's personal secretary, it is certainly laughable and somewhat audacious to make them swear to support equality at the moment so many titles and monarchical distinctions had been re-established. Indeed, Napoleon might end anarchy and turmoil within the boundaries of the French state but brought war, oppression and death to the rest of the continent. As any other emperor or king, he turned out to be one of the main obstacles to freedom and peace in Europe and millions of people died for that on the battlefields.

XI. But beyond that, it is interesting to notice that the prescriptive oath includes *the integrity of the French territory*. Indeed, it depicts the

---

[82]   Fauvelet de Bourrienne, Louis Antoine, *Memoirs of Napoleon Bonaparte*, H. Colburn and R. Bentley, 1831. P. 298.

notion of "equality" of the French empire: to be equal means that all Europeans had to become French speaking French. Equality was understood as cultural uniformity and political centralization. In these terms "equality" was leveled with obedience and submission.

PC. This proclamation tried to impose what was not preexistent either accepted. The French Crown was not a unitary state before 1789 and therefore out of twenty eight million inhabitants only three million spoke French correctly, as their first language. About six million people did not speak a word of French; during the French Revolution the French language became a political tool that the government would use to centralize the state and only through this process the French language became, for the first time, the foundation of the French identity.[83]

XI. Abbé Henri Grégoire was one of the first theorists of such linguistic standardization. He is the author of a series of reports that culminated in 1794 that convinced the Revolutionary Convention to adopt the imposition of standard French as the sole official language of the French state. Grégoire was one of the first declaring that the linguistic diversity was an obstacle for political unity. Before the riots that occurred in the Basque republics in 1790 that faced such an idea of empire, Grégoire wrote a series of questionnaires inquiring how languages as Basque, Breton, Corsican, German or Occitan could be eradicated. By compiling the answers to the questionnaires, Grégoire finally finished his 1794 report to the revolutionary assembly on "annihilating patois" by proclaiming that reading, writing or speaking Basque or any other language besides French made people counterrevolutionary, reactionary or even uncultured and, on the contrary, speaking French turned the masses into civilized, refined or sophisticated citizens. Therefore, in the name of regeneration, culture and universalism, it was imperative to impose French as the common language to all areas of the empire. The rest of the languages of the state, named "patois" and consequently considered substandard, had to disappear.

---

[83]   Nadeau, Jean-Benoît; Barlow, Julie, *The Story of French*, Macmillan, New York, 2006. Pp. 136-137.

PC. Yes, this author, considered to be an icon of universalism, even suggested that women, identified as reactionary and too devout, could not be regenerated by any means and that Jews had to be physically, morally and politically enlightened.

The idea that states should become strong unitary states under one single constitutional code and composed by a single and homogenous people speaking one only language was assumed by the Spanish liberals and so, the first attempts to create a new Spanish central state adopted in their constitutions the idea that the Spanish language should be the only official language of the state. In this context, the termination of the Basque states' political independence and the imposition of strange political laws and cultural uses ultimately ignited the Basque nationalism.

XI. It was not easy to make languages disappear because at the beginning of the nineteenth century neither Spanish nor French were the mother tongues of the Basques, so both languages had to be imposed. Here are some of the first political decrees of the new French state on language policy regarding the Basque language:

1. Decree of October 21, 1793 (*30 vendémiaire an II*) requiring the obligatoriness of primary education in the French language, *dans toutes les parties de la République, l'instruction ne se fait qu'en langue français*.[84]

2. Report of the Committee of Public Salvation of January 27, 1794 (*Rapport et projet de décret présentés au nom du comité de salut public sur les idiomes étrangers, et l'enseignement de la langue française, par Barère; 8 pluviose an II*), also known as *Rapport Barère*, on concerning the generalization of French through education.

3. Report of the National Convention of June 4, 1794 (*Rapport sur la nécessité et les moyens d'anéantir les patois et d'universaliser l'usage de la langue française; 16 prairial an II*), also known as *Rapport Grégoire*, on the necessity of eliminating the "patois" or regional languages and universalizing the French language.

---

[84]   On 17 December 1783 the Committee for Public Safety prohibited the use of German in Alsace.

[121]

4. Circular 72 of June 16, 1794 (*Circulaire 72 du 28 prairial an II*) enforcing Report of January 27, 1794, for which reason French was thus adopted as the only official language of the public education system.

5. Decree of July 20, 1794 (*Décret du 2 thermidor an II, sur la langue française*) on the use of French in the administration of the state, threatening imprisonment for those who disobeyed.

6. Decree of 19 December 1794 (*Décret du 29 frimaire an II*), on the approval of the first plan of education, in French.

7. Decree of the Convention on the exclusive use of the French language in education of Novermber 17, 1794 (*Décret du 27 brumaire an III sur les écoles primaires*) upon the initiative of Joseph Lakanal. Education would be imparted solely in French and it would focus on revolutionary values and the love for an indivisible country.

8. Law of May 1, 1802 (*Loi générale sur l'Instruction publique créant les lycées et l'Inspection générale 11 floréal an X*), by Napoleon Bonaparte, as *premier consul*, creating the first network of secondary schools in the country, with the same linguistic regulations of previous laws. Thus, in virtue of article six of title three, *Des écoles secondaires*, classes were to be taught in French as previously done, and instructors would teach French and Latin grammar.

9. Law Guizot of 28 June 1833 on the creation of the municipal primary school in French (*Loi du 28 juin 1833, dite loi Guizot, porte sur l'instruction primaire*). Order of the Inspector of the circumscription of the city of Maule (Zuberoa) on the exclusion of the Basque language from education.

10. Order of the prefect of the Low Pyrenees of 1846 on the substitution of Basque by French in Primary Education: "Our schools, particularly in the Basque Country, have as their objective to substitute the Basque language for the French language."[85]

---

[85] In French, "Nos écoles en Pays Basque ont particulièrement pour objet de substituer la langue française au basque." A similar idea applied for other nations of the state. : "Nos écoles, dans la Basse-Bretgne, ont particulièrement pour objet de substituer la langue française

11. Law Falloux of March 15, 1850 (*Loi du 15 mars 1850 relative à l'enseignement*), on education by which the exclusive use of the French language in the schools is regulated.

12. Law on the organization of Primary Education of March 28, 1882 (*Loi No 11 696 du 28 Mars 1882 qui rend l'Enseignement primaire obligatoire. Promulguée au Journal officiel du 29 mars 1882*). Primary Education would be offered exclusively in French. Exclusion of any other language from the educational system.

13. Laws Ferry of 16 June 1881 and March 28 1882 (*Loi du 16 juin 1881 qui établit la gratuité absolue de l'enseignement primaire & Loi du 28 mars 1882 sur l'enseignement primaire obligatoire*) by which the obligatory use of French in the public education system, excluding any other, was stated.

PC. These are only some examples. The French legislature passed hundreds of laws in the nineteenth century and will pass even more in the twentieth century in the same matter, affecting all the languages of the state not being French. Today all of them are minority languages and some are at the edge of extinction.

Similar laws were passed by the first Spanish governments in the nineteenth century.

XI. Here are some of the dispositions on linguistic policy adopted by the novice Spanish state between 1766 and 1875:

1. Order by the Count of Aranda, President of the Council of Castile on the prohibition against printing books in any language except Spanish. November 1, 1766.

2. Royal letter by Charles the Third regulating by its seventh article that in all schools of the kingdom, teachers should teach only in Spanish. June 23, 1768.

3. Royal letter by Charles the Third on the obligation of writing the account books in Spanish. December 24, 1772.

4. Order by Charles the Fourth to the Real Council of the Kingdom of Navarre on the readmission of publications in the Basque language. 1800.

---

au breton et ce serait incontestablement un bienfait." Préfet des Cotes du Nord, 1846.

5. Instructions for the adjustment of theaters and companies outside the Court on the prohibition against performing works that are not written in Spanish. March 11, 1801.

6. Law Moyano of public instruction on the exclusion of the Basque language from the education system: *Spanish grammar and Spanish spelling by the Spanish Language Academy will be the unique and obligatory text in public education.* September 7, 1857.

7. Law for the profession of notary (article 25) on the exclusion of the Basque language from all legal writings. May 28, 1862.

8. Royal Order of Isabel the Second on the prohibition against presenting any piece of theater in any language but in Spanish. January 15, 1867.

And a long etcetera. Professor Urrutia and myself have located more than 300 norms against the use of the Basque language passed in the Spanish and the French states from the beginning of the nineteenth century to the end of the twentieth century.[86] We calculate that there may be more than one thousand norms that directly affect the language rights of the Basques and the rest of the citizens of the Spanish and French states who are neither Spanish nor French such as Bretons, Catalans, Galicians, Occitans and, Corsicans, among many others.

PC. The Basque republics (the Brotherhood of Araba, the Signory of Bizkaia, the Province of Gipuzkoa, the Countries of Lapurdi and Zuberoa and both Kingdoms of Navarre) were positioned between two revolutionary processes at the end of the 18th century: the French Revolution and the Spanish Liberal Revolution. The ancient Basque political systems were incompatible with the new model of state.

Such a development of the events had logical political, economic, social and cultural consequences for the Basque society. Politically, the revolutionary process meant the end of the independence of the seven Basque states. Economically, the

---

[86]   Irujo, Xabier, Iñigo Urrutia, *A Legal History of the Basque Language (1789-2009)*, Eusko Ikaskuntza / Society for Basque Studies – Stanford University, Donostia/San Sebastián, 2009.

Basque people had to face the Industrial Revolution in a problematic political context marked by four long wars and a pressing administrative and social chaos. Socially, the customary political system that was almost completely vanished during the 19th century, forced the Basques to face, together with the political and economic processes, a deep process of social changes: family structure and social relationship, marriages, inheritance system, administration of public lands... everything was rearranged according to the French and the Spanish new Civil Codes that were imposed in the Basques states, the Napoleonic *Code Civil* of 1804 (for the Northern Kingdom of Navarre, Lapurdi and Zuberoa) and the Spanish *Código Civil* of 1889 (for Araba, Bizkaia, Gipuzkoa and the Southern Kingdom Navarre; even if the original Basque civil laws were respected to some extent). Finally, the Basque language suffered the worst recession in its history delaying its normal development until the second half of the 20th century. For the first time in history the Basque language was going to become the second language of the Basque people, after Spanish.

XI. Obviously the Basque states reacted to the new legal impositions.

PC. On August 26, 1789, the Declaration of the rights of man and citizen (*Déclaration des Droits de l'Homme et du Citoyen*) was passed by the French National Assembly. An exquisite document on human rights shaped on the Bill of Rights of Virginia... But the political rights were taken from the Basques and the cultural rights were out of it.

Between January and May 1789, the three Basque republics within the French republic wrote the *Cahiers de doléances* or *Record of Complaints*. In them the Basque states proclaimed that they had their own political system with their characteristic institutions. The sovereignty of the three states resided in the people gathered in their respective assemblies and, consequently, no change could be done in them without the approval of their legislative chambers. On 28 March 1789 the Third Estate of the Parliament of the Kingdom of Navarre proposed a project of union of the three Northern Basque states within the new French state. According to the project, all three of them would conserve their own institutions after the required political reforms.

TABLEAU

DE

LA CONSTITUTION

DU ROYAUME

DE NAVARRE,

ET DE SES RAPPORTS

AVEC LA FRANCE;

IMPRIMÉ PAR ORDRE DES ÉTATS-GÉNÉRAUX
DE NAVARRE,

*Avec un Difcours Préliminaire & des Notes , par
M. DE POLVEREL, Avocat au Parlement,
Syndic Député du Royaume de Navarre.*

A PARIS,

De l'Imprimerie de J. Ch. DESAINT, Imprimeur
du Châtelet , rue de la Harpe , N°. 133

Cover of the book published by the Parliament of the Kingdom of
Navarre in 1789 in which the representatives of the people of Navarre
expressed in assembly that they did not need the French constitution for
they had their own, the Code of Laws of Navarre. Source: Irujo Ametzaga
archive.

XI. However, none of the claims of the Basque representatives was attended in Paris.

PC. On December 4, 14 & 22, 1789 new laws on territorial administration and electoral systems were passed; between February 8 and March 4, 1790, the *département* of the *Basses-Pyrénées* (Low Pyrenees) was created including the three northern Basque republics and August 4, 1790, the first project of municipal reorganization of the Basque states was presented. According to the new project the three northern Basque states were dissolved and incorporated into a French *département*. Contrary to which was requested by the Basque representatives at the National Assembly, the new territorial unit was not exclusively Basque, since it was shared with the former territories of Guyenne and Béarn. The revolutionary Assembly tried to dilute the population and the territories of the ancient states by generating historically, culturally and politically heterogeneous administrative entities. Therefore, the *département* of the *Basses-Pyrénées* was divided into six districts (Uztaritz, Saint Palais, Maule, Orthez, Oleron and Pau) and forty cantons.

XI. And, thus the insurrection against the revolution occurred.

PC. The riot against the Revolutionary Assembly happened in spring 1794. About 4,000 Basque men, women and children were driven out of the Basque Country, many of them dying on their way to the Landes.

However, it was not the end of the Basque demands. In 1803 Dominique Joseph Garat, former representative of the Biltzar (or national assembly of Lapurdi) presented emperor Napoleon Bonaparte the proposition of a Federated Basque Republic under the name of New Phoenicia and, when five years after that the assembly of Spaniard notables promoted by Bonaparte in Baiona in June 1808 wrote a constitution for the Spanish state, the four Basque representatives proposed to the emperor the *Foruak* (ancient Basque laws) to be respected in their integrity. On July 6-8, 1808, the new constitution (*Acte Constitutionnel de l'Espagne*) was passed. Article 144 reads, *the legal codes of the provinces of Navarra, Bizkaia, Gipuzkoa and Araba will be discussed during the first session of the parliament in order to determine what is deemed more appropriate to the interests of these provinces and the nation.*

XI. Napoleon had different political projects in mind for the Basque territories. On 12 October 1810, the Emperor revealed his desire to politically incorporate the four Basque republics into the French Empire, as shown in his letter to Marshal Louis Alexandre Berthier, *My Cousin. Write to General Caffarelli (…). You will desire him to set on foot an inquiry into the conduct of General Avril at Bilbao, and of General Barthélemy at Santander. He is even to tell me his opinion of General Thouvenot. He must take means of suppressing instantly every kind of abuse. Let him know confidentially that I intend to annex Biscay*[87] *to France; that it is not to be mentioned, but that it must influence his conduct. Impart the same secret to General Reille with respect to Navarre. Desire these two Generals to arrest all the military commanders who are guilty of peculation, to inquire into past abuses, and to have the funds which were collected for the benefit of private individuals restored.*[88]

PC. However, after the liberal revolution the resultant French state was first an empire and then an autocratic monarchy ruled by the *Charte constitutionnelle de 1814* (Constitutional Chart of 1814), passed on June 4, 1814. According to the new constitution France was a nation and a state under the shape of a monarchy. Therefore, under the new law the old Basque states were no longer political entities. All citizens of the state were considered "Frenchmen" (art. 1 and 3); though, the legislative was a Chamber of Pairs (*Chambre des pairs*) integrated by the deputies elected by the king (art. 27). Also the noblemen would recover their old titles and the king was free to recognize new ones, although it did not affect their rights and duties in relation to the rest of the citizens (art. 71). Again, in order to become elector, citizens (only men) had to be forty years old and pay a direct tax of 1,000 francs; for the right to vote (census

---

[87]   Biscay or "Bizkaia" meant "Araba, Bizkaia and Gipuzkoa" for the Emperor, as may be seen in many letters to his Generals. See, Bonaparte, Napoleon, *The Confidential Correspondence of Napoleon Bonaparte with His Brother Joseph*, D. Appleton and Company, 1856. Pp. 83 & 86.

[88]   Bonaparte, Napoleon, *The Confidential Correspondence of Napoleon Bonaparte with His Brother Joseph*, D. Appleton and Company, 1856. P. 153. See also, Tone, John Lawrence, *The Fatal Knot: The Guerrilla War in Navarre and the Defeat of Napoleon in Spain*, UNC Press, 1994. P. 218.

suffrage) citizens had to be thirty years old and pay a direct tax of 300 francs (Royal ordinances of July 13, 1815, and September 5, 1816, lowered the age of electors to twenty one and the one of parliamentary candidates to twenty five). The king was the only head of the executive (art. 14) and also had the power to propose the laws (art. 16). One legislative was composed of the chamber of pairs (art. 24-34) and the chamber of deputies of the provinces (art. 35-53). Finally, all citizens had the duty of accomplishing the military service (art. 12), a law that would never be accepted by the Basques.

XI. Similar political process was undertaken by the southern Basque states.

PC. Yes. During the Napoleonic invasion of the Iberian Peninsula the Central Defense Board of the Crown of Castile (*Suprema Junta Gubernativa del Reino*) ordered on 28 October 1809 the celebration of *Cortes* or parliamentary assembly in order to elaborate a constitutional draft. Due to the course of the war, the Cortes had to meet far from the battle-front in the Island of Leon at first and in Cádiz thereafter. Approximately three hundred deputies coming from all the republics and territories of the Crown met in Cádiz for two years. Deputy Diego Muñoz Torrero was named secretary of the commission in charge of elaborating the Spanish constitution. On September 24, 1810, the sessions of the assembly were opened and the deputies soon were divided in two main parties or factions (in addition to many other intermediate positions): Liberal and Conservative. The Liberals defended the elaboration of a constitution similar to the revolutionary one of 1791. The Basque deputies were willing to face changes in the constitutions of the Basque territories but without resigning the sovereignty of their territories (confederate state). This positioning placed them closer to the Conservative Party, since liberalism was primarily characterized by a strong centralist and homogenizing spirit. On March 19, 1812, the first liberal constitution was finally passed the day of San Joseph of 1812, which is the reason why it was named "La Pepa." It would never be enforced but it contains the fundamental aspects of the Spanish central state to be created.

XI. As in the French Constitution of 1791 the concept of equality was also confused in the Constitution of 1812 with the idea of uniformity, therefore, for the citizens to be equal they had to be uniform, standardized: same law, same institutions, same symbols, same language, same customs and same beliefs for all of them, independent of their primary customs, culture or laws. Cultural rights were not among the rights of the new constitution. The constitution tacitly imposed the Spanish language as the sole language of the state. As we have seen further laws prohibited the use of any other language in public administration (education, administration of justice…). In sum, the Constitution was requesting from Basques, Catalans and Galician to become Spanish, by law.

PC. Although the principle of unity of the state is not explicitly mentioned in the constitutional text, the resultant state was a strongly centralized monarchy with equal codes for every one of the territories or areas within it.[89] The concept of citizenship is different from the one adopted by the revolutionary constitution of 1791. In this case "citizen" is synonym of "Spanish", excluding the rest of the nationalities of the territory from legality. And, accordingly, "Nation" was understood as the population of the Spanish state, including all the peoples of the overseas (the Americas and the Philippines).[90] The cultural concept of "nation" and the political notion of "state" were mixed and confused into one only idea.

As in the revolutionary constitution of 1791, sovereignty was understood as the common will of all the Spaniards or "the common will of the elected representatives gathered in assembly".[91] The territory of the state would be therefore divided into electoral districts, and Spain was considered thereafter, for the first time in

---

[89]   Title 1, *de la nación española y de los españoles*, Chapter 1, *de la nación española*, Article 3.

[90]   Literally, *la Nación española es la reunión de todos los españoles de ambos hemisferios*. In, Title 1, *de la nación española y de los españoles*, Chapter 1, *de la nación española*, Article 1.

[91]   Literally, *la soberanía reside esencialmente en la Nación, y por lo mismo pertenece a ésta exclusivamente el derecho de establecer sus leyes fundamentales*. Title 1, *de la nación española y de los españoles*, Chapter 1, de la nación española, Article 3.

history, an indissoluble territorial and administrative unity. The standardization of the laws and legislative procedures entailed that the ancient institutions of the four southern Basque states were univocally repealed.[92] The Basque parliaments, courts of justice and city councils were dismantled.

Monument to the Ancient Laws in Iruñea/Pamplona, a symbol of the ancient liberties of the Kingdom of Navarre. Source: Irujo Ametzaga archive.

The Spanish state was divided into "provinces" (new administrative units) so the Basque states became two different "provinces": Navarre and the Vascongadas (including Araba, Bizkaia and Gipuzkoa).[93] Every "province" was to be uniformly administered with new institutions dependant on the central government of the state in Madrid. Also, municipal organization would be equal and uniform for all the cities in the state. It has to be mentioned that due to the federal origin of the Basque states

---

92   Title 1, *de la nación española y de los españoles*, Chapter 1, de la nación española, Article 3.
93   Title 2, *del territorio de las Españas, su religión y gobierno y de los ciudadanos españoles*, Chapter 1, *del territorio de las Españas*, Article 1.

some Basque cities such as Lizarra or Tolosa or valleys such as Baztan or Erronkari had had their own written ordinances for more than seven hundred years.[94]

The chief of the executive was the king, titled for the first time "king of the Spains,"[95] and consequently the titles of Lord of Bizkaia, Lord of Araba, King of Gipuzkoa and King of Navarre were unilaterally abolished. Under the new Constitution all citizens had to accomplish the military service.[96] A new universal tax system for the entire state was to be passed[97] and, consistent with the principle of uniformity, the Constitution states that the civil code, the criminal code and trade code will be the same for all the monarchy, subject to the variations that due to particular circumstances the parliament may approve.[98]

XI. Obviously these measures were not welcomed in the Basque Country.

PC. Right. On October 1, 1833, the War of the Seven Years (1833-1839) broke out. The three states on the north of the country, including the Northern Kingdom of Naverre, Lapurdi and Zuberoa, lost their political independence in 1789 during the French Revolution and the subsequent formation of the French state and the Empire (1789-1804). The four states to the south, Araba, Bizkaia, Gipuzkoa and Navarre, lost their political independence after the Seven Years War (1833-1839).

The government of the Southern Kingdom of Navarre, controlled after the Seven Years War by the Liberal Party, signed the Treaty of Union with the government of the new Spanish state. The treaty was euphemistically called Agreed Law (*Ley Paccionada*)

---

[94] Title 6, *del gobierno interior de las provincias y de los pueblos*, Chapter 1, *de los ayuntamientos.*

[95] Literally, *Rey de las Españas*. Preamble of the Constitution.

[96] *Está asimismo obligado todo español a defender la Patria con las armas, cuando sea llamado por la ley.* Title 1, *de la nación española y de los españoles,* Chapter 2, *de los españoles,* Article 9.

[97] *También está obligado todo español, sin distinción alguna, a contribuir en proporción de sus haberes para los gastos del Estado.* Title 1, *de la nación española y de los españoles,* Chapter 2, *de los españoles,* Article 8.

[98] Title 5, *de los tribunales y de la administración de justicia, en lo civil y criminal,* Chapter 1, *de los tribunales,* Article 258.

and came into force on 16 August 1841. The Treaty unified the Crowns of Navarre and Castilia and formed the Spanish Parliament which, in the practice meant the elimination of the Navarrese parliament, the end of Navarrese independence and the creation of a new state, the Spanish state under complete Spanish control. The Navarrese never accepted the Agreed Law of 1841. As a consequence, after the First Carlist War (1833-1839) and the partial abolition of the ancient Basque laws, the Basque states went to war again in 1872 claiming devolution. After the Second Carlist War (1872-1876), the Spanish government canceled the ancient laws and passed the Law of Abrogation of the Basque Laws of 21 July 1876.

XI. What, from your point of view, is the political significance of the abrogation of the Basque legal codes?

PC. Let me answer your question by reading what the Earl of Carnavon wrote on the abrogation of the Basque laws:

> *At length worn out by the indomitable opposition of the people, the Queen's generals fraudulently guaranteed the preservation of rights which they knew their own Government would not confirm, but which they doubted their own ability to suppress. The last act of the tragedy was worthy of the first; a war of injustice was crowned by a deed of the basest perfidy, and the laws which governed a land of freemen for a thousand years were at length abrogated. In an age of greater civilisation than any which had preceded it —in an age of greater supposed deference to the claims of justice- this most unjust and cruel act was committed*[99].

After the defeat of devolution in the battlefields and in the interminable discussions at the offices of the Spanish government in Madrid and on the battlefields in the Basque Country in 1876, the Basque political nationalism arose as an alternative to war. The first Basque nationalist political party, *Asociación Euskara de Navarra* (Basque Association of Navarre) was created in 1878, only two years after the end of the Second Carlist War.

---

[99]   Herbert, Henry J. G. Earl of Carnavon, *Portugal and Galicia with a Review of the Social and Political State of the Basque Provinces*, John Murray, London, 1848.

Estanislao Aranzadi Izkue, one of the leaders of the *Asociación Euskara de Navarra* (Basque Association of Navarre) with his son Manuel Aranzadi Irujo. Source: Irujo Ametzaga archive.

Led by Sabino Arana, a new Basque nationalist political party, *Euzko Alderdi Jeltzalea - Partido Nacionalista Vasco* (EAJ-PNV) was created soon after, in 1894.

The Basque Nationalist Party was born out of a desire for total devolution, and independence.[100] The main political aim of the first Basque nationalist political forces was to recover the lost liberties and, closely connected to that, the main cultural goal was to protect the Basque culture and more specifically the Basque language from disappearing.

XI. Which do you consider were the main ideological principles of the Basque Nationalist Party created by Sabino Arana Goiri?

---

[100]   Devolution of the ancient laws and, therefore, independence.

Sabino Arana Goiri, founder of the Basque Nationalist Party in 1894. Source: Basque Archive of the University of Nevada, Reno.

PC. The Basque Nationalist Party developed its political activity between 1893 and 1937 through a complex political process, however, there are certain ideological principles and strategic aims that can be traced during all this period of time:

[135]

- *Jaungoikoa eta Lege Zaharrak* (God and Ancient Laws). The motto of the Carlist Party[101] was adopted by the Basque Nationalist Party asking for a complete devolution. In other words, this political force called for the restoration of the Basques' own political system as it was established before the French and the Spanish revolutions.

- *Euskotarren aberria Euskadi da* (Euskadi is the motherland of the Basques). According to Arana the Basques were an ethnic group and a culture (of which the language is a fundamental element) with a privative history, reason why the Basques should have the right to organize themselves into an independent state.

- Europeism. At the beginning of the twentieth century the Basque Nationalist Party included in its program the demand that the Basque Country should be a federated state within a political Pan-European confederation of states.

- Democracy, human rights and republicanism. The Basque Nationalist Party defended human rights as the main political aspiration of the state and the federal republic as the most perfect political system.

- Catholicism and lay state. The Basque Nationalist Party was a Catholic party that defended separation between church and state.

- Christian-Democracy. Socially, the Basque Nationalist Party became one of the first Christian-Democratic parties in Europe.

And so, some of the main goals of the first Basque political nationalism were the following:

---

[101]   The Carlist Party was a confessional (Catholic) and conservative political movement seeking the establishment of a separate line of the Bourbon family on the Spanish throne as a means of conserving the ancient laws of the Basque states. Devolution was therefore the main political goal of the Carlists. The Carlist Party was the political force leading the Carlists Wars in the Basque Country in 1833 and 1876.

- To organize the political instruments in order to accomplish the constitution of an independent Basque state.
- In the context of a dramatic process of industrial reconversion, to achieve and ensure the maximum social, economic, political and cultural welfare benefit for all Basques.
- To implement the presence of Basque nationalist candidates in the Basque institutions (at first only in the Basque institutions and then, also in the state-wide institutions such as the Spanish parliament or even the Spanish government and, in the international organizations such as the European Communities).
- To permanently influence public opinion stimulating the participation of the citizens and social groups in the construction of a future for the Basque Country.

XI. After the Second Carlist War (1872-1876), and the definitive suppression of the ancient laws in 1876, the Basque states negotiated with the Spanish government to restore some of their lost political and economic rights (such as the civil laws). As a result, the *Conciertos Económicos* (Economic Agreements) were passed. The *Conciertos Económicos* gave the four Basque states (now "provinces" within the Spanish state) the right to impose a lump sum (the "Cupo" or installment) in lieu of taxation, on the principle that the total amount paid by the Basque people should be proportionally equal to the taxing burden in other regions of the Spanish state. Indirect taxes on tobacco, petrol, explosives, and other products produced in monopolistic markets were set at a national rate and could not be subject to the "Concierto" or agreement. The four Basque territories each paid a fixed annual sum ("Cupo") into the treasury of the Spanish state and, in exchange, they were exempt from internal taxation by the central government.[102] The payments were periodically adjusted by

---

[102]   Origins of the Basque agitation. Report by U.S. Ambassador to the Spanish Republic, Claude G. Bowers to the Secretary of State. Madrid, September 10, 1934. National Archives and Records Administration, College Park, U.S. Ambassador Claude G. Bowers Files (Files 852.00/…, Boxes 3687 to 3701), Document 852.00/2021. Pp. 3-4.

common agreement between the provincial administration and the state. The Basque provinces were the only regions to have such agreements with the central Spanish government, and they are still in force today.

PC. And, almost half a century after the end of the Second Carlist War (1872-1876) and after several riots, the Basques were given political autonomy. On October 7, 1936, the autonomous Basque state was created, and one day later, the first Basque government was formed led by President Jose Antonio Agirre:

> *Today an autonomous Euzkadi Government takes office. As night fell yesterday amidst a silence broken only by the rustle of autumn leaves, the first President elect of the Basque people, Don Jose Antonio Agirre, stood under the ancient oak tree at Guernica and in the presence of representatives of the people took the oath that is as old as the tree. First in Basque, then in Spanish, he said, "Humbly before God, but erect on Basque soil, beneath the Oak of Biscay, on the memory of my ancestors I swear to fulfill my duties faithfully." The Governor of Biscay then conferred office on the new President in the name of the central Government and called upon him to make known his Cabinet. This is composed of eleven members.*[103]

XI. The Basques have retained their autonomy to the present. However, the political conflict remains unsolved.

Nowadays, the four southern states constitute two autonomous communities within the Spanish state: the Basque Autonomous Community and the Chartered Community of Navarre. The Basques in both communities enjoy their own Executive and Legislature and collect their own taxes in exchange for the above mentioned donation to the Spanish state. But, notwithstanding, by 2011 61 percent of the political parties represented at the Basque parliament and 28 percent of those

---

[103] Report on the Basque Autonomy No 1223. Report by U.S. Ambassador to the Spanish Republic, Claude G. Bowers to the Secretary of State. Donibane Lohitzune, October 12, 1936. National Archives and Records Administration, College Park, U.S. Ambassador Claude G. Bowers Files (Files 852.00/..., Boxes 3687 to 3701), Document 852.00/3553. Pp. 1-2.

represented at the parliament of Navarre requested the right of self determination for the Basque Country.

Lehendakari (President) Agirre taking the presidential oath in Gernika in 1936. Source: Archive of the Basque Nationalism/Sabino Arana Foundation.

PC. Successive Spanish and French governments could have deprived the Basques of their laws, their trade and international relations, but it is very difficult to take from a people their soul. The ancient Basque codes, charters, books of law, were the reflection of the customs of the Basque culture, they represented through the centuries the way a nation has understood life and death, and this is something that cannot be erased from the memory of men by passing a bill of abrogation. One thousand years of history explain the aim of independence of the freemen and freewomen of the Basque Country.

Let me finish by quoting the following article, written in 1937 for the *Time* magazine:

> *No other people have an organization so close to the Swiss conception of the State as the Basques. Most of us know that Switzerland took over the form of her Constitution from the United States; but few*

know that the 18th century Americans on their part turned to the traditional laws of the Basques. The old Basque Country, too, was a confederacy of independent cantons, though these units were called by a different name. As early as the ninth century these cantons existed in approximately their present day outlines and each of them had its own laws. They were each ruled by a 'Sire', a kind of Prince, and all were obligated to give armed help to any canton should it be attacked by an enemy from outside. If, however, one of these 'Sires' wanted to jump at his neighbor's throat, he had to do it on his own account or risk.

Three of these cantons lay north of the Pyrenees and were finally annexed by France in 1789; and the other provinces - Alava, Guipuzcoa, Navarra and Vizcaya - for centuries enjoyed autonomy under sovereignty of Spain. But in 1876 they were deprived of their autonomous status as a result of the last Carlist war, and they came under the direct authority of Madrid. Alien people with alien customs arrived and forced their will and their habits upon the free men of Euzkadi. The Basques did not forget it through the many years and the Spaniards have remained alien invaders to the Basques up to the present day. (…)

Basque separatism aiming a complete independence never quite disappeared during the past hundred years. After the end of the Carlist war, however, there was a period in which Basque aspirations seemed to have been silenced forever. Then, in the nineties, Sabino Arana Goiri, a leader inspired by high ideals, succeeded in reawakening the Basque provinces, but he died in 1903 when only 38 years of age. His brother carried on to liberate the Basques, and today Euzkadi has regained what seems to be a very precarious autonomy.

Gernika, April 26, 1937

Xabier Irujo. Gernika was a symbol far before the bombing of the city on April 26, 1937.

Pete Cenarrusa. Yes, Gernika had been for at least the end of the 18th century the symbol of the ancient liberties, the icon of an old democracy facing a new promising age, the Enlightenment.

As we have already mentioned, kings and emperors came to Gernika and knelt down beneath the Tree of Gernika, in front of the popular assembly of the free men and women of Bizkaia and, with their consent, they had to take the oath and promise that they would not take their laws away from them nor add to them nor give them any new ones unless they should do so in Bizkaia, and with the approval of the General assembly (Biltzar) of the Bizkaians.

In 1810, a century before the town was reduced to rubble by the Luftwaffe, in the midst of an age of political, economic, cultural and social commotion, the English poet William Wordsworth dedicated a poem to the oak of the ancient Basque egalitarianism:

> *Oak of Guernica! Tree of holier power*
> *Than that which in Dodona did enshrine*
> *(So faith too fondly deemed) a voice divine*
> *Heard from the depths of its aerial bower-*
> *How canst thou flourish at this blighting hour?*
> *What hope, what joy can sunshine bring to thee,*
> *Or the soft breezes from the Atlantic sea,*
> *The dews of morn, or April's tender shower?*
> *Stroke merciful and welcome would that be*
> *Which should extend thy branches on the ground,*
> *If never more within their shady round*
> *Those lofty-minded Lawgivers shall meet,*
> *Peasant and lord, in their appointed seat,*
> *Guardians of Biscay's ancient liberty.*

Also Jose Maria Iparragirre, exiled by the Spanish authorities, composed in 1853 what is still considered today the unofficial anthem of the Basque Country, the *Gernikako arbola* (The Tree of Gernika):

The tree of Gernika
Is the blessed symbol
That every Basque
So closely loves.
Saintly tree: spread
Your fruit by the world
While we pay
Fervent admiration to you.

Tradition tells us
That the Tree of Gernika
Was planted by God
More than one thousand years ago.
Saintly tree: do not fall,
For without your sweet shade,
Complete, certain,
Our perdition will be.

You will not fall, oh oak!
If the noble Council of Bizkaia
Fulfills its duties.
Their children have to reconcile
And thus the four sisters
Will support you
So the Basque people
Will peacefully live free.

XI. Gernika was also a political emblem for the Basques. At some stage in a celebration in tribute to Victor Hugo that took place in Paris on February 27, 1881, a group of Basques, some of them members of the Asociación Euskara de Navarra (Basque Association of Navarre) and coming from different points of Europe and America, took with them a Basque national flag whose design was based on the one used by some Basque battalions under

[142]

Jauregi and Mina during the Napoleonic Wars in the Basque Country (1808-1814) and, even before, during the War of the Convention (1793-1795).

The Tree of Gernika today. Source: Irujo Ametzaga archive.

This first Basque national flag was used in America for the first time on November 1, 1882, in the course of the celebration of the Fiestas Euskaras (Basque Festivals) that took place in Buenos Aires. That day the Plaza Euskara (Basque square) was inaugurated, a seed of the tree of Gernika was sowed and the Basque flag was raised while the Gernikako Arbola by Iparragirre was toned. Three national symbols with an obvious political intention were then used during this celebration: the national flag, the Gernikako Arbola as a national anthem and, finally, the mention of all the Basques as a cultural, historical and political unity under the common and general denomination of "euskaros" (Basques) and the subsequent reference to "Euskaria" making reference to Euskal Herria (Basque Country). The flag was also used by other groups of the Basque diaspora in Europe and in the Americas.

However, the world mainly knows Gernika not as a symbol of Basque liberties or ancient democracy, but for the events that took place during the Market Day Massacre.

PC. That is because the events that took place on April 26, 1937 represent a symbol of human suffering, oppression and mass murder for all the innocent victims of previous wars. As proclaimed in 1940 by Telesforo Monzon, Minister of the Interior and Public Safety of the Basque Government, the bombing took Gernika from us and turned it into a universal icon.

XI. On July 17, 1936 a group of Spanish generals led a coup d'état in Melilla with the intention of overthrowing the government of the Spanish Republic and organizing a totalitarian regime. The military coup did not succeed as the insurgents were not able to capture Madrid. However, the Republican forces could not crush the rebels and thus began the so called "Spanish Civil War", a war that lasted three years (1936-39) and that is considered to be the prologue to World War Two.

U.S. Ambassador Claude G. Bowers stated that the war was not a "civil" conflict because as early as July 1936 the German and Italian regimes decided to militarily assist the Spanish Nationalists by sending them men and war materials in great quantities. Indeed, by April 1937, 89 percent of the planes of the Spanish Nationalists were of German and Italian origin.

The majority of the Spanish clergy supported the uprising. Indeed, nearly 90 percent of the Spanish episcopacy supported the coup by signing a letter to the Pope written by the major ecclesiastical authority in the Spanish state, the Prime Archbishop of Toledo, Isidro Gomá. This *Collective Letter of the Spanish Episcopacy on the Civil War* was published on July 1, 1937 and distributed to Catholics all over the world in order to gain supporters for the insurrection at the international level, and especially in order to gain the favor of the Vatican for the rebels.

As we have already mentioned, on October 7, 1936 the autonomous Basque state was created under the presidency of Jose Antonio Agirre. The war was already being fought and the Basque Nationalist forces had already decided to fight together with the Spanish democrats against Spanish National-Catholicism, German Nazism and Italian Fascism.

The leaders of the insurgent Movimiento Nacional (National Movement) initially believed that the Basque Nationalist Party, the major political party in the Basque Country at the time, being Christian-Democrat and conservative, would provide support for the military uprising. This calculation was based on four basic facts: 1) Both political forces (National Movement and Basque nationalism) were mainly conservative; 2) both forces were Catholic; 3) both were opposed to the government of the Spanish Republic and, 4) both the Carlist Party[104] and the Basque Nationalist Party have their roots in the same 19th century historical process and consequently share some ideological principles, such as the vindication of restitution (the restoration of the ancient Basque laws that were abolished in 1876).

On September 8, 1936, a day after the Basque Government was created, an official call for the Basque nationalists to join the uprising was transmitted by radio:

> *You cannot in any way contribute neither much nor little, nor directly nor indirectly, to the fissure of the Spanish Army and the corpses of non-combatant officers and employees of the military, "Requetés," members of the Falange and the civil militia, that in raising the authentic two-colored Spanish flag, fight heroically for the Religion and the Fatherland. Oh! If the Marxists prevail, once the docks of Religion, moral and decency are broken, the sweeping wave would sink all of us in its furious impetus. There would not be salvation for the Catholics, and it would at all costs try to erase the last vestige of God! What a difference in what happened in the provinces that resolutely joined the Rescuing Movement of the Spanish Army! (...) The Crucifix has been restituted to its position of honor in the schools, the venerated image of the Sacred Heart has returned to the throne that previously occupied the city councils and regional governments. The rights of the Sacred Church are respected. Priests, monks and nuns are respected, supported, loved (...) Stop fighting the victorious Spanish Army, support it, cooperate with him, save the life of all so that we all, forgetting hatreds and resentments, can live in peace and sacred freedom.[105]*

---

[104]   The Carlist party was a historical monarchic and strongly conservative Basque political party (whose origin may be searched for back to the beginning of the 19th century) which first political goal was devolution.

[105]   Hernando, Bernardino M., *Delirios de cruzada*, Ediciones 99, Madrid, 1977. Pp. 107.

Rally pro statute of autonomy for the Basque Country. In the photograph, Manuel Irujo giving a speech in the bullring of Lizarra/Estella together with Jose Antonio Agirre and Fortunato Agirre, Mayor of the city who was later shot by the rebels. Source: Irujo Ametzaga archive.

In spite of those appeals, the Basque nationalists quickly demonstrated that they would back the democratically elected Republican government. In fact, on July 19, 1936, only hours after the uprising in Morocco, parliamentary members Manuel Irujo and Joxe Mari Lasarte, after hearing mass in the church of the Capuchinos in Donostia, transmitted a wireless message describing the Basque Nationalist Party's support for the democratic forces and demanding that the civil governor of Gipuzkoa, Jesús Artola Goikoetxea, do the same thing. Furthermore, on July 21, the Basque Nationalist Party published an official notice in two newspapers, *Euzkadi* and *La Gaceta del Norte*, emphasizing its opposition to the military coup d'état:

> *Before the events happening in the Spanish state that can have such a direct and painful repercussion on the Basque Country and its destiny, the Basque Nationalist Party declares —without renouncing its ideology, that today solemnly ratifies- that the fight between citizenship and Fascism, between the Republic and the Monarchy, having been raised, its principles irrevocably move the party to fall on the side of citizenship and the Republic, keeping ourselves with the*

[146]

democratic and republican regime which was inherent to our people during centuries of freedom.[106]

Why do you think the Basque Nationalism opted to join the republicans of the Popular Front?

PC. Although the two factions shared some similarities, they also had many differences, some of which were extreme.

Although it is truth that both forces opposed the Republican government, the causes of the confrontation were completely different. The National Movement objected to the Popular Front, a coalition of leftist political forces, for they considered the Republican government's policy of decentralization an assault on the unity of the state and an attempt to dismantle the country. That was one of the main causes that led to the political union of conservative political forces, the ecclesiastical hierarchy and the Army. Pressed by the Basque and Catalan nationalist forces, the first Republican government held a plebiscite to grant a Statute of Autonomy to Catalonia.

XI. Yes, nearly 90 percent of the population voted for the statute of autonomy of Catalonia (592,961 votes in favor versus 3,276 against), which took effect in 1932. Consequently, a Catalan autonomous government, known as the Generalitat was formed, and the Catalan language was declared an official language of the region along with Castilian. Five years later, in October 1936, the Basque Statute of Autonomy was passed, and the Basque government under the presidency of Lehendakari (President) Jose Antonio Agirre was created. The creation of these two autonomous governments led by nationalist political forces and the announcement of a possible third independent government in Galicia, provoked lively and divergent reactions among the different factions of the Spanish nationalists.

PC. Exactly. The Basque nationalists, by contrast, opposed each of the Spanish Republican governments, whether rightist or leftist, for one fundamental reason: the denial of the right to self-determination for the Basque Country. The main political

---

[106]   *La Gaceta del Norte*, Bilbao, July 21, Tuesday, 1936.

aspiration of Basque nationalism was the creation of an independent Basque state. The diverse Basque nationalist forces insistently demanded from the central government the right to self-determination so that the Basque population could decide its own political future. The various republican governments' distrust of the Basque nationalists delayed approval of a Statute of Autonomy for the Basque Country and the formation of the Basque government until October 1936. The nationalists, without renouncing the right to self-determination, accepted the statute as a first step to more political autonomy. So while conservative forces viewed the policy of decentralization as an inadmissible concession, the Basque nationalists saw it as a timid step toward an independent Basque Federal Republic.

XI. The National Movement considered the secularization of political life and the rise to power of a predominantly liberal regime that advocated freedom of religion and a lay education system a "political disease." After the first draft of the Constitution of 1931 declared the strict separation of church and state in Article 26, Manuel Azaña, the Minister of War and future president of the Spanish Republic, declared on October 13, 1931 that "Spain is no longer Catholic." Pope Pius XI expressed his strong opposition to the separation of church and state in his encyclical *Dilectissima nobis* on June 3, 1933:

> *But, returning to the deplorable laws regarding religious confessions and Congregations, We learned with great sorrow that therein, at the beginning, it is openly declared that the State has no official religion, thus reaffirming that separation of State from Church, which was, alas, decreed in the new Spanish Constitution. We shall not delay here to repeat that it is a serious error to affirm that this separation is licit and good in itself, especially in a nation almost totally Catholic (...) But if the pretension of excluding from public life God the Creator and Provident Ruler of that same society is impious and absurd for any people whatsoever, it is particularly repugnant to find this exclusion of God and Church from the life of the Spanish Nation, where the Church always and rightly has held the most*

important and most beneficially active part in legislation, in schools, and in all other private and public institutions.[107]

PC. The Holy See also criticized the Popular Front's reforms of the education system, which limited intervention by the church, which had previously administered the system through its diverse religious communities:

They were not satisfied with the recent law by which they raged so fiercely against the great and meritorious Society of Jesus; they wished to give another and very serious blow to all Religious Orders and Congregations by forbidding them to teach. Thus was accomplished a work of deplorable ingratitude and clear injustice. In fact, the liberty which is granted to all, to exercise the right to teach, is taken from one class of citizens guilty only of having embraced a life of renunciation and perfection. Did they perhaps wish to inflict upon the Religious, who have left and sacrificed everything to dedicate themselves only to teaching and the education of the young as an apostolic mission, the stigma of incapacity or inferiority in the teaching field? Nevertheless, experience has demonstrated with what care, with what competence, priests always have fulfilled their duty, with what magnificent results for the instruction of the intellect as well as for the education of the heart they have crowned their patient labor. This is luminously proved by the number of persons, truly famous in all fields of human science and at the same time exemplary Catholics, who have been formed at religious schools. This is also proved by the great advances made in Spain thanks to such schools, and by the records of their students. Finally, this is also confirmed by the confidence that they have enjoyed from parents who, having received from God the right and duty of educating their own children, have also the sacrosanct liberty of choosing those who must efficaciously cooperate in their education.[108]

---

[107]   *Dilectissima nobis,* encyclical of Pope Pius XI on oppression of the Church of Spain to the eminent Cardinals: Francisco Vidal y Barraquer, Archbishops of Tarragona, Eustaquio Ilundain y Esteban, Archbishops of Seville, and the other Archbishops and Bishops and all the clergy and people of Spain. Rome, June 3, 1933.

[108]   *Dilectissima nobis,* encyclical of Pope Pius XI on oppression of the Church of Spain to the eminent Cardinals: Francisco Vidal y Barraquer, Archbishops of Tarragona, Eustaquio Ilundain y Esteban, Archbishops of

XI. On the contrary, even if the Basque Nationalist Party, a Christian-Democrat political force, did not support the economic reforms of the Spanish Popular Front and opposed the measures adopted by the Popular Front against the Society of Jesus, it was not opposed to necessary social reforms. Moreover, in October 1936 the Basque Nationalist Party formed a coalition government with the Socialist Party and other leftist forces such as Repoublican Left (IR, Izquierda Republicana), Republican Union (RU, Unión Republicana), the Communist Party (PC, Partido Comunista) and Basque Nationalist Action (EAE-ANV, Eusko Abertzale Ekintza - Acción Nacionalista Vasca), a Basque nationalist and leftist political force. That is, the Basque Nationalist Party did not utterly and confrontationally oppose the social policies of the Popular Front, though certain differences of opinion led sometimes to political disputes between the parties.

PC. And meanwhile landowners viewed the agrarian reforms promoted by the leftist parties as an aggressive attack on their interests. The law 200 of 1936, which outlined the legal framework for the agrarian reforms of the Popular Front, was based on the principle that private property must have a social benefit. This law gave the Spanish government authority to appropriate uncultivated lands and offer parcels to laborers who worked on land that did not belong to them. At the same time, the law prohibited government evacuations of farmers who invaded uncultivated lands. It also provided for the loss of ownership if land went uncultivated for ten years. In those cases, the land could be expropriated by the state and given to farmers not owning any land. A group of some of Spain's largest landowners including the Catholic Church, one of the country's biggest landholders, organized an alliance called the Patriotic Association to oppose the National Economic Reform.

XI. Indeed, Pope Pius XI addressed the issue in the encyclical *Dilectissima nobis*:

Seville, and the other Archbishops and Bishops and all the clergy and people of Spain. Rome, June 3, 1933.

[150]

The Constitution recognizes in all citizens the legitimate faculty of possession and, as reflected in the legislation of civilized countries, guarantees safeguards for the exercise of such important right arising from nature itself. Nevertheless, even on this point, an exception was created to the detriment of the Catholic Church, depriving her, with open injustice, of all property. No regard is paid to the wishes of those making donations in wills; no account is taken of the spiritual and holy ends connected with such properties, and no respect is shown in any way to rights long ago acquired and founded on indisputable juridical titles. All buildings, episcopal residences, parish houses, seminaries and monasteries no longer are recognized as the free property of the Catholic Church, but are declared - with words that badly hide the nature of the usurpation - public and national property.[109]

PC. The predominantly conservative ecclesiastical and military hierarchies viewed socialism, communism and anarchism with distrust. In fact, one of the Popular Front's first measures under the presidency of Manuel Azaña was to grant amnesty to all the prisoners who had participated in the 1934 laborers' riot and other leftist strikes between 1931 and 1936.

XI. The political concept of the state was also divergent.

PC. The leaders of the National Movement and the main instigators of the military coup d'état (the Catholic hierarchy and the military) preserved a strongly centralized, hierarchic and authoritarian government. Although the National Movement encompassed groups with diverse beliefs (National-Catholic, Monarchist, Carlist monarchist, Fascist, Nazi or simply ultraconservative) all these political forces backed the concept of the "organic state," a government whose institutions derive from and depend on the power of a single supreme chief of state. The Spanish organic state constituted a dictatorship with the following characteristics:

---

[109]   *Dilectissima nobis,* encyclical of Pope Pius XI on oppression of the Church of Spain to the eminent Cardinals: Francisco Vidal y Barraquer, Archbishops of Tarragona, Eustaquio Ilundain y Esteban, Archbishops of Seville, and the other Archbishops and Bishops and all the clergy and people of Spain. Rome, June 3, 1933.

1. Totalitarian government backed by the military and ecclesiastical hierarchies. In virtue of this idea of state, the parliament should be an advisory body, and political parties should be outlawed with the exception of a single one, in this case the Falange (Phalange or Phalanx), an extreme-right pseudo-fascist force. Human rights had to be suppressed, including the rights to free association, free thought, opinion and creed. The Francoist government also would suppress the writ of habeas corpus and most other procedural rights in court cases where the police or military forces considered it opportune. The right of citizenship was also revoked from "all those who do not deserve to continue being Spanish," which caused among exiled Republicans the problem of lack of citizenship: *the economic sanctions will be supplemented with others of different nature, such as the incapacity to hold certain public positions or the prohibition of living close to the previous places of residence. In certain cases of significant gravity the sanctions could mean the loss of the citizenship for those who do not deserve to continue being Spanish.*[110] The criminal code was redesigned, capital punishment was employed and concentration and work camps for prisoners were created.

2. The union of church and state in the form of a Catholic confessional state in which the Church would maintain significant authority over the educational system and over civil matters (mostly with regard to marriage and, by extension, family and women). The role of the church in state matters was delineated in the Concordat signed between the Vatican and the government of Generalissimo Franco in 1953.

XI. As stated by U.S. Ambassador to the Spanish Republic Claude G. Bowers, *the difference between the Basque Catholic and the Carlist [monarchist Catholics], is that the latter want Church domination of the State*

---

[110]   Ley de Responsabilidaded Políticas, *Heraldo de Aragón*, February 28, 1939. Also, Díaz-Plaja, Fernando, *La Guerra de España en sus Documentos*, Barcelona, 1975. Pp. 596.

[152]

Gernika, April 26, 1937

and the Basques do not.[111] Under a Francoist unitary central government the autonomous governments were overturned. The Basque, Catalan and Galician languages were completely expelled from the legal system and their use was prohibited in all other scopes of public life. Spanish would become again the only language allowed in the education system.

PC. By contrast, the Basque nationalist forces supported a completely different model of state:

1. Democratic government. The two nationalist forces (the Basque Nationalist Party and Basque Nationalist Action) supported the idea of a federal republic, a decentralized democratic state, based on a parliamentary system of political parties as the guarantor of human rights.
2. Decentralization of the state. Although the Basque nationalists promoted the right to self-determination as a path towards political independence, the Basque state would have to be part of a federal republic among other European nations.
3. Membership in the community of European nations with economic and political openness in the international sphere, as opposed to Generalissimo Franco's closed-off autarky.

In the line of Woodrow Wilson's Fourteen Points, the president of the Basque National Council in London Manuel Irujo defended in 1941 the formation of a Community of Nations sustained by the right to self-determination, a European federation that confronted totalitarian regimes during times of war and, military threats and despotism during times of peace:

If that solution is the best, we should not try to oppose it to other ones that we could describe as good, in the assumption -probable- that it is not possible to try it meanwhile it is unavoidable to subjugate

---

111   Report by Ambassador Claude G. Bowers to the U.S. Secretary of State. May 5, 1937. National Archives and Records Administration, College Park, U.S. Ambassador Claude G. Bowers Files (Files 852.00/…, Boxes 3687 to 3701), Document 852.00/5427.

Germany and Italy; we will willingly join the Western Confederation, located between the Rhine and Gibraltar, integrated by the present states of Holland, Luxembourg, Belgium, France, Spain and Portugal, and perhaps German Rhineland. This confederation brings together 100 million inhabitants. 150 million if we include their colonial empires. They would be 250 million human beings under a great confederal law. This enormous super-state would take from the Rhine, the central Atlantic river in Europe, to the Congo, the central Atlantic river in Africa. The conception is difficult, wonderful, splendid. Important problems will be solved: The Galician-Portuguese, the Basque at both sides of the Pyrenees, the conflict of Wallonia, the unity of Morocco, the affective, spiritual incorporation of all the Latin American Republics to a state organization without the fear of a new Spanish imperialism. The colonial problems of Portugal and Holland, so many times discussed, would be solved also. Catalonia and Andalusia would be the privileged countries of the Confederation, due to their possibilities in Africa and their geographic proximity to Africa, antecedent of their historical and racial kinship. The Iberian Peninsula would fulfill the geopolitical objective of being a bridge between two continents and a barrier between two seas, a reality that has always been denied.[112]

XI. After the outbreak of World War Two, Irujo also foresaw the evolution of the European Community and its advantages:

The most interesting inter-ally phenomenon is the common nexus of England and France that already constitutes a super-state. The currency continues being called "pound" and "franc" but the game of the currency is the same one, the credit is distributed the same, the loss and the rise of the two are the same, the instruments of change has been unified in fact. Just like the currency, all the remaining services are coordinated every day, not only of the military, but those of propaganda, information, economy, foreign trade, etc. France and England are today, already, in fact, the United States of Western Europe. The English and the French people support this work with decision and without any doubt. It will be very difficult to find the party or the man who faces the responsibility of stopping it. The

---

[112]   Letter by Manuel Irujo to Francisco Belaustegigoitia, London, September 16, 1941.

English and French sovereignty is yielding every day its position to the ally in facets really separated from the course of the war. The managers of this work have not been the socialist parties, but the democrats. But the socialists are behind, they support it with decision and they sustain it. Follow with attention this subject. The allied triumph is the triumph of the allied federation. The doctrine of Federal Europe has not had but general ideological adhesions, but without advancing in the field of politics. Simultaneously, England and France, without invoking doctrines but realities, federate, bind and unite in fact, with bonds that never before were set off between any other sovereign and independent countries. Today England and France are less independent from each other than our Basque states and the Crown of Castile were historically.[113]

PC. Also the concept of Christianity was completely opposed. The National Movement and the Christian-Democrat Basque nationalists maintained very different views of the Catholic faith. The Spanish ecclesiastical hierarchy promoted a Catholic faith marked by a hierarchic, dogmatic militarism with strains of fanaticism. Catholicism strongly saturated with militarism, the writings of Cardinal Gomá and Bishop Pla i Deniel, among other Catholic church hierarchs who supported the military coup d'état, are characterized by glorification of the military and prolific use of military terms. Religious and military images even commingled in public ceremonies. The internal organization of the Spanish Catholic Church resembled a hierarchical military order, with severe penalties for interfering with its structure. Sixteen Basque priests were shot in 1936 in the Basque Country because of their ideology which diverged from the new political and ecclesiastical order.[114] As reported by U.S. Ambassador Claude G. Bowers:

---

[113]   Letter by Manuel Irujo to Juan Ajuriagerra, London, April 12, 1940.

[114]   This is the list of the priests shot by the Spanish army in the Basque Country: Martín Lekuona and Gervasio Albizu, vicars of the parish of Rentería, assassinated on October 8, 1936. Jose Ariztimuño ("Aitzol"), Alexander Mendikute and Jose Adarraga, shot on October 17, 1936 in Hernani. Jose Arin, arcipreste of Mondragón, shot on October 24, 1936 in the cemetery of Oihartzun. Jose Peñagarikano, vicar of Markina, shot on October 27, 1936. Zelestino Onaindia, vicar of Elgoibar, shot on October 28, 1936 (prosecutors did not find his brother, Alberto, Canon of

Apropos of the killing of priests, which from the press one could conclude has been confined to the loyalists, we now have the statement given by Don Alberto de Onaindia y Zuluaga, the Canon of Valladolid, long before the war one of the most foremost Catholic propagandists of the Basque Country. He gives a list of Basque priests, supporters of the Government, who have been shot by the Franco forces in Pamplona and Vitoria. These include: Fr. Adarraga, aged 64; Fr. Iturri-Castillo, aged 29; Fr. Onaindia, aged 38, brother of the Canon; Fr. Peñagaricano, aged 65; Fr. Arin, aged 65; Fr. Mendikute, aged 42; Fr. Guridi, aged 39; Fr. Markiegi, aged 30; Fr. Lekuona, aged 29; Fr. Albisu, aged 62; Fr. Sagarna, aged 29; Fr. Otano, aged 40; Fr. Aristimuño, aged 40.[115]

XI. Religion in general and Catholicism in particular was studied, taught and understood mostly in terms of dogmas. Catechism was valued for indoctrination, while reading and studying the Bible on one's own was condemned. Dogmatism and fanaticism would even drive Spain's Catholic hierarchy to accept collaboration with the Axis powers, Nazi Germany and Fascist Italy, in the war against the Republican forces and during WWII.

PC. Unity of church and state or the creation of a confessional state was one of the pillars of the "New Order." The exclusivity of the Catholic religion within the state was one of the most important features of the dictatorship. After the coup, tens of thousands of teachers and professors were demoted and dismissed. The rest were forced to swear allegiance to the ideological

---

Valladolid, so he was shot instead). Jose Iturri, parish priest of Marín. Aniceto Eguren, Jose Markiegi, Leonardo Guridi and Jose Sagarna, priests, shot on October 24, 1936; in October 1936 fathers Lupo, Otano and Roman were also shot, the latter a superior at the convent of the Carmelite of Amorebieta. In, Anasagasti, Iñaki, "Santidad, ¿Y los curas vascos?", *Galeuzca-ren Biltzarra*, 2006.

[115]   The Religious Phase. Report by U.S. Ambassador to the Spanish republic, Claude G. Bowers to the Secretary of State. Donibane Lohitzune, February 24, 1937. National Archives and Records Administration, College Park, U.S. Ambassador Claude G. Bowers Files (Files 852.00/…, Boxes 3687 to 3701), Document 852.00/4889. P. 5.

principles of the regime and to the Catholic creed in particular. Article 2 of the Law of Education specified that teachers had to instruct their students in the Fascist principles of the Phalange. In a literal interpretation of the motto of General Millán Astray "¡Viva la muerte! ¡Muera la cultura!" (Long live death! Death to culture!), 6,000 teachers were shot, another 7,000 imprisoned and more than 40,000 fired according to the data provided by the Basque Government in 1954.

And this militaristic strain of Catholicism climaxed in the Basque Country. Cardinal Gomá and other members of the ecclesiastical hierarchy turned the aspiration for political unity into a Catholic dogma, and it permeated ecclesiastical speeches and sermons. Even now, sixty years later, distant echoes of this are heard; the archbishop of Toledo, Monsignor Antonio Cañizares, referenced the statute of Catalonia in a speech about the Virgin Mary in Toledo in December 2005: *I put in the hands of the Immaculate Maria our Spain, that has the Immaculate as the patron who unites all the peoples of Spain in an unshakeable unit that certainly is threatened.*

Along with the concept of National-Catholicism (Nacionalcatolicismo), race, Spanishness and Catholicism were lumped together into a single idea. For Cardinal Gomá the Spanish Catholic creed was defined by its religiosity and racial superiority, for example, in its transformation of Native American societies during Spanish colonial conquests by means of racial mingling. In a speech delivered in Buenos Aires on October 12, 1934, the cardinal outlined his theory of the generosity and redemption offered by the injection of Spanish blood into the Americas:

Blood fusion, because Spain did with the native Americans what no nation in the world did with the conquered peoples: prevented the boarding of unmarried Spaniard women so that the Spanish men married indigenous women, giving birth therefore to the Creole race, in which, like in Garcilaso de la Vega, a representative of the new people arose in these virgin lands, the robustness of the Spanish soul raised to its current level the weak Indian race. And the Spaniard who in his own lot denied Jews and Arabs the purple shining of his blood, did not have shyness to knead it with the Indian blood, so that the new life of America was, with all the force of the word, Hispano-American life. You see the distance that separates Spain from the Saxons, and the Indians of South America from the red skins (...)

America is our work; this work is essentially made of Catholicism. Therefore, there is indeed a relation of equality between race or Spanishness and Catholicism.[116]

XI. Catholicism espoused by the Basque Nationalist Party, as a Christian-Democrat political party with a Christian agenda, was inspired by the Christian humanism of Jacques Maritain, a member of the League of Friends of the Basques since its founding.

PC. The ideological principles of the Basque Christian-Democracy differed from the principles of the National Movement and the National-Catholiscism, as explained above. The vast majority of Basque clergy positioned themselves on the side of the Republic, democracy and human rights. The clergy faced many forms of persecution, including sanctions, arrests and exile, not to mention executions, after the occupation of the country by the National Movement. It should be noted that the Basque Nationalist Party was one of the first Christian-Democrat political forces in Europe, which is why the militants of the party openly accepted Christian humanism and the so-called "social doctrine of the Catholic church." Basque Christianity (understood from the perspective of the Basque Nationalist Party, the main Christian-Democrat force in the country in 1936) was based on two basic principles:

1. A lay social state. From the Christian socialist perspective, the state was created for the benefit of its citizens, not the reverse. In the words of Maritain, "man does not exist for the state; but the state for man." Thus, the Basque Nationalist Party and Basque Nationalist Action advocated for the separation of church and state and a public system of lay education (without excluding or prohibiting private religious education). They also encouraged the creation of unions to improve the situation of underprivileged workers.

2. A democratic state. The Basque nationalist forces believed that the Fascist, Nazi and National-Catholic ideologies

---

[116]   Gomá, Isidro, "Apología de la Hispanidad", speech given in the Theater Columbus of Buenos Aires in the commemorative evening of the "Day of the Spanish race", October 12, 1934.

were explicitly opposed to faith and Christian humanism. According to the Basque nationalist leaders the only suitable political system from a Christian point of view was —and still is— a state founded on democracy and representative government. In the words of Maritain: *during twenty centuries, preaching the Gospel to the nations and facing the different powers to defend the freedom of the spirit, the Church has taught the freedom of man. No matter how much the present times can be miserable, those that love the Church and freedom have reasons to be glad due to the clarity of the historical situation that we are confronted with. The great drama of the present days is the confrontation of man and the totalitarian state, which is nothing but the old spurious God of the Empire, without submission to the law, that bends everything to its adoration.*[117]

XI. We may add that also strategically the two political forces (National Movement and Basque Nationalism) favored very different strategies to counter the Republican government.

PC. Yes indeed. The National Movement embraced a strategy that viewed war as a "crusade" and considered it necessary to impose political ideas and religious beliefs on citizens. The military regime continually violated human rights during the war and the thirty six years of dictatorship that followed. The Basque nationalist forces aimed for a peaceful, political solution based on a respect for human rights, which is the reason they could not support a military rebellion against a legitimate government elected by the people. From this point of view, it was not ideologically tolerable, nor Christian, to support the National Movement or the Nazi and Fascist parties on the international level. This belief, more than any other, inspired the opposition of the Basque nationalist bloc to the National Movement.

XI. The confrontation was therefore inevitable.

---

[117]   Maritain, Jacques, *El hombre y el estado*, Encuentro Ediciones, Madrid, 1997.

PC. And also expected: the U.S. embassy in Madrid telephoned Secretary of State Cordell Hull by special permission on July 17th informing that a coup d'état was planned for noon.[118]

XI. Although the territories of Bizkaia and Gipuzkoa where Basque nationalism was the major political force remained loyal to the Republican government, the National Movement rebels prevailed quickly in Navarre and Araba with the help of a strong military command, backing from the ecclesiastical hierarchy and support from the Carlist Party.

PC. The rebels established a brutally repressive regime from the early hours of the uprising. An estimated 3,000 people were executed in Navarre during the first year of war from 1936 to 1937. The regime's execution of war prisoners on the battlefield, in prisons and in concentration camps must be added to that total. Additionally, the persecution of Basque political leaders or anyone even accused of being involved in politics did not end in June 1937.[119] After the Nazis gained control over France, many Basque refugees were arrested or shot by the German Nazi or French Vichy authorities working in close co-operation with the Spanish police forces.

XI. On September 13, 1936, the rebel forces took over Donostia, the capital city of Gipuzkoa. Since the Basque Government was not created yet and consequently the military were facing only an under-equipped and non-disciplined militia, General Emilio Mola, in charge of the Army of the North and, together with General Francisco Franco, one of the main leaders of the military uprising, pledged that he would take over Bilbao only one week later.

PC. Mola was wrong. After a long winter, in spring 1937, the Basque forces still resisted. Indeed, this was one of the main

---

[118] Telegram by U.S. Ambassador to the Spanish Republic, Claude G. Bowers, to the U.S. State Department. Donostia, July 18, 1936. National Archives and Records Administration, College Park, U.S. Ambassador Claude G. Bowers Files (Files 852.00/..., Boxes 3687 to 3701), Document 852.00/2174. P. 1.
[119] Bilbao was taken over on June 19, 1937.

reasons for requesting the intervention of the Luftwaffe at the Basque front.

XI. Let's explain that the military rebel command never thought in 1936 that the uprising was going to become a war. The initial plan was to rapidly capture Madrid and take control of the Spanish government in few weeks. However, the expected fall of Madrid did not happen, and more and more Italian and German war units were sent to war. Italian troops sent to war by Benito Mussolini were under the denomination of Corpo Truppe Volontarie and were basically infantry, artillery and air units. They were initially divided in two groups, the Camicie Nere or Black Shirts and the Group March 23, but both were finally combined into a single unit known as the Penne Nere or Black Feathers under the command of General Ettore Bastico. As reported by the British secret services in the Fisher Memorandum, 15,000 Italian troops had been shipped during the first three weeks of January 1937, which brought the total to approximately 51,000 Italian troops at the beginning of February 1937.[120]

Hitler sent the first Nazi units in support of the rebels as early as in July 1936; by November 1937 the German units, mostly air corps, known as the Condor Legion arrived under the command of Major General Hugo Sperrle. According to data provided by the U.S. and British secret services in early 1937, the Condor Legion had approximately 140 planes and 5,000 soldiers ready for action during the war (approximately 17 percent of the German air force). Altogether, the German regime sent about 500 planes and 16,000 to 19,000 "volunteers."

After the initial failure to capture Madrid, it is understandable why the National Movement was willing to obtain German and Italian military support, but which was, in your opinion, the main reason for Hitler and Mussolini to assist the rebels?

---

[120]   Memorandum by G. A. Fisher on the departure of Italian volunteers. In, Medlicott, W. N.; Douglas, Dakin (Eds.), Documents on British Foreign Policy (1919-1939), Second Series, Volume XVIII, European Affairs (January 2 – June 30, 1937), Her Majesty's Stationery Office, London, 1980. P. 70.

Hitler sent the *Condor Legion* to reinforce Franco's army. They were responsible for the bombing of Gernika and other attacks over open cities in the Basque Country. In the photograph, Adolf Hitler, Hermann Goering and troops of the Condor Legion in Berlin. Source: Archive of the Basque Nationalism/Sabino Arana Foundation.

PC. There were various reasons, mainly economic and political but also strategic. It is obvious that there was a close political or ideological identity between the National Movement or, in general, the Spanish National-Catholicism, and Nazism or Fascism. Also, the Italian and German regimes were interested in the raw material that could be acquired at low prices from the Spanish rebels in exchange of military assistance. Hermann Wilhelm Goering, in charge of the financial operations of the Reich, ordered the creation of two corporations, Rohstoff-Waren-Kompensation Handelsgesellschaft (Rowak) in Berlin and Sociedad Hispano-Marroqui de Transportes (Hisma) in Sevilla to regulate trade between the Spanish and the German regimes.[121]

---

[121]   This was part of the struggle within the Nazi government for the control of the Ministry of Economy between Hermann W. Goering and Hjalmar H. G. Schacht (1877-1970), President of the Reichsbank between 1933 and 1939. For this subject see, Simpson, Amos E., "The Struggle for Control of the German Economy, 1936-37", *The Journal of Modern History*, Vol. 31, No. 1, March 1959. Pp. 37-45.

But, apart from that, the main incentive for intervention was strategic. Both the German and the Italian regimes were preparing WWII and they needed their military capability to be tested in combat. As stated by Goering at Nuremberg in 1946:

> *When the Civil War broke out in Spain, Franco sent a call for help to Germany and asked for support, particularly in the air. One should not forget that Franco with his troops was stationed in Africa and that he could not get the troops across, as the fleet was in the hands of the Communists, or, as they called themselves at the time, the competent Revolutionary Government in Spain. The decisive factor was, first of all, to get his troops over to Spain. The Fuhrer thought the matter over. I urged him to give support under all circumstances, firstly, in order to prevent the further spread of communism in that theater and, secondly, to test my young Luftwaffe at this opportunity in this or that technical respect. With the permission of the Fuehrer, I sent a large part of my transport fleet and a number of experimental fighter units, bombers, and antiaircraft guns; and in that way I had an opportunity to ascertain, under combat conditions, whether the material was equal to the task. In order that the personnel, too, might gather a certain amount of experience, I saw to it that there was a continuous flow, that is, that new people were constantly being sent and others recalled.*[122]

XI. However, the impressive military assistance operations in March 1937 concluded with the disastrous defeat of the Italian-Spanish combined rebel units at the battle of Guadalajara (March 8-23, 1937), which prevented the capture of Madrid.

PC. Yes, and that leads us to the tragedy of Gernika. After the catastrophic defeat of the Italian forces at Guadalajara, Mussolini had the Italian command at war informed that none of them should return home alive unless they achieved victory. And while a military victory was necessary to the Italians in order to "clean" their honor, Generalissimo Franco also needed to capture a major city in order to balance the war. In this sense, Franco decided to

---

[122]   Goering, Hermann Wilhelm, *Proceedings at the Nuremberg Trials*, Dr. Stahmer, March 14, 1946.

focus his forces' principal attack on the Basque front, and by capturing Bilbao secure the northern front.

However, apart from the pure military or strategic reasons, also political and economic reasons led Franco to center his military effort against the Basque Country. On the one hand, he and the Nazis needed the iron ore from the Basque mines and the industrial capability of the Basque industries. On the other, as stated by U.S. ambassador Bowers, the assault on Bilbao had more to do with propaganda than anything else. The insurgents continually claimed that they were fighting against "atheists and communists" and "the burners of churches and killers of priests." However, the Basque government and the Basque nationalists were Catholic and notably respectful of the church, even more, the Basque Catholic Church was positioned with the democratic elected government:

> *The fact reported generally, and positively known, that there has been no interference with worship in the Basque Country, that priests and nuns walk the streets in their religious garb without meeting with discourtesy, has interfered considerably with the success of the religious part of the insurgent propaganda. And when a dozen or fifteen Basque priests went to Ireland to combat the propaganda there, the hate of the Carlists began to center on their fellow Catholics in the Basque Country.*[123]

XI. A rapid military victory was then necessary.

PC. Yes, and also expected. The Basque forces were completely outnumbered and were lacking air force assistance.

XI. On March 21, Franco started the offensive over the Basque Country. Generals Juan Vigón, head of the General Staff, Emilio Mola, head of the Northern Combined Army and Generalfeldmarschall Wolfram von Richthofen, commander-in-chief of the Condor Legion, met on March 22 for first time to plan

---

[123]   Report by Ambassador Claude Bowers to the Secretary of State, Donibane Lohitzune, April 12, 1937. National Archives and Records Administration, College Park, U.S. Ambassador Claude G. Bowers Files (Files 852.00/..., Boxes 3687 to 3701), Document 852.00/5238. Pp. 9-10.

the military operations. By March 26 the attack was designed. The basic idea was to attack from the east (from Gipuzkoa) and from the south (from Araba) towards Bilbao. After the first attack, in about two days, the Basque forces would be forced to retreat through the line Durango-Otxandio. After capturing Durango, the path to Bilbao would be open. Once again, at the view of the outstanding military predominance, Mola advanced that Bilbao would be captured in no more than three weeks.

PC. And three weeks after the beginning of the spring offensive against the Basque troops, the rebels had not completely advanced. And that became tragic for the Basques.

XI. Yes. Both Sperrle and Richthofen held that the main task of the air force in battle was not bombarding the frontlines but the rearguard. According to the German command the strategic targets of the raids should be three:

1. To destroy sources of ammunition and food supply.
2. To destroy means of communication and cause interruption of the transportation of troops and war material.
3. To destroy the enemy's morale by terrorizing and demoralizing civilians.

Consequently, as written by Richthofen in his war diary, the German air force would attack the "local reserves" located far from the frontline "without considering the damage to the civilian population."

PC. Under the doctrine of General Erich F. W. Ludendorff's, *Total War spares no one, respects nothing. All weapons will be employed, especially the most cruel, which are the most effective. The future war will be conducted until complete annihilation, not only of the enemy's army, but also of the civilian population.*[124]

---

[124]   Ludendorff, General Erich F. W., *The Nation at War*, Hutchinson & Co., ltd, 1936.

Wolfram von Richthofen, chief of staff of the Condor Legion and author of the bombing of Gernika in 1937. Source: Archive of the Basque Nationalism/Sabino Arana Foundation.

XI. Since the infantry was not advancing at the speed initially planned, the combined rebel command planned a moral strike, the bombing of a city without much strategic importance but moral relevance. Indeed, many factors came together in the decision of bombing Gernika. Goering designed a ghastly test. In his own words he called it a "practical demonstration." He wanted to measure how quickly and effectively a medium size city could be completely destroyed and measure how many people could be killed. Under this scope the bombing was "a war experiment." The method was called saturation bombing or "carpet bombing" and consisted of successive pulverizing waves of bombers flying very low and in close formations while releasing their shells simultaneously on the same target area.[125] Opposed to the precision bombing "carpet bombing" is as described by C. J. Horn a euphemism meaning to direct a carpet of bombs to obliterate a target. The Germans called it "a controlled vivisectional experiment in modern bombing tactics."[126]

On the other hand, the German command was interested in measuring the limits of the "strategic terror"; according to the theoretical essays on total war, strategic terror was particularly effective if the enemy forces consisted of untrained and poorly equipped militia, and that was the case of the Basque army: scarcely equipped, the Basque army was in essence a defense force of volunteers with no air force and almost no antiaircraft.

And, finally, another important element came to play a relevant role in the bombing: the internal fight for power in Berlin. Hermann Wilhelm Goering, commander of the Luftwaffe, foresaw the participation of the Luftwaffe at war as a unique opportunity to show Hitler how lethal and determinative could become the use of the air force in the next world war. And, he could also expect that his budget and, accordingly, his personal power within the Reich would become proportionally prevalent. Indeed, General Field Marshall Werner von Blomberg, Minister of War and Commander-in-chief of the German armed forces, was not informed about the attack against Gernika. Only nine months after the attack Goering and Himmler got him to resign all of his duties within the German army. And soon afterwards Goering became the second strong man of the Reich.

---

[125]   Adolf Galland, member of the General Staff of the Condor Legion during the war of 1936 enthusiastically described in his memoirs the effect of such air raids. In, Galland, Adolf, *The First and the Last: The Rise and Fall of the German Fighter Forces, 1938-1945*, Holt, 1954. P. 16.

[126]   Spencer C. Tucker et alia, *World War II*, ABC-CLIO, 2005. P. 256.

Hugo Sperrle, commander of the Condor Legion. Source: National Archives and Records Administration.

PC. It was important then that the experiment to be carried out ornately, under no adverse conditions and running any unnecessary risks: the rebel air command needed a city with no antiaircraft, an easy target. And Gernika was an open city.

XI. Yes. Gernika was chosen as the target for the experiment for five main reasons:

1. It was a town of about 6,000 souls, however, there were two hospitals and many refugees came there escaping from the rebel troops advancing from the east. As a consequence, the town was approximately the size required for the experiment (about 10,000 people).
2. April 26, 1937, was chosen for the weekly market day was celebrated on Mondays and more people than usual could be expected to be outside, in the streets.
3. The city was completely undefended. There were no antiaircraft, not even heavy automatic machine guns capable of bringing down a bomber so the planes could fly low and slow enough.
4. The city was only to 7.5 miles from the front. So it was going to be conquered just after the raid, before anyone could touch the evidence of the experiment and before the international Red Cross or any other international agency could inform the world about the massacre. Indeed, the city was captured only two days after the attack, on April 29 in the morning, which is the reason why even today the number of victims remains uncertain.
5. Gernika was the traditional capital of the Basques, where deputies of the independent republic of Biscay met biennially under the Holy Tree to legislate. In this sense, the effect of the strategic terror could be superior in the moral of the Basque militia.

PC. It was planned in order to cause the greatest level of destruction.

XI. Yes, even the tactic of the bombardment was far more exhaustive and meticulous than a simple carpet bombing. War correspondent George L. Steer reported that the shelling took place according to the following scheme:

1. The first wave of bombs launched would send the people under cover.

2. A second wave dropped heavy explosive bombs together with incendiary bombs so the people already in the refuges would burn or asphyxiate. The incendiary bombs were not heavy enough to penetrate the roofs of the buildings, consequently, they had to be released after the heavy explosive bombs had already cracked roofs and walls. That way the incendiary liquid went through the cracks and burned it all.

3. After a brief pause a second interval would surprise the survivors, who would have believed that they were safe and would have come out of cover.

4. Finally, once the smoke of the first raid had cleared, the third and last wave of fighters would machine-gun the last surviving inhabitants. This utter act of brutality had also a strategic meaning: in a real battleground the survivors would be infantry units trying to reorganize. It was the moment for crushing them by attacking while they were still inoperative.

Gernika fews days after the bombing. Source: Archive of the Basque Nationalism/Sabino Arana Foundation.

PC. It was a test of the blitz technique which, three years later would be used to tear down Warsaw, Rotterdam and many other European cities. In Hitler's own words, Warsaw had to be pacified,

[170]

that is, razed to the ground and, the old market place of the Polish capital was also reduced to ashes by the Luftwaffe.

George Steer who arrived in Gernika only few hours after the attack, described it in his own words for *The Times,*

> *The Nazi planes came over in waves, blasting the houses from their foundations with heavy bombs, loosing showers of glittering two-pound aluminum incendiary bombs to turn the "Holy City" to a furnace. Skimming the roof tops, fighting planes followed with all machine guns popping, harrying terrified peasants through the fields, sending them sprawling in their own blood. Over 800 men, women and children were killed.*[127]

Ruins of Warsaw, bombed following the same scheme as in Gernika. In the image the Market Place. Source: M. Swierczynski.

XI. Imanol Agirre Delgado, a ten years old boy was in Gernika that day, under the bombs. Months later he was sent by his parents to

---

[127]   Steer, George, "Foreign News: Babies, Bombs & Battleships," *The Times,* London, Monday, May 10, 1937.

one of the many Basque children refugee camps in England. While there he was told to write a short account of his life in Gernika and he wrote one of the most heartbreaking descriptions of the massacre:

> *The bells always rang, "he says", when planes passed over on their way to bomb Bilbao. We got used to it. That day, too, when the town was full of peasants and cattle for the market the bells rang, but nobody took much notice. Suddenly there were crashes. I saw spurts of flame and smoke coming from the far side of the town. To the shelters! To the shelters! People began to run in all directions in a wild panic. I ran with a friend and my uncle towards a small factory where shell-parts were made. There was a high wall we could get behind. Bombs were dropping without a stop; we were almost choked with smoke and dust. But no bomb hit the factory. Factories are the safest places to be, far safer than hospitals. My uncle called out: "Let's run to the fields", and he started off across the street. A plane swooped down and he fell on his side with blood spurting from his head. There was nothing to do and we were frightened, so we left him. Later we both ran out through the orchards and up to the hills where we sheltered under a tree. It wasn't much protection, but it saved our lives. The planes, five of them, circled round us for about twenty minutes on and off. We heard the machine-gun rattle, but they didn't hit us. We saw terrible things. One man near us had been hunting. He ran across to take shelter in a hut and we saw the planes kill both him and his dog. We saw a family of people we knew from our street run into a wood. There was the mother with two children and the old grandmother. The planes circled about the wood for a long time and at last frightened them out of it. They took shelter in a ditch. We saw the old granny cover up the little boy with her apron. The planes came low and killed them all in the ditch, except the little boy. He soon got up and began to wander across a field, crying. They got him too. It was terrible; we were both crying so much we could not speak. Everybody was being killed, there were bodies all over the fields. We had to pick them up in baskets afterwards. A lot of them. After an age the planes went away and we went back into Guernica. It was all smoking ruins. I went to what had been our house and nothing was left, not even a piece you could preserve to remind you of your home. There was a doctor driving about in his car helping to pick up the wounded. I don't know how he escaped death. Sixty people had been*

killed in a half-built refuge. The airmen had played jokes, too, and dropped spanners and hammers. One dropped a wicker basket with food in it which hit a friend of mine. Then they dropped some leaflets. They promised us bread and a warm hearth if we surrendered. The warm hearth will be like Guernica, I expect...[128]

PC. Appalling. 800 deaths according to George L. Steer (on April 28th, two days after the bombing) and 1,654 deaths according to the Basque Government (on Jun 4th, after subsequent deaths were recorded).

XI. I know that you met, among other survivors of the attack, Pedro Beitia.

PC. Yes. I met Pedro Beitia years later in Boise. He was an aide to the Secretary of Defense of the Basque autonomous government and one of the eyewitnesses of the attack. Thirty six years later his testimony still was heartrending. Senator Franck Church requested Beitia's piece entitled "Guernica: I Was There" which appeared in the Washington Post Outlook Section on April 1, 1973, to be printed in the Congressional Records.

I can speak with some authority about that ghastly holocaust because I was there.
At the time the aerial raid occurred on the afternoon of April 26, 1937, I was an administrative assistant to the Secretary of Defense of the Basque autonomous government at Bilbao, 20 miles from Guernica. At about 4:45 p.m. I received a call from the Guernica stationmaster reporting that planes of the Luftwaffe's Condor Legion had launched an intense raid against his city. I immediately set out for Guernica by car.

---

[128]   Imanol Agirre was one of the sons of Gernika who was evacuated to England on board the *Habana*. He wrote this letter at the Stoneham Camp (East Sussex) in July 1937. Most probably he was not even 10 years old. In, Cloud, Yvonne (Born Yvonne Kapp); Ellis, Richard, *The Basque Children in England. An Account of their Life at North Stoneham Camp*, Victor Gollancz Ltd., London 1937. Pp. 56-57. A translation into Spanish of this beautiful description into Spanish can be found at, Atxaga, Bernardo, *De Gernika a Guernica*, Ediciones de la Central, Barcelona, 2007.

I arrived at its outskirts at 6:30 p.m., but found that I could not enter because Germans were still attacking the city, which by then was completely enveloped by flames from the hundreds of incendiary bombs I could see falling on it. When the raid ceased about an hour later, I was able to enter. The Dantesque horror I witnessed during the subsequent twelve hours I stayed there is still vivid in my memory.[129]

And another eyewitness, Catholic Canon Alberto Onaindia,[130] also described the bombing. Two days after the attack Onaindia wrote a letter to Cardinal Isidro Gomá who was assisting the rebels:

I arrive from Bilbao horrified after having personally witnessed the dreadful crime that was perpetrated against the peaceful town of Guernica, a symbol of the secular traditions of the Basque people. German aircrafts bombed the population for almost three long hours. Fighters and bombers, with two and three engines, dropped shrapnel and incendiary bombs while the people, crazy of terror, fled by the roads and the mountains while being machine-gunned by the planes. My car was also machine-gunned and several bombs fell around it which caused several casualties. Three hours of horror and Dantesque scenes. Children and women sunk in the gutters, mothers praying loudly, a Christian Catholic people being murdered by criminals who do not feel the slightest sentiment of humanity. Mr. Cardinal, for dignity, for honor to the Gospel, for the very mercy of Christ, such a heinous, unprecedented, apocalyptic, Dantesque crime should not be committed. The town was completely afire and the poor people who had sought refugee in the shelters were forced to move out and then were machine-gunned. There will be thousands of victims. Patients were burned alive, wounded people buried and reduced to ashes. At one o'clock at night I left and everything was scorching. No one was

---

[129]   *Congressional Records.* Proceedings and Debates of the 93d Congress, First Session (April 3 to April 11), Vol. 119, Part 9, No 56. Pp. 11571-11572. Washington, Tuesday, April 10, 1973.

[130]   Zelestino Onaindia, vicar of Elgoibar, was one of the priest shot by the rebels on October 28, 1936. Prosecutors did not find his brother Alberto, Canon of Valladolid, so he was shot instead.

screaming or crying in horror. We were insensitive statues of so much pain. Never could anyone suspect that war was that.[131]

XI. Cardinal Gomá did not answer to Onaindia but a week later. In contrast to Imanol Agirre or Onaindia, the Cardinal just pointed out that the destruction of Gernika was the logical consequence of their sins, the reparation the Basques deserve for their perversity in opposing the Saintly Crusade led by Generalissimo Franco.

In the same line as Gomá, Colonel von Richthofen, responsible for the execution of the attack, depicted the macabre event in precise military terms as "absolutely fabulous:"

Guernica, city of 5,000 inhabitants, literally leveled. Attack was launched with 250 kg bombs and firebombs, these about 1/3 of the total. When the first Junkers arrived, there was already smoke everywhere (from the experimental bomber squadron, which attacked first with three planes). Nobody could see roads, bridges, or suburban targets anymore, so they just dumped their bombs in the midst of it all. The 250s knocked down a number of houses and destroyed the municipal water system. The firebombs now had time to do their work. The type of construction of the houses —tile roofs, wooden decks, and half-timbered walls- facilitated their total destruction. Inhabitants were generally out of the town because of a festival[132]; most of those fled at the outset of the attack. A small number died in wrecked shelters. Bomb craters in the streets are still to be seen. Absolutely fabulous! City was completely closed off for at least 24 hours; that would have guaranteed immediate conquest if troops had attacked right away. But at least it has been a complete technical success[133] with our 250s and EC.Bs.[134]

---

[131]   Letter by Alberto Onaindia to Cardinal Isidro Gomá. Donibane Lohitzune, April 28, 1937. In, *Historia de la Iglesia en España (1931-1939)*, Vol. 2, RIALP, Madrid, 1993. P. 252-253.

[132]   It is not true. Indeed it should say the contrary "Inhabitants were in the city, out in the streets." The lapse is intended.

[133]   Another member of the Condor Legion general staff, Erwin Jaenecke, considered the bombing a triumph: *Guernica was a total success of the German air force. The only way for the withdrawal of the entire red coast was cut in full by the fire and a pile of rubble of two meters on the roads.* Report by Erwin Jaenecke in the curse of a visit to Gernika. May 18, 1937. In, Maier, Klaus

Ruins of Gernika. Source: Archive of the Basque Nationalism/Sabino Arana Foundation.

The material damage was enormous. According to the data provided by the office in charge of the reconstruction of the town, 100 percent of the buildings in downtown Gernika were completely razed, that means that 85.22 percent of the buildings of the entire town were completely destroyed and most of the remainder were partially damaged.

A., *Guernica. La intervención alemana en España y el "caso Guernica"*, Sedmay, Madrid, 1976. P. 180.
[134]   Richthofen's War Diary, quoted by Clay Large, David, *Between Two Fires: Europe's Path in the 1930s*, W. W. Norton & Company, New York & London, 1990. P. 256.

PC. The attack had an unexpected international impact. Along with the journalist at war, Steer (*The Times*), Holme (*Reuters*), Monks (*Daily Express*) and Corman (*Ce Soir*), most American, British and French newspapers published news of the bombing several days after the attack. Most newspapers in democratic Europe and the United States accepted the thesis that the massacre had been ordered and executed by the combined German, Italian and Spanish rebel armies and expressed their disapproval. Indeed, the bombing changed public opinion and the position of the American Catholic Church, which had previously opposed the Republican forces, slowly started to change. Indeed, among the many that stood before the massacre, Christian columnist Dorothy Thompson wrote the following for the American press,

> *What is now happening there is the ruthless, coldblooded, vicious extermination of one of the rare peoples of the earth, the Basques. This little people is one of the few rare and absolutely pure races left in Europe, having a beautiful language and literature, beautiful bodies and faces, a people proud, independent and free, whose history is as old as Europe's, and who, during all its centuries, have minded their own business, tilling the soil, building a domestic architecture of purest design and exquisite proportions, and churches which are among the gems of civilization. They are Catholics of deepest piety, and Ignatius Loyola, founder of that most intellectual of Catholic orders, the Society of Jesus, is their son. To sit by and not to protest with all the breath in one's body rules one out of the ranks of civilized and Christian society. Good God! The game laws of most of our States prohibit the shooting of birds from airplanes. It is unsportsmanlike.*[135]

XI. Though, the Spanish government always denied the bombing. At first, before the international reaction, General Franco's Press Office reported that the bombings were in general executed by German planes. However, Joachim von Ribbentrop, German ambassador in London, aware of the possible repercussions of the Gernika massacre within the ecclesiastical hierarchy and in the

---

[135]   In, Steer, George, "Foreign News: Babies, Bombs & Battleships," *The Times*, London, Monday, May 10, 1937.

international political arena, instructed Spanish officials to deny that the Germans were responsible for the destruction of the city. Consequently, General Wilhelm Faupel, German Ambassador to Franco, was instructed to persuade Franco to issue "an immediate and energetic denial." Franco never did so, but Francoist press, together with the Italian, German and Portuguese press denied that any bombing had happened and even accused the Basque nationalist troops of having set afire the city while in retreat.

PC. This was the Spanish official version until Franco's death. Even if Hermann Goering, interrogated at Nuremberg by Joseph Maier (Chief of the Briefing Analysis Section) and Sander (Chief of the Analysis Interrogation Section) about the massacre answered that it had been "a lamentable event" —and added- "we could not do otherwise. At that time, such experiments could not be carried out elsewhere."

Still in 1973, thirty-six years after the attack, the Spanish government absolutely denied the bombing. That's why Senator Franck Church requested in 1973 Pedro Beitia's testimony to be printed in the Congressional Records,

> *This distinguished journalist, who for several reasons cannot be identified, says that before anyone in Salamanca other than a handful of senior officers at Franco's headquarters knew what had happened in Guernica, he was summoned to the office of Luis Bolin, Franco's press chief and author of a book on which Mr. Hart's article was based. Bolin ordered him, under penalty of losing his press credentials and being ousted from Spain, to report that Basques and "Asturian dynamiters" had deliberately blown up Guernica's buildings, that there were no bomb craters in the city's streets, and the like. That conversation was on April 28, two days before Franco's troops had entered the city.*
> *The American journalist said he suggested to Bolin, a shouting, irascible man given to purple-faced rages and much revolver drawing, that foreign correspondents already in the area be allowed to visit the city. Bolin replied, "No. Army orders." When the journalists wrote the dispatch Bolin insisted on he attributed his information directly to Franco spokesmen, which lead Bolin to tear up his copy in a frenzy, wave his pistol at him, and ordered him to write another.*

Foreign newsmen were finally admitted to Guernica many days after the bombing, though they were guided through the town by a circuitous route allowed to look at only a limited area and the famous Tree of Guernica, the symbol of Basque nationalism. Save for such guided tours, Guernica remained a closed town to newsmen wanting to research the bombing for months afterwards.

None of the correspondents after 1937 ever took seriously Bolin's claim that the defenders had blown up the town. Several, in the months immediately following Guernica, had occasion in Salamanca or elsewhere to talk to officers of the German Luftwaffe's Condor Legion who made no secret of their connection with the Guernica bombing. The Germans claimed it had been requested by the Franco forces who worried that the Basques intended to make a stand in the town.[136]

PC. Also the Germans denied that the aim was to destroy a city. Some pilots still insist that their target was the bridge of Errenteria. Lieutenant Colonel Karl von Knauer, in command of one of the Junker Ju52 bomber squads during the attack, wrote in his war diary that a sortie carried out against the bridge of Errenteria in Gernika had had a "good effect"[137]. Also Adolph Galland subscribed that the target was the bridge[138]. However, the bridge was untouched.

During WWII when I served as a fighter pilot in the U.S. Marine Corps, I trained many young men to shoot down German and Japanese planes. I also taught them dive-bombing so they could accurately destroy bridges or sink ships. I can attest, definitely, it is not necessary to mobilize about thirty to fifty planes and release between 31,000 and 41,000 kilos of explosive and incendiary projectiles during three hours to destroy a 70-foot-long bridge over a river no more than five feet deep. Furthermore, it is certainly hard to believe that the aim was to destroy the bridge, for, bearing in mind that after dropping such an amount of bombs the

---

[136] *Congressional Records.* Proceedings and Debates of the 93d Congress, First Session (April 3 to April 11), Vol. 119, Part 9, No 56. Pp. 11571-11572. Washington, Tuesday, April 10, 1973.

[137] In, Clay Large, David, *Between Two Fires: Europe's Path in the 1930s*, W. W. Norton & Company, New York & London, 1990. P. 256.

[138] Galland, Adolph, *The First And The Last: The Rise And Fall Of The German Fighter Forces 1938-1945*, Ballantine Books, New York, 1957. P. 42.

bridge remained untouched, both Richthofen and Knauer coincide in affirming that the attack was a "tactic success."

Chuck Winder, senator for Idaho (District N°14, Ada County) and a former U.S. Navy pilot during the Vietnam War and several other former war pilots agree with me that:

1. The standard procedure for blowing a bridge (about 70 feet long and 32 feet wide) from the air, in an open town with no antiaircraft batteries or any other defenses (such as pursuit planes), does not involve twenty-four bombers and twenty-three fighters for a period of time of three and a half hours launching a total of between thirty and forty tons of bombs (at least a third of them incendiary).
2. That destroying a bridge of such characteristics is a simple static target that could be achieved with a single dive bomber or even with a bomber.
3. That, at the view of the results (the bridge was not even touched and the city was completely destroyed with a result of 74 percent of all buildings demolished), it seems that the real aim of the bombing was not to destroy the bridge but to drive the Basques into surrender by terror bombing.

Basically, if after launching such amount of bombs and making use of such machinery a pilot does not destroy a bridge, I would not let him fly my plane.

XI. It has to be underlined -I may add- that one of the main eyewitnesses of the attack, Canon Alberto Onaindia and also Francisco Lazkano, survived because they hid from the bombers precisely under the bridge of Errenteria and other bridges in the nearby area.

PC. Claud Clockburn stated once: *Never believe anything until it has been officially denied.* Maybe because of the nature and consequences of the massacre, maybe because for first time in the course of a war a city was bombed following such a strategic scheme, maybe because the European and American public previewed for first time that Hitler and Mussolini were carrying out an experiment and that the war in the Basque Country and in Spain was just a prologue for an imminent WWII, or maybe because the sordid refusal of the bombing, the fact is that the massacre of Gernika provoked the first deep impact of Basque politics in the United States.

The *Chicago Daily Tribune* and *The Bakersfield Californian* were among the first newspapers worldwide to make news of the bombing public. The event was depicted as "the worst air raid yet" on April 27, the very morning after the attack. In the following days many other American newspapers printed stories, among them *The New York Times* ("Historic Basque Town Wiped out; Rebel fliers machine-gun civilians," April 28), *The Lowel Sun* ("Rebels hammer Bilbao's gates," April 29), *New Castle News* ("Will evacuate citizens from city of Bilbao," April 29), *Oakland Tribune* ("Nazi flayed," April 29), *The Portsmouth Times* ("British Foreign Office frowns on Navy's plan to evacuate women, children from Bilbao," April 29), *The Oshkosh Northwestern* ("Bombarded town," April 30) and the *Winnipeg Free Press* ("Mass killing," April 30). Many other newspapers began to print articles from the major American news agencies, *The Associated Press*, *United Press* and *Universal News Service*. Most of the American-wide newspapers, such as the *Washington Post* and *The New York Herald Tribune*, published heart breaking articles on the blitz.

XI. And here we witness the very early connections between Idaho and Basque politics. Republican Senator for Idaho William E. Borah was one of the first ones to take up the bombing of Gernika in the U.S. Congress.

PC. Yes, on May 6, 1937, Senator Borah proclaimed in Congress that,

> *This is the logic of fascism. This is the logic of the system which is founded upon force. This is not courage but cowardice, not government but brute savagery, not war but butchery. We have to go back to the days of Attila to find anything to compare with this ruthless destruction of helpless men, women and children. It is a repudiation of civilization. It rejects all the principles and precepts of justice and humanity, born, of centuries of sacrifice and struggle for the light. It is a reversion to the savagery of the cave man. It is an attempt to found government upon the primitive passions of the horde.*

From Ethiopia let us go to Spain. Here fascism presents to the world its masterpiece. It has hung upon the wall of civilization a painting that will never come down -never fade out of the memories of men. So long as men, and women may be interested in searching out from the pages of history outstanding acts of cruelty and instances of needless destruction of human life they will linger longest and with the greatest horror over the savage story of the Fascist war in Spain. We have always been familiar with those stories of unspeakable barbarity, which come down to us from the dim pages of oriental history. But those things happened long before men had felt the humanizing effect of centuries of Christian civilization.

The butcheries of helpless women and children in Spain occurred in the very morning of the twentieth century. During the French Revolution the city of Lyons was marked for destruction, and Barre cried from the rostrum, "Let the plow pass over her." This has many times been cited as the most revolting instance of mass murder in all history. But it must now give place to Guernica, the ancient Basque capital.

Modern warfare, with its improved instruments of destruction of both property and life, is revolting at best. But it remained for the Fascist warfare to select the deadliest weapons which the ingenuity of man has contrived and to show to the world how thorough and effective these weapons are when used for the destruction of women and children. How effective are airplanes when throwing bombs and hand grenades into homes; how airplanes, swooping low like winged monsters can massacre thousands of innocent children without endangering in the slightest the lives of the brave assailants; and how of the same time they can set a noncombatant city on fire and leave the streets covered with the charred bodies of the slain, While the Intrepid Fascist soldiers escape without a wound. Fascism boasts of courage, of the bravery of its soldiers; boasts, how it makes men of its adherents, and tells other peoples that fascism makes heroes of the young. And, as evidence of the fulfillment of its creed, It points to the subjugation of the wholly, weak and disarmed Ethiopia. And now doubtless will take pride in the successful slaughter of women and children throughout Spain.

No language can describe the scene at Guernica and Guernica was not a single instance, it was simply a culmination of a long line of unspeakable atrocities. It was not a military, maneuver. The city was a long distance from the battle line. The attack had no

[182]

legitimate military objective. An unarmed, noncombatant city was singled out for the most revolting instance of mass massacre of modern times. It was Fascist strategy.

Mr. President, I have no choice between communism and fascism. The latter is supposed to be more respectable than the former and finds a more ready entrée into respectable society. But they are both enemies of every vital liberty and every right and, privilege of the average man or woman. Both reduce the average citizen to a state of political and economic serfdom. Both succeed in breeding and fostering discontent in all the different nations in the world. Both have their active propagandists in our own country.

Mr. President, the world is torn and tortured with religious and race persecutions, with a speech of brutality almost without precedent. The people are being taxed in every land almost beyond endurance for greater and costlier weapons of destruction. These things are in a marked degree the fruits of the systems which are built upon force and at enmity with human liberty. With conditions in other lands we can have little to say. But their systems should not be permitted to introduce themselves into this country without full knowledge of all the facts. From time to time the facts will be given.[139]

XI. Borah's intervention ignited a bitter debate that lasted several weeks regarding the German and Italian participation in the war.

PC. Yes. Senator Gerald P. Nye of North Dakota believed there was no doubt that Italy and Germany were carrying out an undeclared war on the Spanish Republic. But Senator Key Pittman of Nevada, Chairman of the Senate Committee on Foreign Relations, objected to Nye's statements and claimed that there was no evidence of such support. Pittman was lying. U.S. ambassador to the Spanish Republic Claude G. Bowers had been sending weekly reports since the beginning of the war showing that German and Italian troops had been shipped to war. In addition, Horace H. Fuller, military attaché at the U.S. embassy in Paris, had

---

[139]   *Challenge to Democracy. Fascism and Communism* by Senator William E. Borah. In, *Congressional Record. Proceedings and debates of the First Session of the First Session of the 75th Congress of the USA.* Volume 81, Part 4, April 19, 1937, to May 18, 1937, United States Government Printing Office, Washington, 1937. P. 4237.

reported to the U.S. State Department on February 23, 1937, that his counterpart at the German embassy in Paris had told him that there were between 40,000 and 50,000 Italian and thousands of German troops[140] fighting for Generalissimo Franco. In view of the quantity and precision of the documentation sent by Bowers and received by the State Department, we only may conclude that both Pittman and U.S. Secretary of State Cordell Hull were openly lying to the U.S. when repeatedly stating in Congress that there was no evidence of the German participation at war.

Thousands of POW in hands of the rebels died in concentration, labor or prisoner camps as well as in war hospitals. Source: Archive of the Basque Nationalism/Sabino Arana Foundation.

The beginning of the Spring Offensive against the Basques and the massacres of Durango (March 31) and Gernika (April 26) awakened the debate in Congress regarding Nazi and Fascist intervention. At this point Senator Borah of Idaho addressed the first statement on the bombing on May 6, pointing out that combating Communism did not mean helping Fascism. On May 17 Senator Matthew M. Neely of West Virginia introduced into the Congressional Record an editorial entitled "The Unmasking in Spain" and, the same day Evangelic Bishop Francis J. McConnell

---

140   There were about seven hundred German pilots at war at once during the war.

sent to U.S. Secretary of State Cordell Hull, on behalf of ninety citizens, an appeal to the conscience of the world on *the anguishing news of the ruthless bombardment of non-combatant men, women and children at Gernika.*

The ancient Basque city of Guernica has been razed to the ground by Fascist Insurgent airplanes. Unfortified and unarmed, its houses, churches, and defenseless inhabitants -10,000 men, women and children including refugees- were bombed and machine-gunned for nearly four hours without ceasing. The toll of slaughtered innocents exceeds 800 persons. This is the crime of Guernica. And this is the unspeakable crime of War on Women and Children, waged with a brutality and callousness unparalleled in modern times.

The massacre of Guernica has been confirmed in all its horror by such survivors as Canon Alberto Onaindia of Valladolid Cathedral and by foreign correspondents. One of them a distinguished staff member of the London Times, described the machine-gunning of helpless civilians and added: "The only counter measures the Basques could employ -for they did not possess sufficient airplanes to face the Insurgent fleet- were those provided by the heroism of the Basque clergy. The clergymen blessed and preyed for kneeling crowds — socialists, anarchists and communists in addition to the declared faithful- in crumbling dug-outs" (built for safety from air raids).

Will the prayers of Guernica's dead and dying go unanswered? Or will 300,000 civilians, women and children, soon meet a similar fate in Bilbao without the voices of civilized peoples being raised in overwhelming protest?

We refuse to condone such atrocities by our silence. We do not attempt to assess the contending causes which now struggle for mastery in Spain, but we do insist that this ruthless aerial warfare upon women and children stands outside the pale of morality and of civilization. We insist that there is not such thing as partisanship where this kind of mass murder occurs, or is permitted to occur. We denounce the monstrous crime of Guernica in the name of justice and humanity. We demand a revival of that noble world conscience which manifested itself in the days of persecution of the Jews in Russia and again when the Armenian people lay postrate before the Turks.

For these reasons we call upon all men of good will to protect this immense crime in the name of all that is sacred to human morality and human decency and in the name of Almighty God.[141]

XI. It is remarkable that, considering that the Basques are mostly Catholic, the massacre at Gernika was denounced by the Commission of Evangelism while in May and June 1937 Catholic Cardinal William H. O'Connell was openly defending General Franco as the leader of a Saintly Crusade against evil. Indeed, the Vatican was also openly favoring the uprising.

PC. On June 2, a group of seven congressmen led by O'Connell and John T. Bernard, requested President Roosevelt to adopt measures against Germany and Italy under the Neutrality Act of 1937. The resolution passed by the Senate stated that:

Whereas the Neutrality Act of 1937 prohibits the export of arms, ammunition, and implements of war to belligerent countries;

Whereas a white paper, providing within the limits of human knowledge that Italy has attacked the democratic Spanish government, a recognized friendly nation, by force of arms, has been presented to the nations of the world;

Whereas Germany and Italy have withdrawn from the non-intervention committee, and

Whereas the German bombardment of Almería, the latest Nazi outrage, with its ruthless destruction of men, women, and children, constitutes an act of war:

Now, therefore, be it resolved by the Senate and House of Representatives of the United States of America in Congress assembled, that the President is hereby requested to proclaim Italy and Germany nations at war as defined by the Neutrality Act of 1937 and to invoke the terms of that Act accordingly.[142]

---

[141]   Letter by Senator Francis McConnell to the U.S. Secretary of State. Washington DC, May 17, 1937. National Archives and Records Administration, College Park, U.S. Ambassador Claude G. Bowers Files (Files 852.00/..., Boxes 3687 to 3701), Document 852.00/5466.

[142]   Joint Resolution 390, 75th Congress, 1st Session, House of Representatives, June 1, 1937.

XI. What happened at the U.S. Congress was an image, a reflection of what was happening in Europe. In 1936 no one wanted to be responsible for igniting WWII but every European political leader knew that war was almost inevitable. It was a question of time and, when the war was set off by the National Movement in July 1936, the danger of an open international conflict became close and real. The main reason to avoid military confrontation in 1936 was that the future Axis powers and the Allies considered that they were not prepared yet for such an international war.

In view of this danger, just fifteen days after the insurrection started in July 17, the French government appealed to the British, Italian and German administrations to create a system of non-intervention and by early August the French received the assent of them all. The resulting strategy was named "the Non-Intervention Agreement" even though it was not an agreement (since no document was signed) and it did not intend to stop foreign intervention (but to cover up intervention and avoid an open international conflict). The agreement affected equally trade of war materiel with any of the parties at war, republicans or rebels,

Animated by the desire to avoid every complication which may prejudice maintenance of good relations between nations,

Declares the following:

The Government of His Majesty, in so far as it is concerned, prohibits direct or indirect exportation, re-exportation and transit, to a destination in Spain, the Spanish possessions or the Spanish zone of Morocco, of all arms, munitions and materials of war, as well as all aircrafts, assembled or dismantled, and all vessels of war, such are the enumerated in the appended Order in Council of 1931;
This prohibition applies to contracts in process of execution;
The Government of His Majesty will keep the other Governments participating in this understanding informed of all measures taken by it to give effect to the present declaration.

The Government of His Majesty, in so far as it is concerned, will put this declaration into effect as soon as the French Government, the German Government, the Italian Government, the Government of

the U.S.S.R. and the Portuguese Government shall likewise have adhered to it.[143]

PC. The U.S. Neutrality Act passed in Congress at the beginning of 1937 was shaped by the image of this accord.

XI. An accord that not only did not stop intervention at all but incited it. Even though the German regime had adopted the Non-Intervention accord on August 17, Hitler and Mussolini had decided to ship war material and troops to the rebels almost a month earlier. Indeed, the Non-Intervention accord solidified Hitler's and Mussolini's presumption that Franco's victory was guaranteed: while the rebels could assume that they were going to receive strong military support (for the German and Italian regimes were going to continue shipping war materiel and troops), the Spanish Republican government could only expect a weak political reaction at the League of Nations (for Great Britain and the French republic, natural allies of the Spanish democracy, were not interested in showing any participation).

PC. U.S. ambassador Bowers had always shown himself very critical of the non-intervention system and the Neutrality Act. In his Memoirs he wrote,

> *The Non-intervention Pact was proving itself a dishonest farce. The Fascist powers fought just openly, defiantly, with arms; most of the democracies fought just as effectively, if unconsciously, as collaborationists of the Fascist under the mocking cloak of "non-intervention." When men of good minds assumed that Italy, Germany, and even Portugal were observing the pact, the dishonesty of the pretense stood out like a sore thumb. This pact has become a mockery by October, 1936. It denied the Spanish government the arms and ammunition turning a blind eye to the glaring violations by Germany and Italy. Arms and ammunition poured into the Portuguese ports consigned to Franco, and without inspection at the customs were hurried through to Franco's forces. It was common*

---

[143]   Padelford, Norman J., *International Law and Diplomacy in the Spanish Civil Strife*, The Macmillan Company, New York, 1939. Pp. 206-207.

knowledge. Later, deliveries were made openly through Cádiz, Vigo, Pasajes and Malaga. On September 16, 1936, John Whittaker, Knickerbocker, and Floyd Gibbons, war correspondents, informed me that rebel aviation consisted largely of German bombers and Italian pursuit planes, and that in Seville they had seen German officers in the cafés.[144]

XI. And in the line of Senator Nye's accusations on Pittman's and Hull's statements at the U.S. Congress, Bowers adds that British Foreign Secretary Anthony Eden was lying to the British people at the Chamber of the Commons in 1937 when stating that there was "no evidence" of foreign participation, that there was "no evidence" that the rebel combined air force had bombed Gernika,

All this was in the shoddy days when British ministers were assuring the House of Commons, on their responsibility as ministers of the Crown, that they had "no information" that any Italians were in Spain. I knew that the British Embassy in Hendaye was informing London on the contrary.[145]

So, after the bombing of Gernika and only due to the growing international denunciation of the accord and its ineffectiveness against foreign participation, the Non-Intervention Committee was forced to make a public statement denouncing the shelling of open towns "by both parties at war." However, only one day after Gernika was bombed, a company of one thousand German soldiers landed in Donostia/San Sebastián in plain daylight. In early December, a new German shipment of war material and troops was sent to the Spanish front, and British and French officials could only "deplore" it without any means to stop it:

Then, early in December, 1936, when German soldiers, technicians, engineers, and aviators landed in Cádiz, the British government "deplored it" —and hastened the passage of a law making it a crime to sell arms or ammunition to the loyalist government! The delectable

---

[144]   Bowers, Claude, *My Mission to Spain*, Simon and Schuster, New York, 1954. Pp. 325.
[145]   Ibid. Pp. 325.

Ribbentrop, later to be hung at Nuremberg for his crimes, thereupon informed the Non-Intervention Committee of the pleasure of Hitler that steps had been taken to prevent "intervention." Thus the collaboration with the axis powers in the war of extermination against democracy in Spain was complete.[146]

Senator Frank Church of Idaho with his wife Bethine Clark beneath the Tree of Gernika in 1978. Source: Cenarrusa archive.

PC. For obvious reasons the Non-intervention Committee tried to emphasize the "civil" nature of the conflict. The press supported the idea that the conflict was a "Spanish Civil War," even though every one of the pilots who bombed Gernika and Durango were Italian or German. U.S. Congressman Jerry J. O'Connell of Montana also denounced it by claiming, together with ambassador Bowers, that the war was not a "civil conflict" but the prologue to WWII:

Just last week I sent a letter, signed by myself and three colleagues in this House, and addressed to Secretary Hull. We called the attention of the Secretary of State to the massacre of Guernica, reported by all the foreign correspondents of accredited newspapers to be the work of German planes, German bombs and German pilots. We asked the

---

146   Ibid. Pp. 326.

State Department to take official notice of what is common knowledge, namely, that Germany and Italy are in fact belligerents in the war of invasion now going on in Spain.[147]

XI. Children were among the first victims of the bombings. At the beginning of the conflict children taken out of the biggest cities and schools were placed in places such as Gernika or Durango, far enough from the frontlines and, consequently, out of danger. Nevertheless, due to the notion of "strategic terror" and "total warfare" developed by the rebels, a high number of children were counted among the victims of the bombings. The Basque Government then started the plans for evacuating civilians en mass. Consequently, approximately 120,000 Basque citizens were evacuated between May and October 1937 from the Basque Country (26 percent of them children), primarily to Great Britain, the French Republic and Belgium.

Camp for Basque refugee children in England. 1937. Source: Archive of the Basque Nationalism/Sabino Arana Foundation.

---

[147]   *Congressional Record. Appendix of the First Session of the 75th Congress of the USA. Volume 81, Part 9, January 5, 1937 to May 19, 1937*, United States Government Printing Office, Washington, 1937. Pp. 1131.

In total, approximately 32,000 children under seventeen years of age, nearly 20 percent of the children in the area controlled by the Basque Government, were evacuated from the Basque Country by ship between the end of April and June 1937. According to data provided by the U.S. consul at Bilbao, William E. Chapman, 15,000 children had been evacuated from Bilbao by May 26. By June 14, the noncombatants evacuated numbered nearly 30,000.[148] About 50 percent of the children were evacuated alone, for they had lost both parents or their fathers were in prison; many of them never returned to their families or lost track of them during the war.

PC. No Basque children were taken here, to the United States. The American Board of Guardians for Basque Refugee Children, created in May 1937, hoped to ship five hundred children to New York by the end of June. The children were to be hosted by Basque families or by a nursery school in New York under the care of Basque priests, nurses and teachers. The children would remain in New York during the war and, if necessary, after the war (if their parents were missing or in prison). However, when everything was ready and the Board of Guardians for Basque Refugee Children had collected the necessary funds to cover the operation, Catholic Cardinal William H. O'Connell of Boston lobbied against this will.

By mobilizing the Councils of the Knights of Columbus (CKC) in Massachusetts O'Connell got the State department to stop the plans for evacuation. Numerous CKC councils in Massachusetts and Maine sent telegrams to both the State Department and the House of Representatives opposing the evacuation of children. Other Catholic organizations in O'Connell's diocese joined the campaign, among them the Franciscan Friars of the Atonement, the League of Catholic Women, the Congress of Catholic Women, the Women's Philomatheia Club, the Ladies Catholic Benevolent Association of

---

[148]   Memorandum for the Ambassador by U.S. Consul in Bilbao William E. Chapman to U.S. Ambassador Claude G. Bowers. Donibane Lohitzune, June 14, 1937. National Archives and Records Administration, College Park, Bilbao Consulate General Records (1936-1946). Box 4, 1937. P. 2.

the State of Illinois and the Catholic Alumni Sodality of Boston. They all opposed the project as "Red propaganda,"

> *The Adams Council Knights of Columbus disapprove of State Department waiving immigration law allowing Basque Children entering United States without parents. We believe that this is just another piece of Communistic propaganda instituted by the followers of the Loyalists group in Spain who are seeking sympathetic support in United States. We protest this monstrous undertaking.*[149]

O'Connell also influenced the Catholic representative for Massachusetts John W. McCormack, Massachusetts Senator David Ignatius Walsh and Massachusetts' Governor Charles Francis Hurley. They all lobbied to stop admission into the United States of five hundred refugee children, the first victims of the Nazi bombings in the Basque Country at Gernika, Durango and Bilbao.

In spite of these efforts O'Connell did not stop the action of many Americans to help these children and in 1938 a delegation of the Basque Government in exile visited Idaho. During the visit of the delegates Anton Irala and Manuel Sota, two Basque festivals were organized for helping Basque refugees in the French republic. Later, a Pro-Refugees Committee was formed and chaired by Marciano Uriarte in order to raise money for these children or war. Again on Christmas 1938, as part of the annual dance of the Basque sheepherders in Boise the documentary Gernika was displayed and local media echoed the event. However, Juanita Iriondo and Marciano Uriarte reported that people gradually cooled down because of the Fascist propaganda in Idaho, and new subscriptions were cancelled.

XI. It was a bad time for the victims but things were going to change.

---

[149]   Telegram by Grand Knight of Adams Council of the Knights of Columbus J. P. McAndrews to U.S. Representative Allen T. Treadway. Adams (Massachusetts), May 25, 1937. National Archives and Records Administration, College Park, U.S. Ambassador Claude G. Bowers Files (Files 852.48/…), Document 852.48/93.

Iconic image of the Tree of Gernika taken in the 60s. A young man praying beneath the tree during the Franco years. The identity of the man in the picture remains an intriguing mystery. Source: Irujo Ametzaga archive.

PC. Years after the bombing… here in Boise, on the west lawn of Idaho's Capitol is an oak tree from the Tree of Gernika brought to America in 1981 from the Basque Country, as a symbol of Basque freedom and independence but also as a symbol of human suffering. We may end by quoting Senator Borah, of Idaho,

> *There is no tenet of democracy which fascism does not challenge. There is not a vital principle of free government with which this ruthless creed is not in conflict. It is built and professes to be built upon the ruins of democracy. It is grounded in force. It could not survive a fortnight in the atmosphere of free discussion. It meets criticism by sending its critics to island prisons compared with which Dante's hell has its advantages. Under its reign individual judgment, individual liberty, are looked upon as heresies calling for chains or the prison cell. The citizen, with his rights and his privileges, his individual outlook, and his aspirations is under this system transformed into a cog, a soulless cog, in a vast machine called the state.*[150]

---

[150]   *Challenge to Democracy. Fascism and Communism* by Senator William E. Borah. In, *Congressional Record. Proceedings and debates of the First Session of the First Session of the 75th Congress of the USA.* Volume 81, Part 4, April 19, 1937, to May 18, 1937, United States Government Printing Office, Washington, 1937. P. 4237.

On the cooperation between the Basque secret services and the U.S. Office of Strategic Services

Xabier Irujo. As we have mentioned the Luftwaffe had bombed Gernika because such a strike would make the untrained Basque militia flee and thus the gates of Bilbao would be open in a matter of days. But it would take almost two more months to make the 25 mile path that separates Gernika from Bilbao. After the capture of Bilbao on June 19, 1937 the war in the Basque Country was over.

Pete Cenarrusa. Let me quote the last message of Lehendakari (President) Jose Antonio Agirre to the Basque peoples in Turtzios/Trucios, before leaving to go into exile,

> I have reached with the Basque troops the last border of the Basque Country. I have remained among them admiring the temper of our people, whose spirit will never be defeated. And before leaving our land I protest on their behalf before the world for the plundering that the Basques have been subject to in the middle of the twentieth century, depriving us of our homeland, to which we are entitled, for it is ours and because we endearingly love it. And I also protest, because to carry out the dispossession the Spanish fascism has required foreign mercenary forces and elements of war coming from Germany and Italy. Our enemies invoke the right of conquest. We deny this right forever. The territory is under enemy control but not the soul of the Basque peoples: our spirit will never be conquered.
>
> We have acted nobly, our conduct has not changed, not even at the last moment. We have left Bilbao and its sources of production intact. We have freed prisoners with generosity that is paid in exchange by the enemy with persecution and executions. No dispossession is imputable to the Basque army.
>
> The Basque people look forward to its future, its soul belongs to us. Our conduct is the one of our country. We will come back to regain the land of our fathers, to restore the banned language,

the outraged law and the stolen liberties. What has Fascism ever promised to the Basque Country? Nothing, therefore after capturing Bilbao the Fascists have cancelled not only our Basque political autonomy but also our Economic Agreement, the only one of our remaining historic liberties that was respected even in times of the monarchy. I also protest this dispossession, interpreting the feelings of subjugated peoples who are not allowed to speak.

My people face the sea and confront a double menace. I cannot believe that our friends or our enemies are going to remain silent. Is it such a crime that a people defend their freedom? Since for defending it, for being worthy of our homeland, hundreds of thousands of Basques today suffer anguish and deprivation. I do not want to believe that the world is not any longer sensitive.

The Basque government retains its duties, as well in the Basque Country as wherever it may be in the future. It is the legitimate government of the Basques because it interprets the feel of a nation which has not been defeated but temporarily overwhelmed and outraged. And the affection of our fellow citizens will accompany you until the day of victory.[151]

XI. After the Republican army was defeated in April 1939, the Basque Government had to make a decision about its future: to dissolve and renounce fighting or to act from exile and face, together with the rest of the European and American democracies, the totalitarian forces. The decision of going on fighting came to be obvious for the Basque Government was among the first governments in Europe facing the German Nazis and the Italian Fascists and, after three years, in 1939 the Basque Government considered itself to be at war with all the enemies of democracy in Europe.

PC. Besides, European and American leaders knew that WWII was about to break out.

XI. And the Basque Government was committed to taking an active role in the upcoming world war, both politically and militarily. However, since it was not possible to maintain the

---

[151] Agirre, José Antonio, *Obras completas de José Antonio de Aguirre y Lecube*, Sendoa, Donostia, 1981. P. 632. Translated by the author.

remains of the Basque army out of the Basque Country after the war was over, the Basque Government decided to organize a Secret Service organization and so act within the Basque homeland and abroad.

Dance of the death soldier. Performed in Boise (Idaho) during the celebration of the First *Aberri Eguna* (Day of the Basque Country) in 1974. Source: Achabal archive.

So, after the war ended in April 1939, the Basque government of Lehendakari Jose Antonio Agirre went into exile and transferred its central offices from Barcelona to Paris. A day after the occupation of Poland, the Basque government declared that it was virtually at war with the German, the Italian and the Spanish regimes and on the side of the democratic states.

After the German occupation of Paris in June 1940, the Basque government was forced to evacuate its office in Paris. While fleeing the Gestapo, President Agirre disappeared in June 1940 in Dunkirk, and Manuel Irujo assumed the temporary presidency of the Basque National Council, an institution that replaced the Basque government until the reappearance of Agirre a year-and-a-half later.

PC. President Agirre could not be evacuated at Dunkirk in 1940, where the British Intelligence had promised to do their best to take him to London. Therefore he was facing certain death at hands of the Gestapo and the Spanish intelligence. Thousands of people had suffered retaliation and many others had been shot, for instance, the minister of the Spanish government Julián Zugazagoitia, the minister of the Basque government Alfredo Espinosa, and the president of the Government of Catalonia, Lluís Companys. Espinosa was captured and shot in 1937 and both Zugazagoitia and Companys were captured by the Gestapo and given to the Spanish authorities to be shot in 1940. In order to escape from the Gestapo, Agirre decided to go to Berlin. On January 13th, 1941, Agirre even assisted at a speech by Hitler at the centric Kurfursterndamm Boulevard, and during that spring he eye-witnessed some of the first bombings of the city by the RAF.[152]

XI. During this period, Manuel Irujo, former minister of justice of the Republic, created, together with other Basques exiled in London, the Basque National Council. The three main aims of Irujo were to organize a provisional Basque government meanwhile Agirre was hidden and so, to keep alive a legitimate Basque political organization in exile; to help the evacuation of all Basque refugees in occupied Europe and, to sign a political and strategic agreement with both the British Foreign Office and the French government in exile. The Basque proposal was the following:

- The Basque secret service would collaborate with the British Intelligence in their common struggle against Nazism, Fascism and Francoism.
- The collaboration would only happen if there was a previous political agreement on the independence of the Basque Country.
- The thousands of Basque refugees in Europe and America would be helped by the British officials in these countries.
- All the operations would be financed by the British government.

---

[152]   Aguirre, Jose Antonio, *Escape via Berlin. Eluding Franco in Hitler's Europe*, University of Nevada Press, Reno, 1991.

- The Basque agents would operate under direct Basque command.
- The Basque language would be the official language of the Basque Secret Services.
- The Basque agents would operate fundamentally in Europe but also in South and Central America.
- The main target would be to dissolve the Nazi and Fascist spy networks in Europe and Latin America.

PC. In less than a month the Basque National Council and the British government had accorded their first agreements on military collaboration. Robert J. G. Boothby, representing the British government, and Jose Ignacio Lizaso, representing the Basque National Council, signed the first agreement on July 29, 1940, which spelled out that the British government was committed to defending the independence of the Basque Country if the Spanish government went to war on the side of the Axis powers. The following is the document signed by both parties:

Most secret. Formula

H. M. Government sympathizes with the cause of the Basque peoples, in their claim for liberty and independence.
In the event of hostilities breaking out between the British and Spanish Governments, H. M. Government will immediately recognize the Basque National Council as the Provisional Basque Government.
In the event of a British victory, H. M. Government will undertake to do everything in their power to secure the constitution and security of a Basque State.
The delimitation of frontiers is a matter for settlement later on.[153]

XI. Despite the agreement, the document was never approved by Churchill, who preferred to maintain economic cooperation with

---

[153]   Letter by Jose Ignacio Lizaso to Commandant P. Carey of the British Admiralty's Naval Intelligence Division (NID), London, July 30, 1940. Also a copy of the document in the letter by Jose Ignacio Lizaso to Ramón Sota, London, July 9, 1941.

Franco's regime rather than confront the possibility of a military operation on the Iberian Peninsula.

It was a purely practical decision: it was much cheaper to pay General Franco not to go into WWII with the Axis than to finance a military campaign in these countries during an eventual operation for the liberation of the continent. Consequently, Churchill signed a number of commercial pacts with Franco that the British government maintained even after the occupation of France in June 1940, when the Spanish state declared itself a "nonbelligerent state" rather than a "neutral state."

PC. Moreover, these Hispanic-British agreements were preserved even after the Spanish government signed agreements of military cooperation with Nazi Germany (supporting the German navy by facilitating provisions for U-boats in Spanish ports); even after Franco sent the División Azul (Blue Division) to the Russian front.

XI. Yes, between July 14 and 20, 1941, a contingent of around 40,000 troops arrived at the German headquarters in Bavaria to be sent to the Russian front on August 10. The Spanish Blue Division remained in Russia for nearly two years, until October 1943. After the first German defeats in Europe and Africa, the division was reduced to a small force of about 1,800 men under the command of Colonel Antonio Navarro. On March 3, 1944, after the first heavy German defeats at the Russian front, the Spanish government issued an order of repatriation for all of the contingents.

PC. In spite of the British position, the Basque National Council also signed cooperation agreements with the Conseil de Défense de l'Empire Français (Council of Defense of the French Empire) led by General Charles De Gaulle. By virtue of the agreements, a Basque force was going to be created within the army of the Free France. And, four years later the Gernika Battalion fought during WWII within the French Army in the battle of the Médoc in April 1945, during the campaign for the liberation of the French Republic.

Soldier of the Gernika Battalion in 1945. The Gernika Battalion took part in the operations for the liberation of the Medoc in April 1945. Archive of the Basque Nationalism/Sabino Arana Foundation.

XI. I interviewed Jose Elizalde, a soldier of the Gernika Battalion who decided to go into WWII to take revenge for what had happened in Gernika.

PC. Idahoan Joe Eiguren was one of them too. While I was joining the Marines, he declared to me his intention to join the U.S. Army to fight the Germans and their allies. Gernika was on his mind when fighting the Germans:

On July 4th of 1944, we were approaching the Germans, and General Omar Bradley issued an order that at noon on that day, as a celebration of the 4th of July, every soldier of every unit, whether it was a rifle, bazooka or short-range artillery, or long-range 155 Howitzers, was to fire one shot towards the enemy. At noon on that day, we did. Everybody fired a shot towards the Germans. From then on, we kept on moving. I was really proud that I was in that Army and this might sound silly, but I was not afraid at all. I was actually eager to meet the enemy, for as we were moving, every place I looked were our equipment-tanks, waiting for the enemy, in case of an attack, our artillery, anti-tank guns, just everything. I thought to myself, "Who could stop us with all this equipment that we have?" In addition to the equipment that I saw, I was eager to meet the Germans, because it was always so strong in my mind what the Legion Condor had done in the Basque Country. I thought this is going to give me a chance to see how rough these guys are with all this fighting equipment that we have and the Basques did not have. On July 6th, about two or three o'clock in the afternoon, as we were moving cautiously towards the firing line, the fireworks started.[154]

XI. President Jose Antonio Agirre had reappeared in Montevideo, Uruguay on October 1941 after a year-and-a-half of travel through Nazi Germany. The Basque government was reinstituted, and the central offices were transferred from London to New York until the liberation of Paris in 1944. In October 1941, and, even more so after the bombing of Pearl Harbor on December 7, 1941, the Basque government initiated diplomatic and strategic negotiations with President Roosevelt's administration.

---

[154]   Eiguren, Joseph, *Kashpar*, Joseph Eiguren, Boise, 1988. P. 109.

The two administrations agreed to initiate a partnership between their intelligence agencies, the Basque Secret Services and the Office of Strategic Services (OSS), which would continue from May 1942 until the end of 1949. The Basque-American agreement comprised four main points:

- The Basque secret services would collaborate with the U.S. Office of Strategic Services.
- The Basque secret services would operate under direct Basque command.
- The Basque secret services would operate in South and Central America, in Europe and also in the Philippines.
- The main target was to dissolve the German and Spanish spy networks in Latin America and, the Japanese in the Philippines.

PC. It was, in essence, the agreement proposed by the Basque National Council to the British in 1940. However, there was no political agreement.

XI. Yes, and this became a hot issue that led to an intense discussion between Agirre and Irujo. Manuel Irujo did not like the idea of negotiating the participation of Basque troops without a previous political agreement. Besides, Irujo understood that the political future for the Basque Country was a European matter to be discussed with the European governments. However, Agirre knew that it was not possible to reach an agreement with the Roosevelt administration including a political statement on the independence of the Basque Country. Agirre was certain that it was not necessary to include a political declaration in the agreement since after the war the U.S administration was going to support the Basque political claims against the Francoist regime anyway.

PC. Beginning in 1944, Franco's international approach began to change drastically in light of Germany's decline in military and political importance in Europe. Franco, as early as June 1942, described to Carlton J. H. Hayes, ambassador of the United States in Madrid, his "theory of the two wars," the one at the Western front in which Spain remained neutral, and the one at the Eastern front against communism, in which Spain was involved both politically and militarily.

In any case, at the end of World War II in May 1945, Franco's government was sanctioned for its association with the German and Italian totalitarian governments. Between July 17 and August 2, 1945, representatives from the chief Allied governments, Great Britain, the Soviet Union and the United States, met in Potsdam and decided to deny Spain's admission into the international organizations to be created after the war:

> *The three governments, nevertheless, feel forced to make clear that, on the other hand, they will not favor the entrance, if asked for it, of the present Spanish government, since, having established with the support of the powers of the Axis, by its origins, its nature, its performance and its intimate association with the attacking states, does not have the necessary requirements to justify its participation in quality of a member.*[155]

XI. Accordingly, the Spanish state would not be accepted into the United Nations, which would recommend the retirement of all of Madrid's ambassadors, consuls and international diplomats. The U.N. approved the Project of Resolution on Spain (Document A/40), which had three main points:

> *The Assembly remembers that the Conference of San Francisco adopted a resolution in accordance with which paragraph 2, article 4, chapter II of the Chart of the United Nations will not be applied to those states whose regimes have been taken to power with the help of troops of the countries that have fought against the United Nations while those regimes continue in power.*
>
> *The Assembly remembers that, in the Conference of Potsdam, the governments of the United Kingdom, the United States of North America and the Soviet Union, declared that they would not support a demand of entering the United Nations by the present Spanish government whom, having been founded with the support of the powers of the Axis, does not have, by virtue of its origins, its nature, its*

---

[155]   Jiménez de Aberasturi, Juan Carlos, *De la Guerra Civil a la Guerra Fría (1937-1947)*, Txertoa, Donostia, 2001.

performance and its intimate association with the attacking states, the necessary qualifications to justify its admission.

The General Assembly, in having made these two declarations, recommends to the members of the United Nations that it consider its letter and its spirit in their future relations with Spain.[156]

On March 4, 1946, the British, French and American governments, all three members of the U.N. Security Council, signed a public denunciation of the Spanish regime, although they declared their refusal to interfere in Spain's internal affairs:

The governments of France, the United Kingdom, and the United States of America have exchanged views with regard to the present Spanish Government and their relations with that regime. It is agreed that so long as General Franco continues in control of Spain, the Spanish people cannot anticipate full and cordial association with those nations of the world which have, by common effort, brought defeat to German Nazism and Italian Fascism, which aided the present Spanish regime in its rise to power and after which the regime was patterned.

There is no intention of interfering in the internal affairs of Spain. The Spanish people themselves must in the long run work out their own destiny. In spite of the present regime's repressive measures against orderly efforts of the Spanish people to organize and give expression to their political aspirations, the three Governments are hopeful that the Spanish people will not again be subjected to the horrors and bitterness of civil strife.

On the contrary, it is hoped that leading patriotic and liberal-minded Spaniards may soon find means to bring about a peaceful withdrawal of Franco, the abolition of the Falange, and the establishment of an interim or caretaker government under which the Spanish people may have an opportunity freely to determine the type of government they wish to have and to choose their leaders. Political amnesty, return of exiled Spaniards, freedom of assembly and political association and provision for free public elections are essential. An interim government which would be and would remain dedicated to

---

[156]   *El problema de España ante el mundo internacional. Resolución aprobada por la 1ª Asamblea General de Naciones Unidas. Texto y discusión de la misma*, p. 13, Spanish Republic, Ministry of State, London, 1946.

these ends should receive the recognition and support of all freedom-loving peoples.

Such recognition would include full diplomatic relations and the taking of such practical measures to assist in the solution of Spain's economic problems as may be practicable in the circumstances prevailing. Such measures are not now possible. The question of the maintenance or termination by the Governments of France the United Kingdom, and the United States of diplomatic relations with the present Spanish regime is a matter to be decided in the light of events and after taking into account the efforts of the Spanish people to achieve their own freedom.[157]

PC. The Cold War would dramatically change the international political scene.

XI. However, the administration of President Harry S. Truman (1945-1953), despite pressure from the Republican-controlled Congress, refused to support conservative dictatorships as a way to fight communism.

PC. Yes. The U.S. began to pay more attention to the potential military benefits of working with Spain. The Join Chiefs of Staff commissioned a study, "Drumbeat," which concluded in August 1947 that from a military point of view it would be in the United States' best interests to furnish Spain with economic aid and to have friendlier relations. But the proposal to do this went nowhere. President Truman was both anti-fascist and anti-communist and was opposed to the whole idea of allying with a fascist state. He called the report "decidedly militaristic and in my opinion not realistic with present conditions." He made famous his statement "I won't fight tyranny with tyranny." The U.S. Congress also applied pressure on the Executive Branch to reconsider its policy towards Spain, but Truman used his power of veto.

XI. Senator Joseph McCarthy of Wisconsin and Senator Pat McCarran of Nevada initiated the Witch Hunt, an anti-communist crusade. As mentioned by Edward T. Lampson, specialist in European affairs, and Pauline Mian, analyst in European affairs for

---

[157]   Statement released by the U.S. State Department, March 4, 1946.

the Foreign Affairs Division, the change of attitude towards the Spanish regime did not stem from a change in the Spanish state itself but from the onset of the Cold War. It reflected a fear that there was a new threat to peace in Europe and the enemy was no longer fascism, but communism.[158]

PC. Senator Joseph McCarthy was strongly in favor of an alliance with the Spanish dictatorship, claiming that there was no war on God's earth to defend the richest prize for which Communist Russia was aiming – the industrial heart of Europe – unless the American government used "those two great wells of tough anti-Communist manpower," that is, the Western German and Spanish governments.

XI. On April 27, 1950, Senator McCarran proposed that Congress approve a $50 million payment to Spain, though the measure was rejected on a 42-35 vote. Only three months later, after the beginning of the Korean War, McCarran proposed an amendment to the 1948 treaty of economic cooperation with the Spanish regime (the Economic Cooperation Act of 1948), which authorized a $100 million grant to Spain. Congress approved McCarran's second proposal 65-15 on August 1, 1950. Almost the entire Democratic leadership in the Senate supported the proposal. And $100 million were added to the funds agreed upon in the General Appropriation Bill for the third year of the European Cooperation Administration (ECA). The effect of the Korean War (Jun 25, 1950-July 27, 1953) on diplomatic relations between the Spanish state and the United States turned out to be significant.

Consequently, on 3 November 1950 the U.N. passed a resolution repealing part of the earlier 1946 resolution condemning the Spanish regime. The resolution resolved:

---

[158]   "Current Spanish–U.S. Negotiations", Report by Edward T. Lampson, Specialist in European Affairs, and Pauline Mian, Analyst in European Affairs for the Foreign Affairs Division. Washington, October 15, 1975. In, Boise State University Library, Frank Church Collection, MSS 56, Box 43, Fol. 14.

- To revoke the recommendation for the withdrawal of Ambassadors and Ministers from Madrid, contained in the General Assembly resolution of December 12, 1946.

- To revoke the recommendation intended to debar the Spanish regime from membership in international agencies established by or brought into relationship with the United Nations, which recommendation is a part of the same resolution adopted by the General Assembly in 1946 concerning relations of Members of the United Nations with the Spanish government.

Senator Frank Church met with Manuel Irujo at the Basque Center in Caracas (Venezuela) in the early seventies. Source: Cenarrusa archive.

PC. McCarran's proposal provoked criticism from President Truman and the House later reduced the sum to $62.5 million. When the bill was signed on September 6, President Truman declared that he would consider the provision as an "authorization" and not as a "directive," and that the loan would be made available to the Spanish government "whenever such loans will serve the interests of the United States in its conduct of foreign relations."[159]

XI. However, credits were gradually extended to Franco. In 1951 the Export-Import Bank extended four separate credits totaling $17.2 million, and credits were also provided under the General Appropriations Act of 1951, which ultimately led to the Pact of Madrid of 1953. President Truman and the State Department were concerned by the political and moral implications of such a rapprochement and by the diplomatic repercussions such a move would have with the Western European allies of the United States. But in 1953 the Vatican signed the Concordat with the Spanish government and the new Republican Executive Branch led by President Dwight D. Eisenhower opened negotiations which culminated in the signing of the Pact of Madrid on economic and military cooperation on September 26, 1953.

The defense and economic arrangements of 1953 were embodied in three executive agreements (a Defense Agreement, an Economic Aid Agreement, and a Defense Assistance Agreement) signed in Madrid on September 26, 1953, collectively known as the Pact of Madrid. The Pact of Madrid represented a reversal of a U.S. policy in force since the end of World War II of ostracizing Franco Spain as a fascist state.[160]

Two years later, in 1955, the Spanish state was admitted into the United Nations, which would allow Franco to prolong his dictatorship until his death in 1975. For the first time, the Basque government faced the possibility of a long exile. None knew then that Generalissimo Franco was going to be in power until November 20, 1975.

---

[159] "Current Spanish–U.S. Negotiations", Report by Edward T. Lampson, Specialist in European Affairs, and Pauline Mian, Analyst in European Affairs for the Foreign Affairs Division. Washington, October 15, 1975. In, Boise State University Library, Frank Church Collection, MSS 56, Box 43, Fol. 14.

[160] Ibid.

On the long Spanish dictatorship

Pete Cenarrusa. Forty years of brutal repression of the Basque people (1936-1975) followed the coup d'état of July 1936. Beginning with the killing of thousands of prisoners of war during their period of confinement at concentration fields, Basques (and also Spanish, Galicians and Catalans) would suffer four decades of death, prison and exile. The Spanish state became a big prison and politically, economically, socially and culturally the Spanish state went back to indexes lower than the ones shown in the early 20th century.

Xabier Irujo. Yes. The new state set up after the war, the "grid-state" as Cardinal Isidro Gomá called it (*Grid-state, unaware of the contours and reliefs on the national body*), was indeed a centralist state organized according to the most conservative Spanish nationalist ideology.[161] The result was a totalitarian state with a strong military presence. It was also supposed to be culturally uniform, since the National Movement envisioned Spain as a single indissoluble nation:

> But this is a domestic struggle; struggle that has its natural origin in what has been called the differential fact, not of the Hispanic races, of which there is only one, the product of twenty centuries of history in which all the ethnic differences have been fused, the blood and spirit, the invading peoples, but also the culture, temperament, historical atavisms that have been intensified because of past and present political errors and perhaps by the clandestine action of hidden international forces, that with their aspirations try to balkanize Spain, breaking simultaneously the political and religious mold that formed our national unit. But this will pass. It will pass due to the frustration or the fatigue of the anxious ones, or due to the good

---

161   "Estado-cuadrícula, desconocedor de contornos y relieves del cuerpo nacional". Gomá, Isidro, *El caso de España, Instrucción a sus diocesanos y respuesta a unas consultas sobre la guerra actual*, Iruñea, 1936.

sense of the peoples and the prudence of the governors that have found the balance that allows the free game of the regional life within the unity of the great fatherland. I believe that, except for some crazy people who have this chauvinist fever, there is no Spanish national who does not know that Spain cannot be divided into pieces without these pieces, sooner or later, entering into the orbit of attraction of another political world, of another state, and no good Spanish national will ever agree to this.[162]

In few words, as in any other military dictatorship, the state became a *cuartelillo* or police headquarters under a *caudillo* or chief.

PC. Under the unique authority of Generalissimo Franco, officially named the "Caudillo of Spain by the grace of God," and in line with Franco's assertion that "our regime is founded on bayonets and blood, not on hypocritical elections," the new Spanish state was a military totalitarian government whose main characteristics were:

1. Concentration of all political authority and control over the armed forces in the person of General Franco. That meant subordination of the legislative and the judiciary to the executive.
2. Absence of a constitution, which was replaced by the rules and orders of the "Generalissimo."
3. Prohibition of all political parties and persecution of former members or supporters of the Catalan, Galician and Basque nationalist parties and socialist, communist and anarchist political forces. One sole political party was legal, the *Falange Española Tradicionalista y de las JONS*.
4. Strong state centralization. Consequently, the Basque Statute of Autonomy was repealed as well as the administrative institutions in Bizkaia and Gipuzkoa, which were deemed to be "traitor provinces." That meant the

---

[162] Gomá, Isidro, "Apología de la Hispanidad," speech given in the Theater Columbus of Buenos Aires on the commemorative evening of the "Day of the Spanish race," October 12, 1934.

end of any path toward political autonomy in the Basque Country, Catalonia and Galicia.

5. Eradication of national distinctiveness. Spanish became the only official language of the state for all purposes. People were fined or arrested for speaking languages other than Spanish and it was prohibited to print books in any of the minority languages.

6. Abundant use of violence, protracted use of police brutality, threats to intimidate and coerce potential political opposition and, militarization of justice and civil society.

Just Before Speaking Begins

GOV. ROBERT E. SMYLIE grabs the hand of Speaker Pete Cenarrusa as he moves to the podium to deliver his message to the special session of the Idaho Legislature.

Pete T. Cenarrusa acting as Speaker of the House. "Speaking," an icon of democracy, is something forbidden in dictatorships. From *The Idaho Statesman*.

XI. And that all meant imprisonment or execution of the political opposition. The meticulous study of Altaffaylla Kultur Taldea[163] details the name, surname and place of execution of 3,164 people, mostly civilians, in Navarre during the war (1936-1939). Purges also occurred in other Basque territories. At the same time, thousands of people were imprisoned or interned in concentration camps and tens of thousands, among them 32,000 children, went into exile. Capital punishment was legalized and used abundantly by military courts martial, although during the first years of the uprising the majority of executions took place without any trials.

PC. Unity of church and state and religious education in the hands of the Catholic Church was other of the main aspects of the Spanish regime. The new state was declared to be Catholic, and freedom of public worship was strongly restricted. On August 25, 1953, Alberto Martín Artajo, secretary of state, and Domenico Tardini, secretary of the Roman curia, signed an order by which relations between church and state were regulated. The document was centered on the idea that religious freedom was a heretical principle as understood in the encyclical *Syllabus de errorum* written by Pius IX in 1864, which condemned the freedom of creed and the severance of church and state. As Bowers wrote in a report entitled "The Burgos Attitude on Religious and Intellectual Freedom," Protestants and Jews were described as "the enemies of the Catholic Church". In U.S. Ambassador Claude G. Bowers words, *this reference to Protestantism is, as you know, in strict accord with the traditional attitude of the Hierarchy in Spain toward the Protestant religion which was not tolerated under the monarchy*.[164]

XI. And censorship. Control over the mass media was complete by 1936 and a strict system of censorship was established. As early as August 1936, a National Defense Council cabinet known as the Press and Propaganda Office was created in the zone controlled by

---

[163]   Altaffaylla Kultur Taldea, *Navarra 1936: de la esperanza al terror*, Altaffaylla Kultur Taldea, 2001.
[164]   The Burgos Attitude on Religious and Intellectual Freedom. Report by U.S. Ambassador to the Spanish Republic, Claude G. Bowers to the Secretary of State. Donibane Lohitzune, March 1, 1938. National Archives and Records Administration, College Park, U.S. Ambassador Claude G. Bowers Files (Files 852.404/...), Document 852.404/95. P. 2.

the military. Later, "purifying commissions" were also created by the new regime:

> *The purifying Commissions of our New State (...) will order the retirement of books, pamphlets, magazines, publications, engravings and forms that contain in their text prints or stamps showing dissolvent ideas, immoral concepts, propaganda of Marxist doctrines, and whatever means lack of respect to the dignity of our glorious Army, attacks to the unity of the fatherland, disrespect to the Catholic religion and whatever is against the meaning and aims of our national Crusade.*[165]

Long after the war, Franco's government maintained the Law of Press, which noted in its introduction that the journalist is an "apostle of the thought and the faith of the nation." The first article also stated that, the organization, monitoring and control of the National Institution of the Mass Media were state issues.

No intellectual freedom, no freedom of speech. The regime also created the Commission for the Purification of Libraries, which acted under the Department of Justice. In an article in the *Hoja Oficial del Lunes de Guipúzcoa* of 28 February 1938, the commission published a list of books prohibited by the state. Bowers noted with some astonishment that Thomas Carlyle's "Heroes and Hero Worship," studied in American high schools, and the works of John Dewey, were among the forbidden texts. The works of Honoré de Balzac, Alexandre Dumas, Gustave Flaubert, Anatole France and all Russian novelists were also banned:

> *This early inauguration of an official censorship over the reading of the public bears out my conviction that should the insurgents finally win it will mean the end of civil, religious and intellectual freedom in so far as governmental decrees can affect it.*[166]

---

[165] *Decreto para la regulación de la prensa y la propaganda,* January 1937.

[166] The Burgos Attitude on Religious and Intellectual Freedom. Report by U.S. Ambassador to the Spanish Republic, Claude G. Bowers to the Secretary of State. Donibane Lohitzune, March 1, 1938. National Archives and Records Administration, College Park, U.S. Ambassador Claude G. Bowers Files (Files 852.404/...), Document 852.404/95. P. 5.

PC. In summary, quoting U.S. ambassador Claude G. Bowers:

In a lengthy decree issued by General Franco on August 5 at Salamanca no doubt is left as to the purely autocratic character of the State he has in mind. Much of the phrasing is mystical, and to my mind meaningless, more calculated to confuse the average person than to enlighten him. But one thing stands out clearly and in so many words, General Franco is to have absolute power even to the extent of naming his successor. As the Chief of the new organization, the Falange Española Tradicionalista y de las JONS, there is to be no limitation to his power.

The purpose of the new State proposed is "to give back to Spain the profound sense of the indestructible unity of destiny, and a resolved faith in the Catholic and imperial mission as a protagonist of history; to establish an economic regime superior to the interests of individuals, groups or classes for the multiplication of wealth." (...)

Such, in outline is the new State proposed. It is a combination of Fascist and military dictatorship of the most uncompromising sort. It definitely ends the following features of the democratic republic it is intended to displace:

It ends Republic.
It ends democracy in Spain.
It ends parliamentary government.
It ends constitutional government.
It ends the separation of Church and State.
It ends the plan for a public school system.
It is feudalism grafted on to the 20th century.[167]

XI. The question of whether to recognize the Spanish military regime in November 1936 provoked strong reactions in both European and American countries. Premature recognition of the Spanish military regime was widely considered an act of

---

[167]   Franco Outlines His New State. Report by U.S. Ambassador to the Spanish Republic, Claude G. Bowers to the Secretary of State. Donibane Lohitzune, March 1, 1938. National Archives and Records Administration, College Park, U.S. Ambassador Claude G. Bowers Files (Files 852.01/...), Document 852.01/239. Pp. 1-6.

intervention.[168] In the United States, groups like the American Friends of Spanish Democracy opposed such recognition. However, in April 1939, once the war was over, a government that had declared its intention to destroy democracy and establish a military dictatorship would be recognized by all democratic states. As in 1936, the decision to recognize Generalissimo Franco's government in 1939 also generated protests in the democratic states.

PC. Yes indeed; U.S. recognition on April 1, 1939 was followed by several protests. Notably, the Lawyers Committee of the American Bar submitted a forty page memorandum to the State Department and the House of Representatives. Written by Paul J. Kern, the memorandum detailed five main reasons to reject recognition of the Spanish regime:

1. It was a key tenet of American foreign policy to refuse recognition of a government established and maintained by force against the will of the people.
2. It was a key tenet to avoid recognition until there was convincing evidence of the establishment of civil tranquility and domestic order.
3. It was inconsistent with a policy of opposing aggression and invasion.
4. It would reverse the traditional American policy of condemning governments guilty of moral outrages.
5. It was contrary to U.S. interests.[169]

XI. And the Basque culture and language was also affected by the new regime. A prohibition on the Basque language in Spain and France was nothing new. For almost 150 years (1789-1936), regimes in both countries had pursued policies designed to

---

168 Communication by the American Friends of Spanish Democracy to the U.S. Secretary of State. December 8, 1936. National Archives and Records Administration, College Park, U.S. Ambassador Claude G. Bowers Files (Files 852.01/...), Document 852.01/179.

169 Lawyers Committee on American Relations with Spain, *Memorandum on the Relationship of the United States Government to the Franco Regime*, Washington, April 1, 1939.

strengthen a single official language while excluding others from state administration and public and private education. Consequently, the Catalan, Galician and Basque languages were prohibited, excluded or simply forgotten.

Plaza Urrutia in Grand Junction, Colorado. One of the many Basque Pilota courts in the American West. Many Basques were exiled, escaped or simply decided to leave the Basque Country during the Francoist dictatorship (1936-1975) due to the economic depression and the political situation. Source: Center for Basque Studies archive.

The modern French state, created as a "unitary and indivisible" political entity after the revolution of 1789, adopted a series of proscriptive measures against the Basque language. French officials never passed any laws "forbidding" or "condemning" the use of the Basque language after 1794. They simply excluded any language but French. By contrast, the Spanish state, created after the First (1833-1839) and Second (1872-1876) Carlist Wars, approved a long list of prohibitions on the Basque language.

The weakening of the Basque language, which had started in 1839 and gathered speed after 1876, the year in which the Basque territories were definitively subsumed within the Spanish state, dramatically accelerated after the coup d'état in 1936. New regulations drastically reduced the number of books published in Basque. At the same time, the number of Basque speakers decreased remarkably during the thirty-nine years of dictatorship.

General Severiano Martínez Anido, the strongly reactionary minister of the interior,[170] was well-known for his brutality.[171] While head of the Home Office, an average of fifteen political murders occurred every week in Barcelona under his orders.[172] In 1938, the General issued orders intended to end the use of the Basque language in the Basque Country.

---

[170] Literally, *Ministro de Orden Público*, minister of public order.

[171] He defined his antiterrorist policy as follows: *I settled social conflicts Barcelona without making use of the Police and the Civil Guard. What I did was to lift the spirit of the citizenship, by vanishing cowardice, and recommending to the free workers that for every one that fell ten labor unionists should die.* Zamora, July 17, 1927.

[172] Woodcock George, *Anarchism. A History of the Libertarian Ideas and Movements*, Broadview Press, Peterborough, Ontario, 2004. P. 317.

[221]

The Basque Country, a nation politically divided into two states

Xabier Irujo. Among the papers of Senator Len Jordan there is a note on the Basques that reads as follows:

> *In the shadows of the Pyrenees mountains, between France and Spain, there lives a small group of people known as the Basques. Though they are politically divided into French and Spanish Basques, they are neither French nor Spanish. They all share common racial qualities, a common language, and a common culture. They lived in this region since a time long before either France or Spain became a political entity. There are multitude of ancient legends and modern theories to explain the origin of these people, but all that can be said with certainty is that neither the Basques themselves nor anybody else knows exactly where they came from.*[173]

Generalissimo Franco died on 20 November 1975 consequently closing one of the worst and bloodiest periods of the history of the Basque Country, the 39-years-long Francoist dictatorship (1936-1975). The death of the dictator opened an interesting chapter of the history of the Basque nation. What do you remember of that post-Francoist period?

Pete Cenarrusa. Senator Len Jordan was a good friend of mine. The dictator had died but, de facto, the Spanish state continued being a military dictatorship until 1978. According to Franco's will, King Juan Carlos Borbón became head of the state and Carlos Arias Navarro continued in his duty as head of the Spanish government. Under the circumstances and basically due to the international pressure, Arias Navarro (Franco's political heir) was forced to introduce the first reforms in the system after almost forty years of political immobility. However, the new government

---

[173]   Len Jordan Collection, Boise State University Library, Special Collections, MSS 6, Box 186, Folder 28.

tried to stop by any means any move toward democracy, opposing, among many other things, the legalization of political parties, specially the Basque nationalist ones. His refusal to give an answer to the demands of the Basque political groups, led to a series of pro-amnesty and pro-democracy demonstrations after which he had to resign and, in July 1976 he was substituted by Adolfo Suárez at the head of the Spanish government.

Although Suárez was a member of the *Cortes*, the consultative parliament under the dictators' rule, and also secretary general of the official party of the dictatorship, he was a democrat. But he had a great challenge to face. The Spanish state was still a dictatorial regime, so he himself was representing a government that had gained power by virtue of a coup d'état against a democratically instituted Republic and that had won a war in coalition with the Nazi Germany and the Fascist Italy. I felt at that time that, unlike Arias Navarro, Suárez did want to institute a move toward democracy but I also felt that the idea these people had of democracy differed much from our idea of democracy, freedom and liberties.

XI. Are you referring to the American idea of democracy?

PC. Right. By 1976 the United States had had two centuries of democracy. Since the Spanish state was first created after the Second Carlist War in 1876, it had only known five years of democracy during the short Republican period (1931-1936). Accepting that our system may have the imperfections due to any human creation, it is clear that the members of a Francoist government did not have the political formation and could not share the democratic principles that are substantial to our systems.

XI. An entire generation of Spaniards had been educated in the principles of the dictatorship so we may say that Franco died in 1975, but not completely.

PC. Moreover, I may say that he is still alive in the minds of many Spaniards. The idea of a central homogeneous state, the idea of a single culture, the denial of dialogue as a means to achieve political goals and the National-Catholic notion that the unity of the Spanish state is something sacred, beyond human rights, and that therefore Basque or Catalan political nationalisms are some kind of sin, is indeed still alive, and to some extent still ruling Spanish politics today.

For instance, Antonio M. Rouco Varela, Archbishop of Madrid and Cardinal of the Catholic Church, wrote a book in 2006 entitled *Spain and the Catholic Church* in which he defends the idea that the unity of Spain is a pre-positive law, prior to the constitution, even above the will of the people. According to Cardinal Rouco Varela, Spain was generated as a human community since time immemorial and therefore it is not acceptable from a Christian point of view for this social, cultural and political unit to be broken. On the contrary, every Christian, *by virtue of Christian love*, has the duty to promote and consolidate the unity of the Spanish state. From this point of view, the unity of the state is a question of Christian charity, a great blessing not to be missed.

Well, it is obvious that this way of understanding religion and politics (National-Catholicism) is far from the Jeffersonian concept of democracy. And we must take into account that Cardinal Rouco Varela is currently the head of the Spanish Catholic Church, President of the Spanish Episcopal Conference (CEE, Conferencia Episcopal Española), in other words, he represents a major school of thought of the Spanish Church.

XI. So, in view of the events of 1976 your feeling was that the transition from the dictatorial regime into a democratic system was going to be highly conditioned by the ideological circumstances of the Spanish political class integrating the *Cortes*.

PC. Yes. There was a certain threat of a coup d'état such as the one that occurred a few years later headed by the Lieutenant Colonel of the Guardia Civil Antonio Tejero on February 23, 1981. On that occasion two hundred members of the paramilitary Guardia Civil stormed the Spanish Parliament, firing automatic weapons and took about 350 MPs hostage for about twenty four hours. I remember that day very well. I read in the newspapers that a Madrid radio broadcast said the council of state had been told "Tejero will not obey any orders other than those of the King or Lt. General Jaime Milans del Bosch," commander of the Valencia region who had declared the state of emergency in Valencia and moved army combat cars, mobile antiaircraft and troop carriers into the center of the city. According to the reports, Tejero telephoned Milans del Bosch immediately after the seizure of the parliament building and said, "My general, no news. All is in order, all is in order." Then he shouted "Long live Spain!" and hung up.[174] The military coup occurred against a background of increasing political instability mainly caused by the debate regarding the political rights of the Basques.

Coup d'état. Antonio Tejero at the Spanish parliament on February 23, 1981. Source: Anasagasti archive.

XI. The question that Suárez had to face was then how to make the transition into democracy while avoiding a discussion on the Spanish monarchy (model of state) or on right for self-determination of the nations within the Spanish state (unity of the state).

PC. Exactly. And it is certainly difficult to take steps in politics in a democratic way by avoiding debate and parliamentary discussion.

---

[174] Wheeler, Fenton, "Spanish Parliament Seized," *Boston Globe*, Boston, Tuesday, February 24, 1981.

XI. What would have been from your point of view the most appropriate procedure to switch from the Franco regime to a democratic system?

PC. If we take a look at our own history, Benjamin Franklin first proposed the celebration of a continental congress in 1773. The First Continental Congress convened in Philadelphia's Carpenters Hall on 5 September 1774 and the Second Continental Congress met from 10 May 1775 until the ratification of the Articles of Confederation on 1 March 1781.

The adoption of the Constitution of the United States took four basic stages:

1. On 21 February 1787, the Congress called a Convention of state delegates at Philadelphia for the purpose of revising the Articles of Confederation.
2. The Constitutional Convention began deliberations on 25 May and the constitution was drafted and adopted by the Constitutional Convention on September 17.
3. After General George Washington's defeat of Lord Cornwallis at Yorktown on 19 October 1781, and the end of the American Revolutionary War, the Constituion was ratified by conventions in each of the states of the Union in the name of the people of the United States;
4. Finally, elections had to be held in accordance to the constitution. The Electoral College elected George Washington unanimously as the first President of the United States in 1789.

XI. The Spanish transition was not carried out in the manner you have described. Basically, it took seven steps:

1. An ad hoc committee was appointed directly by the head of the already totalitarian government with the mission of drafting a law (the Law of Political Reformation) that was going to be the legal framework of the future constitution. That is, the Law of Political Reformation (LPR) was conceived as a law superior to the constitution itself for the Spanish constitution had to adapt the principles included in it. This was extremely unusual for it is a

[227]

commonly accepted political principle that where a constitutional document exists it represents a form of law superior to all other laws in the state;

2. The ad hoc committee drafted the LPR according to which the Spanish state had to be a democratic monarchy. This way the government avoided the referendum (on monarchy or republic);

3. The LPR was then passed by referendum. The citizenship could then elect if they wanted to vote that law in (yes to the LPR) or return to dictatorship (no to the LPR) which, in essence, constitutes political blackmail;

4. Only then elections were called and the elected representatives constituted the Spanish Constitutional Convention;

5. However, in order to avoid uninvited debates, the drafting of the constitution was reserved for an ad hoc committee formed by MPs representing the main Spanish political forces but with no Basque nationalist presence. The constitution was drafted, as said, according to the political framework established by the LPR;

6. The constitution was passed by referendum and, finally,

7. Elections were held.

PC. Right.

XI. The first step taken by the government headed by Suárez was to adopt the Law of Political Reformation on November 18, 1976. As said, the law was conceived as a political framework (more of a guideline or a recommendation) for the future democratically established parliament in charge of writing the first Spanish democratic Constitution. In other words, the members of the parliament and the drafters of the Spanish Constitution would have to accept the limits imposed by the LPR that the future Spanish state had to be a democratic monarchy under King Juan Carlos Borbón according to the following three political principles:

1. Democracy based on the following principles:
    *   Supremacy of law as expression of the sovereign will of the people.
    *   Inviolability of the fundamental rights of individuals.

[228]

- The power to draw up and approve laws resides in the parliament.
2. The Parliament would be bicameral, composed of a congress of deputies (350 seats) and senate (270) elected for a term of four years.
3. The new state would be a parliamentarian system, by virtue of which the Congress would elect the head of the government.

In addition, as ruled by the LPR, the constitutional reform initiative would be in the first instance in the hands of the government and in the second instance the congress would have the right (and the duty) of ratifying the decision of the executive branch. A constitutional amendment would require approval by an absolute majority of the members of congress and the senate.

The LPR was ratified by referendum a month later, on December 15, 1976.

From left to right, Admiral Luis Carrero Blanco, vice-president of the Spanish Council from 1967 to 1973; General Franco, the dictator; Torcuato Fernández-Miranda, Director-General of University Education in the 1950s, Secretary General of the National Movement from 1969 to 1974, and tutor for the political education of Prince Juan Carlos Borbón; prince Juan Carlos Borbón, King of the Spanish state from 1975. Source: Anasagasti archive.

PC. Such a law was certainly hard to understand. The LPR was designed by Suárez together with the King in order to guarantee that the following democratic regime was going to be a Monarchy and not a Republic. It should be borne in mind that the Spanish state prior to the dictatorship of Generalissimo Franco was a Republic in 1936, established and supported by popular will, that Franco dissolved with the aid of Hitler and Mussolini. By the LPR, the courts complied with the decision of Generalissimo Franco, one of the principal architects of the destruction of the Republic, that the future Spanish state would be a monarchy and his personal decision that at his death Juan Carlos Borbón would become head of state.

The LPR was put above the system itself, indeed, the LPR was beyond the will of the people in charge of drafting the future constitution for the drafters had to accept the three basic principles included in it. From my point of view, the will of the citizenry was not respected and the LPR violated the democratic principle of popular sovereignty, by accepting the decisions of the executive of a dictatorial regime, on something as basic to a democratic system as the form the state would take: the future Spanish state would be a monarchy. Our core political value is *representative democracy*, that is, the idea that citizens have a duty to aid the state by freely drafting laws at parliament or assembly and they must resist corruption of the system, especially by means of monarchism and aristocracy. Moreover, the referendum on the LPR was passed only a month after this law was adopted, giving absolutely no time to anyone to discuss or to debate its merits or lack thereof.

XI. The next step was to call for democratic elections and to organize the first democratic parliament in charge of drafting the constitution. General elections were held on June 15, 1977 with 78 percent participation. The Union for Democratic Center (Unión de Centro Democrático, UCD), the centrist party led by Adolfo Suárez, prevailed in Spain. UCD got 34.6 percent of the votes and 166 seats at the new Spanish Congress. The Spanish Worker's Socialist Party (Partido Socialista Obrero Español, PSOE) became the second strongest group with 29.3 percent of the votes and 118 seats. In the Basque Country the Basque Nationalist Party (Euzko Alderdi Jeltzalea – Partido Nacionalista Vasco, EAJ-PNV) became the strongest party and got 1.7 percent of the votes of the Spanish state as a whole, resulting eight seats at the Spanish Congress.

The Congress voted for Suárez as the new president of the government and so the new democratic executive was formed. But the Congress was facing a big issue, there was not a constitution and, consequently, the institutions of the state were still the ones of the former dictatorial regime, including the army and the police, strongly against any change to democracy. The next step was to create a Committee within the new Congress in charge of drafting the Constitution. In order to avoid the presence of Basque nationalists on the Committee, known as Ponencia Constitucional (Constitutional Committee), the Spanish Congress accorded that the minimum requirement to have a presence at the Committee was to have at least 2.5 percent of the votes. Consequently, the Basque Nationalist Party would not have a seat at the Ponencia Constitucional. In the end only five political parties had a seat at the Ponencial Constitucional, namely, UCD (three representatives), PSOE (one representative), Spanish Communist Party (Partido Comunista, PC) one representative, Democratic Pact for Catalonia (Pacte Democràtic per Catalunya, PDC) one representative, and, finally, the right winged Popular Alliance (Alianza Popular, AP) one seat.

After the constitution was drafted, it was adopted by the Congress and passed in referendum on 6 December 1978. The referendum was held with 67.1 percent participation. The constitution was endorsed by 87.87 percent of the votes (58.97 percent of the census) vs. 7.83 percent (5.25 percent of the census) who said "no." The constitution came into force on 29 December 1978 after being sanctioned by the King (December 27). The Spanish state was now a kingdom, a parliamentary monarchy.

PC. I remember that the eight representatives of the Basque Nationalist Party abandoned the Congress when the vote for the constitution took place in protest of the lack of democratic character in the process. In the referendum on the constitution citizenship could not but stand for the constitution drafted by the Ponencia Constitucional (that made of the Spanish state a constitutional monarchy) or vote against it, which meant a de facto return to dictatorship. As you have pointed out, from this point of view the referendum was political blackmail.

[231]

XI. This is why the Basque Nationalist Party called for abstention in the Basque Country.

Arantzazu Ametzaga, member of the Basque Nationalist Party (EAJ-PNV), in a speech calling for abstention at the constitutional referendum in 1978. The flier reads: "The rights of the Basque nation are not present in the constitution. Consequently, the Basque people will not vote in the referendum [for the Spanish Constitution]." Source: Irujo Ametzaga archive.

As a consequence, abstention reached 55.35 percent in the Basque Country, in other words, only 44.65 percent of the Basques voted at the Spanish constitutional referendum. 69.12 percent of voters (30.86 percent of the census) voted "yes" to the constitution and 23.54 percent of voters (10.5 percent of the census) said "no" to the constitution in Araba, Bizkaia and Gipuzkoa. In Navarre, 50.38 percent voted "yes" to the constitution and 11.29 percent "no"; the abstention reached 33.42 percent of the votes in Navarre. And, consequently, with regard to the Basque Country, the Spanish constitution failed to win the majority support of the people.

The Basque Country, a nation politically divided into two states

	Yes %	No %	Abstention
Araba	42,33%	11,38%	52,09%
Bizkaia	30,93%	9,41%	64,85%
Gipuzkoa	27,75%	12,95%	69,51%
Navarre	50,38%	11,29%	33,42%

Results of the referendum on the Spanish Constitution in the Basque Country on December 6, 1978.

According to the Spanish Constitution the King (hereditary and non elected political title) is the head of state and the president (or prime minister) is the head of government. As in most European countries, a parliamentary system rules in the Spanish state where the president is not elected directly by the people but by the members of the parliament (MPs). In other words, in the context of general elections, people vote for political parties and consequently each political party gains a number of MPs or seats at parliament. This is the product of a voting system known as proportional representation. Then, the MPs elect the president by majority of votes within the parliament. In a parliamentary system, the government is an executive committee appointed or commissioned by the parliament. If a political party gains majority, the government may be composed of one single party, however, a common solution is to seek absolute majority (parliamentary stability) through multi-party coalitions or arrangements. Since the members of the cabinet are appointed by the president, a certain political party may agree with another or several other political parties on the distribution of the members of the executive branch according to their political strength or number of elected representatives at parliament. As a consequence, the resulting government may be composed by MPs from different political parties. In other cases, different political parties may agree on a political arrangement according to which a political party or a group of parties may support the candidate of another political party in exchange of certain political demands but without having a representative in the mono-color executive branch (the government or the cabinet).

Meeting of EAJ-PNV in commemoration of Sabino Arana, founder of the Basque Nationalist Party. Bilbao, November 25, 1977. Source: Anasagasti archive.

According to the LPR the Spanish parliament is a bicameral legislature. The Congress (Congreso) has 350 members and the Senate (Senado) has 264 members. Congressmen and senators are elected at General Elections for four-year terms from the autonomous communities according to their population. Apart from general elections (for the Spanish parliament and government), the Spanish citizens also vote at municipal elections (for the city councils), autonomic elections (for the regional parliaments and governments), European elections (for the European parliament).

PC. The president is thus both the chief executive and the chief legislator.

XI. Yes. And that may become problematic under certain circumstances. In 2000 the Popular Party (PP) gained 10,321,178 votes, and got 183 seats at Congress (52.28 percent). The Spanish Workers' Socialist Party (PSOE), with 7.918.752 votes, had 125 seats (35.72 percent) and, other ten political forces had 42 seats (12 percent). The result was that José María Aznar was elected president with absolute majority and, as a consequence, the leader of the main political party of the state (PP) became, at the same time, the head of government and leader of the parliament: too much power in the hands of a single person. Under such circumstances the principle of separation of executive and legislative powers is debased.

PC. It may be considered a dictatorship within democracy if we consider that according to the principle of party obedience (*obediencia de partido*) the MPs are expected to vote according to the guidelines established by the leader.

XI. Yes, at this point the Spanish parliamentary system differs from the American one at a very critical point. While within the U.S. houses certain Democratic or Republican representatives may on occasion support initiatives of the opposing party, in the Spanish parliament the result of the voting is always known due to the fact that all MPs of each political force are almost always going to vote in agreement to their leaders. In some cases, political parties may even force their MPs to resign for having voted against the party's instructions.

PC. But, although the Spanish constitution came into force in December 1978, the whole issue of the political rights of the Basque nation remained unsolved. According to the Preliminary Title, Section 2 of the new Spanish Constitution the Spanish state was considered an indissoluble nation but recognized some historical rights to Basques, Catalans and Galicians:

> *The Constitution is based on the indissoluble unity of the Spanish Nation, the common and indivisible homeland of all Spaniards; it recognizes and guarantees the right to self-government of the nationalities and regions of which it is composed and the solidarity among them all.*

In May 1977 six different Basque political parties signed an Agreement on Political Autonomy prior to the general elections on June 15, 1977, whereby they undertook to promote, support and approve the drafting of a statute of autonomy for the Basque Country as a whole. And soon after, on June 19, 1977, the Assembly of Basque Parliamentarians was formed under the tree of Gernika, including all the deputies and senators elected in Araba,

[235]

Bizkaia, Gipuzkoa but only three of the nine Navarrese members of the parliament. You know of course that one of them, Manuel Irujo, was elected president of the Assembly.

XI. Certainly.

PC. However, by then the decision of separating the four Basque states into two different autonomous states was adopted. In the future Araba, Bizkaia and Gipuzkoa would be part of the Basque Autonomous Community (BAC) and Navarre would become the Chartered Community of Navarre (CCN). This way the southern Basque Country or Hegoalde was divided into two different autonomous states.

XI. Yes. On 19 December 1977, the Parliamentary Assembly unanimously approved the draft decree for a transitional pre-autonomous status for the Basque Country. Immediately afterward, in a sort of race against the clock, the central government drafted the Royal Decree 1/1978, on January 4, approving pre-autonomy for Araba, Bizkaia and Gipuzkoa and following the adoption of that decree the Basque Parliamentary Assembly created the Basque General Council, a sort of Basque pre-executive branch.

The following approval of the statute for the Basque Autonomous Community took place in three steps:

1. From November 20, 1978 to December 24, 1978 (one month): preparation of the draft statute.
2. From July 2, 1979 to July 18, 1979 (two weeks): discussion, negotiation and approval of draft statutes at the congress and senate of the Spanish state.
3. From October 5, 1979, to October 25, 1979, (three weeks): election and subsequent referendum on the statute of the Basque Country.

On October 25, 1979 the referendum to ratify the statutes of autonomy of the Basque Country and Catalonia took place. In Catalonia (with the participation of 59.70 percent of the census) the statute was approved by the 88.14 percent of the votes. In Araba, Bizkaia and Gipuzkoa (participation of 59.77 percent of the census) the Basque statute was approved by 90.29 percent of the votes.

A multitude of demonstrations took place in the 1970s and the 1980s. Under the motto "Peace and freedom for the Basque Country" the demonstration pictured here was called in Bilbao in February 1981 after the killing of Joseba Arregi at the Spanish police headquarters. Also in February, ETA kidnapped and executed Engineer José María Ryan and Lieutenant Colonel Antonio Tejero stormed into Congress. Source: Anasagasti archive.

Three years later, on June 30, 1982, the statute of autonomy of the Chartered Community of Navarre known as *Ley orgánica de reintegración y amejoramiento del régimen foral de Navarra* (LORAFNA) was passed.

Basque flag in the city hall of South San Francisco during the celebration of a Basque festival in 2007. Source: Irujo Ametzaga archive.

The resulting Spanish state was thus divided into seventeen autonomous asymmetric communities and two autonomous cities. The basic institutional law (the constitution) of the autonomous community is the Statute of Autonomy. The government of every autonomous community comprises a Parliament (legislative assembly) whose members are elected by universal suffrage (proportional representation), a Government (executive), headed by a President (known as Lehendakari in the BAC), elected by the autonomous Parliament (and nominated by the King acting as head of state).

However, as already mentioned, the Spanish state is asymmetric, meaning that the Basque Autonomous Communities have more powers than other autonomous communities of the state. For instance, the three Basque territories at the BAC have their own government known as Aldundia (or Diputación in

Spanish). Araba, Bizkaia and Gipuzkoa also have territorial parliaments called Biltzar Nagusiak (Juntas Generales in Spanish). The autonomous communities have authority over: schools, universities, health, social services, culture, urban and rural development and, in the Basque territories, also policing, tax collection and their own civil code. The Basque autonomies also have two official languages, Basque and Spanish.

Also, judiciary power was never passed to the autonomous communities and therefore the Spanish state cannot be considered a federal state.

PC. The resulting political formula of the transition into democracy of the Spanish state was considered a maximum for many Spaniards, while it was considered the minimum for most Basque nationalists who still prefer independence.

In the words of Charles Herrington, Office of the Governor of Idaho, in a Briefing Memorandum sent to Cecil D. Andrus, Governor of the State of Idaho, on April 23, 1992, Basques are like Americans, they prefer self-government:

> *Share Regional Pride.*
> *U.S. states, under the U.S. federal system, are self-governing. Most local issues in the U.S. are handled by state and local governments. State and local governments are responsible for educating and protecting their citizens and building and maintaining transportation systems. State laws are passed by state legislatures. State and local taxes raise the money needed to build schools and roads. Police are hired and fired by state and local jurisdictions. We understand why the Basque Country insists on having a parliament, fiscal autonomy, and control over the police.*[175]

---

[175] Briefing Memorandum by Charles Herrington, Office of the Governor of Idaho, to Cecil D. Andrus, Governor of the State of Idaho, Boise, April 23, 1992. In, Boise State University Library, Cecil D. Andrus Collection, MSS 141, Box 374, Fol. 6.

Map of the nations in Europe. The Basque Country, Euskal Herria, is between Occitania, Cantabria, Castile and Aragon. If we compare the official map of Europe with the map of the European nations, we see that the second one has many more "colors" on it. Indeed, there are more than sixty nations within the European Union and only twenty seven states; there are more than 230 European languages and only 23 official communitarian (official) languages. Source: Organization for the European Minorities.

XI. And, what about the Northern Basque Country?

PC. At the other side of the Pyrenees, the République française does not recognize any historical or politic rights to the Basques. Defined as an indivisible nation, the French constitution came into effect on September 28, 1958. Unlike the Spanish state, the French state is a republic and therefore the President, elected for a five-year term by direct universal suffrage is the head of state (head of the executive in relation to foreign affairs and defense). The Prime Minister (head of government) and the members of the Cabinet are appointed by the President. The legislature is composed by a bicameral chamber, the Assemblée Nationale and the Sénat with no territorial representation. The National Assembly (Assemblée Nationale) has 577 members, elected for five-year terms from single-member constituencies. The Senate (Sénat) has 321 members. Of these, 309 are elected for nine-year terms by electoral colleges in each Département. Twelve members are appointed to represent French citizens abroad, but none represent the Basques, Catalans, Britons or Occitans as such.

The République française is a model of extreme centralization. The territory divided into symmetric Regions and Départements and the Basque historical territories of Lapurdi, Behe Nafarroa and Zuberoa are diluted into a wider political unit called Pyrénées-Atlantiques. The one hundred departments are grouped into twenty-two metropolitan and four overseas regions. All regions have identical legal status and they are subdivided into 342 Arrondissements (districts). Each Département is administered by a Conseil Général (an assembly elected for six years by universal suffrage) and an executive (since 1982 the President of the council). The Préfet (prefect), appointed by the president of the state, is the representative of the central government. The prefect is assisted by one or more sub-prefects based in districts of each Département divided as we have mentioned into one to seven Arrondissements. The capital city of an arrondissement is called the Sous-préfecture (subprefecture). The public official in charge is called the Sous-préfet (sub-prefect). The Départements are further divided into communes governed by municipal councils.

The Basque language does not have any official status and hence its situation is critical.

XI. The political situation of the Basque nation, divided into two states and three different administrations, does not solve the Basque political conflict. We may leave the discussion of the main aspects of the Basque political conflict for a further session.

On political violence

Xabier Irujo. As it happened in Ireland, in Tyrol, in Scotland, in Flanders, in Brittany, in Corsica or in almost any part of Europe – (and probably of the world) in which a nation or a group has been politically oppressed for a long period of time, violence has arisen. And we are still suffering violence in the Basque Country.

Pete Cenarrusa. Right, violence begets violence. *Euskadi ta Askatasuna* (ETA, Basque Country and Freedom) is a product of the Francoist repression, the effect of a dictatorship that lasted for too long. In order to understand ETA we have to understand the economic, political, social and cultural circumstances which caused its creation.

A group called EKIN was formed in 1954 as a result of the ideological and strategic disagreements with the Basque Nationalist Party to solve the Basque conflict with better and more effective methods. That group became ETA in 1958.

I remember that here in Idaho I met certain special Basque Country patriots who attended a Basque Festival in Boise. I invited Jose Luis Alvarez Enparantza (Txillardegi), Mikel Munioa, Jokin Echevarria and Angel Arregi to fly with me in my airplane to Hailey-Sun Valley to see the country and visit my parents, who were retired and living in Hailey. The distance to Hailey is about 150 miles, flying directly over the mountains. At about one-half the distance to our destination, the air got very rough, because of high winds over the mountains. The aircraft jumped up and down, which caused some concern with my passengers. I said to Txillardegi, "this aircraft is like a wild horse, it's bucking like a bronco." Everybody tightened their seat belts, but since I had flown in much rougher air before, I began to laugh to ease their concern and let them know we were perfectly safe. My father met us at the airport - we had a nice visit with my parents and they got a good view of Sun Valley on our way back to Boise. With my passengers tightly belted in we rode the "wild horse" safely back to Boise.

As Txillardegi told me during that trip, in its first fighting phase, ETA did not intend to kill anyone and had a program to claim national rights as well as a minimum demise in regard to the problem of the Basque workers. ETA was not established nor designed to initiate any violence. In fact, the first fourteen years of existence of ETA (1954-1968) there was not a single fatality associated with ETA's activities. The first action of importance consisted of the sabotage to a railroad convoy.

However, in the fifth assembly (1966-67) ETA took a dramatic course, in which the organization decided to create a military front. According to a Communiqué to the American People and the Basque Workers of America by ETA, dated in Boise (Idaho) on June 3, 1972, the goals of ETA were basically three, and violence was not going to be any longer avoided as a means to obtain such goals:

1. *Realize that the Basque workers (factories, farmers and fishermen) are the backbone of our struggle.*
2. *Demonstrate the National and Social contradiction.*
3. *Build one Basque culture as a whole liberation of the Basque country.*

Strategically the assembly decided the formation of four fronts (worker, cultural, political and military).[176]

XI. On 7 June 1968 a young Basque by the name of Xabier Etxebarrieta was shot dead. Two months later, on August 2, Melitón Manzanas, police chief of the Social Investigation Brigade of Donostia, was shot dead. Thereafter, the victims of ETA were predominantly members of the Spanish police forces and the military.

PC. 1968 and 1969 were very violent years in the Basque Country. 1,953 people were detained and 342 people escaped to exile. Only in 1969 the Tribunal de Orden Público imposed 223 years of prison to 93 different defendants. According to the data provided by Justo Sarria, President of Anaiak Danok, an organization created

---

[176]   Communiqué to the American People and the Basque Workers of America by ETA, Boise (Idaho), June 3, 1972. In, Boise State University Library, Pete Cenarrusa Collection, MSS 240, Box 3, Fol. 18.

in Boise to help people who had suffered some type of violence, five people were killed by the Spanish police in the Basque Country in 1969 and four more in 1970. Apart from that, many other people were imprisoned or tortured:

General Statistics of the Repression in the Basque Country in 1969[177]

Individuals detained	1,953
Individuals imprisoned	862
Individuals tortured	510
Individuals in exile	342
Years of prison imposed by Tribunal	786
Fines imposed (in pesetas)	6,650,000

General Statistics of the Repression in the Basque Country in 1970

Wounded by gunshot of the police	16
Death penalties	9
Individuals detained	831
Individuals imprisoned	396
Individuals tortured	257
Individuals exiled	128
Individuals receiving judgment	416
Individuals declared rebels	149
Years of prison imposed by Tribunal	1,104
Fines imposed (in pesetas)	25,930,000
Confiscations	63
Confiscation of vehicles	37
Closing of businesses of Basque nationalists	143

XI. On September 19, 1970, during the opening session of the world pilota championship celebrated in Donostia, Joseba Elosegi, a former Basque soldier who witnessed the bombing of Gernika, burned himself in front of Franco to protest about the political

---

[177]   Letter by Justo Sarria to Senator Frank Church, Boise, November 19, 1975. In, Boise State University Library, Frank Church Collection, MSS 56, Box 43, Fol. 14.

[245]

situation in the Basque Country. Elosegi survived but suffered severe wounds provoked by the self-inflicted fire.

PC. At the end of October 1970 a court martial against sixteen Basque nationalists took place at Burgos, Spain. It was very soon known as "The Burgos Trials." Thirty-two men and women were to be tried by a Spanish court martial, including sixteen who escaped to other countries in absentia. Among the defendants there were three women and two Roman Catholic priests, however, one of the women who had been in custody for a year and a half could not be in court as a result of tortures inflicted during interrogation. According to the indictments, they were all accused of collaborating in the assassination of Melitón Manzanas.

XI. It was a show of power of the regime.

PC. Yes, a Kangaroo Court. The defense lawyers were not given the right to defend their clients; it was not a legal decision but a strictly political verdict. The chief prosecutor, Carlos Granados Mezquita, in summing up his appeal for death sentences, urged on December 22 that those advocating separatism "be sent to a volcanic and desert Island where, like slavering dogs, they would be obliged to scratch their nourishment from the soil with their fingernails." It was not a metaphor. The Spanish regime had sent prisoners to concentration camps in Fuerteventura and other volcanic and desert islands in the past.

XI. The prosecutor had demanded death sentences against six of the sixteen defendants, three of them being given double sentences, and faced death by garroting if found guilty on charges of military rebellion or terrorism. The prosecutor was demanding jail sentences totaling more than 700 years for the rest with prison terms ranging from six to seventy years. However, the trial was expected to last only a few hours.

As pointed out by Frank Church, the Spanish military authorities ordered that the court martial should be held in secret (closed session) because - they said - the Concordat between Franco's government and the Vatican required that in any judicial proceedings in which priests were involved, the trial should be conducted in this manner. But the Holy See demanded the Spanish government that the court martial in this case be held in public.[178] But it was not.

Many democracies all over the world protested the manner in which the trial at Burgos was conducted.

PC. Yes. I personally got on the phone with our State Department and was told by the assistant secretary of state in charge of European Affairs that the United States could not get involved in the affairs of another nation. I told the secretary that the U.S. should go along with the many other nations who were pleading with Franco to spare the lives of the six accused Basques.

I contacted the governors of Idaho, Nevada and Oregon and the Congressional Delegation of Idaho (senators Church and Jordan and representatives McClure and Hansen) for help. I also thought it was a good idea to send a letter over governor Samuelson's signature to U.S. Secretary of State William P. Rogers in an attempt to get state department support for clemency. And Samuelson wrote to Franco in these terms:

November 27, 1970
His Excellency Generalismo Francisco Franco
Palacio de El Pardo
Madrid, Spain

On behalf of the citizens of Idaho and especially of its large Basque community, whose ancestors pioneered our state, I respectfully request, Your Excellency, that the forthcoming trial to be held at Burgos against sixteen Basque Nationalists, in which six death sentences and seven hundred and fifty years are demanded by the prosecution, be transferred from a military to a civil court.

I am not asking clemency for the prisoners but only that they have the right of due process of law in a free and open court so that their guilt can be removed or established.

---

[178]   Communication to Frank Church, Paris, October 9, 1970. In, Boise State University Library, Frank Church Collection, MSS 56, Box 43, Fol. 15.

Reports of alleged confessions extracted by torture have produced strong reaction in our state among whose citizens are relatives of some of the prisoners and therefore I associate myself with the pleas addressed to you from many quarters including the Vatican and the Basque Bishops of Bilbao and San Sebastian in their joint pastoral letter of last Sunday in order that the due process be observed in this case before an open civil court.

Respectfully,
Don Samuelson
Governor of Idaho

I approached people in McClure's office and suggested the attached text be sent to Secretary Rogers. On December 4, 1970, Frank Church sent a telegram to Secretary of State William P. Rogers urging him to use his good and influential offices to encourage the Spanish government to deal compassionately with the Basques on trial in Burgos.

Since this was world-wide news, the wire services UPI and AP called me and asked me if the Basques of Idaho were going to protest. By that evening with the aid of the wire services, the local radio and TV, around two hundred people gathered at the Basque Center on Grove Street and protested the actions by the Burgos Military Court and asked Governor Samuelson to send a cablegram in protest, which he did. A well known Basque was to go on national television that night to protest, but President Nixon's administration put a stop to it.

I was on the telephone again with the State Department to pass on the information from Boise, but the Department stayed with their original position.

XI. The trial began on December 3, 1970 and on December 1 ETA kidnapped Eugen Beihl, honorary West German consul in Donostia. On December 3 the state of exception was declared in Gipuzkoa for three months. In addition to the considerable powers the police already enjoyed, they were empowered to arrest persons at will and detain or to deport them indefinitely and, to carry out searches anywhere anytime. On December 7 the trial was stopped under the excuse of the court's judge advocate Captain Antonio Troncoso's illness. It ended on the 9th when Mario Onaindia cried out, "Gora Euskadi Askatuta" [Long life to the Basque Country] and other defendants started to sing patriotic songs.

PC. Yes. I was very well acquainted with the uncle of one of the accused who lived in Boise. From him I learned that his nephew became so exasperated that he arose as did Patrick Henry when he said, "give me liberty or give me death," and cried out, "Gora Euskadi Askatuta" (long live the Basque Country). The Civil Guard immediately charged to subdue the proceedings. The court proceedings came to a halt.

The defense lawyers and the defendants used every occasion to put the police on trial by describing tortures they said were inflicted on the Basque prisoners, and by using the trial as a forum for the Basque cause against the centralist powers of the Franco regime. Bilbao, Donostia and other Basque centers went into demonstrations and strikes. The issue has flared elsewhere as other opposition groups, underground or in the open, took advantage of the Basque rebellion to stage sit-ins, strikes and demonstrations in Madrid, Barcelona, Granada and other cities.

XI. Eugen Beihl was freed by ETA on Christmas Eve but on December 28 the commander of the Burgos military region, Lieutenant General Tomás García Rebull, ratified the sentences. Mario Onandia was one of three who were sentenced to two death sentences each.

PC. Yes, we all were very concerned but, amazingly, the morning that the six prisoners were to be executed by a firing squad, the State Department telephoned me in my office and told me that they were pleased to report that the Department had been on the phone all morning with Madrid and that Franco had given the order to halt the executions and instead to sentence the accused to terms of thirty years each. On December 30 Franco commuted the death sentences to thirty years in prison. Frank Church announced the commutation of the death sentences to the U.S. Senate:

> *Mr. President, I have just received word that Generalissimo Franco of Spain has commuted the death sentences imposed on six young Basque separatists. This is good news, indeed. I hope that this liberal gesture coming as it does during this holiday season, is only the first*

step toward humanizing the Spanish Government's treatment of the two and a half million Basques residing within the country. Yesterday I announced to the Senate that I would submit today a sense of the Senate resolution concerning the continued injustice, intolerance, and repression suffered by the Basque community.[179]

And the resolution read as follows:

Resolution Concerning the Continued Injustice, Intolerance, and Repression Suffered by the Basque Community of Spain

Resolved, that the Senate hereby expresses its gravest concern over the continued injustice, intolerance and repression to which the Basque community in Spain has been subjected by the Government of that nation. This has been manifested most recently in Burgos where Basque civilians were tried by a military tribunal, which sentenced six Basques to death and nine others to a total of 351 years in prison. The harsh punishment dealt out, together with the method of the trial, has aroused sympathy and protest throughout the world.

Therefore, the Senate respectfully urges the President (1) to convey to the Government of Spain, with whom the United States has friendly and normal relations, the gravest concern of the Senate over this latest example or injustice and repression toward a minority; (2) to urge the Government of Spain to set aside the harsh sentences imposed by the military tribunal, and to furnish the accused with a new trial in an open civil court, and (3) to urge the Spanish Government to provide full and equitable treatment to all Basque citizens residing within the country[180].

In 1972 the Idaho Legislature sent a petition to Congress (Senate Joint Memorial No. 115 of April 6, 1972) asking the government of Spain to extend human rights principles to all

---

[179]   Church, Frank, "The Basque Community of Spain." In, *Congressional Records. Proceedings and Debates of the 91ˢᵗ Congress, Second Session*, Vol. 116, Nº 210, Washington, Wednesday, December 30, 1970. Pp. 21548-21554.

[180]   *Congressional Records. Proceedings and Debates of the 91st Congress, Second Session*, Vol. 116, Nº 210, Washington, Wednesday, December 30, 1970. P. 21548.

Basques and Spaniards and to allow amnesty for those imprisoned or exiled for political activities. John Peavey who served in the Idaho Senate from 1969 to 1976 and from 1978 to 1994, introduced the Memorial in the Idaho Senate and Frank Church included the petition in the Congressional Records. This first Memorial of 1972 tried to foster dialogue between Basque and Spanish to work out a compromise to stop terrorism and solve the Basque political conflict.

XI. However, the Burgos Trials made ETA much stronger.

PC. Yes. Only three years after the Burgos Trials ETA was strong enough as to kill Admiral Luis Carrero Blanco, on 20 December 1973. He was vice-president of the Spanish state council from 1967 and on 8 June 1973 he was named by Franco prime minister of the regime and, thus, his successor. It has been calculated that ETA members used up to 200 lbs of explosives in a tunnel excavated under the street. When Carrero Blanco was crossing over the duct, the blast propelled his Dodge 3700 over a six-story building, and it landed on a second floor balcony on the other side. I remember that I read that the violence of the explosion had made of Carrero Blanco "the first Spanish astronaut."

XI. In 1973 five people were sentenced to death by the regime's martial courts. And in this occasion five of them were shot to death.

PC. Yes that was a very violent period of time. I remember the case of Jose Antonio Garmendia. The murder of the policeman Gregorio Posadas Zurrón took place on April 3, 1974 in Azpeitia. As Justo Sarria pointed out, on June 2, 1974 Juan Maria Labordeta Vergara, a militant member of ETA, declared before a police court that he knew with certainty that Javier Aya and Garmendia had conspired to murder a policeman on an anniversary date set aside in commemoration of all those of ETA who had been killed by the police. On the 5th of June, Labordeta further stated that his confession on June 2 had been induced by the use of force and torture. On June 6, Labordeta declared before a military judge that he could not recall the statement made to the police on the 2nd of June.

[251]

On August 28, 1974 Garmendia was detained in Donostia in a shoot-out with the Guardia Civil and as a result of the incident he was shot in the head. However, Garmendia was interrogated after being captured, before he was taken to hospital. Later on, Garmendia had brain surgery and part of his brain was removed by Dr. Arrazola.[181] Angel Otaegi was arrested from information extracted from Garmendia by means of Sodium Penthanol. The whole process was so inhuman:

> *The process lasted exactly five hours. The accusations of the prosecutor were based always on the supposed declarations of Garmendia which was taken while he was in grave condition after he had been shot in the head. The defense --under the direction of Attorney Bandres--denied the accusations of the prosecution and presented as witnesses, Dr. Arrazola who attended to Garmendia and confirmed the deficient state of mind of the accused, and also four other persons who did not recognize Garmendia as one of the two authors of the bullets which caused the death of the police officer Gregorio Posadas. Bandres emphasized with numerous proofs of the state of unconsciousness of Garmendia at the time of questioning and pointed out that upon regaining his mental awareness, Garmendia denied the accusations. In addition, since on the day of the execution of Posadas, Garmendia was not even in Spain, the defense asked for pardon for his client, Garmendia. Angel Otaegi was asked whether or not he knew Garmendia before he was arrested---he declared that he saw Garmendia for the first time in jail, and denied all accusations which were made against him by the prosecutor. Legally, things are clear; but, in spite of all this, the Military Prosecutor asked for the death penalty for both. The last doubts have disappeared; in spite of that which is apparent, the Tribunal nor the judge decided anything; all was contrived beforehand.[182]*

XI. Just seven months before Franco died the Spanish regime decreed once again the state of exception in the Basque Country in April 1975, leading to thousands of arrests and extensive use of

---

[181]   Letter by Justo Sarria, President of Anaiak Danok, to Frank Church, Senator of Idaho, Boise, August 27, 1975. In, In, Boise State University Library, Pete Cenarrusa Collection, MSS 240, Box 14, Fol. 9.
[182]   Ibid.

torture attested to by Amnesty International. As part of this campaign by the Spanish authorities, two young ETA activists—Juan Paredes Manot ("Txiki") and Angel Otaegi—together with three GRAPO (First of October Antifascist Resistance Groups) members, were executed in September.[183]

PC. According to the data provided by Justo Sarria, four people were killed by the police in 1974:

General Statistics of the Repression in 1974[184]

Wounded by gunfire	30
Individuals detained	1,116
Individuals imprisoned	315
Individuals receiving judgment (military and civil)	105
Years of prison imposed	786
Confiscations	38
Fines imposed (in pesetas)	32,162,559
Individuals in exile or escaped	320

On October 6, 1975, at Congress, Senator Frank Church spoke in the following terms:

Mr. President, from around the world voices of protest have been heard this week over the execution by the Spanish Government of five men accused of terrorist activities. I add my voice to their number. But I would go much further. It is important for us to realize that these executions are not an isolated incident but only the most obvious act in a pattern of repression against the Basque people particularly. Behind the grim headlines lies the reality of years of persecution of the Basque minority and in recent step up of terror and torture by the Government. I call the Senate attention to a report made public at the United Nations Wednesday by Amnesty International, a worldwide

---

183   Letamendia, Francisco, "ETA: Political Violence, Its Historical Evolution, and Conflict Resolution," Ibarra, Pedro and Xabier Irujo, *Basque Political Systems*, Center for Basque Studies, University of Nevada, Reno, 2011, p. 191.

184   Letter by Justo Sarria to Senator Frank Church, Boise, November 19, 1975. In, Boise State University Library, Frank Church Collection, MSS 56, Box 43, Fol. 14.

human rights movement, independent of any Government, political faction or religious creed. Amnesty International works for the release of men and women imprisoned anywhere for their beliefs, color, ethnic origin, or religion, provided they have neither used nor advocated for violence. In July of this year Amnesty International sent a mission to Spain to investigate allegations of torture reported to have occurred during a 3-month period in two of the four Basque provinces. Despite the refusal by the Spanish Government to allow access to some of the prisoners who allegedly suffered the worst torture, the mission obtained conclusive evidence of the following:

First. Massive illegal detentions took place in the two provinces, probably of several thousand persons;

Second. The mission received convincing evidence that torture systematically used against a minimum of 250 Basque detainees. One victim told of 30 sessions of torture in 21 days of continuous imprisonment; and,

Third. Three major police forces·participated in the torture of the Basques and regularly circumvented Spanish law by transferring prisoners from one province to another, holding them without cause and re-arresting prisoners.

The report is tough reading -a description of cruel tortures intended not only to extract confessions and information from their victims but to intimidate the Basque people in every possible way. But it is important that we understand the lengths to which the Spanish Government will go to suppress the Basques. In the light of this evidence, we in the United States should do more than protest, we should seek to avoid complicity in the suppression of the Basques through supporting of the Franco Government. Our Government should do everything possible to separate himself from these acts of the Franco regime. In the months and perhaps years ahead, when the Generalissimo seeks to maintain the present form of Government even after his passing, let us hope we are sufficiently wise to avoid either the illusion or the fact of support for the conduct I have just discussed. The execution which took place last week may be only the beginning. Fifteen more Basques are expected try go on trial and at least three are expected to receive death sentences. While we may wish to respect the internal laws of other countries in criminal matters, when human rights are so flagrantly abused as in Franco Spain it is time to speak out. The Spanish Government should recognize that the international outcry expresses the universal desire for civil liberties and human dignity. When citizens of a country such as Spain are prevented through fear from expressing themselves in an open society, it is time for us to speak on behalf.[185]

XI. ETA became especially active after the dictator's death (November 20, 1975).

Period	Franco 1968-1975	UCD 1976-1981	PSOE 1982-1995	PP 1996-2004	PSOE 2004-2011	Total
Victims (deaths)	45	291	411	70	12	829
Kidnaps	7	40	40	3	8	98

Total number of mortal victims of ETA (1968-2011) according to the data provided by the Spanish ministry of the interior. 486 (59 percent) were members of the Spanish police or military forces and 343 (41 percent) were civilians.

ETA caused approximately a death a week between 1978 and 1980. The number of blasts and victims increased at the end of the 1970s (one death every four days in 1980). From 1981 to 1987 ETA killed 231 people, one person every eleven days or an average of 33 persons per year. But 1987 was a turning point. On June 19, 1987, after placing an explosive device in Hipercor, a department store in Barcelona, members of ETA warned in advance, but for some reason the call was unattended and the attack caused 21 deaths and 35 other people were seriously wounded, all of them civilians.

In 1983 the Spanish paramilitary unit known as the Antiterrorist Liberation Groups (GAL, *Grupos Antiterroristas de Liberación*) was created by officials of the Spanish government and members of the Spanish police department to fight ETA. The

---

[185] Church, Frank, "Spanish Government Threat to The Basque People." In, *Congressional Records. Proceedings and Debates of the 94ʰ Congress, Second Session*, Vol. 122, N° 89, Washington, Monday, October 6, 1975. Pp. 17562-17566.

GAL caused nearly twenty-seven deaths between 1983 and 1987. This episode is known to be part of the "dirty war" against ETA. On January 12, 1988, six months after the attack against Hipercor and the disbanding of the GAL, all the political parties represented in the Basque parliament except Herri Batasuna signed the Agreement on Normalization and Pacification of the Basque Country known as the Ajuria Enea Pact. On January 8, 1989, ETA declared a two weeks truce and begun meetings with members of the Spanish government in Algiers that lasted until April 6, 1989.

After 1991 ETA started to lose popular support and began a process of decline that has lasted for almost ten years now.

There have been sixteen ceasefires and processes of dialogue between ETA and the Spanish government from 1981 to 2007. Since 1984, when the Vice-president Alfonso Guerra expressed that negotiating with ETA was possible, a sector of the PSOE has historically defended political negotiation with ETA. Spanish President Felipe González denied the possibility of any negotiation on political terms with ETA, but he defended "to maintain the dialogue" with the purpose of obtaining the disappearance of the organization. However, the Popular Party, after the failure of the negotiations in 1998, has always stigmatized processes of dialogue defending the complete defeat of ETA through police action. For instance, when ETA announced a truce in 2006, Mariano Rajoy, leader of the Popular Party, stated that it was not possible to negotiate politically or to pay a political price to a terrorist organization because in that case terrorism could become a political instrument and terrorists would win the battle.

Against this point of view, all Basque nationalist political parties and organizations call for an immediate cease of hostilities and the organization of a round of conversations. In this sense, the pastoral letter written by the Basque bishops of Bilbao, Donostia and Gasteiz in December 1987 on the political negotiation as a way of reaching peace, raised blisters among the Catholic bishops of the state since, as we have mentioned, some members of the upper echelons of the Spanish Catholic Church defend the thesis that the unity of the Spanish state is a question of divine origin.

On September 1998 ETA announced a unilateral truce. It lasted for a year and a half. On March 22, 2006, ETA announced a second unilateral truce that lasted scarcely a year. After these two failures, violence still had a place in Basque politics. Before the last call for a cesaefire, ETA killed for the last time on March 16, 2010.

PC. The Idaho legislature has, on three occasions, in 1972, 2002 and 2006, dealt with the problem of peace in the Basque Country and we have consequently passed three Memorials asking for the cessation of all violence in the Basque Country. In the first draft of the Memorial HJM 14 of 2002, we asked that all violence cease. The reason for this wording was that there is not only violence perpetrated by ETA in the Basque Country but also by the Spanish police and the paramilitary groups such as the GAL. We found no difference between these two types of violence (terrorism or state terrorism).

But then the Spanish Ministry of the Exterior ordered the Spanish ambassador to Washington to "disarm" the initiative. Almost immediately Javier Rupérez, Spanish Ambassador to the United States pulled out all stops to kill the Memorial objecting that the resolution was a "gratuitously unfriendly gesture." I was in contact with the Chair of the State Affairs Committee Sen. Sheila Sorensen and she consented to meet in my office (Sec. of State of Idaho) with Representative Dave Bieter, Lobbyist Roy Eiguren and Ben Ysursa (Chief Deputy Sec. of State).

The Ambassador had protested to Senator Sorensen that ETA was not mentioned in the Memorial and that ETA should be mentioned emphatically as terrorists. Aznar's message to Rupérez was clear: the Memorial had to emphasize that ETA was a Spanish home affair, and that ETA and Al-Qaeda were part of the same problem, that blasts by ETA and the September 11 attacks were part of the same worldwide phenomenon. I do not have to clarify how insane these suggestions were to all of us. Moreover, it was quite impolite to assert that we, Idahoan congressmen, were *people who are not fully informed.* Or to read that *the good intentions and will of the vast majority of the members of the legislature was grotesquely manipulated.* In the end, it was quite offensive to be told what our House should pass or not, and why.

Summarizing, no one at Madrid was going to tell us Idahoans what we should or should not say, proclaim and adopt at Congress and so the Idaho's legislature passed unanimously. The Joint Memorial 14 was passed in March 2002, calling for an immediate cessation of all violence occurring in and near the

Basque homeland, and asking a peace process to be immediately undertaken between the governments of Spain and France, the Basque Autonomous Government, and other groups committed to peace.

As I expressed in the statement of purposes, through this joint memorial the Idaho legislature stands with the Basques and all Idahoans in opposing all violence in the Basque Country and calling for the immediate convocation of a process to bring about a lasting peace. In view of the events that have taken place in the Basque Country since 1968 it seems clear to us that the definitive end of ETA requires a political process of dialogue, in other words, a political conflict requires political measures to be solved. Even in the improbable case that ETA was finally defeated by police action or in the event that ETA decided unilaterally to disband, the Basque political conflict would remain unsolved.

As far as I have seen in the last forty years in which I have been involved in Basque politics, there are three significant political obstacles for reaching an agreement on the side of the Spanish authorities who have the key for the solution:

1. The successive Spanish governments have been highly reluctant to open a process for political dialogue and when they have done it, they have not been able to reach an agreement and materialize it in a covenant. It is a principle of conflict resolution that both parties have to feel that they are strong enough and at the same time weak enough to aspire for and desire a peaceful cessation of the conflict. In 1988, during the negotiations that took place in Algiers that lasted until April 1989, ETA felt stronger, too powerful for surrendering their guns. Today the Spanish government feels that ETA may be defeated without the need for a process of political dialogue.

2. Non-Spanish rulers seem to accept that ETA is the product of an unsolved political conflict and not its origin. ETA was created in 1958 and, as we have already discussed, the Basque political conflict goes back at least 222 years. In the course of a conversation with the Spanish ambassador to the United States Javier Rupérez in Boise, he told me that there is no such thing as a Basque political conflict. I remember discussing this point with Reverend

Alec Reid, well known for his role in the Northern Ireland peace process, who had come to Boise State University to give a talk on the Basque conflict. During our conversation we noticed that unlike in the United Kingdom, among French or Spanish politicians it was common to deny the existence of political problems dealing with the Basques, Catalans or Bretons. However, denying the existence of the problem itself, is hardly going to solve it.

3. Strong Spanish and French territorial nationalism. The Spanish National-Catholicism is a deeply rooted political phenomenon, a strong feeling of national identity by virtue of which the unity of the state prevails over human rights or even economic welfare for it is understood and even lived as a divine design, preceding human politics. The new shape of the National-Catholicism is the Patriotic-Constitutionalism adopted by the 14th Congress of the Popular Party in January 2002. According to this doctrine, *we believe that Spain is a great country, a nation formed through the centuries that in its long history has accumulated a certain place in the world. A nation with a plural identity which is not ethnic but political, historical and cultural; derivative of its contribution to the culture and history of the world from its own constitutive plurality and its historical roots in two worlds, Europe and the Americas.*[186] The idea that Spain is the product of a timeless divine design and that therefore to break the unity of the state has to be considered a sin against Christianity is still alive, and obviously makes dialogue even more difficult.

XI. After a series of conversations, the Basque Nationalist party (EAJ-PNV), Eusko Alkartasuna (EA) and ETA signed an agreement intended to promote a ceasefire and an ensuing process of political negotiation in August 1998:

Euskadi Ta Askatasuna, Eusko Alkartasuna and Euzko Alderdi Jeltzalea-Basque Nationalist Party, taking into account the situation in the Basque Country, and seeking to start a new era in

---

[186]   *El patriotismo constitucional. Ponencia en el XIV Congreso del Partido Popular.*

[259]

relation to the conflict with Spain, have signed this Framework Agreement:

1. *The signatories commit to take steps to achieve an effective and sovereign institutional structure [an independent state] including the territories of Araba, Bizkaia, Gipuzkoa, Lapurdi, Navarre and Zuberoa. The signatories will bring together all political and social forces that share this goal, the process of creating this central institutional structure, advocating and encouraging any initiative that seeks to overcome the current institutional and inter-state partition [of the Basque Country].*

2. *The signatories, together with the forces in support [of the restitution] of the political rights of the Basques and the political construction of the Basque Country, based on basic and minimum needs, commit to bind agreements pursuant to long-term and short-term strategies, and to promote dynamics [in that sense].*

3. *EAJ-PNV and EA commit to leave their agreements with the parties aimed at the destruction of the Basque Country and the construction of Spain (PP and PSOE).*

4. *Euskadi ta Askatasuna (ETA), meanwhile, commits to start an indefinite ceasefire. Although a general and undefined ceasefire, ETA keeps the right of maintaining the supply works and the right to defend itself in the course of a hypothetical fighting.*

Subsequent to the August agreement, twenty-three Basque nationalist parties, labor unions, and grassroots groups, and United Left (IU) signed the Lizarra-Garazi Declaration on 12 September 1998.

In the view of the factors that had propitiated the Good Friday Agreement on 10 April 1998 in Northern Ireland, the signatories of the Lizarra-Garazi declaration accepted the political origins and political nature of the Basque conflict and, as a result, that its resolution also should be achieved through a process of political negotiation. The signatories also understood that, if there was no process of negotiation, the armed conflict in the Basque Country could be endlessly prolonged. Having this into account, the parties agreed that a process of deliberation, dialogue and negotiation should be fostered, always attempting not to exclude anyone from these talks. In sum, all the signatories agreed that a political solution can only be achieved through a process of open dialogue and negotiations, without excluding any of the implicated parties and with the participation of all Basque society. The goal was thus to generate an atmosphere of relaxation that would help building a process intended to bring a solution to the Basque political conflict with the inclusion of all existing political and social traditions as a way to reduce resistance from those who previously promoted exclusive dialogue or politics of isolation.

Participants emphasized that exclusion was one of the main causes of political violence and that, as a consequence, inclusiveness had to become the key to peace. Thus, a durable peace process would need to involve international mediators that would play a significant role by supporting and directly taking part in the resolution of the conflict. In this sense, support given by different institutions of the European Union, United Nations or foreign administrations was to be encouraged.

Taking into account that territoriality and political sovereignty constituted two of the fundamental questions to be unraveled, the recognition of the right of the citizens of the Basque Country to self-determination was to bring depth to the content of democracy (creating new formulas of sovereignty such as the concept of free-association) as well as the methods for implementing these rights (giving the citizens the word or the celebration of referenda).

The process was to be propitiated in two phases. A preliminary phase (an open and public national debate) with no preconditions prior to multilateral talks and, a subsequent resolution phase with the willingness to compromise when dealing with the causes of the conflict that would be carried out under a condition of absence of all expressions of violence (permanent ceasefire). There should not be limited agendas and negotiations had to consider and give response to all the questions which constituted the core of the conflict. In other words, the parties involved in the process agreed that negotiations for resolution should bear no specific clauses, should respect the plurality of opinions and should give Basque citizens the last word to decide their own future, and make the final decision.

The pact encouraged ETA to call for a truce and, four days later, on 16 September, ETA announced an indefinite and unconditional ceasefire that was to begin two days later. The Spanish Government showed willingness to initiate talks and in May 1999 a meeting was held in Switzerland which, although the efforts, happened to be unsuccessful. In November 1999 ETA announced the end of the truce and on 21 January 2000 killed Lt. Col. Pedro Antonio Blanco. All signatories of the Lizarra-Garazi Agreement condemned the attack except Herri Batasuna, which caused the cancelation of the agreement and the end of the process.

The Lizarra-Garazi Agreement generated great expectations. The Basque nationalist forces had formed a new coalition government under President Juan Jose Ibarretxe and the signatories of the Agreement got to involve a large sector of the Basque society in the peace process. The declaration of ETA to continue the armed struggle and the subsequent assassination caused disappointment in the Basque Country and Herri Batasuna achieved the worst electoral results ever in May 2001, losing more than 80,000 votes and seven seats, half of its political representation in the Basque Autonomous Community. A group of members of Herri Batasuna split and created a new political party called Aralar, which rejected political violence.

PC. Political misunderstanding, lack of responsibility and the absence of political leaders with vision frustrated one of the greatest opportunities for peace of the last decades in the Basque Country.

XI. Right. Never before neither after had the Basques lived with such intensity and hope a peace process. We had to wait for six years to be able to generate a new social and political scenario for dialogue. Six long and difficult years. From 2000 on, especially after the September 11 attacks in 2001, to 2004, the Popular Party's administration led by President José María Aznar reactivated the "judicial war" against ETA by amending the Criminal Code and introducing tough anti-terror legislation under the cover of the global War on Terror that would possibilitate the banning of political parties, the closing of newspapers and the indiscriminate arrest of thousands of people without warrants and reducing the limits of judicial intervention to the absolute minimum.

After years of uncertainty, on March 11, 2004, at 7:37 am, the simultaneous explosion of ten bombs distributed in four suburban trains in Madrid killed 191 people and injured a further 1,800. It was the most serious terrorist attack ever carried out in the Spanish state. On March 14, general elections were due to be held, therefore the political implications of the attack led to a serious crisis in the two days following the incident. The PP's political evaluation of the events was the following: If the attack had been carried out by an Islamic group, this would damage the PP for its insistence on taking part in the War in Iraq against the wishes of a majority of the Spanish people; if, on the other hand, the attack had been perpetrated by ETA, this would benefit the PP for a number of reasons (it had led the fight against ETA, if it was ETA, then this would justify the PP's reforms of the Penal Code already undertaken, as well as facilitating further reform and curbs on individual rights, and all this would benefit the PP electorally); consequently, and until at least one day after holding the elections, the Spanish government attempted to maintain the theory that ETA had been behind the attacks.

As a result, at 1 o'clock on March 11, the day of the attacks, Aznar called a press conference at which he claimed ETA was responsible. Half an hour later, Minister for the Interior Ángel Acebes corroborated the notion that ETA was behind the attacks and that it had achieved its objective. At the same time, instructions were sent out to the Spanish delegate at the United Nations to seek a resolution condemning ETA. This all took place despite the fact that two hours previously, at 10:30 am, Arnaldo Otegi, the principal spokesperson for Batasuna had declared before the media that ETA was not responsible for the bombings. At 2:30 pm, Aznar reiterated, without mentioning the word "ETA," that the Basque organization had provoked the attacks. By that time, approximately 2:15–3:30 pm, the police had finished inspecting a suspicious van found near the scene of the events in which detonators habitually used by Islamic groups had been found, together with a copy of the Koran and a cassette tape with voices speaking in Arabic on it. Despite all this, at 5:30 pm, Ana Palacios, the foreign minister, dispatched a telegram to all Spanish embassies so that they would refute any doubts as to the perpetrator of the

[263]

attacks and state that ETA alone committed the atrocity. This message was also extended to the media, in a clear violation of freedom of information.

At 8:20 pm, Acebes announced publicly that the detonators had been found but still maintained that ETA was responsible. At 9:30 pm, the Islamic group Abu Hafs al Misri claimed responsibility for the attacks in a British newspaper. In spite of this, however, at 11:30 am on March 12, Aznar, appearing once more before the media, underscored the notion that ETA was the principal suspect and the "most logical option," and at 4:04 pm, he considered the claim by Abu Hafs al Misri to be "dubious." Once again, at 4 pm, Acebes stated that ETA was the main suspect. Meanwhile, a demonstration to be held through the provincial capitals of the state was called for that same evening under the banner, "With the Victims, With the Constitution, For the Defeat of Terrorism" (in a clear reference to the defense of the constitution as opposed to any Basque right of self-determination). Despite this, and pointing out their personal disagreement with the slogan, all Basque political parties except Batasuna joined the demonstration. I myself was there. In Madrid, two million people joined the demonstration, led by the Spanish prince, the president and ministers and, the leaders of the remaining political parties. And, while we all were marching, at 6:30 pm, ETA declared publicly that it had nothing to do with the attacks and condemned them.

Despite the claims of Abu Hafs al Misri and ETA's denial of any involvement, on March 13, a day of electoral reflection prior to holding the vote the next day (when all campaigning must legally cease), at 2:30 pm, Acebes insisted on the fact that ETA had taken part in the attacks for the fourth time in front of the media.

Although opinion polls prior to the attacks had predicted victory for the PP, on March 14, the PSOE won the elections, gaining 164 seats in Congress as opposed to the PP's 148. That same day, the PSOE (with 61 seats) claimed a clear victory over the PP (with 37) in autonomous elections in Andalusia. Catalan nationalist force Esquerra Republicana de Catalunya (ERC) achieved a dramatic victory in Catalunya. ERC's vote jumped by 335 percent and got more than 457,000 new votes, totaling 652.196, increasing its representation from one single depute to eight representatives in Madrid. The Basque Country happened to be the only community in the Spanish state where nor the PSOE neither the PP won the elections. Basque nationalist party EA and Catalan nationalist party ERC requested from the socialist government an amendment to the constitution regarding the Political statute of the Community of the Basque Country. In Navarre, Basque nationalist forces EA, EAJ-PNV and Aralar created a coalition called Nafarroari Bai (Na-Bai, "Yes to Navarre") that got historical results: 18 percent of the votes at the CCN and a representative in Madrid.

Amnesty International, while denouncing the bombings, also criticized the attempts to manipulate information by the PP government. And on May 20, a full session of Congress passed unanimously a bill to create a commission to investigate the events of March 11 and clarify government actions; a commission whose hardly clarifying findings (for lack of evidence) were published on July 7, 2005. On 27 April 2004, the new Spanish president, José Luis Rodríguez Zapatero (PSOE), appeared before Congress to explain his government's decision to withdraw troops from Iraq.

PC. Two years later, on 22 March 2006, ETA announced a permanent ceasefire to "promote a democratic process in the Basque Country" starting on Friday, 24 March 2006.

XI. Yes. Following the announcement of a ceasefire, Spanish President Jose Luis Rodríguez Zapatero (PSOE) and opposition leader Mariano Rajoy (PP) gathered at the Moncloa Palace in Madrid on March 28, and a few days later, Rodríguez Zapatero met with the Basque President Juan Jose Ibarretxe. The truce had some international impact and Pope Benedict XVI appealed for prayers for peace in the Basque Country and called on Spaniards to work for peace. On April 6 Rodríguez Zapatero met with UN Secretary General Kofi Annan.

PC. On April 12, ETA issued a communiqué conditioning the achievement of peace to the previous achievements of political goals such as self-determination or territorial demands. We knew that at that point the peace process required further international support and we also knew that the Spanish Socialist government led by Jose Luis Rodríguez Zapatero was far more predisposed than the previous Aznar administration to initiate talks. Thus, on

April 12 the members of the Second Regular Session of the Fifty-eighth Idaho Legislature, the House of Representatives and the Senate extended for third time in history its encouragement and support to the Basque, French and Spanish governments in their ongoing efforts to establish a process to bring a lasting peace, as well as to enhance an appropriate degree of governmental autonomy for the Basque people.

XI. Yes, and following the support of Idaho's Legislature, President Ibarretxe met with Arnaldo Otegi, leader of the outlawed party Batasuna in the palace of Ajuria Enea on April 19. A week later Ibarretxe presented the Plan for Peace and Coexistence aiming to settle a durable peace process in the Basque Country that was agreed between EAJ-PNV, EA and IU. The Plan anticipated a solidarity law for terrorism victims by recognizing their status and highlighted the necessity to prevent torture in Spanish and French prisons and the importance of bringing Basque prisoners back to Basque prisons. The plan was to be presented and discussed in the Basque Parliament in order to include suggestions from the Constitutionalist political parties (PSOE and PP). The plan was based on five central points: defense and promotion of human rights, solidarity with victims, recovery of historic memory, reward victims of the dictatorship (1936-1975) and, preventing torture and other expressions of state terrorism. In Ibarretxe's words the plan was the contribution of the Basque Government to the peace process, always trying to recognize and alleviate social and personal suffering and preventing new violations of human rights, for no peace process can be built on oblivion.

On 21 May President Rodríguez Zapatero declared that the Spanish executive had concluded the verification of the ceasefire and announced the forthcoming launch of talks with ETA and, finally, on 29 June the Spanish executive announced the start of a complex negotiation process with ETA, but underlined that the Spanish government would not pay a political price and would not repeal Organic Law 6/2002, of 27 June that had allowed the banning of Batasuna and other Basque political parties. Delegates of the Spanish government, ETA and neutral international mediators met in Oslo, Geneva and other cities. William Douglass, former member of the Center for Basque Studies of the University of Nevada, Reno, was among these international mediators.

PC. However, by mid August things started to deteriorate. On August 18 ETA claimed in a public statement that the peace process was in crisis, and blamed it on EAJ-PNV and PSOE. The Ermua Forum (Foro de Ermua) and Dignity and Justice (Dignidad y Justicia), two activist associations opposing peace talks with ETA, asked the Supreme Court of the Basque Country to act against President Juan Jose Ibarretxe and members of Batasuna for meeting on April 19 and, on June 10 the High Court of Justice of the Basque Country agreed to hear the cause. On October 23, ETA members stole more than 350 guns from a warehouse in Vauvert (France) and, a day later, thirty-eight members of Batasuna were indicted for alleged links with ETA.

XI. With the intent of reactivating the process, the European Parliament passed a motion supporting the peace process on 25 October. The document was carefully written, on terms acceptable to the Spanish executive and to the Spanish political opposition led by the Popular Party:

The European Parliament, (…)

1. *Endorses the statement by the European Council of 23 and 24 March 2006 under the Austrian Presidency that 'the European Council welcomed the reports of the President of the Spanish Government on the announcement of a permanent ceasefire made by the terrorist group ETA';*

2. *Supports the statement by the President of the European Parliament, Josep Borrell, of 22 March 2006, to the effect that 'this is good news for Spanish society and the whole of Europe, showing that terrorism can be fought by the force of democracy, that this is a time to show calmness and caution; a time to remember the many victims of terrorism; and a time for hope, for the unity of all the political forces of democracy';*

3. *Calls on the Council and Commission to take appropriate action;*

4. *Condemns violence as it is morally unacceptable and absolutely incompatible with democracy;*

5. *Expresses its solidarity with the victims of terrorism;*

6. *Supports the fight against terrorism and the peace initiative in the Basque Country undertaken by the Spanish democratic institutions within the framework of their exclusive competences;*
7. *Instructs its President to forward this resolution to the Council, the Commission and the governments of the Member States.*[187]

However, under the pressure of the Spanish Popular Party, the European People's Party voted against the motion.

On November 4, ETA warned the government in a statement that the truce would be broken if the Spanish executive did not meet their commitments and, two days later Rodríguez Zapatero said that they had not made any concessions to ETA. On December 5 Batasuna declared that under the given conditions the peace process could not continue and on 22 December declared that there had been no significant change to solve the crisis that the process had faced for the last six months.

Finally, on 30 December 2006, ETA detonated a truck bomb loaded with more than 1,000 lbs of explosives in the Madrid Barajas Airport, resulting in two deaths and a five-story parking structure demolished. Few days later ETA declared that it had not been their intention to kill anyone, but the Spanish executive declared that the peace process had been ruined and, on 5 June 2007 ETA announced the end of the permanent ceasefire.

PC. The Ermua Forum (Foro de Ermua) and Dignity and Justice (Dignidad y Justicia) asked in November 2006 the Supreme Court of the Basque Country to act against President Juan Jose Ibarretxe (member of the EAJ-PNV), Patxi Lopez and Adolfo Ares (members of the PSOE) for meeting with Batasuna leaders. Subsequently, in October 2007 the Supreme Court opened proceedings against Ibarretxe, Lopez and Ares for meeting publicly with former leaders of the outlawed Batasuna during ETA's ceasefire in 2006.

XI. Right. Investigating magistrate Roberto Saiz said that the facts may constitute "a crime of disobedience," as defined in article 556 of the Spanish Criminal Code, and that the meetings occurred

---

[187]   *European Parliament resolution on the peace process in Spain*, October 17, 2006. B6-0527/2006. See also, PE 379.689/rev.v01-00.

despite Batasuna was outlawed and dissolved by the Spanish Supreme Court in March 2003. Saiz also accused Batasuna leaders Arnaldo Otegi, Pernando Barrena, Juan José Petrikorena, Rufi Etxebarria and Olatz Peterson. Meetings between Lehendakari Ibarretxe and members of Batasuna took place on 19 April 2006 and 22 January 2007, while the socialist leaders met with the leaders of the nationalist left on 6 July 2006. Only after two years, the Supreme Court agreed on 13 January 2010 upholding the decision of the Court of Justice of the Basque Country to file the case against Ibarretxe, understanding that the facts do not constitute a crime.[188]

Madrid Barajas Airport after the attack of 30 December 2006. Source: Enrique Dans.

PC. We are living now another period of hope.

XI. Right. On June 8, 2007, two days after ETA announced publicly the rupture of the truce in force since March 24, 2006, Arnaldo Otegi, leader of Batasuna, was arrested and in October 4,

---

[188]   "Spain court orders trial over ETA talks," *Associated Press*, October 30, 2007.

2007, the Spanish police arrested twenty-three other members of the Ezker Abertzalea (Nationalist Left, the name under which Batasuna is known after being outlawed in 2003). In October 2009, leaders of the Ezker Abertzalea publicly announced their intention to support a strategy based exclusively on "the use of purely political and peaceful ways" in the struggle for independence. But within days, on 13 October 2009, Judge Baltasar Garzon ordered the arrest of all the top leaders of the Ezker Abertzalea, Arnaldo Otegi, Rafa Díez, Rufi Etxeberria, Sonia Jacinto, Arkaitz Rodriguez and five other leaders under the charge of attempting to reconstruct Batasuna at ETA's orders.

Year	Blasts	Deaths	Wounded	Kidnappings
2006	1	2	11	1
2007	11	2	8	4
2008	31	4	74	3
2009	14	3	70	0
2010	1	1	0	0
2011	0	0	0	0
Last six years	58	12	163	8

Attacks by ETA in the last six years.

PC. The actions of the crusading Spanish "superjudges" Garzón and Del Olmo have never helped any peace process nor have they improved the Basque political conflict from any perspective. In fact in May 2010, the Supreme Judicial Council (the highest body of the Spanish judiciary) suspended Judge Baltasar Garzón for alleged malfeasance in three separate cases, one in connection with the financing of courses organized at New York University.

XI. But despite the setbacks, in November 2009 the Ezker Abertzalea issued the Altsasu Declaration calling for a new peace process. Also, the first contacts between Lokarri, the Basque Citizen Network for Agreement and Consultation, and South African lawyer Brian Currin who was instrumental in the establishment of the Truth and Reconciliation Commission, date back to 2009. At the same time, Basque Friendship Group (BFG), the group supporting a peace process for the Basques in the

European Parliament, viewed the Altsasu Declaration with great optimism and this fact led to a new declaration by the Ezker Abertzalea on February 16, 2010, included in the document Zutik Euskal Herria (Basque Country Stand Up).

By virtue of the Altsasu Declaration, the Ezker Abertzalea committed itself to support "a democratic process under political and democratic means" and calls for the political collaboration of all the political forces seeking independence in the Basque Country. ETA, publicly welcomed the reflection contained in the Altsasu Declaration and Zutik Euskal Herria.

Following these events, on February 14, 2010 the International Contact Group (ICG) promoted by Brian Currin to expedite, facilitate and enable the achievement of political normalization in the Basque Country was presented officially in Bilbao. The members of the ICG are Silvia Casale, Pierre Hazan, Raymond Kendall, Nuala O'Loan and Alberto Spektorowski. And on March 29, 2010, Currin made public at the European Parliament, the Brussels Declaration of the ICG, a petition endorsed by four Nobel laureates (former South African President Frederick de Klerk, Archbishop Desmond Tutu, former Irish Prime Minister John Hume and Betty Williams), the Nelson Mandela Foundation, Mary Robinson, Albert Reynolds and sixteen other persons who specialize in peace processes and conflict resolution, asked the Spanish government to respond by filing a new negotiating process in the case that the truce finally materialized.

On June 20, 2010 Eusko Alkartasuna (EA) and former members of Batasuna signed the Lortu Arte agreement, the basis for a strategic agreement between political forces seeking independence and the cessation of any kind of violence in the Basque Country. By virtue of the agreement, the signatory parties agreed to peacefully defend the independence of the Basque Country in pure political and democratic terms. And, on September 3, EA and Batasuna prepared a document that set the conditions to tackle a negotiating process under eight conditions:

1. The ceasefire must be permanent and have international verification;

2. All Basque political forces must agree to participate in the subsequent political negotiations process by accepting the six ground rules known as the George Mitchell Principles;

3. The basic civil and political rights (freedom of assembly, freedom of association, universal suffrage, freedom of expression...) should be respected;

4. Consequently, the Spanish government should repeal the Law of Political Parties under which Batasuna and other Basque political parties were outlawed;

5. All forces must accept and stick to the Universal Declaration Human Rights, the International Covenants on civil and political rights and on social, economic and cultural rights (including the right of self-determination);

6. The Spanish government should give up non-democratic prison policies such as dispersion, isolation, refusal to grant paroles and imprisonment of those who are severely ill;

7. Deletion of measures including judicial proceedings that violate basic civil and political rights and free political activity such as the closure of newspapers or the banning of political parties;

8. Work to provide reparation and reconciliation for all victims.

PC. And finally, ETA announced a unilateral ceasefire on September 5, 2010.

XI. Indeed. After ETA's announce Currin visited the Basque Country and declared that ETA should give a positive response to the Brussels Declaration for the ICG to begin its work. And on September 26, 2010 EA and Batasuna, political parties that have led the ceasefire process, signed the Gernika Agreement, endorsed by three more political forces (Aralar, Alternatiba and AB) and twenty-three social agents. The Gernika Agreement basically calls again for a unilateral, permanent and internationally verifiably ceasefire, requests that the Spanish government repeal the Law of Political Parties, end the practice of torture and terminate the current prison policy and, finally, the agreement asks for the opening of a political negotiation process based on the Mitchell Principles. The agreement literally expresses that its aim is "to seek agreements among all political cultures on the recognition of both the Basque national reality and the right to decide of the Basque peoples," and requests respect for the democratic will of the Basque people on their decision upon the legal-institutional political model and what type of relationship they will have with the French and Spanish states, without excluding independence from the negotiation.

PC. With some slight variants what the European group Friendship is asking for today is what the House of Representatives and the Senate of Idaho requested in 2006, namely, 1) to respond with responsibility to the initiative and to engage in a process leading to peace talks; 2) to request that the European states act accordingly and, more specifically that the Spanish government seize upon this goal during its forthcoming EU Presidency; 3) to adhere to the idea that the only valid solution must pass through the multilateral agreement based on dialogue and on peaceful and democratic means; 4) to release Arnaldo Otegi and other imprisoned leaders who could help in the peace process and, finally, 5) to grant the right to decide on the Basques (self-determination).

XI. And, after these first successful steps, on 12 November 2010 Brian Currin advanced in the course of a press conference in Bilbao that ETA may declare a ceasefire before Christmas and made public the mandate and role of the ICG that included:

- *To promote facilitate and enable the legalization of Abertzale Left;*
- *To encourage confidence building measures such as:*
  a) *Overcoming special measures of restrictions on political activity and,*
  b) *Adapting the penitentiary policy to the new transformed political situation;*
- *To encourage and assist the parties, for as long as required, with the preparation and development of an agenda for political dialogue;*
- *To encourage, facilitate and enable, for as long as required by the parties, all-inclusive multi-party talks and negotiations, which would be subject to the Mitchell Principles, without conditions and with no pre-determined outcome. The objective of the multi-party talks and*

negotiations would be the achievement of an all-Inclusive agreement to overcome the political conflict;

• *To mediate, if called upon by the parties, In the event of deadlocks;*
• *To generally build confidence in the minds of the public that a successful peace process is indeed possible.*[189]

In a letter to political and social representatives signed in Pretoria, on 21 March 2011, the ICG added that the group was also ready and able to share skills and expertise with the people of the Basque Country, their leaders and institutions including advocacy and lobbying, advice on national and international criminal justice, information and assistance with transitional justice and reconciliation processes, advice on rights of victims, remedies for victims and enforcement mechanisms, guidance on penitentiary reform in a post conflict environment, guidance on application of international and regional human rights treaties and conventions, advice on and assistance with prisoner release processes, guidance on ceasefire verification processes and establishment of appropriate body, if required.[190]

The general secretary of the Spanish Worker's Socialist Party (PSOE) in Araba, Txarli Prieto, disavowed Currin by pointing out that "no one has called him" and that "he is putting his foot in issues that are not of his concern."[191]

A new step was taken on December 4, 2010 when former leaders of Batasuna, EA, Aralar and EAJ-PNV, among other persons, presented in Durango a new platform under the name Movement for the Civil Rights in Euskal Herria which aims to promote the peace process and achieve the end of terrorism to move towards independence by peaceful means. The statement was read by the professor of the University of the Basque Country and Former Distinguished Scholar of the Center for Basque Studies at the University of Nevada, Reno, Pedro Ibarra, in line with the principles extracted in his book *Relational Democracy* thus urging the Basque society to take direct part in the mobilizations called under the slogan "Eskubide Guztiak denontzat" (civil rights for all).

---

[189]   http://icgbasque.org/mandate/
[190]   Ibid.
[191]   "El PSE cree que Currin 'patina' sobre un terreno que no le corresponde", Europa Press, November 13, 2010.

As Currin had predicted, on January 8, 2011 ETA announced a unilateral and internationally verifiable truce (that was made public on January 10):

With this declaration ETA, the Basque socialist revolutionary organisation for national liberation, wishes to give news of its decision to the Basque Country:

In recent months, from Brussels to Gernika, well known personalities on the world level and many Basque social and political actors, have stressed the need to bring a just and democratic solution to the centuries-old conflict.
ETA agrees. The solution will come through the democratic process with dialogue and negotiation as its tools and with its compass pointed towards the will of the Basque people.

- *The democratic process has to overcome all situations of denial and violations of rights and must respond to the key elements at the heart of the political conflict, namely territorial sovereignty and self-determination.*
- *It is the task of the Basque social and political actors to reach agreements in order to come to an agreed formulation concerning the recognition of the Basque Country and of the right to decide, ensuring that all political projects, including independence, are possible. At the end of the process, Basque citizens must have their say and a right to decide on their future without any limit or interference.*
- *All parties have to commit themselves to respect the agreements reached as well as the decision of the Basque people, and to put in place guarantees and mechanisms to this end.*

Therefore, ETA has decided to declare a permanent and general ceasefire which will be verifiable by the international community. This is ETA's firm commitment towards a process to achieve a lasting resolution and towards an end to the armed confrontation.
It is time to act with historical responsibility. ETA calls upon those governing Spain and France to end all repressive measures and to leave aside for once and for all their position of denial towards the Basque Country.

ETA will continue its indefatigable struggle and efforts to promote and to bring to a conclusion the democratic process until there is a truly democratic situation in the Basque Country.
Long live the free Basque country! Long live the Socialist Basque country!

MPs from the European Free Alliance and other parties of the European Parliament's Basque Friendship Group (BFG)[192] joined forces and held a press conference on 19 January 2011 in Strasbourg to welcome ETA's announcement of a ceasefire and to call for the EU institutions to play an active role in resolving the conflict, in the following terms:

We understand that the Abertzale Left has to be legal for a multiparty talks process to take place. We also believe that prison and security policies should be adapted to the new situation and be used as tools for the resolution of the conflict rather than for its perpetuation.
As members of the European Parliament we would like to recall the motion on the Basque issue approved by this institution in October 2006 and stress the role that in our opinion all European institutions should play. The Parliament called on the Commission to take appropriate action to promote peace in the Basque Country.
Furthermore, European Institutions should begin to act and prepare for the resolution of this conflict. The Irish case is an example of how Europe can help overcoming difficult situations, the peace program has been described as an important factor for reconciliation in Ireland, Europe has to collaborate also in the resolution of the Basque conflict.[193]

On May 4, the International Contact Group for the Basque Country (ICG) made public a press release announcing that in contact with business associations in the Basque Country the group could confirm the cessation of so called "revolutionary tax"

---

[192]   Oriol Junqueras (ERC, Catalonia), Bairbre de Brun (Sinn Fein, Ireland), François Alfonsi (PNC/Europe Ecologie), Tatjana Zdanoka (PCTVL, Latvia), Catherine Greze (Europe Ecologie).
[193]   Basque Friendship Group (BFG), "Press conference 19/01/2011 on ETA's cease-fire 10/01/2011," Strasbourg, 19 January, 2011.

as an integral part of the ceasefire. And, only a week later, on May 11, the ICG made public a statement addressed to Spanish president José Luis Rodríguez to foster negotiation: "Today, we make a plea to the Spanish President: Mr. Zapatero, do not miss this historic opportunity to help end the last violent political conflict in Europe. Do whatever you can to ensure that Sortu is given a chance to prove its commitment to peace and democracy, especially in the light of the decision by the Constitutional Court to unban Bildu; relax stringent security laws to enable an all-inclusive political environment in the Basque Country; engage with an international body to verify ETA's ceasefire and facilitate the decommissioning of arms."[194]

And, after demanding months of negotiations, Lokarri (the Basque Citizen Network for Agreement and Consultation), the ICG, the Berghof Foundation for Conflict Studies, Conciliation Resources (an international non-governmental organization working to prevent violent conflict, promote justice and build lasting peace in war torn societies), the Desmond and Leah Tutu Legacy Foundation and the Norwegian Peacebuilding Resource Centre (NOREF) held the conference in Donostia on Monday 17th October designed to promote a resolution to the Basque conflict. The meeting took place from 1:00 to 5:00 PM at the Human Rights Institute located in the Aiete Palace, summer residence of General Franco during the dictatorship.

The four-hour conference was headed by former UN General Secretary and 2001 Nobel Peace Prize Kofi Annan, along with former French Minister of the Interior and Defense and member of the Constitutional Council since 2001 Pierre Joxe, former Irish Prime Minister Patrick Bartholomew "Bertie" Ahern, former Norwegian Prime Minister Gro Harlem Brundtland and, President of Sinn Fein Gerry Adams. Former British Prime Minister Tony Blair apologized for not being able to attend the conference but Jonathan Powell, former British Cabinet Head, attended the conference in his place. Also, representatives of all Basque nationalist political forces assisted.

---

[194]   International Contact Group for the Basque Country (ICG), "President Zapatero, help to end violence now," May 11, 2011.

PC. By contrast, the Spanish socialist government and leading opposition party Partido Popular (PP, Popular Party) did not attend the one-day meeting. Moreover, in order to avoid the presence at the conference of President of the Basque Country Patxi López, who is a member of the Spanish Worker's Socialist Party (PSOE), the Basque government scheduled his visit to New York to present *Canal Vasco*, a TV channel that brings Basque-language television to the Basque community residing in the Americas, precisely on these October days. From New York, President López declared that "no conference is needed to defeat terrorism." Yolanda Barcina, president of the Chartered Community of Navarre (CCN), did not assist either. Juan Luis Sánchez de Muniain, spokesman of the Navarrese government, declared on October 18 that "the Government of Navarre has been absent from what has occurred in Donostia."[195]

XI. The conference passed the Donostia Declaration read in English by Ahern calling on ETA to definitively put down arms and to the Spanish and French governments to welcome dialogue as a means to help solve the conflict. This resolution, that may be one of the last steps for finishing an armed conflict lasting four decades, reads as follows:

> *We have come to the Basque Country today because we believe it is time to end, and it is possible to end, the last armed confrontation in Europe.*
> *We believe this can now be achieved, with the support of citizens and their political representatives, as well as the support of Europe and the wider international community. We want to state clearly that we have not come here to impose anything or claim that we have the right or the authority to tell the citizens of this country, or relevant actors and political representatives, what they should do.*
> *Rather, we have come here in good faith, with the hope of offering ideas drawn from our own experiences of resolving long conflicts that afflicted our own societies and peoples, as well as others we have helped resolve.*

---

[195] "Las víctimas escribirán el final de ETA, no los asesinos," Diario de Noticias de Navarra, Tuesday, October 18, 2011.

We know from our own experience that it is never easy to end violence and conflict and secure lasting peace. It requires courage, willingness to take risks, profound commitment, generosity and statesmanship.

Peace comes when the power of reconciliation outweighs the habits of hate; when the possibility of the present and future is infinitely greater than the bitterness of the past.

We also know from our own experience that when a genuine opportunity for peace arises it must be seized. The growing demand of the citizens of this country and their political representatives to resolve this conflict through dialogue, democracy and complete non-violence has created this opportunity.

Because of all of this, we believe it is today possible to end more than fifty years of violence and attain a just and lasting peace.

In light of this:

1. *We call upon ETA to make a public declaration of the definitive cessation of all armed action and to request talks with the governments of Spain and France to address exclusively the consequences of the conflict.*

2. *If such a declaration is made we urge the governments of Spain and France to welcome it and agree to talks exclusively to deal with the consequences of the conflict.*

3. *We urge that major steps be taken to promote reconciliation, recognize, compensate and assist all victims, recognize the harm that has been done and seek to heal personal and social wounds.*

4. *In our experience of resolving conflicts there are often other issues that, if addressed, can assist in the attainment of lasting peace. We suggest that non violent actors and political representatives meet and discuss political and other related issues, in consultation with the citizenry, that could contribute to a new era without conflict. In our experience third party observers or facilitators help such dialogue. Here, such dialogue could also be assisted by international facilitators, if that were desired by those involved.*

5. *We are willing to form a committee to follow up these recommendations.*[196]

---

196   Donostia, 17 October 2011. In, http://icgbasque.org/

PC. One day later, Jimmy Carter and George Mitchell endorsed the declaration and British newspaper *The Guardian* announced that ETA was expected to announce a definitive end within days after the peace conference.

However, most Spanish politicians reacted skeptically to the suggestion ETA would dissolve, with some angry about international peace brokers coming to discuss the end of violence in the Basque Country from abroad. "They don't have a bloody clue what country they are in or what type of conflict has gone on," declared Esteban Gonzalez Pons, former spokesman of the Popular Party (PP) and head of this party's list in Valencia, which polls put on course for a landslide victory in the Spanish general elections of November 2011.[197]

ABC, the third largest general-interest daily newspaper in the Spanish state, with circulations of over 240,000, covered the event on the first page under the headline "In the service of ETA. Mediators assume in the final communiqué of the Peace Conference-trap the roadmap proposed by the terrorist group in the Anoeta Offer."[198] And, one day later, included a new article under the headline "Carter, Blair and Mitchell also subscribe ETA's plan."[199]

XI. Right. This was one of the major problems that the peace process had to face in the days following the Conference of Donostia. As the BBC remarked, the conference was seen as a possible prelude to ETA's dissolution but neither the Spanish Government nor ETA were represented.

The Conference was held on October 17 and on November 20 the Spanish general elections were to be held. Political analysts and polls indicated that the Popular Party (PP), unreservedly opposed to any negotiation with ETA, was expected to win by a large margin. ETA's statement on ending the armed

---

[197] "San Sebastian Peace Conference could prompt ETA to make statement," *EITB*, Donostia, October 17, 2011.

[198] "Al servicio de ETA. Los mediadores asumen en el comunicado final de la Conferencia-trampa de paz la hoja de ruta propuesta por la banda terrorista en la 'oferta de Anoeta,'" *ABC*, October 18, 2011.

[199] "Carter, Blair y Mitchell también suscriben el plan de ETA," *ABC*, October 19, 2011.

struggle was expected therefore before the elections in order to allow a minimum time frame to get back on track the peace process before the PP could complicate or even block all avenues for negotiation from government.

"In the service of ETA." Headline of the Spanish newspaper ABC on October 17, 2011. In the photograph, from left to right, Jonathan Powell, Gro Harlem Brundtland, Kofi Annan, Gerry Adams and, Bertie Ahern moments before reading the Donostia Declaration.

PC. And ETA made public her Declaration of a definitive end to armed activity on October 20, three days after the Peace Conference and announced the "definitive cessation of all armed action" using the exact same words as in the Declaration of the mentioned Peace Conference. By this communiqué ETA closed a cycle of violence of forty-three years and fifty-two years of existence:

> *ETA, socialist revolutionary Basque organization of national liberation, desires through this declaration to announce its decision:*
> *ETA considers that the international conference held recently in the Euskal Herria [Basque Country] is an initiative of great political transcendence. The agreed resolution brings together the ingredients for an integrated solution to the conflict and has the support of large sectors of Basque society and of the international community.*
> *In Euskal Herria, a new political age is opening. We face a historic opportunity to obtain a just and democratic solution to the age-old political conflict.*
> *Faced with violence and repression, dialogue and agreement must characterize the new age. The recognition of Euskal Herria and respect for popular will must prevail over any imposition. This is the will of the majority of Basque citizens.*
> *The struggle of many years has created this opportunity. It has not been an easy road. The rawness of the struggle has claimed many companions forever. Others are suffering jail or exile. To these our recognition and heartfelt homage. From here on, the road will not be easy either. Facing the imposition which still remains, every step, every achievement, will be fruit of the effort and struggle of Basque citizens. Throughout the years Euskal Herria has accumulated the experience and strength necessary to tackle this road and it also has the determination to do it.*
> *It is time to look to the future with hope, it is also time to act with responsibility and valor.*
> *Because of all this, ETA has decided on the definitive cessation of its armed activity. ETA makes a call to the governments of Spain and France to open a process of direct dialogue which has as its aim the resolution of the consequences of the conflict and thus the conclusion of the armed conflict. With this historic declaration, ETA demonstrates its clear, firm and definitive purpose.*
> *ETA finally calls on Basque society to get involved in this process until peace and liberty are achieved.*
>
> *Long live the free Euskal Herria, Long live Basque socialism, no rest until independence and socialism are achived.*

On political violence

In Euskal Herria, 20 October 2011
Euskadi Ta Askatasuna[200]

XI. All Basque nationalist parties welcomed ETA's farewell to arms and, in line with the judgment and belief of the international mediators, requested from both ETA and the Spanish and French governments to foster contacts and dialogue and, to agree on the definitive dissolution of ETA on terms to be negotiated with the authorities in Madrid and Paris.

On the contrary, most of Spanish leaders expressed their satisfaction but declared that it was a victory of the Spanish democracy over terrorism achieved through law enforcement and police activity rather than through mediation and dialogue. Indeed, nor the PSOE neither the PP were thoroughly involved in the negotiations preceding ETA's announcement and appeared very critical with the mediators' efforts to bring ETA to a definitive ceasefire. The Popular Party, widely expected to win general elections on November 20, strongly opposed any negotiation process, insisting that ETA should disarm and surrender. Mariano Rajoy, president of the PP, argued that ETA's declaration was "good news because there had been no political concessions made." Moreover, if elected president of the Spanish government, Rajoy will have to face strong pressure from hard-line elements within the PP, including the families of PP politicians killed or extorted by ETA, who will only accept ETA's dissolution and total surrender. For instance, Esperanza Aguirre, president of the government of Madrid, stated that "ETA's communiqués have zero credibility" and added that "the crimes of assassins do not prescribe just because they claim that they are not going to kill anymore."

Regarding ETA's declaration, most Spanish political leaders underlined that ETA members, contrary to demands made by the Spanish government and the associations of victims of terrorism, offered no apology to the victims. In addition, ETA's spokespersons did not renounce to their political goals of independence and socialism but reasserted them in their communiqué. Finally, ETA did not declare her total dissolution

200   "Declaration of a definitive end to armed activity," *BBC News*, October 20, 2011.

and unconditional surrender, and did not give up arms. Spanish political leaders also pointed out that ETA had blocked negotiating periods and truces in the past. For instance, after calling the permanent ceasefire in March 2006 ETA resumed attacks with a shocking blast at the Madrid-Barajas airport on December 30, 2006.

We must not forget either that social and political support for home-grown violence has steadily receded in the Basque Country in the last two decades, especially after the fiasco of the Lizarra-Garazi Agreement in 1999 and, after the attacks of September 11 two years later. In 2009 the main leaders of the Ezker Abertzalea announced their intention to support a strategy based exclusively on the use of purely political and peaceful ways and, for first time, requested from ETA to halt terrorist activity and to put down the arms. Simultaneously, the police campaign against ETA and the indiscriminate application of anti-terror measures further reduced the group's operational potential. In these circumstances the Spanish and French governments and most leaders of the main Spanish and French political parties do not see any pressing need for making strategic, political or legal concessions to ETA in the course of a negotiation process.

PC. If the new Spanish government to emerge after November's general election and the French administration decide to take an uncompromising stance in the peace talks that could frustrate the peace efforts.

XI. Yes. However, Currin declared that he had confidence in the Spanish and French leaders, including Rajoy, and stated that "he is a perceptive, intelligent and responsible person. I am sure he will take the step to lead this process to its natural conclusion."[201]

The European institution also favored dialogue and negotiation. President of the European Parliament Jerzy Buzek stated that he welcomed ETA's declaration of the end of its armed activity, which had to be verified, fully confirmed and followed up. He added that ETA must disarm and dissolve but also underlined

---

[201]   "Eta declares halt to armed conflict. Basque separatist group renounces use of arms after year in which it has observed unilateral ceasefire," *The Guardian*, Thursday, October 20, 2011.

that the European Union had full trust in the capacity of the Spanish authorities to verify this announcement and stated that there is no place for violence in the European Union. In sum, Buzek called for competent and skilled measures in order to end up Europe's last major terrorist group's actions in a time of economic crisis and budgetary readjustments.

PC. U.S. State Department spokesman Mark Toner declined immediate comments on ETA's declaration and stated that the U.S. administration was not in a position to determine the validity or the intent of the announcement and that the U.S. government would collaborate with the Spanish government. However, former U.S. President Bill Clinton, married to Secretary of State Hillary Clinton, urged ETA to implement an unconditional and complete renunciation of all violence, and to lay down the arms.

XI. As soon as ETA's farewell to arms was made public you started promoting Joint Memorial No. 14 in Idaho.

PC. Yes. As you well know, we started to work in October 2011, after the Donostia Declaration and the subsequent farewell to arms by ETA were made public.

XI. As in previous cases (1972, 2002 and 2006), the present Memorial encourages the Basque, Spanish, French and U.S. governments to promote peace, democracy and the right to self-determination as essential steps to solve definitively the Basque political conflict.

PC. Right. In Idaho we understand that the resolution of a political conflict requires a political solution. The Basques should hold a referendum on the political future of the Basque Country like the one to be carried out in Scotland in 2014. Just so we know what the Basque citizens want, to maintain the status quo, more competences (devolution) or full independence. This is the only fully democratic and satisfactory solution to our conflict.

XI. In fact, we included a reference to the referendum in Scotland in the first two drafts of the Memorial.

PC. Exactly. The drafters of the Memorial understand that there are three basic problems regarding the Basque political conflict. The main one may be the lack of democracy in the Spanish and French political systems. We understand that violence in Euskadi is a phenomenon inherited from the dictatorship. In the Spanish case, there has been no time in thirty-seven years to root political democracy and much less social democracy, that is, democratic thinking and democratic political culture that makes it possible within states such as the Spanish or the French a referendum on the independence of the Basque Country such as, the one to be carried out in Scotland within two years. The second big problem is the lack of peace in the Basque Country. In this sense, the Memorial sets the principle that only through dialogue are we able to bring a stable peace and to avoid further bloodshed. This requires the recognition of all victims of the conflict and acting accordingly in order to give a proper solution to the problems caused by decades marked by the use of violence, much before 1968, since July 1936. The third problem is the lack of a political solution to solve the Basque political conflict. In order to build a long lasting peace, we must have a correct diagnosis of the political problem and its origins and only then we will be in the position of giving a satisfactory solution to the conflict. The institutional future of the Basque Country, which is the heart of Basque political conflict, has to be addressed by giving the Basques a voice and the chance of deciding on it.

XI. And this is precisely the aim of the 2012 Memorial, to make a recommendation to the parties involved in the conflict to take steps.

PC. Yes. The present Memorial is a non-binding recommendation of the State of Idaho to the two Basque executives and the American, Spanish and French governments on this particular issue. Through this statement the state of Idaho, through their representatives in both Houses, has recommended to the U.S. government and the secretary of state and to the European Parliament to which it was directly issued, to take the necessary steps to definitively solve two issues that have affected the Basques for two centuries such as the existence of violence and the lack of a proper institutional framework.

Sixty-first Idaho Legislature passed House Joint Memorial No. 14 on March 22, 2012. Pete Cenarrusa, in the gallery, receiving a standing ovation from the members of the Idaho House of Representatives. Source: Cenarrusa archive.

As stated in the Statement of Purpose (Rs 21,542), the intent of this Joint Memorial passed by both chambers is to extend support from Idaho to the governments of the United States, Spain, France and the European Union as well as to the governments of the Basque and Navarrese autonomous states, in its continuing efforts to establish a negotiation process to achieve a lasting and a stable peace and the recognition of all victims of violence in Euskadi.

XI. Do you think that the steps made these months in the Basque Country are bringing a lasting peace, reconciliation and political and democratic normalization?

PC. I would have great faith in the actions taken by the people making the Brussels and Donostia declarations to seek a lasting peace. I would have great faith also in the people who made possible the Gernika agreement of 25 September 2010. They all have to be positive about stopping the last armed conflict in Europe. However, we all have to be conscious that nothing is irreversible in life but death and that, consequently, we have to keep on working for peace. The Spanish and French Governments haven't taken any public steps since ETA declared the permanent end of all armed activity in October 2011. The do-nothing policy of the governments is one of the biggest handicaps right now. The illegalization of political parties like Sortu and the imprisonment of political leaders is not the best strategy for fostering peace and dialogue. This is another big handicap in the peace process. All this is part of the lack of a democratic political culture in a society that has undergone forty years of dictatorship, until 1975. Democratic values and the full respect of human rights are political tenets that can only be implemented by a prolonged practice of democracy.

XI. In your opinion, what are the steps to solve the political conflict and achieve a lasting peace in the Basque Country?

PC. I am 94 years old and I have served in politics for 52 years. I want to leave a legacy to the Basques of the next generation. The only possible solution to the Basque political conflict is the celebration of a referendum and the subsequent construction of an independent Basque Republic within the European Union based on the free will of the Basques, supported by a Basque constitution that includes the political principles and values and legal institutions that shaped their ancient Basque legal codes passed in their open assemblies since the eleventh century when the first written legal charter was passed on Basque soil. An independent state based on the principles of freedom, equality before the law, resignation to the right of conquest, social welfare and security of the cultural rights, among these, the right that belongs to the Basques as a nation to perpetuate their language and customs, generation after generation. The Basques must regain the right to be subjects of their own history and stop being objects of the histories of other nations similarly as spelled out in the Declaration of Independence of the United States.

XI. The 2002 Memorial was vociferously opposed by the Spanish ambassador during a trip to Boise and prompted the intervention of then national security adviser Condoleezza Rice.

PC. It was Javier Ruperez, former Spanish ambassador in Washington who wrote an article saying that members of the Idaho legislature and, in general, Basques in Idaho do not know what really is happening on their soil. Unlike Ruperez I do not believe in absolute truths, much less when dealing with politics, apart from the full respect of human rights among which the respect for the others' opinion is included. I assume that people learn from their mistakes so I do not expect a reaction like the one ten years ago. However, before the 2012 Memorial was presented to be discussed and passed, we had a meeting with Phil Reberger, former chief of staff to governor Dirk Kempthorne, and he advised us to contact the state department through Idaho senator Jim Risch. So we did and in a matter of days we had a positive answer from the secretary of state. That does not necessarily mean that the Obama administration is going to take steps to promote dialogue in the Basque Country, but it shows that the state department shares our view that only through the promotion of dialogue can we build a lasting peace in the Basque homeland.

Also, the current political situation is different. Both the government and the secretary of state of the United States have taken a turn as regard to international relations and many other urgent issues. The Bush administration was unable or unwilling to understand the relevance of the former Memorial and Condoleezza Rice herself attempted to stop the legislative initiative of Idaho. She failed but our request did not find fertile ground in Washington. Today the situation is different and the secretary of state not only has not opposed but has collaborated with us in this effort. With respect to the Basque and Navarrese communities, the situation is also different. President López does not seem to be as active as former President Ibarretxe was in this aspect. However, we expect an answer in good faith and the strong commitment of the Basque institutions to promote the ongoing effort.

XI. In your opinion, what should the international community do at this point, after ETA's farewell to arms?

PC. The International Conference held last October in Donostia engaged many international leaders such as Kofi Annan, Gerry Adams, Jonathan Powell, Gro Harlem, Bertie Ahern and Pierre Joxe who made the Donostia Declaration of five points to achieve peace, reconciliation and a political and democratic solution to the conflict. I am not certain if they will be able to persuade the Spanish and French governments to set talks with ETA, to take steps to the liberation of political prisoners, to accept what Basque political parties decide in a process of political dialogue at a multi-party table or to accept what the Basque people decide in a referendum for the political future of the Basque nation, but I am certain that the only solution to a political conflict is to act accordingly to the people's will and that, if the Spanish and the French administrations do not give the Basques their word, the Basque political conflict won't be solved.

XI. There are currently two international groups The International Contact Group (to promote dialogue between Basque political parties) and The International Verification Group (to verify the cessation of ETA's armed activity) working now in the Basque Country. The participation of international actors and institutions in the peace process is very important as it ensures that the process is internationally refereed and therefore that every point of view and each position has a channel and that as a consequence a solution is reached. There are many lessons that the Basque people had learned in this regard. Some of the worst crimes the Basques have seen throughout the nineteenth and twentieth centuries have occurred under the umbrella of "non-intervention" or the principle of "non-interference in the internal affairs of the states."

Sixty-first Idaho Legislature passed Senate Joint Memorial No. 14 on March 26, 2012. In the gallery, Roy Eiguren, Freda Coates Cenarrusa and Pete Cenarrusa. Source: Cenarrusa archive.

PC. Yes, the participation of international observers or mediators in the peace process is an essential element not just in the case of the Basque political conflict but, going back to the last three decades, in the case of South Africa, Northern Ireland, Palestine and many other world scenarios. ETA's declaration has opened the path to peace.

XI. In fact, this is just the first step towards peace. For many years the Basque society has called for a farewell to arms and, has got to bring ETA to the repudiation of violence; we should now be able to bring dialogue, foster negotiation and build peace. And we should have in mind that peace is a goal, not a solution. Peace and reconciliation must be the goal of the peace process.

PC. Yes. The announcement of ETA's cessation does not solve the Basque political conflict that fired up more than two hundred years ago, in 1789, and so predates the creation of ETA. However, it may terminate one of the most dramatic periods of the last seventy-five years of Basque history (1936-2011) and a long cycle of violence.

XI. Right. We have to make clear also that the proclamation of ETA announcing its dissolution does not represent either the culmination of the peace process. Negotiation in the context of a post-conflict environment includes a further process of verification of the ceasefire necessarily involving national and international policing, reparations to the victims, reform of penitentiary policy and amnesty. That entails the instruction and implementation of a transitional justice period including both judicial and non-judicial approaches with a focus on the promotion of human rights, halting ongoing human rights abuses and preserving and enhancing peace. It is also a period for reconciliation, a time for fostering individual and national understanding. Political transition from a social context marked by repression and political violence to stability requires from every one of the Basque citizens to show each other and the world that Basques renounce to violence and can and will achieve peace.

PC. That brings me to mind Eleanor Roosevelt's assertion: "We have to face the fact that either all of us are going to die together or we are going to learn to live together and if we are to live together we have to talk."[202]

XI. Right. In this context, the concept of justice has to be revisited, for the full and successful implementation of justice requires mobilization, commitment and a great deal of dialogue. In Desmond Tutu's words, "there are different kinds of justice. Retributive justice is largely Western. The African understanding is far more restorative - not so much to punish as to redress or restore a balance that has been knocked askew."[203] The concept of restorative justice, largely implemented by the South Africa Truth and Reconciliation Commission, is an approach to justice that focuses on the needs of victims, the rehabilitation of offenders and,

---

[202]   Toor, Rachel, *Eleanor Roosevelt*, Chelsea House Publishers, New York, 1989. Pp. 101.
[203]   Tutu, Desmond, "Recovering from Apartheid," *The New Yorker*, November 18, 1996.

the readjustment of the social framework after decades of violence. It has the advantage that it is a more flexible concept of justice and that focuses on social reconstruction, basic needs in the post-violent stage of a peace process.

In this context, the first problem arises when we try to determine who the victims are. People killed or injured as a consequence of terrorist activity certainly are, but also people tortured by police agents, some of whom died or resulted injured. No matter the society or the chronological setting, bringing victims and offenders together is not simple, neither painless. And it will demand a great social effort and much time.

PC. We must now have hope.

On ideologies and political formulas. Political parties in the Basque Country today

Xabier Irujo. The Basque national question, the Basque political conflict, is 222 years old today, in 2011. Since the French Revolution took place in 1789, the Basque Country has been a nation divided into two states with diverse political parties on both sides of the boundary and, as a consequence, different solutions, dissimilar political formulas and unlike ideologies at the southern and northern feet of the Pyrenees. However, despite this diversity, the same political and cultural problems have fostered the presence of the same Basque nationalist political parties in both the Spanish and the French states providing uniformity to this complex political reality to the extent that we live and undergo a single Basque political conflict and a single Basque political question on both sides of the Pyrenees.

Pete Cenarrusa. Yes, indeed there are many parallels between politics on both sides of the Pyrenees. The same Basque nationalist political parties defend the same rights for the Basque people in both the northern and the southern Basque Country. As a result, the political discourse of the state-wide parties in both the French republic and the Spanish monarchy tend to be the same, protesting with a similar political discourse and identical strategies, for the political and cultural rights of the Basques. That is, the key issues of the Basque political conflict are the same in both states: 1) political debate regarding the cultural rights of the Basques and, in particular, the right of the Basques that their language has the same legal status as French and Spanish; 2) political debate regarding the right of the Basques to form an independent state and, finally, 3) the problem of terrorism and the various forms of political violence.

XI. However, the Basques do not have their own institutions within the French state to defend their political demands and the administrative organization of the republic and its electoral system does not allow the formation of relevant nationalist political forces.

PC. Right. The administrative framework has historically imposed and still imposes serious restrictions to the developing of a strong Basque nationalist movement at the northern bank of the Pyrenean mountains.

XI. Yet, apart from the differences that we may observe at both sides of the country, there are also strategic and ideological differences among the diverse political forces in the Basque Country. That is, there is more than one Basque nationalist ideology and also several Spanish or French constitutionalist or nationalist creeds and, even if the political parties are the same, the political reality partially differs from the Basque Autonomous Community (BAC) to the Chartered Community of Navarre (CCN) and Iparralde.

The three different administrations of the Basque Country today.

PC. Yes. There is a strong tendency, often borne of self-interest, to simplify the various nuances of the Basque nationalism. For example, ETA is frequently called "the Basque separatist group" somehow suggesting that the only pro-independence movement in the Basque Country is of a violent nature or that somehow every political movement seeking independence must necessarily be violent, which is far from being true. However, a general analysis of the political doctrines in the Basque Country should be done regarding the three administrative units in which the country is today divided, namely, 1) the Basque Autonomous Community (BAC) comprising the ancient states of Araba, Bizkaia and Gipuzkoa, 2) the Chartered Community of Navarre, comprising the southern kingdom of Navarre and, 3) Iparralde (Northern Basque Country), comprising Lapurdi, Behe Nafarroa (the northern Kingdom of Navarre) and Zuberoa.

XI. If we focus our analysis on the Basque Autonomous Community (BAC) comprising Araba, Bizkaia and Gipuzkoa, we observe three political blocs, three different groups of parties, namely, the Basque nationalist, the constitutionalist and the leftist blocs. The Basque political nationalism bloc represented a majority at the BAC's parliament until 2009 with 53.44 percent of the seats; the constitutionalist bloc had 40.08 percent and the leftist bloc 5.37 percent of the seats. From your point of view which are the main characteristics of the Basque nationalist bloc?

PC. The Basque nationalist bloc includes all the political parties that defend the right of self-determination for the Basque people as a way to obtain the independence of Euskadi, the Basque Country. These political parties are the Basque Nationalist Party (EAJ-PNV), Aralar, Eusko Alkartasuna (EA), Batasuna (currently outlawed in the Spanish state) and Batzarre. Except Batzarre, all of these political parties have a presence in the entire Basque Country (BAC and CCN in the southern part of the country and also in Iparralde) and they all are non-state wide (Spanish or French) parties and they do not intend to be so.

Territoriality, sovereignty, national identity, historic rights and devolution, human rights and the survival of the Basque language and culture are some of the basic pillars of the secessionist political programs. Furthermore, all Basque nationalist parties are republican and defend some form of European political federation, the project of 'Europe of the One Hundred Flags,' which is a political project defended by of the European Free Alliance, a coalition of European political parties and also a European political party itself.

These political parties defend the position that the Basque Country is a nation divided into two multi-national states and that the Basque Country has lived for the last two centuries in a political, economic, social and cultural struggle. As a consequence, independence is defended as the only political means of guaranteeing the survival of the Basque language and Basque culture. However, even if the final goal is independence, the Basque Nationalist Party, Aralar and Eusko Alkartasuna (and, up to an extent also Batasuna) backed the plan by President Juan Jose Ibarretxe in 2004 and 2008 who proposed a new framework relation with the Spanish state in the form of a free associated Basque state, with recognition of an eventual and future unlimited exercise of the right of self-determination. That is, even if these political parties defend independence they are open to negotiate other political alternatives with the Spanish or French governments as alternative steps towards that end.

Parliament of the Basque Autonomous Community in Gasteiz/Vitoria.
Source: Diario de Noticias.

Regarding the Basque nationalist political bloc, it is also important to notice that the position of these five political parties as regards the use of political violence in the Basque Country results in Batasuna being excluded from electoral coalitions formed by the other secessionist parties until 2011. This way, at the CCN the Basque Nationalist Party, Aralar, Eusko Alkartasuna (EA) and Batzarre formed a coalition called Nafarroa Bai (NaBai) with the omission of Batasuna. However, after the ceasefire of September 2010, Eusko Alkartasuna and Batasuna, together with Alternatiba, formed a coalition called Bildu that saw very good results in the elections of May 22, 2011 and fostered ETA's declaration of a "definitive cessation of its armed activity" of October 20.

Finally, it is also important to underline that the electoral results differ geographically as well as in of the nature of their elections. In general terms Basque nationalist political parties have better results in the local or autonomic (Basque) elections than in general (state-wide) elections. Likewise, Basque nationalist political parties predominate in small to medium size populations. Meanwhile, state-wide political parties such as the Spanish Workers' Socialist Party (PSOE) and the Popular Party (PP) obtain better results in large provincial capitals. However, among the four big cities of Hegoalde (the Southern Basque Country), only one is governed by constitutional forces, namely Gasteiz/Vitoria where the PP governs. In Iruñea/Pamplona, the regionalist political party Union of the Navarrese People (UPN) is the main force. Interestingly, the most populated city of the Basque Country, Bilbao, has always been governed by a Basque nationalist party, EAJ-PNV and, Bildu (a coalition of Basque nationalist political forces) is the first political party in Donostia/San Sebastián, the third largest city in the Basque Country.

In the municipal elections of May 22 2011, the Basque nationalist parties achieved very good results. EAJ-PNV got 30.73 percent of the votes, the Basque nationalist coalition Bildu got 26.03 percent and Aralar 2.89 percent. Thus, in total, the Basque nationalist forces got 59.65 percent of the votes at the municipal elections. The leftist bloc lost some support and IU-EB got 3.20 percent of the votes. The PSE, PSOE's branch in the Basque Country, got 16.71 percent of the votes and the PP 13.83 percent, that is, altogether the constitutionalist bloc got 30.54 percent of the votes. The elections for the regional parliaments at the BAC were also held on May 22, 2011 with identical results: the Basque nationalist bloc got 61.14 percent of the votes, the leftist bloc 3.39 percent and the constitutionalist bloc 31.8 percent.

The Basque nationalist bloc got also very good results in the CCN. The Basque nationalist bloc got 28.44 percent of the votes (4.84 percent more than in 2007), the leftist bloc got 5.7 percent (1.4 percent more than in 2007) and the regionalist and constitutionalist bloc got 57.6 percent of the total votes (34.5 percent for the regionalists and 23.1 percent for the constitutionalists).

XI. The Basque nationalist political forces represented at the parliament of the BAC are the four that follow:

The Basque Nationalist Party (EAJ-PNV) is the first political force in the Basque Autonomous Community and also in the Basque Country as a whole. It is known as Euzko Alderdi Jeltzalea (EAJ) in Basque and Partido Nacionalista Vasco (PNV) in Spanish. The Basque Nationalist Party, created in 1895 by Sabino Arana Goiri, is a nationalist Christian Democrat force, pro-European and republican. With regard to the Basque language, EAJ-PNV defends the official status of the Basque language in the entire Euskal Herria demanding the same legal status for the Basque language as that of French and Spanish.

Since the end of the dictatorship of Generalissimo Franco in 1975, EAJ-PNV has won the support of between 25 percent and 40 percent of the population in the BAC. In the April 17 2005 elections to the parliament of the BAC the coalition EAJ-PNV and Eusko Alkartasuna (EA) gained 468,117 votes, i.e. 38.67 percent of the total valid votes and 29 of the 75 seats of the parliament (22 of which corresponded to EAJ-PNV and 7 to EA). Led by Juan Jose Ibarretxe, a member of EAJ-PNV, the coalition formed by three political parties (EAJ-PNV, EA and IU-EBB) won an absolute majority and governed from 2005 to 2009 in the BAC. In the Basque Parliament elections of March 1 2009, EAJ-PNV received 399,600 votes, or 38.56 percent of the total, and 30 seats in parliament. As we have pointed out, in the elections of 22 May 2011, the Basque nationalist parties achieved very good results. In the BAC, EAJ-PNV got 30.73 percent of the votes in the municipal elections and 31.66 percent in the elections for the regional parliaments of Araba, Bizkaia and Gipuzkoa. EAJ-PNV is also represented at the Chartered Community of Navarre (CCN). In the elections of May 2003, the coalition EA/PNV won 22,824 votes, 7.43 percent of the total valid votes, and 4 seats at parliament (three of which corresponded to EA and one to EAJ-PNV). In 2007, EAJ-PNV was integrated into the coalition Nafarroa Bai (NaBai) which is in 2011 the third strongest political force in Navarre. In the parliament elections of May 22, 2011 the coalition NaBai had very good results: 15.14 percent of the votes and eight seats at the Navarrese parliament.

EAJ-PNV led all governments of the BAC from 1978 to 2009. Between 1979 and 1984 the Basque Nationalist Party governed, headed by Lehendakari (President) Carlos Garaikoetxea. After the division of the party in 1985, EAJ-PNV governed in coalition with the Spanish Socialist Party (PSE) from 1984 to 1998 under Lehendakari Jose Antonio Ardanza. Finally, between 1998 and 2009, under the presidency of Juan Jose Ibarretxe, EAJ-PNV has governed in coalition with EA and IU-EBB. In Navarre, EAJ-PNV is within the coalition NaBai and, at the European level, the Basque Nationalist Party is part of the Coalition for Europe which has two seats at the European parliament. The Coalition for Europe is formed by different centrist moderate nationalist or regionalist political parties: Democratic Convergence of Catalonia (CDC, Convergència Democràtica de Catalunya), Democratic Union of Catalonia (UDC, Unió Democràtica de Catalunya), Nationalist Bloc of Valencia (BNV, Bloc Nacionalista Valencià), Majorcan Union (UM, Unió Mallorquina), Menorcan Union (UMe, Unió Menorquina) Canary Coalition (CC, Coalición Canaria) and the Andalusian Party (PA, Partido Andalucista). Currently Iñigo Urkullu is the president of EAJ-PNV.

In the context of a crisis within the Basque nationalism a new political party called Basque Solidarity (EA, Eusko Alkartasuna) emerged in 1986 as a division of EAJ-PNV led by Carlos Garaikoetxea, former Lehendakari of the BAC. Eusko Alkartasuna is a social democratic, Basque nationalist, pro-European and republican political party. With regard to the Basque language, EA defends the same official legal status for the Basque language as the one that the French and Spanish languages enjoy today on both sides of the Pyrenees, in the entire Basque Country.

In the Basque parliament elections celebrated on 17 April 2005, the coalition formed by EAJ-PNV and EA won 468,117 votes, i.e. 38.67 percent of the total valid votes (winning 29 seats in the parliament, 7 of which corresponded to EA and 22 to EAJ-PNV). In the 2009 Basque parliament elections, EA went alone, and dropped dramatically to 38,198 votes (3.69 percent), losing about 10,000 votes compared to the overall results of 2008 and, hence, got a single seat in the parliament of the BAC. The poor results prompted the schism within EA and Iñaki Galdos created Alkarbide, a political force claiming a coalition with EAJ-PNV. In the elections of May 2003 in Navarre, EA in coalition with EAJ-PNV won 22,824 votes, 7.43 percent of the total valid votes, and 4 seats at the parliament of the CCN (three of which corresponded to EA and 1 to EAJ-PNV). In 2007 EA joined the coalition Nafarroa Bai (NaBai) that currently is the second largest political force in Navarre. EA has lost nearly 40 percent of the electoral support between 1986 and 1998: from 15.84 percent to 8.69 percent in the BAC and from 7.1 percent to 4.56 percent at the CCN.

However, in the elections of 22 May 2011, headed by Pello Urizar, EA joined and led the coalition Bildu, and achieved very good results: 26.03 percent in the municipal elections and 25.94 percent in the elections for the regional parliaments of Araba, Bizkaia, and Gipuzkoa. At the CCN, Bildu saw very good results also, with 13.3 percent of the votes and seven seats at the Navarrese parliament.

Between 1998 and 2009, EA governed at the BAC in coalition with EAJ-PNV and IU-EBB. At European level, EA is integrated into the coalition European Free Alliance (EFA) that has 7 seats at the European parliament. According to article 3 of the statutes of EFA, this political party stands for European unity and the creation of a European union of free peoples based on the principle of subsidiarity which calls for solidarity with each other and other peoples of the world and for the defense of human rights and the rights of peoples, in particular the right to self-determination. The European Free Alliance is formed of different progressive social democrat nationalist or regionalist political parties advocating for full political independence or some form of devolution or self-governance for their country, among them, the Galician nationalist Bloc (BNG, Bloque Nacionalista Galego), the Council of Aragon (CHA, Chunta Aragonesista), Esquerra Republicana de Catalunya (ERC, Republican Left of Catalonia), Occitan Party (PÒc, Partit Occitan), The Party of Wales (Plaid, Plaid Cymru), the Scottish National Party (SNP), South Tyrolean Freedom (STF, Südtiroler Freiheit) and the Breton Democratic Union (UDB, Union Démocratique Bretonne). In partnership with the European Green Party, the coalition Greens-EFA is the fourth political force at the European Parliament with 55 seats (out of a total of 736, or 7.4 percent). Currently the president of EA is Pello Urizar.

Batasuna, founded in 1978 as Herri Batasuna (HB) is a coalition of left-wing Basque nationalist parties ranging from Marxist to socialist, Basque nationalist, pro-European and republican. The coalition has changed its name several times, known as Herri Batasuna (HB) between 1978 and 1998, Euskal Herritarrok (EH) between 1998 and 2001 and Batasuna between 2001 and 2003; the coalition was represented by the Communist Party of the Basque Lands (EHAK, Euskal Herrialdeetako Alderdi Komunista) at the parliament of the BAC between 2005 and 2008 and by the Basque Nationalist Action party (EAE/ANV, Euskal Abertzale Ekintza/Acción Nacionalista Vasca) between 2007 and 2008 (municipal elections and general councils at the BAC). With regard to the Basque language Batasuna defends the legas status of the Basque language in the whole Basque Country.

Batasuna's support in the elections to the parliament of the BAC oscillates between its best 18.33 percent in 1990 and the lowest 10.12 percent in 2001. Considered the political branch of Euskadi Ta Askatasuna (ETA) by the Spanish courts of justice, on March 17, 2003, the Spanish Supreme Court agreed to outlaw HB, EH and Batasuna and ordered its dissolution under the charge of having violated the law on political parties. Batasuna was also included in the European Union's list of terrorist organizations of 29 May 2006. In 2008 EHAK and EAE/ANV were also outlawed. When it was outlawed Batasuna had 143,139 votes at the BAC (10.12 percent of the total valid votes) and 7 MPs at the Basque Parliament; EHAK obtained 12.44 percent of the seats at the parliament of the BAC in 2005. In Navarre, Batasuna had 47,271 votes (10.44 percent) and 8 MPs at the Navarrese Parliament in 2003.

Batasuna never formed coalitions of government at the BAC or at the CCN until 2011. This was due mainly to its ambiguous policy regarding the use of violence with political goals. In 2009 Batasuna started calling for the end of violence and, under the current political agreement between EA and leaders of the outlawed Batasuna of June 20, 2010 Batasuna formally requested of ETA a unilateral, permanent and verifiable ceasefire that was finally announced on September 5, 2010. As a consequence EA and Batasuna promoted the subsequent Gernika Agreement of 26 September, signed by five political forces and 23 social actors aiming to find an end to political violence in the Basque Country. The former spokesman for Batasuna, Arnaldo Otegi, was arrested in June 2007 but was released soon after in August 2008. In October 2009 he was arrested again and he is currently in prison. Due to the outlawing of Batasuna, this political force has no political representation at the parliaments of the BAC and CCN in 2011. Also, Batasuna is not a member of a European coalition at the European parliament.

As a consequence of the cessation of violence and the subsequent political agreement, EA, Alternatiba, and Batasuna formed the coalition Bildu that, as we have already mentioned, had very good results in the elections of 22 May 2011 (26.03 percent in the municipal elections and 25.94 percent in the elections for the regional parliaments at the BAC and 13.3 percent of the votes and seven seats at the Navarrese parliament in the CCN).

Aralar is a political party created in June 2000 from the division of Batasuna after the breakdown of the truce of 1998 by ETA and, subsequently, the rupture of the Lizarra-Garazi Agreement. Highly critical with the activity of ETA, Aralar is a Marxist oriented, Basque nationalist, pro-European and republican force. Like the rest of the Basque nationalist forces, Aralar defends the official status of the Basque language in the entire Basque Country, in equal legal conditions as the French and Spanish languages.

In the BAC parliament elections of 17 April 2005 Aralar received 28,180 votes, i.e. 2.33 percent of the total valid votes and a seat at the Basque Parliament (out of 75). However, in the 2009 elections Aralar won 62,514 votes, 6.03 percent of the total, gaining 4 seats at the parliament of the BAC. Aralar did not achieve good results on May 22, 2011, and only got 3.54 percent of the votes in the elections for the regional parliaments and 2.89 percent in the municipal elections. Aralar is a particularly strong political formation in the CCN, where at the elections in May 2003 received 24.068 votes, 7.83 percent of the total votes and 4 seats at the Navarrese parliament, slightly ahead of the coalition EA/EAJ-PNV that won 22,824 votes (i.e., 7.43 percent and 4 seats). In 2007 Aralar joined with EA, EAJ-PNV and Batzarre the coalition Nafarroa Bai (NaBai) that currently is the third political force in Navarre (15.14 percent of the votes on May 22, 2011 and eight seats at the Navarrese parliament).

Aralar joined, together with Eusko Alkartasuna, the coalition Greens-EFA in 2009. In the European elections of June 2009 the coalition won 6 percent of the votes and the candidate of the coalition Iñaki Irazabalbeitia obtained representation at the European Parliament, who thus took his seat for a period of ten months. The general coordinator of Aralar is Patxi Zabaleta and Aintzane Ezenarro is the leader of this political force at the parliament of the BAC.

PC. The leftist bloc is composed of a single political party: Izquierda Unida/Ezker Batua (IU-EB) or United Left, created in 1986.

IU-EB is a leftist, Marxist oriented, pro-European and Republican political force. Not being a Basque nationalist party, IU-EB presents separated lists at the BAC and at the CCN elections and has no political presence in Iparralde. United Left defends a Spanish federal republic as the state model and, as a consequence, also defends the right of self-determination for the Basque people as a means to solve the Basque political conflict. With regard to the Basque language, IU-EB has been in favor of the legal equality of Basque and Spanish in the CAB and has maintained a passive stance in this regard in the CCN. With no representation in Iparralde, IU-EB has no policy regarding the revitalization of the Basque language in the French state.

Unlike the political parties that we have analyzed so far, IU-EB is a state wide political party and, consequently, it has a presence throughout the Spanish state. At the BAC, IU-EB in alliance with the Greens forms the coalition EB-Berdeak (IU-EBB). In the 17 April 2005 BAC parliamentary elections IU-EBB got 65,023 votes, i.e. 5.37 percent of the total valid votes, getting 3 seats at the parliament (out of a total of 75 seats). Between 2005 and 2009 IU-EBB was part of a coalition government with the nationalist forces EAJ-PNV and EA. However, due to a major internal crisis which resulted in a split and the creation of the political party, Alternatiba, led by Oscar Matute, in the course of the Basque parliamentary elections of 2009 IU-EBB received 36,373 votes, that is, 3.51 percent of the total valid votes and a single representative. IU-EBB did not achieve good results on May 22, 2011 either, winning only 3.2 percent in the municipal elections and 3.39 percent in the elections for the regional parliaments at the BAC. However, Alternatiba had very good results within the Bildu coalition (with EA). In the same 2011 elections they won 26.03 percent in the municipal elections and 25.94 percent in the elections for the regional parliaments at the BAC. At the state level IU also faces a severe internal crisis.

IU-EBB is part of the European United Left/Nordic Green Left (EUL-NGL) coalition, a parliamentary group formed by leftist, socialist and communist elements that with 35 MPs is the sixth force in the European parliament. Currently, the general coordinator of IU-EB is Mikel Arana, a member of the parliament at the BAC.

XI. The third bloc, the constitutionalist bloc, is composed of three political parties, Partido Socialista Obrero Español (PSOE), Partido Popular (PP) and Unión Progreso y Democracia (UPyD). This bloc represented 40.08 percent of the seats at the BAC parliament in 2005. The Spanish constitutionalist parties, with presence throughout the Spanish state as a whole (with no presence in Iparralde) do not consider Navarre or Iparralde to be part of the Basque Country. From this perspective, the Basque Country is the Basque Autonomous Community, a region of the Spanish nation. The mentioned political forces defend that the Spanish state is indivisible and that to give the right of self-determination to the Basque people is simply illegal for it is not granted by the Spanish constitution. Thus, these three political forces, that reject being labeled as Spanish nationalist, claim to be constitutionalist.

Regarding the Basque language, none of the parties has shown a program for its recovery and members of these political forces at the Basque parliament and leaders of UPyD as Rosa Díez or Fernando Savater defend the concept that the Spanish state should have one single official language, Spanish. All these parties are monarchist and, against the project of the Europe of the Peoples defended by the Basque nationalist political forces, the forces of the constitutionalist bloc advocate for a European model based on the alliance of the states.

The Spanish Worker's Socialist Party (PSOE, Partido Socialista Obrero Español), founded in 1879 by the labor union leader Pablo Iglesias, is the oldest still existing Spanish political party. The PSOE is a moderate socialist force that advocates for the model of a decentralized Spanish state in the form of a constitutional monarchy. The Socialist Party also defends a model of European Union based on solidarity between the European states. At the CAB the PSOE adopted the name Socialist Party of Euskadi-Euzkadiko Ezkerra (PSE-EE). The PSE was established in 1993 following the merger of the PSOE and the left-wing Basque nationalist party Euskadiko Ezkerra (EE) that at that time was divided into two groups.

As a party of regional representation, the PSE-EE has no municipal or regional representation outside the BAC, in Navarre or Iparralde. The PSE supports the constitutional monarchy as a model of Spanish state and, like other constitutional forces, denies that the Basque people have the right to self-determination. The PSOE does not advocate for the developing the Basque statute of Autonomy beyond its current constitutional framework. With regard to the situation of the Basque language, the PSE has maintained an ambiguous position sometimes broadcasting the need for a limited revitalization of the Basque language and then objecting to the same proposition on the basis that it is an imposition. With no representation in Iparralde, the PSE-EE has no policy regarding the revitalization of the Basque language in the French state.

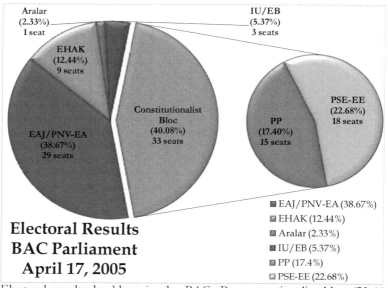

**Electoral Results
BAC Parliament
April 17, 2005**

Electoral results by blocs in the BAC: Basque nationalist bloc (53.44 percent); Leftists or Federalist bloc (5.37 percent) and Constitutionalist bloc (40.08 percent).

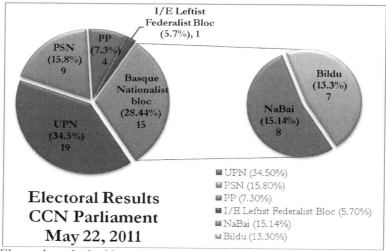

**Electoral Results
CCN Parliament
May 22, 2011**

Electoral results by blocs in Navarre: Regionalists (34.5 percent); Basque nationalist (28.44); Constitutionalist (23.1); Leftists or Federalist (3.39).

Historically, the PSE has won between 18 percent and 23 percent of electoral support in the BAC. After the excision of EAJ-PNV in 1985, the PSE ruled in coalition with EAJ-PNV until 1998. In the 2005 elections to the parliament of the BAC, the PSE-EE won 274,546 votes, i.e. 22.68 percent of the total valid votes, the second political force in the BAC, with 18 seats at parliament (out of a total of 75 seats). In the BAC parliamentary election of 2009, the PSE-EE was the second political force after EAJ-PNV, obtaining 318.112 votes, 30.70 percent of the valid votes, and 25 seats. In coalition with the Popular Party, the PSE currently governs in the BAC under the leadership of Patxi López. With respect to the representation in the European Parliament, the PSOE is part of the Party of the European Socialists (PES) that currently has 162 seats and that within the coalition Progressive Alliance of Socialists and Democrats (S&D) is the second European force behind the conservative European People's Party (EPP) that has 265 seats. The general secretary of the PSE at the BAC is Patxi López and the general secretary of the PSOE is José Luis Rodríguez.

In the elections of May 22, 2011 at the BAC the PSE achieved bad results, 17.17 percent of the votes in the election for the regional parliaments (6.54 percent less than in 2007) and 16.71 percent in the municipal elections (8.16 percent less than in 2007).

The Popular Party (PP, Partido Popular) is a state-wide political party created in 1989 following the demise of Popular Alliance (AP, Alianza Popular), a party created by Manuel Fraga, former minister of industry of the Franco regime. The PP is a conservative, Christian Democratic oriented political force that advocates for a centralized Spanish state model in the form of a constitutional monarchy. As the PSOE, the PP defends a model of European Union based on the solidarity of the European states, without direct participation of the nations without state at the Union's institutions.

As the rest of the state level constitutionalist parties, the PP does not have political representation in Iparralde. The PP supports the constitutional monarchy as the state model of the Spanish state and, like other constitutionalist forces, denies the right to self determination of the Basques. With regard to the situation of the Basque language, the PP has maintained a stance of rejection towards the revitalization of the language, imposing objections to its promotion. Along with the PSE, the PP is against the idea of the Basque language being a communitarian language, that is, one of the official languages of the European Union.

In the last ten years the PP has fluctuated between 17.40 percent and 23.12 percent of the votes at the BAC parliamentary elections. In the 2005 elections the PP won 210,614 votes, i.e. 17.40 percent of the total valid votes and 15 seats at parliament (out of 75). In the elections of March 2009, the Popular Party won 146,148 votes (14.10 percent of the total) and 13 seats at the BAC parliament. Following the political agreement with the PSE, the PP supports the executive led by Patxi López at the BAC. In the elections of May 22, 2011 at the BAC the constitutionalist parties did not achieve good results. The PP won 14.63 percent of the votes in the election for the regional parliaments (2.72 percent less than in 2007) and 13.83 percent in the municipal elections (1.95 percent less than in 2007).

At European level, the PP is part of the European People's Party (EPP) that, including Christian Democratic, conservative and liberal forces, is currently the largest group in the European Parliament with 265 members. Since 2008 the PP in the BAC has been chaired by Antonio Basagoiti.

Union Progress and Democracy (UPyD, Unión Progreso y Democracia), founded in 2007, is a state wide Spanish political party defined by its leader Rosa Díez as "progressive and transversal," i.e., with ideological contributions from liberals and conservatives. UPyD defends a more centralized but federal Spanish state model in the form of a constitutional monarchy. Like the PSOE and the PP, UPyD advocates for a federal model of European Union based on the integrity of the states and the maintenance of the current European state borders without direct participation of the nations without states in the European institutions.

UPyD was born as the political expression of a form of Spanish nationalism that seeks to eliminate linguistic and cultural features for the sake of the unity of Spain that, in the opinion of its leaders, is in danger. From this standpoint "legal equality" equals "cultural unity" and, therefore, the only official state language and culture must be Spanish.

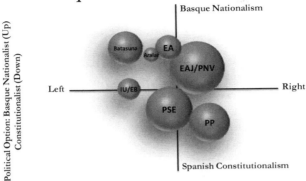

BAC Parliament elections. April 17, 2005

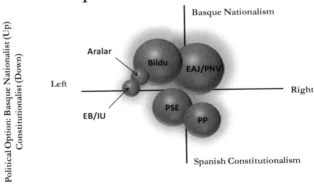

BAC Regional Parliaments elections. May 22, 2011

As a consequence UpyD believes that the state should be more centralized, especially in reference to the political and cultural rights of Basques, Catalans and Galicians. In conclusion, a strongly centralized and culturally homogeneous Spanish state is the ideal political framework and an ad hoc Spanish constitution the only political instrument capable of guaranteeing the resultant equality of all citizens.

UPyD won 22,233 votes in 2009 at the BAC (2.15 percent of the total valid votes) and has currently a seat at parliament. In the elections of May 22, 2011 at the BAC, like the rest of the constitutionalist forces UPyD did not achieve good results. UPyD only won 0.82 percent of the votes in the election for the regional parliaments and 0.65 percent in the municipal elections. Rosa Díez is the leader of this political force.

XI. If we consider the evolution of each of the political blocs in the last twenty-seven years, we conclude that the proportion of the vote has remained, with few alterations, the same. Each one of the blocs has had periods of ascension and phases of decreasing political strength. However, in the long run the secessionist bloc (PNV, EA, Aralar and HB/EH/Batasuna) has increased 5.14 percent. The leftist bloc (EB-Berdeak) has lost 3.61 percent of the popular vote. Meanwhile the constitutionalist bloc (PP, PSE-EE) has remained the same with the support of 32 percent of the votes from 1984 to 2011.

BAC	1984	1986	1990	1994	1998	2001	2005	2011[204]
Secessionist Bloc	56% 43	55% 43	57% 44	55% 41	53% 41	52% 40	53,5% 39	61.14%
Leftist Bloc	7% 6	10% 9	7% 6	9% 6	5% 2	5% 3	5,4% 3	3.39%
Constitutionalist Bloc	32% 26	29% 23	28% 25	33% 28	38% 32	40% 32	39,9% 33	31.8%

Evolution of the political representation at the BAC's parliament between 1984 and 2005 by blocs (proportion of votes and number of seats).

---

[204] Elections for the regional parliaments in Araba, Bizkaia and Gizpuzkoa, in the BAC.

PC. Also in the Chartered Community of Navarre the various political parties can be grouped into different blocs, although the proportion of the political representation of each of them differs from the BAC, i.e., while the secessionist bloc has the support of the 28.44 percent of the Navarrese votes, the constitutionalist bloc holds 23.10 percent of the seats in the parliament of Navarre. The leading bloc at the CCN is the regionalist bloc that, historically linked to the constitutionalist bloc, has in 2011 the support of the 34.5 percent. With 5.7 percent of the votes, the leftist bloc has a similar strength at the CCN and at the BAC.

XI. The leading political bloc in Navarre is the regionalist. This bloc comprised until 2011 two regionalist parties, Unión del Pueblo Navarro (UPN) and Convergencia de Demócratas de Navarra (CDN, that disappeared in 2011). In general terms we may say that 35 percent of the citizens of the CCN vote for Navarrese regionalist and conservative forces, 28 percent for Basque nationalist forces, 23 percent for constitutionalist forces and, about 6 percent for federalist leftist forces.

Navarrese Parliament in Iruñea/Pamplona. Source: Parlamento de Navarra/Nafarroako Parlamentua.

The Union of the Navarrese People (UPN, Unión del Pueblo Navarro) is a regionalist party created in 1979 by its former first president, Jesus Aizpún. UPN is a conservative and regionalist party that, unlike the Basque nationalist coalition Nafarroa Bai (NaBai), which advocates for the incorporation of Navarre, together with the rest of the Basque territories in a single political entity, defends a separate Navarrese identity integrated into the Spanish state. From this standpoint Navarre is not a nation but a historic region with its own political rights within the Spanish state.

UPN defends the constitutional monarchy as the ideal model of Spanish state and, like other constitutional bloc forces, denies that the Basque people have the right to self-determination. However, unlike the core assumptions of the PP, PSOE and UPyD, UPN defends the concept of administrative decentralization and the respect for the historical rights of Navarre as a basis for the coexistence of the various regions of the state. This position is reflected in UPN's defense of the status quo regarding the state of the autonomies. With regard to the situation of the Basque language, its opposition to Basque nationalism has led UPN to maintain a very hostile stance regarding the revitalization of the Basque language in Navarre, imposing serious objections to the promotion of this language. This situation prompted the intervention of the European Bureau for Lesser-Used Languages (EBLUL), whose President Bojan Brezigar expressed in Pamplona in 2004 that the situation at the CCN was "very worrying." According to the authors of the inquiry, Alexia Bos Solé and Johan Haggman, Navarre was the only case in Europe where there had been an actual decline in linguistic rights.

As a regionalist political party, UPN has no political representation outside the CCN. In the elections of May 28, 2003 at the CCN, UPN received 127,460 votes, 41.50 percent of the total valid votes, and 23 seats in the parliament (out of 50). In the elections of May 28, 2007 UPN won 139,122 votes, 42.20 percent of the total, and 22 seats. In the elections of May 22, 2011, UPN won 34.5 percent of the votes and 19 seats at the Navarrese parliament (7.7 percent less than in 2007). However, UPN has consolidated in the last decade as the leading political force in the CCN and has now formed a government with support of the branch of the PSOE in Navarre, the Socialist Party of Navarre

(PSN). Yolanda Barcina is currently the president of UPN and also the president of the Government of Navarre.

The Democratic Convergence of Navarre (CDN, Convergencia de Demócratas de Navarra) was a regional conservative party, of Christian Democratic orientation, created in 1995 by Juan Cruz Alli. From UPN's regionalist position, Navarre is not a nation but a region of Spain, and as a consequence the actual autonomy statute is sufficient. However, there is a faction within UPN that resembles nationalist positions in defending the notion that Navarre is, in fact, a nation. The clash of these two positions within UPN gave rise to a split in the party in 1995 and the creation of CDN.

CDN defended the idea of Navarre as a nation or the Navarrese people as an original and differentiated historical nationality. Consequently, its political program was based on a notion of *Navarridad* (as opposed to the UPN's regionalist *Navarrismo*) and thus it sought to reinforce the national identity of the Navarrese people. *Navarridad* might be defined as a political concept somewhere between regionalism and nationalism. CDN also envisioned greater levels of self-government as part of a process of developing the current statute of autonomy. It therefore accepted and recognized the cultural and historic ties of Navarre with the other Basque territories.

Like UPN, CDN did not have political representation outside the CCN. In 1995 CDN was very successful with 55,153 votes, or 18.55 percent of the total valid votes in Navarre and 10 seats in the Navarrese parliament. However, in the elections of May 2003 CDN lost almost half of its electoral support and with 23,516 votes, 7.70 percent of the total, only won 4 seats at the Navarrese parliament. Then, in the elections of May 2007 CDN fell again, getting 14,418 votes, i.e., 4.4 percent of the total, and a mere two seats at parliament (out of a total of 50 seats). In the elections of May 22, 2011 CDN did not get any representation and the party disappeared. José Andrés Burguete headed this political force in 2011.

The constitutionalist bloc is formed by the Popular Party (PP) and the Navarrese section of the Spanish Workers' Socialist

Party (PSOE) known as the Navarrese Socialist Party (PSN, Partido Socialista de Navarra).

What we have said before about the Popular Party in the BAC applies equally to Navarre. The PP defends the idea that Navarre is a Spanish region that is not part of the Basque Country. Thus, the PP defends the political status quo of an autonomous region of Navarre included in the Spanish state with the current political powers.

In virtue of the electoral pact between the PP and UPN, the PP did not show up for the elections at the CCN thereby giving its votes in the context of the elections to the parliament of Navarre to UPN. In return, the candidates of UPN to the Spanish parliament in Madrid came to be part of the PP's parliamentary group. However, in September 2008 the president of the CCN, Miguel Sanz, announced that UPN could give its support to the central government's budget plan for 2009 if the central government of the PSOE attended UPN's demands on several issues of interest for the Navarrese (i.e., the pass of the high-speed train through Navarre, the improvement of several aspects of the Navarrese Charter or the transfer of the traffic powers to the CCN). As a consequence, on September 30, 2008, the central government announced its intention to increase the state's investment in Navarre by 31.3 percent and UPN agreed to vote in favor of the socialist government's budgetary plan for 2009. However, on 22 October, Santiago Cervera (UPN) voted "no" on the state budgetary plan against the decision of his party (UPN), for which he was suspended from membership in UPN. This led to the final breaking of the electoral agreement between UPN and the PP and, as a consequence, the PP participated in the parliamentary elections in Navarre in 2011 headed by Santiago Cervera.

The Socialist Party of Navarre (PSN) is, as the PSE, part of the Spanish Workers' Socialist Party (PSOE). As a party of regional representation, the PSN has no political representation outside the CCN and, in essence, embraces the same political principles that applied in this case to PSE. That is, Navarre is a Spanish region that is not part of the Basque Country as a whole and, accordingly, Navarre must be an autonomous region included in the Spanish state with its current political powers.

In the parliamentary elections of 1995 in Navarre, the PSN received 62,021 votes, 21.28 percent of the total valid votes, and 11 seats at parliament (out of 50 seats). In May 28, 2003 the PSN got almost identical results, with 65,003 votes, 21.20 percent of the total valid votes and 11 seats at parliament. In the elections of May 2007 the PSN received 74,157 votes, 22.50 percent of the total, and 12 seats. The PSN's tacit support for the minority government of the conservative regionalist coalition UPN-CDN created a serious internal crisis within the Socialist Party of Navarre after the 2007 elections, as the party's executive in Navarre, bowing to political pressures from the PSOE in Madrid, decided to ignore the decision of the assembly of the PSN in Navarre to conclude a government agreement with the Basque nationalist coalition Nafarroa Bai (NaBai), which was the second largest political force in the CCN. The PSN did not get good results in the elections of May 22, 2011, with 15.8 percent of the votes and 9 seats at the Navarrese parliament (6.7 percent less than in 2007). Roberto Jiménez is currently the general secretary of the PSN.

PC. The leftist bloc is composed, as in the BAC, of a single political party: Izquierda Unida (IU), created in 1986. Izquierda Unida de Navarra (IUN) in Spanish and, in Basque, Nafarroako Ezker Batua (NEB) is the name of the party in Navarre (IUN-NEB). As IU-EB, IUN-NEB is part of the statewide coalition United Left (IU, Izquierda Unida). As a party of regional representation, IUN-NEB has no political representation outside the CCN and its social and political assumptions are the same or very close to those of IU-EB.

In the Navarrese parliamentary elections of 1993, IUN-NEB received 27,773 votes, 9.53 percent of the total valid votes, and 5 seats at the parliament of the CCN. In the elections of May 2003 this political force received 26,962 votes, 8.80 percent of the total votes, and four seats, one less than in 1993. In the May 2007 elections the electoral support for IUN-NEB was reduced to 14,337 votes, 4.4 percent of total valid votes cast, with two seats at the parliament of the HNC (of a total of 50 seats). On May 22, 2011, under the name Left (I/E, Izquierda/Ezkerra) won 5.7 percent of the votes and a single seat at the Navarrese parliament. José Miguel Nuin is currently the leader of this political force in Navarre.

Leaders of EA. From left to right, Rafael Larreina speaker of the party; Carlos Garaikoetxea, former president of the BAC and president of EA; Pello Irujo president of EA in Navarre. Source Irujo Ametzaga archive.

XI. The Basque nationalist political forces represented in the parliament of the CCN are Aralar, EA, PNV and Batzarre,[205] which were all included in a single coalition called Nafarroa Bai (NaBai) created in 2002. With chronological oscillations and also with oscillations in the various types of elections (be they local, regional, statewide or European) the principle of Basque nationalism has approximately from 20 percent to 28 percent of the popular support in Navarre.

Being a coalition formed by various Basque nationalist forces NaBai combines different ideologies from Marxist socialism (Aralar, Batzarre), Social Democracy (EA) and Christian Democracy (EAJ-PNV). In this sense, NaBai advocates to ensure equality and basic rights of the people of Navarre to public health,

---

[205] Batzarre is a Marxist-oriented political party founded in 1987 with a presence only on the CCN (in the BAC is called Zutik but has no institutional representation). In the elections of May 2003 in the CCN Batzarre got 7,873 votes, 2.62 percent of the total valid votes and therefore accounted for a seat at parliament. Batzarre got similar results in the 2007 elections that joined the coalition Nafarroa Bai (NaBai).

education, housing, culture and labor services. NaBai defends the existence of a Basque Country with the inclusion of all the Basque territories, Araba, Bizkaia, Gipuzkoa, Lapurdi, Navarre and Zuberoa, and the right of the Basques to the right of self-determination and independence. In relation to the language policy, NaBai advocates for the development of the Basque language in Navarre and the rest of the Basque territories claiming an identical legal status for the three languages spoken in the Basque Country, Basque, French and Spanish.

NaBai was the second political force in Navarre with 77.893 votes, 23.60 percent of the electoral support and 12 seats at the parliament of Navarre in 2007. In light of the electoral results of 2007, NaBai offered PSN the possibility of forming a left-wing coalition government in Navarre as an alternative to UPN. The assembly of PSN in Navarre accepted the proposal but the general direction of the PSOE in Madrid vetoed the resolution and the agreement was thus never signed. As a consequence, the coalition UPN and CDN governs in the CCN since 2007. Uxue Barkos is currently the leader of this political coalition. Patxi Zabaleta serves as the spokesperson of NaBai in the Parliament of Navarre, and Uxue Barkos as the spokesman of NaBai at the Spanish parliament in Madrid and in the city council of Iruñea/Pamplona.

On May 22, 2011, NaBai lost some electoral support before Bildu, an emergent Basque nationalist force formed by EA and members of the former Batasuna. However, with 15.14 percent of the votes and eight MPs, NaBai got good results and it is currently the third political force in the CCN.

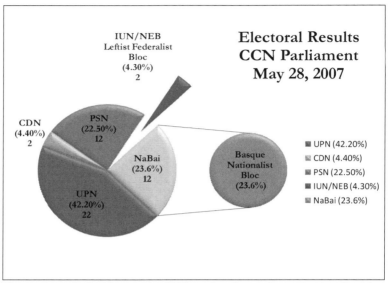

Electoral results in Navarre in 2007: regionalist and constitutionalist bloc (69.1 percent), leftist or federalist bloc (4.3 percent) and Basque nationalist bloc (23.6 percent).

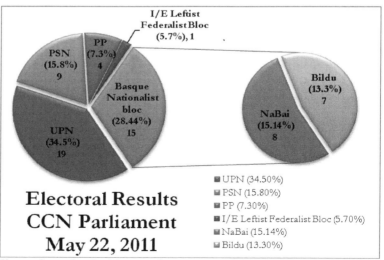

Electoral results in Navarre in 2011: regionalist bloc (34.5 percent), constitutionalist bloc (23.1 percent), leftist or federalist bloc (5.7 percent) and Basque nationalist bloc (28.44 percent).

[320]

PC. The banning of Batasuna in 2003 has meant that this political force has not been present at the Navarrese parliament elections since June 13, 1999. At that time, Batasuna, under the name of Euskal Herritarrok (EH), won 47,271 votes, 15.96 percent of the total valid votes and 8 seats, becoming the third political force in Navarre behind UPN (22 seats) and PSN (11 seats). During the May 2003 elections, Batasuna called for invalid votes; as a consequence, 21,296 invalid votes were registered, 6.5 percent of the votes, which represents approximately 3 seats.

Batasuna is a nationwide Basque political party and, consequently, what we have said about this political force in reference to the BAC also applies to Navarre and Iparralde. Pernando Barrena was the leader of Batasuna in Navarre until he was arrested in February 2008, along with Francisco Jose Urrutia, under the accusation of belonging to a terrorist organization. After spending two years in prison without trial, Barrena was released on bail in February 2010 under the prohibition of making public statements. Txelui Moreno represented Batasuna in the context of the agreement signed with EA in September 2010 for the cessation of violence.

On May 22, 2011, the coalition Bildu, formed by EA and Batasuna got very good results with 13.3 percent of the votes and seven MPs at the Navarrese parliament.

XI. If we consider the evolution of the electoral results in Navarre in the last twenty five years, we conclude that the Basque nationalist bloc has substantially increased its presence at the Navarrese parliament. Each one of the blocs has had ups and downs. However, in the long run the secessionist bloc has increased its strength gaining six seats at the parliament (40 percent more than in 1983). The leftist bloc (IUN-NEB) has maintained its strength with about two seats at parliament (nearly 5 percent of the votes), meanwhile the regionalist and the constitutionalist blocs (UPN, CDN, PP, PSN) have lost eight seats at the Navarrese parliament from 1983 to 2011.

Parliament of the CCN	1983	1987	1991	1995	1999	2003	2007	2011
Secessionist Bloc	9	12	9	7	11	8	12	15
Leftist Bloc	0	1	2	5	3	4	2	1
Regionalist & Constitutionalist Blocs	41	38	39	38	36	38	36	32

Evolution of the seats at the Navarrese parliament by political blocs (1983-2011).

PC. The last administrative section of the Basque Country is Iparralde, namely the three Basque territories today included in the French republic. The institutional reality of the French Republic makes the defense of the Basque nationalist political programs difficult. The Basque historical territories in the Northern Basque Country (Iparralde) are diluted into a bigger political unit called Pyrénées-Atlantiques with approximately 643,000 inhabitants among which, nearly 260,000 are Basques representing only about 40 percent. Pyrénées-Atlantiques (until 1969 known as Basses-Pyrénées) is one of the original 83 departments of the French republic created in 1790 during the French Revolution. It was created from parts of the former territories of Guyenne, Béarn, and the Basque states of the northern Basque Country: the Kingdom of Navarre, the Country of Lapurdi and the Country of Zuberoa. Following the political idea of the drafters of the French constitution, even if all the Basques were affiliated to one single Basque nationalist political party, this force would not gain but 38 percent of the seats at the a general council (conseil général) of the department, an assembly whose members are elected for six years terms by universal suffrage. And the president of the council is the executive of each department.

The Union for French Democracy (UDF, Union pour la Démocratie Française) was the first political force at the Pyrénées-Atlantiques in the cantonal elections of 2004 and the Union for a Popular Movement (UMP, Union pour un Mouvement Populaire) at the elections of 26 March 2008. Jean Castaings, a member of UMP, is the current president of the general council of the Pyrénées-Atlantiques.

XI. Moreover, the different departments are parts of a single region. In our case, the department of the Pyrénées-Atlantiques is part of the Region of Aquitaine. The whole region of Aquitaine has approximately 3,151,000 inhabitants, so that the Basques represent only 8 percent of the total population of the region. Regional councilors are elected for a term of six years. There are 85 members at the regional council of Aquitaine, namely, 36 from the department of the Gironde, 17 from the Pyrénées-Atlantiques, 13 from the Dordogne, 11 from the Landes and 8 from Lot-et-Garonne. That means that the entire department of the Pyrénées-Atlantiques represents only 20 percent of the members at the regional assembly and, as a consequence, the Basques only represent 7.6 percent of the regional assembly. The Chair of the Regional Council for 2010 was entrusted to Alain Rousset (Socialist Party) at the plenary meeting of 26 March 2010.

PC. In such circumstances it is extremely difficult for a Basque nationalist party to reach the minimum 10 percent of the votes required to pass the second electoral round and, as a consequence of this electoral system, only state wide political parties have access to the regional assemblies and departmental general councils. Regarding the case of the Basques, there are very few Basque nationalist representatives being elected at the mentioned institutions. Mitchel Labéguerie was elected a member of the French national assembly in 1962 and Jean Etcheverry-Ainchart was also elected a member of the national assembly and conseiller général from Baigorri as a member of Enbata. Indeed, in 1946, as a member of the national assembly, Etcheverry-Ainchart presented a bill calling for the creation of a Basque Department within the French Republic. But these are exceptions to the norm.

XI. Today, the Basque Nationalist parties in Iparralde are the same as the ones in Hegoalde: EAJ-PNV is called in Iparralde Parti Nationaliste Basque (PNB), Eusko Alkartasuna (EA) and Batasuna is known as Abertzaleen Batasuna (AB). Historically the Basque nationalist political movement in Iparralde has known different coalitions, namely, Enbata,[206] EHAS,[207] EMA,[208] EB.[209] There has

---

[206]   Enbata was a Basque nationalist cultural force created in 1953 by

On Basque politics

been a strong increase in popular support for the Basque nationalist forces in Iparralde in the last four decades that has doubled their votes in this period of time:

1967	1978	1986	1988	1993	1997	2002
Enbata	EHAS	EMA	EMA-EB	AB-EA	AB-EA-PNB	AB-PNB
4.63%	3.59%	3.77%	5.65%	6.65%	9.30%	7.42%
5,035 votes	4,924	5,081	6,756	8,179	11,297	9,503

Evolution of the Basque nationalist vote in Iparralde (1967-2002).

members of the extinct Basque Students' Association (AEB, Association des Etudiants Basques), among them, Mitchel Burucoa, Mixel Labéguerie, Pierre Larzabal, Jean Louis Davant, Jean Fagoaga, Jacques Abeberry, Ximun Haran, Michel Eppherre and other Basque patriots in Iparralde. On April 15 1963, during the celebration of the Aberri Eguna or Day of the Basque Country, Enbata officially became a political party by passing, at the first assembly of the new political force *La Charte d'Itsassou*, a political manifesto according to which the Basque Country is a nation divided into two states that has the right to become an independent state. [207] The EHAS or Euskal Herriko Alderdi Sozialista (Socialist Party of the Basque Country) was a marxist and Basque nationalist political party created in 1975 by Santi Brouard from the unification of two political forces, the Basque Socialist Party (EAS, Euskal Alderdi Sozialista) in Hegoalde and the Peoples' Socialist Party in Iparralde (HAS, Herriko Alderdi Sozialista). In 1977 EHAS and Basque Socialists (ES, Eusko Sozialistek) created the People's Socialist Revolutionary Party (HASI, Herri Alderdi Sozialista Iraultzailea); "Hasi" means in Basque "to begin." In 1978 HASI became part of the Basque Socialist Union (KAS, Koordinadora Abertzale Sozialista) and was incorporated into the coalition Herri Batasuna and, as a consequence of the union, EHAS disappeared in 1979. [208] The Leftist Nationalist Movement (EMA, Ezkerreko Mugimendu Abertzalea), a socialist and nationalist political force, was created in 1985. In 1988 EMA joined Basque Union (EB, Euskal Batasuna) and the coalition got 6.756 votes in Iparralde. EMA and EB were included in the coalition Nationalist Union (AB, Abertzaleen Batasuna) and got 8.179 votes in the elections of 1993. In 1994 all these groups, EMA, EB and HA (Herriaren Alderekin) joined the coalition Abertzaleen Batasuna (AB) and the coalition formed the Federation of Solidary Regions and Peoples (RPS, Régions et Peuples Solidaires) for the European parliament. [209] Basque Union (EB, Euskal Batasuna).

PC. In the regional elections held in March 2010 the Basque nationalist parties increased their electoral strength reaching (in coalition with the strong political force Europe Écologie) about 18 percent of the votes in Iparralde. A historic result.

The largest party in the first round of elections was the Socialist Party (PS, Parti Socialiste) led by Bernard Uthurry with 74,089 votes or 32.71 percent of the total valid votes in the entire department of the Pyrénées-Atlantiques; the second political force was Liaison Committee of the Presidential Majority (MP, Comité de Liaison de la Majorité Présidentielle), a force that supported Nicolas Sarkozy, led by Alain Lamassoure that in the first round won 44,865 votes or 19.81 percent; the third political force, the Democratic Movement (MovDem, Mouvement Démocrate) led by Jean-Jacques Lasserre, got 39,993 votes or 17.66 percent.

As regards the Basque nationalist parties, the results of Europe Écologie (EE),[210] a coalition supported by Eusko Alkartasuna (EA) and led by David Grosclaude, got the support of 11.85 percent of the voters in Iparralde, representing 12,622 votes. Europe Écologie joined the Socialist Party list in the second round but the candidate of EA, Manex Pagola, could not be included in the final list because he was not in the top position of the list proposed by Europe Écologie. With 23,349 votes, 10.31 percent of the votes of the entire department of the Pyrénées-Atlantiques, EE was the fourth largest political force in the first electoral round.

Led by Jean Tellechea and under the name of Régionalisme (Reg), EAJ-PNV has achieved the best results ever. With 7,030 votes, 6.6 percent of the vote in Iparralde and 3.1 percent of the entire department of the Pyrénées-Atlantiques, this political force has doubled its electoral support with respect to the European elections in 2009 in which this political party received about 4,000 votes. In the other four departments of Aquitaine (not including Iparralde) EAJ-PNV had only received 62 votes, so that it represents 0.66 percent of the votes of the entire region of Aquitaine and thus it does not reach the minimum 5 percent in

---

[210] Europe Écologie is a coalition of the following parties: The Greens (Les Verts), Fédération Régions et Peuples Solidaires including Eusko Alkartasuna (EA) and the Occitan Party (PO, Partit Occitan), Civil Society, and independents.

order to ally another list and be able to participate in the second electoral round.

Abertzaleen Batasuna (AB), within the coalition Euskal Herria Bai (EH Bai) led by Peio Etxeberri asked their voters to give a vote of protest and, as a consequence, between 4,000 and 5,000 invalid votes were registered so we can say that about 4 percent of voters followed the instructions of EH Bai in the elections held in March 2010.

On the elections of March 1, 2009

Pete Cenarrusa. We should speak about the Spanish electoral laws and their political consequences regarding the elections of 1 March 2009 for the Basque parliament.

Xabier Irujo. Yes. The question in that occasion was how to get more than 50 percent of the seats at a certain parliament (absolute majority) with barely 40 percent of the votes, 13 percent less than the first political force.

PC. It took two steps:

- Banning a Basque nationalist political party (Batasuna) under the anti-terror law.
- Perturbation of the principles of the Law D'Hont of political representation (proportionality).

XI. Right. Let's focus for now on the second point, the perturbation of the formulas of apportionment. We will discuss the Batasuna case and the *Judicial War* against ETA in other chapter.

The proportional representation voting system adopted in the Spanish state differs from the American or British plurality-majority voting system where the candidate with the best electoral results represents an electoral district. By virtue of the Spanish proportional representation system, the number of seats a political party wins in elections should be proportional to its electoral support. However, unlike in the United States where people vote directly for a candidate, people vote for political parties (lists of candidates). So, in an ideal case, if a political party wins 25 percent of the votes it should have 25 percent of the seats of the Parliament.

PC. It is quite a democratic system.

XI. Yes, indeed. Let's explain it with an example; let's say that elections have been held in the Basque Autonomous Community (BAC) and that there were twelve candidacies and seventy five seats in parliament. And let's say that the results were the following:

Political party	Electoral results in percentage	Percentage of Seats (75 seats)
Party 1	38.67%	29
Party 2	22.68%	17.01
Party 3	17.40%	13.05
Party 4	12.44%	9.33
Party 5	5.37%	4.02
Party 6	2.33%	1.75
Party 7	0.34%	0.25
Party 8	0.33%	0.24
Party 9	0.19%	0.14
Party 10	0.13%	0.09
Party 11	0.10%	0.07
Party 12	0.01%	0.007

The parliament has seventy five seats, so we have a problem, since we cannot divide the seats (we cannot have ten candidates seated on 9.33 seats). To solve this problem, election designers developed different mathematical methods of apportionment (the process of allocating political power among the candidacies). The d'Hondt formula is one of them, named after Victor d'Hondt, the lawyer who developed it in 1878.

PC. Although the formula is named after d'Hondt the same system was invented previously by Thomas Jefferson as a way to allocate seats among the states at Congress after elections.

XI. Right. By applying different algebraic variables we may vary the proportion so each party gets a complete digit (a whole number of seats). Among these variables, it is established that in order to gain parliamentary representation a political party has to have a minimum percentage of votes. So if the minimum is established at

2 percent we automatically eliminate Parties 7 to 12 from the table. As a consequence, the result of the application of the d'Hondt method could have been the following:

Political party	Electoral results in percentage	Proportional allocation of seats (75 seats)	Number of seats allocated
Party 1	38.67%	29	30
Party 2	22.68%	17.01	17
Party 3	17.40%	13.05	13
Party 4	12.44%	9.33	9
Party 5	5.37%	4.02	4
Party 6	2.33%	1.75	2
Party 7	0.34%	0.25	0
Party 8	0.33%	0.24	0
Party 9	0.19%	0.14	0
Party 10	0.13%	0.09	0
Party 11	0.10%	0.07	0
Party 12	0.01%	0.007	0

Once each party has a number of seats, their representatives elect the president of the government. Each representative has a vote so the candidate winning most votes becomes President. This way Party 1 has 30 votes, but Parties 2 and 3 together also have 30 votes, so a coalition between Party 1, 5 and 6, with absolute majority (36 votes out of 75), could be formed. The first candidate of Party 1 would become President and parties 5 and 6 could have one or two ministries of the government and in exchange would vote for the candidate of Party 1.

PC. But the system may be manipulated in many ways, that is, once the proportion is not exact, some parties can easily win "extra" representation by, for instance, altering the size or structure of the constituencies or changing the number of elected representatives per constituency.

XI. Right. And that's exactly what happens in the Spanish system. And here we come to reality. The results that we have mentioned are the ones of the Basque Parliament's elections in 2005, and the political parties are the following:[211]

Political party	Electoral results in percentage	Proportional allocation of seats (75 seats)	Number of seats finally allocated	Distortion in the proportion of allocated seats
Party 1 (PNV & EA)	38.67%	29	29	= 0%
Party 2 (PSOE)	22.68%	17.01	18	+ 0.99%
Party 3 (PP)	17.40%	13.05	15	+ 1.95%
Party 4 (EHAK)	12.44%	9.33	9	- 0.33%
Party 5 (EB/IU)	5.37%	4.02	3	- 1.02%
Party 6 (Aralar)	2.33%	1.75	1	- 0.75%

PC. The two only political parties earning an "extra" representation are the Spanish constitutionalists, that is, the Spanish Workers' Socialist Party (PSOE) and the Popular Party (PP). In total, the Spanish constitutionalist forces were apportioned an extra 2.94 percent. Meanwhile the nationalist and leftist blocs lost 2.1 percent. And this extra apportionment supposed an increment of 3.92 percent of the total votes, as we are going to see.

XI. And not by chance. The results are the product of a meticulously designed variation of the d'Hondt method.

The situation is the following. As we have already seen, political parties in the southern Basque Country are divided into three blocs: Spanish constitutionalists, Basque nationalists and the Leftist bloc. The Basque nationalist bloc represented in 2005 53.44 percent of the votes (resulting from the addition of the Basque

---

[211]   The official data of the Basque elections are available in English at: http://www.euskadi.net/elecciones/indice_i.htm

nationalist political forces PNV, EA, EHAK and Aralar), meanwhile the Spanish constitutionalist bloc represented 40.08 percent. The rest, 5.37 percent corresponded to the leftist bloc, historically linked to Basque nationalism and formed by a single political party, IU-EB or United Left (Federalists). That's why Juan Jose Ibarretxe, member of the Basque Nationalist Party (PNV) was elected president of the Basque autonomous state with the support of all political forces except the PSOE and the PP.

Electoral campaign poster of the socialist party (PSOE) under the motto "Yes, we can" in March 2009. In the photograph, the candidate for president of the Basque Autonomous Community Patxi López (left) and the president of the Spanish government José Luis Rodríguez Zapatero (right). Source: Diario de Noticias.

PC. With the support of 40 percent of the votes, the Spanish constitutionalist forces were never going to win elections, so during the mandate of José María Aznar (2000-2004), two steps were taken in order to gain control of the Basque parliament, that is, in order to obtain 51 percent of the seats at the BAC parliament with 40 percent of the political representation.

XI. An example of the concept of democracy *à la carte*. And here we are again. If we take a look at the results in 2005, we see that even if the Spanish constitutionalist bloc had the support of 40.08 percent of the votes, won 33 seats (PSOE 18 and PP 15), that is, 44 percent of the seats at the Basque Parliament.

PC. It was then necessary to "earn" an extra 7 percent.

XI. Yes. The first step was taken in 2003 by banning Batasuna, and thus eliminating 12.44 percent of the Basque nationalist vote under the charge of terrorism.

PC. By doing so the Spanish constitutional bloc could definitely expect an increase in its number of seats at the Basque parliament. But several things went wrong. A second political party was immediately created in 2005 (EHAK) that won two more seats than the ones obtained by Batasuna four years earlier in the elections of 2001.

Demonstration against the illegalization of Batasuna in April 2011 under the motto "Normalization of the Basque Country: Legalization now". Source: Diario de Noticias.

XI. Right. So for the next elections (2009) Spanish justice had to make sure that no alternative for Batasuna was allowed to run for the parliament.

Even so, this was not enough. It could be reasonably expected that some electoral supporters of Batasuna would give their votes to another Basque nationalist force, so a further perturbation is necessary in order to ensure 51 percent of the seats at the Basque parliament.

First of all we have to mention that according to article 163 of the Spanish Organic Law 5/1985, of June 19, of the General Electoral System, and also according to the Basque Law 6/2000 of October 4, for the amendment of article 11.1 of the Law 5/1990 of June 15, of the Basque Parliament Elections[212] to access the allocation of seats it is required that the electoral list obtains at least 3 percent of the total valid votes cast in the respective constituency. Also, it is crucial to understand that there is not a single constituency for the whole BAC but that there are three separated constituencies, namely, Araba, Gipuzkoa, and Bizkaia.

Demostration against political trials in the Basque Country in July 2011. Source: Diario de Noticias.

The allocation of seats based on the D'Hondt Law is conducted according to the following rules:

1) The system does not take into consideration those lists of candidates that have not obtained at least 3 percent of the valid votes cast in a given constituency.

2) The number of votes obtained by the rest of the lists of candidates (the ones that have obtained 3 percent of the

---

212 *Ley Orgánica 5/1985, de 19 de junio, del Régimen Electoral General* and *Ley 6/2000, de 4 de octubre, para la modificación de la Ley 5/1990, de 15 de junio, de Elecciones al Parlamento Vasco.*

votes or more) are ranked from the highest to the lowest in a column.

3) The number of votes obtained by each candidate is divided by 1, 2, 3, etc., until the number of seats of the constituency, forming a table (with the lists of candidates in the rows and the number of votes resultant of the divisions in the columns). The seats are allocated to the lists of candidates in the table following a decreasing order.

Let's give the practical example provided by article 163 of the law Organic Law 5/1985, of June 19, of the General Electoral System. Let's imagine a 480,000 valid votes cast in a constituency to choose eight deputies. The vote is divided among candidates from six parties. If we take, in decreasing order, the eight biggest numbers (the ones in bold type in the table), we see that Party 1 gets four representatives (four numbers in bold type), Party 2 gets two, and Parties 3 and 4 get one representative each. Parties 5 and 6 do not get any representation. In the case of a tie between two different lists for a given position (same number of votes in two of the cells), the seat shall be allocated to the list with the biggest number of votes overall. If the two lists have an equal number of total votes, the first tie will be broken by drawing lots and the successive ties will be solved alternately. The seats for each candidate shall be given to the candidates listed in the electoral lists in the order of placement in which they appear.

	By 1	By 2	By 3	By 4	By 5	By 6	By 7	By 8
Party 1	**168,000**	**84,000**	**56,000**	**42,000**	33,600	28,000	24,000	21,000
Party 2	**104,000**	**52,000**	34,666	26,000	20,800	17,333	14,857	13,000
Party 3	**72,000**	36,000	24,000	18,000	14,400	12,000	10,285	9,000
Party 4	**64,000**	32,000	21,333	16,000	12,800	10,666	9,142	8,000
Party 5	40,000	20,000	13,333	10,000	8,000	6,666	5,714	5,000
Party 6	32,000	16,000	10,666	8,000	6,400	5,333	4,571	4,000

It is certain that the d'Hondt method favors somewhat the biggest parties in detriment to the smaller ones, but this extra "help" to the biggest parties can be distorted by altering the electoral districts. This is the case in the Basque Autonomous Community (BAC).

The BAC is formed by three historical territories, namely, Araba, Bizkaia, and Gipuzkoa that, as we have already mentioned, represent three separated constituencies. In 2009 Araba had 248,231 constituency members (number of voters entitled by law to vote in Araba). Bizkaia had 952,835 and Gipuzkoa had 574,986. However, each one of the three territories has 25 seats at the Basque parliament, which means that a single seat to parliament in Bizkaia is worth four times more votes than the one in Araba. Taking into account abstention,[213] a seat in Araba was obtained in the 2009 Basque parliament elections with 6,445.52 votes, in Bizkaia with 25,126.16 votes and in Gipuzkoa with 14,077.08 votes. And the constitutionalist political parties in Araba are stronger than the Basque nationalist ones that are stronger in Bizkaia and Gipuzkoa.

If we take a look at the following graphics we can easily notice the "distortion" between popular will and parliamentary representation at the Basque Country in favor of the Spanish constitutional bloc.

In 2005 the Basque nationalist bloc had the support of 53.44 percent of the voters but only obtained 52 percent of the representation at the Basque parliament (1.44 percent reduction), meanwhile the Spanish constitutional bloc won 40.08 percent of the votes and obtained 44 percent of the political representation (4 percent *plus*). The leftist bloc, with 5.37 percent of the votes only got 4 percent of the seats at the Basque parliament (1.37 percent reduction). And the distortion of the popular will in 2009 happened to be even worse.

---

[213]   The electoral participation rate is quite high in the Basque territories, 65.84 percent in Araba, 67.58 percent in Bizkaia and 63.06 percent in Gipuzkoa in the Basque Parliament elections of 2009.

Elections April 17, 2005

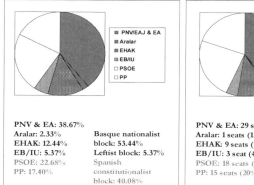
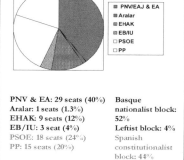

PNV & EA: 38.67%
Aralar: 2.33%
EHAK: 12.44%
EB/IU: 5.37%
PSOE: 22.68%
PP: 17.40%

Basque nationalist
block: 53.44%
Leftist block: 5.37%
Spanish
constitutionalist
block: 40.08%

PNV & EA: 29 seats (40%)
Aralar: 1 seats (1.3%)
EHAK: 9 seats (12%)
EB/IU: 3 seat (4%)
PSOE: 18 seats (24%)
PP: 15 seats (20%)

Basque
nationalist block:
52%
Leftist block: 4%
Spanish
constitutionalist
block: 44%

Percentage of popular votes in elections

Percentage of seats at the parliament (total 75 seats) or political representation

Elections March 1, 2009

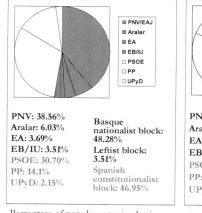
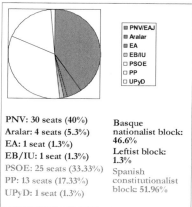

PNV: 38.56%
Aralar: 6.03%
EA: 3.69%
EB/IU: 3.51%
PSOE: 30.70%
PP: 14.1%
UPyD: 2.15%

Basque
nationalist block:
48.28%
Leftist block:
3.51%
Spanish
constitutionalist
block: 46.95%

PNV: 30 seats (40%)
Aralar: 4 seats (5.3%)
EA: 1 seat (1.3%)
EB/IU: 1 seat (1.3%)
PSOE: 25 seats (33.33%)
PP: 13 seats (17.33%)
UPyD: 1 seat (1.3%)

Basque
nationalist block:
46.6%
Leftist block:
1.3%
Spanish
constitutionalist
block: 51.96%

Percentage of popular votes in elections

Percentage of seats at the parliament (total 75 seats) or political representation

Campaign sign for the 2007 elections in the CCN. Roughly half of the EAE/ANV lists were declared illegal and, in 2008 the party was outlawed.

In 2009, after banning a political party (Batasuna, or 12.4 percent of the voters) the Basque nationalist bloc had 48.28 percent of the votes but only obtained 46.6 percent of the representation at the BAC parliament (1.33 percent reduction), meanwhile the Spanish constitutional bloc won 46.95 percent of the votes and obtained 51.96 percent of the representation (5.01 percent *plus*). The leftist bloc, with 3.51 percent of the votes got 1.3 percent of the seats at the Basque parliament (2.21 percent reduction). Overall, the system took from the Basque nationalist and leftist coalition 4.84 percent of the popular representation to give it to the constitutionalist forces. In other words, 4.84 percent of the people who gave their vote to the Basque nationalist or leftist forces were deceived: their votes were taken away from them and their will was ignored.

PC. So, the PSOE and the PP in coalition with 46.9 percent of the popular support governed in the Basque Country by virtue of the over-representation credited to them by an inappropriate application of the formulas of apportionment and the banning of a political party. This is a real life example of what we consider the perturbation of the principles of the Law D'Hont of political representation (proportionality) we mentioned earlier.

On language policies

Xabier Irujo. The Basque conflict is essentially a cultural conflict. The conflict resulting from the clash of three different traditions, the Basque, the French and the Spanish, each of them expressed in its own language. After two hundred years of repression of the Basque language, up to the point of currently being on the edge of disappearing in Iparralde, the Basque nationalist political forces have concluded that the only formula ensuring a future for the Basque culture and the Basque language is by constituting an independent Basque state.

Since the first Spanish constitution was drafted in 1812 and only after hundreds of laws, norms and decrees prohibiting the use of the Basque language were passed, the Spanish constitution of 1978 established on article 3 that,

> 1. *Castilian is the official Spanish language of the State. All Spaniards have the duty to know it and the right to use it.*
> 2. *The other Spanish languages shall also be official in the respective Autonomous Communities in accordance with their Statutes of Autonomy.*
> 3. *The wealth of the different linguistic forms of Spain is a cultural heritage which shall be especially respected and protected.*[214]

In other words, all Basques have the duty of knowing Spanish but only the right of knowing Basque and, as a consequence, Basque is far from being genuinely co-official for the official relationship with any institution of the central state has to

---

214   In the original Spanish:
1. El castellano es la lengua española oficial del Estado. Todos los españoles tienen el deber de conocerla y el derecho a usarla.
2. Las demás lenguas españolas serán también oficiales en las respectivas Comunidades Autónomas de acuerdo con sus Estatutos.
3. La riqueza de las distintas modalidades lingüísticas de España es un patrimonio cultural que será objeto de especial respeto y protección.

be carried out in Spanish, as must many transactions regarding the Basque autonomous state.

Similarly, since 1789 the Basque language has been forbidden or ignored by the French state. Only 200 years after the creation of the French parliament has an amendment to the constitution been proposed stating that *les langues régionales appartiennent au patrimoine de la France*, that is, that the regional languages belong to the patrimony of France.[215] Nothing is said about including them into the educational system or about making their use co-official nor about protecting, promoting or encouraging their use through political measures. Right now, it is just a vague statement.

> *Federalism and Superstition speak low Breton, Emigration and Hatred of the Republic speak German; Counter-revolutionary spirit speaks Italian, and Fanaticism speaks Basque. We have to break these instruments of injury and error.*[216]

This is part of the Report of the Committee of Public Salvation known as *Rapport Barère*, on the convenience of using and of harnessing the French language solely and making the rest of the languages spoken in the French state disappear, among them the Basque language, *the language of Fanaticism*. It was passed and adopted in 1794, and since then the Basque language has been outlawed in the French state whose only official language since then has been French.

---

[215] New article 75.1 of the French constitution. Included under Title 12, *On Territorial Communities*.

[216] Report of the Committee of Public Salvation, Rapport Barère, on the convenience of using the French language solely. 1794. In original French, *Le fédéralisme et la superstition parlent bas-breton; l'émigration et la haine de la République parlent allemand; la contre-révolution parle l'italien, et le fanatisme parle le basque. Cassons ces instruments de dommage et d'erreur.* Irujo, Xabier, Iñigo Urrutia, *A Legal History of the Basque Language (1789-2009)*, Eusko Ikaskuntza / Society for Basque Studies – Stanford University, Donostia/San Sebastián, 2009. P. 97. Also, Gazier, A. (Ed.), *Lettres à Grégoire sur les Patois de France (1790-1794). Documents inédits sur la langue, les mœurs et l'état des esprits dans les diverses régions de la France, au début de la Révolution*, Slatkine Reprints, Genève, 1969. Pp. 94-95.

According to linguistic surveys passed by Henri Grégoire in 1792, out of twenty eight million inhabitants only three million spoke French correctly (11 percent), as their first language. About six million people did not speak a word of French; the political conclusion was obvious, *French had to be imposed.* Consequently, the genesis of the French state after the Revolution in 1789 and the creation of Spanish state after the War of the Seven Years in 1839, carries the imposition of an excluding linguistic policy that accelerated the retreat of the Basque language. Both states, strongly centralist, fed the idea of a single language. The Convention of France declared, through its spokesmen, Monsieur Barère and Monsieur Grégoire, that the Basque language was a "Patois" and, therefore, the language of the antirevolutionary fanaticism and a brake for the development of the ideas of the Enlightenment. So it had to disappear.

Indeed, from the creation of the French state in 1789 and the drafting of the first Spanish constitution in 1812, the Basque language has known no less than five hundred laws, decrees, orders, norms, legal initiatives, recommendations and official reports regarding its elimination or exclusion in both the Spanish and the French states. The norms have always been of three different types:

1. Prohibitions. Laws simply prohibiting the use of the Basque language and consequently punishing its use. We already have mentioned many among the norms passed in the 19th century in the chapter *On the rising of the first Basque political nationalism.* But the Basque society would know many more during the 20th century, especially under the Francoist dictatorship (1939-1975).

2. Exclusions. Some other laws do not prohibit the use of the Basque language but discriminate against its use by prioritizing the use of Spanish and French or just by simply regulating the exclusive use of Spanish and French. The legal result is exactly the same as the one by the laws that prohibit the use of a language. In this sense, the Spanish governments have been historically much more active in using prohibition laws while the French administration has made use of this second way of tacit prohibition.

[341]

3. Omissions. Other laws simply omit the Basque language which, consequently, gets outlawed.

As mentioned, one of the hardest periods of history for the Basque language and, in general for the Basque culture and people, has been the Francoist dictatorship (1936-1975), during which hundreds of measures of different types were taken against the use of the Basque language. Among the official dispositions of the New Regime on linguistic policy we may mention the following ones:

- Ordinance by the Military commandant of Lizarra (Estella) prohibiting the word *agur* (meaning "good-bye" in Basque). September 25, 1936.
- Ordinance by the Governor of Bizkaia and Gipuzkoa to prohibit the use of Basque spellings, so that the characters "k", "tx" and "b" were forbidden. December 7, 1936.
- Public document on the fulfillment of the prohibition of speaking Basque. April 1937.
- Public document on the imposition of sanctions to anyone infringing the dispositions on the prohibition against speaking any language or dialect different from Spanish. May 29, 1937.
- Ordinance by the Commander's office on the prohibition from using the Basque language at church after eight o'clock in the morning. June 1, 1937.
- Agreement on the destitution of the professors occupying the chair of Basque language Tomás Aguirre Urdalleta and Jose de Altuna. Official Bulletin of the Basque Country, November 13, 1937.
- Ordinance by the Delegate of Public Order of Gipuzkoa on the prohibition to hold sermons in Basque. December 17, 1937.
- Ordinance on the prohibition of using names with 'separatist' meaning like "Iñaki" and "Kepa." May 21, 1938. Official Bulletin of the State, May 26, 1938.
- Ordinance by the Ministry of Organization and Trade-union Action on the prohibition of the use of any language other than Spanish in the titles, trade names, statutes, and

in the call and celebration of the assemblies of the dependent organizations of the Ministry of Commerce. May 21, 1938. Official Bulletin of the State, May 26, 1938.

- Ordinance by the Commandant's office on the prohibition to hold sermons in Basque. May 30, 1938.
- Ordinance by the Ministry of Justice on the exclusion of the Basque language from the Registry. August 12, 1938.
- Ordinance by the Ministry of Industry and Commerce on the exclusion of the regional languages from the Registry of the Industrial Property. May 20, 1940.
- Circular of the Civil Governor of Gipuzkoa on the use of Basque names. October 30, 1940.
- Procedural norms for the lodging of appeals before the Court of Marine Preys. December 21, 1940. Article 13 on the exclusion of any language that is not the Spanish. Official Bulletin of the State, December 25, 1940.
- Decree on the Regulation of notaries of June 2, 1944. Article 148 on the exclusion of any language other than Spanish from public documents. Official Bulletin of the State, January 8, 1945.
- Ordinance by the Ministry of Industry and Commerce on the prohibition to designate merchant ships with non-Spanish names. January 15, 1945. Official Bulletin of the State, January 24, 1945.
- Communication N° 2486 by the Fourth Office (*Negociado*) of the Civil Government of Bizkaia, on October 27 1949, requiring that the relatives and owners of the tombs or pantheons with inscriptions in Basque replace such inscriptions by others written in Spanish. October 27, 1949.
- Authorization by the Provincial Delegate of Information and Tourism for the broadcasting of certain programs of the Popular Radio of Loyola in Basque and the prohibition to make publicity in this language. October 30, 1964.
- Law on primary education of February 2, 1967. Article 7 on the exclusion of any language other than Spanish from education.

Pete Cenarrusa. It is said that a language disappears when the people who speak it do not use it anymore; well, that is clear. We should ask though why a person abandons his or her own language or which the circumstances in which such abandonment is produced are. During the Franco years (and decades before him) the use of Basque language was prohibited by the Spanish authorities. By the end of the 19th century it was forbidden in schools. Kids caught speaking Basque were punished by being forced to wear a finger ring. The ring was supposed to be a mark of shame. In 1936, when Franco's fascist troops took the city of Bilbao, the *slogan* was "One Nation: Spain; one language: Spanish," clearly expressing the political ideology and aim. I think that the list of laws that you have brought here does not need further comment. But, there is a report, written by Claude G. Bowers, U.S. Ambassador to the Spanish Republic, that I think deserves quoting in this context, for it provides the point of view of a person directly involved in the political situation of the rising of such an inhuman dictatorship,

It is universally agreed that the Basque language is one of the oldest and purest in the world, having been spoken by the Basques as far as history goes. No race in the world has been more tenacious in the preservation of its language and culture through all the upheavals of the last two thousand years known to history. Great numbers of the Basques speak Basque only, and all of them who speak Spanish also use Basque in their homes. In great numbers of parishes Basque has been used exclusively for a thousand years in religious worship. Under the order of General Anido an exception in the case of worship is permitted in churches in hamlets (…).

This order, the product of a typical military mind, convinced that human nature itself can be changed by bayonets as in Russia or in Germany, is an illustration of the blunders I think certain to be made by the Francoists in the event of a military victory. This attitude towards the Basques from the beginning of the war is hard to reconcile with the Spanish common sense, and it indicates how far the supporters of Franco have gone in their attempt to apply foreign, German and Italian methods to Spain. Instead of attempting to conciliate the Basques, every move being made is calculated permanently and bitterly to alienate them from the proposed new regime. To illustrate:

1. *The first blunder, admitted to me by many Francoists of high standing, was the alignment of the rights against that autonomy, which the Rights themselves had always supported until recently. This drove the Basques to support the Lefts in defense of their ancient rights and privileges.*

2. *The extermination of Guernica, "holy city of the Basques," by the German air force was an almost incredible piece of stupidity, and the impression left on the minds and hearts of the Basques by this barbarous act will never be wiped out.*

3. *Having crushed the Basques, instead of trying to reconcile with them, the Francoists almost immediately entered upon the work of driving all Francoists of Basque blood from all positions that had been held under Franco up to the time of the destruction of their country. Thus, in San Sebastian many Basques who were rebels and who held minor offices were immediately discharged, because they were Basques.*

4. *And now comes the supreme blunder of trying to wipe out the Basque language and culture, something that the efforts of numerous forces have been unable to accomplish in thousands of years. Of course they will not succeed; they will merely make an implacable enemy within the nation.*

5. *In order to cultivate the Basques, who were democrats and not extremists, as is now universally agreed, the Francoists while persecuting them in ways just mentioned, are assiduously cultivating the syndicalist minority, offering it all sorts of inducements to join the Falangists whose plans are so similar.*

The offensiveness of this to the Basques is in fact that the syndicalists are atheists where the Basques are devout Catholics; and that throughout the struggle for the defense of the Basque Country, the syndicalists by their excesses and crimes and refusal to cooperate were a constant embarrassment to the Basque Government in defending its country.[217]

---

[217]   Persecution of the Basques: Forbidding Use of Their Ancient Language. Report by Claude G. Bowers to the U.S. State Department. Donibane Lohitzune, March 24, 1938. National Archives and Records Administration, College Park, U.S. Ambassador Claude G. Bowers Files (Files 852.402/…), Document 852.402/9.

Each of these measures constituted a clear violation of human rights, yet only some of them raised any international outcry, such as the order by the civil governor of Bizkaia on October 27, 1949 demanding the removal of Basque inscriptions from graves, tombs and sepulchers.

While the Basque language was banned in the Basque Country, it was commonly used by the Basques in Idaho and other parts of America. Secretary of State Pete Cenarrusa being gifted a cake in his birthday with an inscription in Basque reading *Happy Birthday to Our Boss*. Source: Cenarrusa archive.

XI. None of these measures were rectified until after Franco's death in November 1975. It wasn't until November 1982 that the first law[218] formalizing the official status of the Basque language was approved and only in the Basque Autonomous Community; the Basque language was not granted an official status in Navarre until 1986.[219]

---

[218]   *Ley 10/1982, de 24 de noviembre, básica de normalización del uso del euskera (Law 10/1982, of November 24 on the normalization of the use of the Basque language)*.
[219]   *Ley foral 18/1986 del "vascuence" en Navarra*. This law of the Basque language in Navarre was passed on December 15, 1986.

Clearly, this mass of regulations on top of the repression of the Basque people, had a significant impact on their language. The Basque government in exile (1937-1975) was forced to design a language policy in the Americas, which was the origin, for instance, of the Basque Studies Department at the Universidad de la República de Uruguay, in Montevideo, in 1944.

There is a theory of the language that lies behind the regulations against the Basque language. There is still today a strong feeling that the Basque language is no more than a nuisance or an obstacle for the unity of the state. This idea is based on the following basic principles compiled and defended for first time as a thesis by Miguel Unamuno but developed through the 19th century since the French Revolution:

- Basque cannot develop: it is a fossil language. From this point of view Basque is a language that has not evolved since prehistory.
- It is very difficult to learn Basque and that's due to the fact that indeed it is a prehistoric language, not useful or suitable anymore for modern life.
- The reason for not having developed through the centuries is internal; according to these authors the Basque language supposedly has a prehistoric grammar that impedes its evolution and survival.
- Consequently, the Basque language is dying and there is nothing to do.
- Even more, to do something to help the Basque language would be unnatural and aberrant. Thus, no one should try to keep it alive for it is a natural death.
- The Basque language is not a culture language: it is only useful for family life.
- Peoples and cultures are culturally superior and inferior; Spanish and French are superior meanwhile the Basque language is inferior for it is not possible to express in Basque what it can be expressed in these other two languages. Also, Basque is only spoken by less than a million inhabitants meanwhile these two languages are spoken by millions of people.

- To think or to speak in Basque is dangerous: it makes people nationalist, Catholic or fanatical (depending on the period of time and the ideology of the regime in force).
- As a natural general consequence, Basque people should speak Spanish or French to become more cultured, less nationalist and to help the Basque language die in a natural way.

We may change the word "Basque" from the paragraph above for any other minority language (Catalan, Corsican, Flemish, Gaelic, Tyrolean, Washoe, Paiute…), and we would have the discourse of hundreds of centralist or assimilationist administrations heading multicultural states all over the world.

PC. Not a long time ago, in November 2007, a Journalist named Keith Johnson published an article in the Wall Street Journal along the very same line of what you have pointed out. Johnson wrote that we Basques were "inquisitors" for wanting to impose the Basque language on anyone… Well, no Basque language was allowed in schools, universities or public administration until thirty years ago, and even today students are not allowed to study in Basque in a big part of the Basque Country, because it is not official, nor in the French state neither in the southern part of Navarre. I believe the situation I've just described is close enough of what we understand by "inquisition." Even today many leaders of the Popular Party still do not condemn the Franco regime's cultural policies. In fact, in October 2007, Jaime Mayor Oreja, former leader of Popular Party of the Basque Country, declared that "he was not going to condemn a regime that still represents a wide sector of Spaniards." On 14 May 2009 he said that his great grandfather was a great man and a visionary for he forbade his grandfather to speak Basque at home and this way they were no longer ignorant…[220] According to this politician for whom it is necessary not to speak Basque in order to speak good Spanish, the Basque people have to understand (and even *encourage* the idea) that Basque should not become an official language of the European

---

[220]   In the original Spanish: *mi bisabuelo se esforzó para que sus hijos no se encerrasen en el granero. Prohibió que hablaran el vasco en casa, para que aprendieran bien el español.*

Union; instead (he argues) they should promote Spanish so it becomes the "second greatest language of the Union."

Parliamentary session of the Idaho's legislature. Source: Cenarrusa archive.

No, certainly Basques do not understand culture and languages in that sense, and Basques have never believed in inquisition. If, as stated by Johnson in his article, more than 80 percent of the courses in schools are taught in Basque, it is solely due to the fact that parents have voluntarily decided to take their children to Basque schools, for no Spanish law imposes anyone to go to one or to the other type of school (where classes are taught in Spanish, in Basque or in both languages). And, as a consequence of the demand of the parents, the administration has to have teachers able to teach in Basque.

One hundred-eighty scholars, mainly linguists, responded to the article by replying point by point on every one of the mistakes, inaccuracies and, finally, fabrications of the piece.[221]

---

[221]   The article may be found in the documental appendix.

Boiseko Ikastola, founded in 1998, is open to both Basque and non-Basque students, 2 to 6 years of age. All classes are taught in Basque. As the web site of the Ikastola underlines, research has shown that exposing children to a second language at an early age gives them an advantage in areas such as mathematics, language and cultural awareness. Source: Irujo Ametzaga archive.

The Basque language is the oldest European language, far from being a regional language it is the Basque national language and does not belong to the patrimony of the French or the Spanish states but to the people, as any other cultural patrimony of humanity. The right to use a language in private and public life is an inalienable right conforming to the principles embodied in the United Nations International Covenant on Civil and Political Rights of 1966. In virtue of Article 7.1 of the European Charter for Regional or Minority Languages passed at Strasbourg on November 5, 1992, in respect of minority languages, within the territories in which such languages are used and according to the situation of each language, the states shall base their policies, legislation and practice on the following objectives and principles:

1. *The recognition of the regional or minority languages as an expression of cultural wealth;*

2. *The respect of the geographical area of each regional or minority language in order to ensure that existing or new administrative*

divisions do not constitute an obstacle to the promotion of the regional or minority language in question;

3. *The need for resolute action to promote regional or minority languages in order to safeguard them;*

4. *The facilitation and/or encouragement of the use of regional or minority languages, in speech and writing, in public and private life;*

5. *The maintenance and development of links, in the fields covered by this Charter, between groups using a regional or minority language and other groups in the State employing a language used in identical or similar form, as well as the establishment of cultural relations with other groups in the State using different languages;*

6. *The provision of appropriate forms and means for the teaching and study of regional or minority languages at all appropriate stages;*

7. *The provision of facilities enabling non-speakers of a regional or minority language living in the area where it is used to learn it if they so desire;*

8. *The promotion of study and research on regional or minority languages at universities or equivalent institutions;*

9. *The promotion of appropriate types of transnational exchanges, in the fields covered by this Charter, for regional or minority languages used in identical or similar form in two or more States.*[222]

Furthermore, by virtue of the Charter the states should undertake to eliminate any unjustified distinction, exclusion, restriction or preference relating to the use of a minority language and intended to discourage or endanger the maintenance or development of it. At the same time, the signatory governments should promote, by appropriate measures, mutual understanding between all the linguistic groups of the country, especially by the inclusion of respect, understanding and tolerance in relation to minority languages among the objectives of education and training provided within their countries and encouragement of the mass media to pursue the same objective.

---

[222]   Woehrling, Jean-Marie, *The European Charter for Regional or Minority Languages: A Critical Commentary*, Council of Europe, Strasbourg, 2005. P. 119.

[351]

Visit of Senator Frank Church to Euzkadi Ikastola, Caracas (Venezuela), 1972. In the photograph the Basque preschool Euzkadi Ikastola that was created in exile in 1962 when teaching in Basque was forbidden in the Basque Country by the authorities of the Francoist regime. The school had more than one hundred students and was finally closed after the death of General Franco, when many of the families exiled in Venezuela came back to the Basque Country. In the photo, third line from below, eighth from the left, Xabier Irujo. Source: Frank Church archive at Boise State University.

XI. Maybe it is for these reasons that the French state is one of the few members of the European Union that has not signed the Charter. There are two points that should be underlined regarding the Charter. First, in determining their policy with regard to minority languages, the governments shall take into consideration the needs and wishes expressed by the groups which use such languages, something that it is completely ignored by the French administration and slightly regarded by the Spanish government or even the Navarrese government in the Chartered Community of Navarre. Secondly, the adoption of special measures in favor of minority languages aimed at promoting equality between the users of these languages and the rest of the population should not be considered to be an act of discrimination against the users of more widely-used languages. Something that both the Spanish Socialist Party and the Popular Party have claimed in the past.

PC. I consider that anyone who is forced to use a second or a third language when dealing with the administrative body of the state is being deprived of the minimum political rights and consequently would seek a new political framework for his or her language and culture. It is logical that after asking for respect and recognition, and having got so little of any of both, the Basques opted for claiming political independence in order to ensure the future of their culture and language.

I think that the poem by Gabriel Aresti, *My father's house*, written in 1963, perfectly represents this idea. Aresti was a Basque poet who was born into a non-Basque-speaking family in Bilbao but who began to study Basque at the age of fourteen on his own:

> *I shall defend*
> *The house of my father.*
> *Against wolves,*
> *Against drought,*
> *Against usury,*
> *Against the Justice,*
> *I shall defend*
> *The house of my father.*
> *I shall lose cattle,*
> *orchards,*
> *and pinewoods;*
> *I shall lose*
> *Interests,*
> *Income,*
> *And dividends,*
> *But I shall defend the house of my father.*
> *They will take away my weapons*
> *And with my hands I shall defend*
> *The house of my father;*
> *They will cut off my hands*
> *And with my arms I shall defend*
> *The house of my father;*
> *They will leave me*
> *Without arms,*

Without shoulders,
And without breasts,
And with my soul I shall defend
The house of my father.
I shall die,
My soul will be lost,
My descendence will be lost,
But the house of my father
Will remain
Standing.

XI. It is sad to see a person or a group of people interested in destroying culture. Languages, cultures, should never be the object of humiliation or punishment but considered as expressions of human heritage. Europe has dozens of languages. "United in diversity" is the motto of the European Union (EU). In fact, the Charter of Fundamental Rights of the EU, adopted in 2000, states that the Union shall respect linguistic diversity. Together with respect for the individual, openness towards other cultures, tolerance and acceptance of others, respect for linguistic diversity is a core value of the EU. This principle applies not only to the twenty-three official languages of the Union but also to the many minority languages spoken by millions of Europeans. In fact, it is a requirement to know at least two official languages to become an EU civil servant. Most of the Swedish citizens speak English, but this does not mean that the Swedish language should not be official. The same case could be applied to Slovenian (2 million speakers), Latvian or Maltese (less than 400.000 speakers), all of them official languages of the EU.

All languages are part of the world heritage. We should never consider diversity a problem but a challenge. I suppose we have to learn to let everyone speak their own languages; the voice in which a nation expresses herself, be it Spanish, French, English or Basque or any other in the world, deserves the respect owed to any culture. A lesson many have yet to learn.

On anti-terror policies and their collateral damage

Xabier Irujo. An important issue brought up by Lehendakari Ibarretxe in the Draft Statute presented at the Basque parliament on 27 September 2002 was the constitution of a Basque Judiciary power. The partisan use of the Judiciary by the Spanish government that between 1995 and 2003 introduced eighteen reforms of the criminal code (an average of more than two amendments per year) requires decentralizing the Judiciary to avoid further deterioration and discrediting of this branch.

The failure of the conversations at Algiers between ETA and the Spanish government promoted a series of measures clearly repressive such as the policy of dispersing ETA prisoners. In 1987 there were 435 ETA prisoners in Spanish prisons, most of them (around 73 percent in the two prisons on the outskirts of Madrid, Herrera de la Mancha and Alcala de Henares). When the negotiations of Algiers failed in 1989 the socialist government started dispersing ETA prisoners all over the prisons of Spain, trying, in this way, to break the unity of action of the organization. This policy of dispersion was also carried out by the French administration. As a result, at the end of 2003 there were 544 prisoners in 51 Spanish jails and 117 in 28 French jails.

Pete Cenarrusa. The policy of dispersal is clearly a violation of the fundamental rights of the inmates who are subjects of rights that should not be the object of negotiation, exchange or manipulation, on the basis of political interests. The policies of dispersal or isolation are examples of additional punishment on the prisoners and their relatives; prisoners should be in the prisons nearest to their social environment and family. According to the data provided by *Gara* in October 2003, altogether the relatives of the prisoners drive distances of over 500,000 miles per week to see their loved ones, that is, the equivalent of nearly 20 turns to the world or a return trip to the moon.

It is a fact that unnecessary or additional punishment may have short term results but in the long run has the effect of fueling further terrorist action. But, most important, it represents a violation of basic positive international and state covenants.

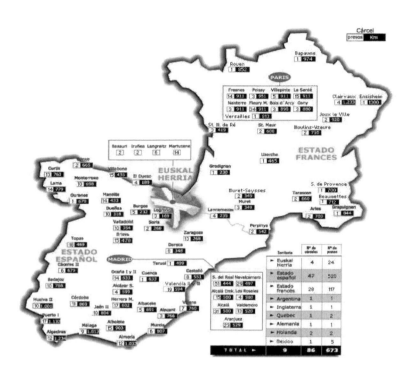

Policy of dispersal of ETA prisoners. From *Gara*, October 2003. In 2003 there were 673 ETA prisoners. In 2011 there are 704 ETA members in jail: 560 in Spanish prisons and 140 in French prisons. There four more prisoners in British, Mexican, Portuguese and Irish jails. 81 of the 560 prisoners in Spanish jails are women (14.5 percent). 438 have been sentenced by the Spanish Court hearing these cases (*Audiencia Nacional*) and 121 have not been sentenced yet (21.6 percent), but they are in prison under the anti-terror legislation. 337 prisoners are held under a high-security regime (*primer grado*); 181 under ordinary regime (*segundo grado*) and, only four have been granted open regime (*tercer grado*) between 2007 and 2011 in virtue of severe health problems.

XI. Article 11 of the Universal Declaration of Human Rights, adopted at the United Nations' General Assembly on December 10, 1948, specifies that,

- *Everyone charged with a penal offense has the right to be presumed innocent until proved guilty according to law in a public trial at which he has had all the guarantees necessary for his defense.*
- *No one shall be held guilty of any penal offense on account of any act or omission which did not constitute a penal offense, under national or international law, at the time when it was committed. Nor shall a heavier penalty be imposed than the one that was applicable at the time the penal offense was committed.*

In the same line, and in line with the international legislation, Article 55.2 of the Spanish Constitution of 1978 establishes that,

An organic law may determine the manner and the circumstances in which, on an individual basis and with the necessary participation of the courts and proper parliamentary control, the rights recognized in section 17, subsection 2, and 18, subsections 2 and 3, may be suspended for specific persons in connection with investigations of the activities of armed bands or terrorist groups.

In other words, only exceptionally and on an individual basis, under compulsory judicial intervention and with proper parliamentary control, can a person charged with terrorism have the rights recognized in articles 17.2, 18.2 and 18.3 of the Spanish constitution temporarily suspended. Article 17.2 states that *preventive arrest* may last no longer than the time strictly necessary in order to carry out the investigations aimed at establishing the events; in any case the person arrested must be set free or handed over to the judicial authorities within a maximum period of seventy-two hours. Article 18.2 states that *the home is inviolable*, and specifies that no entry or search may be made without the consent of the householder or a legal warrant, except in cases of flagrante delicto (principle of *inviolability of the dwelling*). Article 18.3 establishes the privacy of communications is guaranteed, particularly regarding postal, telegraphic and telephonic communications, except in the event of a court order.

In open disregard of the mentioned constitutional guidelines, the Spanish Congress drafted the Organic Law on terrorist crimes on October 29, 1980, which was issued on December 2 in the *Boletín Oficial del Estado* (BOE), the official state bulletin. This law was the implementation of Article 55.2 of the constitution dealing with the suspension of certain rights and freedoms (those contained in Articles 17.2, 18.2 and 18.3). However, the draft was repealed by the Spanish Constitutional Court, and four years later a new Organic Law 9/1984 of December 26, against the actions of armed gangs and terrorist elements was passed. However, on December 16, 1987, the Constitutional Court also declared Organic Law 9/1984 unconstitutional (sentence 199/1987) several provisions of the new anti-terror law.

Pete T. Cenarrusa, as Secretary of State of Idaho, with President Ronald Reagan and his wife Nancy Davis. Boise (Idaho), c. 1985. Source: Cenarrusa archive.

Among the main reasons for declaring various articles of Organic Law 9/1984 unconstitutional we may comment the following:

- Organic Law 9/1984 included the proclamation of "statement in support or in defense of terrorism" as a criminal action. However, Art. 55.2 of the Constitution specifies that the term "armed gangs" must be interpreted restrictively and always in connection, significance and scope with the "terrorist elements" mentioned in the Constitution.

- It allowed the extension of the governmental detention for seven days (168 hours), far beyond the constitutional limit of three days (72 hours).
- It allowed having a person arrested in solitary confinement, even without judicial intervention. This is a flagrant violation of Article 11 of the Universal Declaration of Human Rights, that is, the principle of *Presumption of innocence*. But it also contravened Article 55.2 of the Spanish Constitution that expressly stipulates *the necessary participation of the courts* during the detention of individuals held in custody.
- Organic Law 9/1984 allowed the *entry or search without the consent of the householder or a legal warrant* even in the case where it was not in flagrante delicto. The regulation of the registration or seizure without a warrant directly and patently contravened Article 18.2 of the Spanish constitution and several international covenants regarding the inviolability of the dwelling.
- It allowed the interception of private communications without a warrant.
- Organic Law 9/1984 permitted the closure of mass media under certain conditions.

PC. And these would henceforth become the basic aims of the anti-terror legislation of the Spanish Socialist Party (PSOE) and the Popular Party (PP) in the period 1984-2003. By virtue of the Spanish political principle of *Justicia a la carta*, if there is a law hindering a political goal, the law has to be changed or, if there is not a law permitting the trespass of the limits of certain executive action, then, it should be adopted.

XI. Right. Basically, the reforms of the Spanish Criminal Code and the Procedural law from 1984 to 2003 were intended to legalize the suspension of the habeas corpus (arrest, detention and solitary confinement without a warrant for periods exceeding 72 hours) and also intended to permit or contemplate the legal closure of mass media and political parties which entails the contravention of several fundamental human rights, among many others the following:

- Presumption of innocence.
- The principle of *Nullum crimen, nulla pœna, sine previa lege* (principle of legality of the law).
- Effective judicial protection.
- Right of inviolability of the dwelling.
- Freedom of speech (mainly referring to the closure of mass media or political parties).

The legal basis has been always the over-interpretation of the limits to the executive action in cases of terrorism contemplated in Article 55.2 of the Spanish Constitution. But we should bear in mind that the empowerment of police activity (executive action) above or beyond judicial control known as *favor libertatis* is one of the fundamental characteristics of a dictatorial regime. In this sense, the interception of the communications of a person made by order of a political authority or, failing that, of an administrative authority, comes to be especially adverse to the fundamental rights.

The first reform of the Criminal Code was implemented through the adoption of the Organic Law 3/1988, of May 25, on the reform of the Criminal Code. According to the new law the penalty for the crime of terrorism was stiffened (always applying the most severe degree of penalty).

PC. The imperative aggravation of the sentence entails the restriction of the rights and duties of the judge who is always limited to the most severe sentence. This is a contravention of the right of the defendant to have an individualized case, because each defendant has to be given the most severe punishment no matter the special circumstances of his/her case. And finally, it trivializes any possible extenuating circumstances of the case.

XI. Further on, by virtue of the Organic Law 4/1988, of May 25, of reform of the Code of Criminal Procedure:

- A person may be suspended in the exercise of public office under a committal for trial order that only collects evidence to be confirmed before the judge. This measure explicitly contravenes the principle of presumption of innocence.
- Organic Law 4/1988 legalized the extension of governmental detention without warrant from 72 hours to 120 hours or five days of solitary confinement. Attention was given to the possibility of extending the preventive arrest, which implies de facto the application of the penalty when the suspect has not yet been sentenced in court. Concretely, the protective custody was extended up to four years under the reform of 2003 of the Law on Criminal Procedure of 1988. Summarizing, if a person is suspected by the police of being a terrorist, he or she can be held in preventive arrest for five days completely isolated (no telephone calls and no visits). If after five days the police do not find evidence, that person can still remain in jail or *in protective custody* for a period of up to four years while evidence is collected against him/her.
- Organic Law 4/1988 allows the violation of the home: including arrest, search and seizure of objects without warrant.
- It allows the interception of private communications without a warrant (an order by the Minister of the Interior or the Director of State Security is enough), and also for an unlimited time.
- It allows the implementation of emergency procedures for terrorist offenses.
- It introduces the possibility of creating special courts through the principle of "court immediacy."

PC. The extension of governmental detention without warrant and in complete isolation with no cameras or legal supervision seems to pursue no other purpose but the implementation of torture. Moreover, it is a flagrant violation of the detainee's right to remain silent or to have a lawyer, all of which is contained in Article 9.3 of the International Covenant on Civil and Political Rights of December 16, 1966, as well as in Article 5.3 of the European Convention for the Protection of Human Rights and Fundamental

Freedoms of November 4, 1950, both ratified by the Spanish state on April 27, 1977, and September 26, 1979, respectively.

XI. Yes, indeed. When the Popular Party won elections in 1996, there was not much to invent or implement. Anyhow, after the entry into force of the new Criminal Code of 1995, there have been eighteen reforms to the Criminal Code or the procedural legislation during the government of the Popular Party (1996-2004), among them:

- 1980. Ley orgánica 11/1980, sobre delitos de terrorismo (on crimes of terrorism).
- 1984. Ley orgánica 9/1984, de 26 de diciembre, contra la actuación de bandas armadas y elementos terroristas (on the activities of armed gangs and terrorist elements).
- 1988. Ley orgánica 3/1988, de 25 de mayo, de reforma del código penal (reform of the criminal code).
- 1988. Ley orgánica 4/1988, de 25 de mayo, de reforma de la ley de enjuiciamiento criminal (reform of the law of criminal procedure).
- 1995. Ley orgánica 10/1995, de 23 de noviembre, del código penal (criminal code).
- 2000. Ley orgánica 6/2000 de reforma del código penal (reform of the criminal code).
- 2003. Ley orgánica 7/2003, de 30 de junio, de medidas de reforma para el cumplimiento íntegro y efectivo de las penas (on the full and effective enforcement of the sentences).
- 2003. Ley orgánica 20/2003, de 23 de diciembre, de modificación de la Ley orgánica del Poder Judicial y del Código Penal (reform of the Judicial Power Organization Act and the criminal code).

As in previous cases, by virtue of Organic Law 10/1995, of November 23 (criminal code), the penalties for those who belong, act in the service of or collaborate with armed groups, organizations or groups *whose purpose is to subvert the constitutional order or severely disrupt the public peace*, commit crimes or provoke havoc or fire (defined in Articles 346 and 351 respectively) were stiffened. Under these charges the person would be punished with imprisonment from fifteen to twenty years, as well as subject to the penalties attached to them if there was injury to life and limb or health.

Organic Law 6/2000 on the reform of the criminal code further increased penalties, regulated the punishment of *serious* disturbances in the course of plenary sessions of city councils and included the characterization of the crime of exaltation of terrorism. This further reform of the criminal code also incorporated new provisions to strengthen the implementation of the principles underlying the law of criminal liability of minors involved in terrorist crimes by amending the Organic Law 5/2000 of January 12, on the criminal responsibility of minors.

PC. And after the attacks against the Twin Towers of September 11, the international anti-terror legislation seriously deteriorated.

Immediately after the attack, the United Nations passed UN Resolution 1373 of September 28, 2001, which called upon the member states to adopt specific measures to combat terrorism. A natural and wise measure to adopt. However, from this point on, the Spanish government headed by José María Aznar started pressuring the international community for recognition of the anti-terror measures adopted by the Spanish administrations in the period 1988-2001. And, I have to admit I am ashamed that our Patriot Act is basically an adaptation of one of the worst pieces of legislation of the Spanish state, based primarily on the criminal policies of the Francoist regime and their Military Courts (*Tribunal de Orden Público*). If we carefully study the Patriot Act we find many of the measures that we have mentioned before. Moreover, in May 2004, former ambassador of the Spanish state to the United States for the period 2000-2004 Javier Rupérez was appointed executive director of the Counter-Terrorist Committee (CTC) with full support of the Bush administration. Rupérez is the same person who pressed the U.S. Secretary of State to kill Idaho's joint Memorial of March 13, 2002 and, the one who pointed out that Kofi Annan, Brian Currin and the rest of the signatories of the Donostia Declaration of October 17 2011 were at the service of ETA.

Moreover, we had an official visit all set up with Senator Craig and other Representatives from Idaho, right after the Memorial in fall 2002. George Bush's administration stopped it through the State Department's office. One of the reasons, and maybe one of the main ones, for the Spanish administration to take the Spanish state into the Iraq War was to stop any possibility of having a Basque delegation at Washington DC. The Aznar government's decision to go to war in Iraq was taken simultaneously with the maneuvers to stop our visit to the Congress and the communiqué we received from the office led by Condoleezza Rice. Apart from that, it was an interesting opportunity for the Spanish government to increase influence as showing "expertise" in anti-terror legislation and to include ETA on the list of International Terrorist groups, when ETA has never attacked outside the Spanish or French states and it is clear that it has no connection with Al-Qaeda.

In the context of this exchange of favors, another Spanish diplomat, Inocencio Arias, was appointed (once again with the support of the Bush administration) president of the Antiterrorism Committee of the United Nations between April 2003 and May 2004. In 2004 the Security Council adopted Resolution 1535 of 2004, creating the Executive Directorate of the CTC in order to provide technical advice to the committee on matters covered by resolution 1373 of 2001.

After the adoption of such foreign anti-terror policies, the political role of the United States in the world needs improvement in my thinking. We need dialogue, dialogue, and more dialogue rather than war, and Habeas Corpus instead of *special measures*. All sound minds should work toward avoiding war. The U.S. needs to mend some fences in the world, and we do have that capability insofar as I am concerned.

XI. After the first legislative abuses, the Council of Europe passed the European Framework Decision of the Council of Europe of June 13, 2002 on combating terrorism (2002/475/JAI) inviting Member States to align their legislation, thus introducing a common definition of the crime of "terrorism" according to the international legislation and the basic principles of human rights. The Decision of the Council of Europe established *minimum norms on terrorist crimes* and specified the penalties for terrorist crimes for the member states incorporating them into their legislation before the end of 2002.

PC. But the activity of the Bush administration provided an international umbrella to the Spanish government. Moreover, in exchange for the Spanish support at Iraq, the Bush administration helped implementing a series of measures that started being corrected by President Obama, such as the creation of special prisons or the adoption of exceptional executive actions in case of terrorism.

XI. Right. The PP administration passed Organic Law 7/2003, of June 30, by virtue of which:

- The maximum penalty for terrorist offenses was increased from 30 to 40 years of prison.
- The courts were required to provide benefits to those facing prison for terrorist activities on the totality of the sentence that was imposed to them, only in the cases in which it exceeds twice the maximum penalty, i.e. those sentenced to more than 80 years of imprisonment.
- The new law empowered the state tax agency and the Basque autonomous administrations to investigate the patrimony of persons convicted of terrorist activities, in order to act on personal income (present or future), inheritances or donations they received, thus to compensate the victims of their crimes.
- The persons sentenced to more than five years of prison could not be granted the "third grade prison" (benefits) until they reach a "period of security" of at least half of the complete sentence.
- The law only allowed the reintegration of "active collaborators," that is, "repentant terrorists" under the principle of "withdrawal and denouncement." In orther words, the new law uprooted the benefits of rehabilitation to anyone who did not show an "active collaboration."

PC. And, again, the Popular Party passed Organic Law 20/2003, of December 23, in order to block Lehendakari Ibarretxe's initiative to hold a referendum on constitutional future of the Basque Country.

XI. In the very sense of what you have pointed out at the beginning regarding *justicia a la carta*, that may be translated as *Justice à la carte*, on 23 December 2003 the PP administration promoted a further reform of the criminal code. Such reform set forth the possibility that a public official calling for a referendum might be criminally liable, in a clear allusion to the referendum proposed by the Lehendakari Juan Jose Ibarretxe in September 2001. This way, Ibarretxe's proposal became "manifestly" illegal.[223] The articles of the Criminal Code affected by the reform were the 506 bis, 521 bis and 576 bis. By virtue of the first one, the public official who called or authorized the call of general elections or regional, local or popular consultations could be imprisoned for three to five years and disqualified from holding any public office for six to ten years. By virtue of article 521 bis, the public official promoting and ensuring the realization of illegal referendums could be punished with six months to one year of imprisonment. Finally, Article 576 bis stated that the public official who used public funds or assets, subsidies or aids of any kind to fund illegal associations or dissolved political parties would be subject to a sentence of three to five years of prison.

Organic Law 20/2003, of 23 December was repealed by the Socialist government led by Jose Luis Rodríguez Zapatero through Law 2/2005 of June 22, on the reform of the Criminal Code. The new law expressly stated that articles 506 bis, 521 bis and 576 bis, "referred to actions that are not sufficiently significant to warrant criminal indictment, and even less imprisonment. The criminal law is governed by the principles of minimum intervention and proportionality, as noted by the [Spanish] Constitutional Court that has reiterated that no one can deprive a person of the right of freedom without being strictly necessary. In our system there are other ways to control the law other than criminal proceedings. Thus, the exercise of the powers to convene public consultations or promote those by individuals who do not have the legal attributions to do so is perfectly controllable by means other than the criminal."[224]

---

[223]   *Ley Orgánica 20/2003, de 23 de diciembre, de modificación de la Ley Orgánica del Poder Judicial y del Código Penal*, Article 506 bis.1, Madrid, Dicember 23, 2003.

[224]   *Boletín Oficial del Estado*, No. 149, Thursday 23 June, 2005. P. 21,846.

Pete T. Cenarrusa and Xabier Irujo in Carey (Idaho), May 2009. Source: Irujo Ametzaga archive.

PC. Such manipulation of the judiciary to one's own advantage is not legitimate. If the purpose of combating terrorism is the defense of freedoms and the strengthening of democracy, we cannot resort to practices involving its total destruction because, as Benjamin Franklin said, "who puts security over freedom is in danger of losing both."

And, I should remark that dealing with the Basque Country, these measures seemed to be severely embellished; according to the survey for the year 2007 of the European consortium formed by Gallup Europe, UNICRI, the Max Planck Institute, CEPS/INSTEAD, Luxembourg and GeoX Ltd, the Spanish state stands (2004 data) among the six European countries with fewer number of ideological or political crimes in Europe. The Basque Country has been one of the safest areas of the Spanish state in the last ten years, that is to say, one of the areas with the lowest crime rates in the state and in Europe as a whole (including of course the crimes of terrorism). According to Eurostat data, NSI and Eustat, the crime rate in the Basque Autonomous Community was in 2003 at 36.31 crimes per one thousand inhabitants) while the Spanish average was 49.49 and the European 72.46. Moreover, the Basque Country and Ireland are among the safest areas in Europe.

XI. Overall, if we accept that for obtaining certain goals the disregard of certain human rights is licit, then, we are indeed shielding terrorism. And then we have no moral authority to face violence as a means for attaining political goals. In general, we may conclude that:

- The abusive increasing of penalties does not imply, on its own, any benefit, for example, raising the penalties for terrorism from 30 to 40 years prison.
- The criminalization of the concept of "exaltation of terrorism" may lead to it being used as a political weapon.
- The "legislation of emergency" is particularly dangerous for it introduces concepts and practices characteristic of authoritarian or even totalitarian states in democratic states, giving rise to inquisitorial executive attitudes.
- The restriction of fundamental rights only should apply in the case of the fight against terrorism, although this is a very loose and polysemous definition that may be used against political opponents.
- Without an adequate legal protection, the law leaves *de facto* in the hands of the police (Executive branch) the interpretation of the terms "emergency legislation", "counter-terrorism", "exceptional cases" or "urgent necessity", which contravenes the principle of division of powers since it is the executive power judging if a situation is legally "exceptional" or "urgent."
- As we have said, the empowerment of police activity above or beyond judicial control (*favor libertatis*) is one of the fundamental characteristics of an authoritarian or dictatorial regime. The interception of the communications of a person made by order of a political authority or, failing that, of an administrative authority, seriously contravenes fundamental rights and implies a dangerous practice that could be used with political purposes.

- The indefinite extension of the violation of the right to privacy (of communications) means *de facto* the contravention of this right.
- The application of this kind of anti-terror norm means in practice that the presumption of innocence does not exist anymore, for in order to apply the suspension of fundamental rights to the person it is enough to be suspicious of being involved in terrorist activities.
- The complete isolation of an alleged offender for a period of up to five days without cameras or eye witnesses, (which is a violation of habeas corpus) seems to pursue no other purpose but the implementation of torture. And, as we have already said, it's a violation of the detainee's right to remain silent or to call for a lawyer, rights contained in Article 9.3 of the International Covenant on Civil and Political Rights of December 16, 1966, as well as in Article 5.3 of the European Convention for the Protection of Human Rights and Fundamental Freedoms of November 4, 1950, both ratified by the Spanish state on April 27, 1977, and September 26, 1979, respectively.
- The indiscriminate use of the preventive detention of up to four years in the case of being suspected of belonging to a terrorist gang is also alarming since it unambiguously contravenes the principle of presumption of innocence. The practice shows that the implementation of emergency measures have exceeded the limit of what seems advisable, when, during 2003, Aznar's executive arrested more than 150 people accused of belonging to ETA. According to the data provided by the Spanish Ministry of the Interior between 2000 and 2004 (under the Aznar administration) 686 people were arrested and, between 2004 and 2008 (under President Rodríguez' administration) 545. That represents an average of more than one arrest every two days, which certainly exceeds the constitutional and international principle of "exceptional" measure.
- The implementation of rules on criminal liability of minors and the actions taken under the law 7/2000 on the reform of the Criminal Code do not seem to be guided by the principle of reintegration and rehabilitation of juveniles.

- The regulation of registration or seizure without a warrant is a clear infringement of the principle of inviolability of the dwelling.
- The implementation of emergency procedures for terrorist crimes contradicts the widespread doctrine that special procedures are applied exclusively to facilitate the procedural formalities for minor offenses (not being crimes).
- Granting special benefits to only some of those facing prison for terrorist activities constrains the scope of these benefits and limits the necessary freedom of action of such courts and, moreover, eliminates the universal concept of collective reintegration of prisoners because of the nature of the offense.
- In the same sense, granting the reinsertion only to "active partners", namely the "repentant terrorists" violates the right of reintegration and, therefore, the duty of the authorities to promote reintegration.
- The denial of access to the "third grade" to persons with prison sentences longer than five years until they fulfill the "period of security" of at least half of the sentence, is an added limitation to the right of reintegration, which must be one of the prime aims of a prison system.
- The power of the state tax agencies and the autonomous administrations to carry out inspections and actions on personal incomes, inheritances or donations (past, present or future), in order to compensate the victims, is contrary to the principle of universal property of the family, under which the families of prisoners should not pay for the crimes committed by the material perpetrator.
- The gradual expansion of the "cases of terrorism" carried out through the Organic Law 10/1995 of November 23, the criminal code (Articles 571 to 575, section 2, of terrorist offenses), expands to the scope of "terrorist crimes" certain offenses that currently are considered to be "common crimes."
- The principle of "court immediacy", according to which special courts dealing with terrorism are created, has been one of the main characteristics of the European dictatorial systems of the 20th century.

The Spanish criminal law is particularly punitive in those crimes related to the activity of ETA, which blurs the necessary demarcation line between the criminalization of the terrorist activity on the one hand and respect for the peaceful defense of the political independence of the Basque Country on the other. Indeed, to combat the political proposal of a new statute by Lehendakari Juan Jose Ibarretxe, through a reform of the criminal code, means to reconstitute the concept of "political crime" within a democracy.

In this regard, it is shocking that the government has adopted such extraordinary measures in connection with ETA while not applying similar measures to several collectives involved in other areas of international terrorism, such as organized transnational crime, traffic of illegal drugs, illegal money-laundering, illegal arms trafficking and illegal movement of nuclear, chemical, biological and other potentially deadly materials.

It is true that terrorism generates antiterrorism but it is also true that antiterrorism is also a consequence of political ideologies. Furthermore, even if it is difficult to measure to what extent antiterrorism nourishes terrorism, it certainly does fuel terrorism and the spread of pro-terrorist ideologies. The violation of human rights may bring short-term results, but has a high social, political and economic cost. We all aim for the cease of violence and the end of suffering in the Basque Country and we all have seen that the only periods of true peace and complete ceasefire have occurred during the truces that gave space for dialogue, discussion and parliament.

On the *Egunkaria* and *Batasuna* cases

Xabier Irujo. The Spanish government determined that in order to put an end to ETA it was necessary to terminate the alleged political support that the left wing political party Herri Batasuna (HB, Peoples' Union) was giving to ETA. In 1996 the Popular Party (PP) won elections in Spain and José María Aznar became president of the Spanish government. Only one year later, in December 1997, the National Assembly of HB was sent to prison accused of collaboration with ETA. That same year Arnaldo Otegi was appointed president of HB and changed the name of the party to Euskal Herritarrok (EH, Peoples of the Basque Country).

The imprisonment of the National Assembly of HB was part of the *Judicial War* against ETA and it was followed by political maneuvers to gain control of the General Council of the Judicial Power (CGPJ, Consejo General del Poder Judicial) the governmental organ of the judicial branch of the Spanish state. The CGPJ is composed of the President of the Supreme Court of Justice who presides over the Council and twenty members named for a period of five years by the King by means of a royal decree authenticated by the Minister of Justice. By controlling the nomination of the members of the CGPJ and thus ensuring a majority of members of the Popular Party or close to it, this party could control the executive, the legislative and the judiciary all at the same time. In virtue of this arrangement, in 1999 Emilio Olavarria, member of the Basque Nationalist Party (EAJ-PNV), was censured by the PP. The outcome was that the CGPJ, an independent body of the judiciary created to ensure the independence of judges and magistrates in the exercise of its functions, was therefore controlled by a single political party.

Pete Cenarrusa. On March 12, 2000, the Popular Party won elections with 44.5% of the votes and 183 out of 350 seats at the Spanish parliament, that is, 52.3% of the parliamentary representation. Within a parliamentary system such as the Spanish one, members of the parliament elect the president of the government, therefore, José María Aznar was appointed president of the Spanish state. This way, Aznar who was president of the major political party of the state (controlling 52.3% of the votes at parliament), became the head of the executive branch and, by controlling the CGPJ, he also had the judiciary on his side. The following four years became a dictatorship within a democracy because the three branches of the state were under a single head.

The first step in the path to make political parties illegal was taken on December 8, 2000, by adopting the Pact for Liberties and Against Terrorism (*Pacto de las Libertades y contra el Terrorismo*). By virtue of that agreement the Socialist Party (PSOE) agreed to second any initiative of the Popular Party in the context of the *Judicial War* against ETA and only one year later the Spanish government drafted a law to outlaw political parties.

XI. Yes. On June 27, 2002, the Organic Law 6/2002 of Political Parties came into force. By virtue of the Pact for Liberties and Against Terrorism the law was passed with the support of 95 percent of the votes at the Spanish parliament (PP and PSOE). On August 26, 2002 the Spanish congress controlled by PP and the PSOE requested the Supreme Court to make Herri Batasuna illegal by means of the new law. And, consequently, on March 28, 2003 the Supreme Court announced that Herri Batasuna, Euskal Herritarrok and Batasuna (three names for the same political party) were illegal and thus ordered the immediate cease of their activities. At the same time, Judge of the National Audience Baltasar Garzón decreed the suspension of the activities of the members of this party at the Basque parliament. That is, twenty four years after the Spanish constitution was passed, the Spanish Congress voted for a law which establishes the legal mechanisms to outlaw a political party, according to the wording of the law *while respecting the principle of minimum intervention that follows from the constitution.*

In 2003 Batasuna had 143,139 votes in the Basque Autonomous Community (10.12 percent) and seven seats at the Basque parliament. Batasuna had 47,271 votes (10.44 percent) in the Chartered Community of Navarre and eight MPs at the Navarrese parliament. The new law banned 10 percent of the votes in the Basque Country.

PC. The outlawing of a political party means to completely remove the opportunity for freedom of association. From my point of view freedom of association is a basic individual right to come together with other individuals and collectively express, promote, pursue and defend common interests and it is guaranteed by the First Amendment to the U.S. Constitution. Freedom of association is included in the Universal Declaration of Human Rights of 1948 (Art. 20), in the European Convention for the Protection of Human Rights and Fundamental Freedoms of 1950 (Art. 11). According to the U.S. Constitutional Court freedom of association is closely connected to freedom of speech. It is the right to choose to enter into and maintain certain human relationships and expressive associations; it is a fundamental element of personal liberty. Thus, groups such as political parties have the basic right to engage in activities protected by the First Amendment, namely, freedom of speech, freedom of assembly and freedom of petitioning the government for a redress of grievances, and the free exercise of religion.

I received the following letter at my office, on Thursday, September 05, 2002:

By the time I was able to make a comment regarding the outlawing of Batasuna, that process had already taken place. I am quite disappointed in the Spanish Government and in the international community for allowing such a thing to happen, it is not only anti-democratic, it also sheds light on the fact that the Spanish government is unwilling to negotiate and more than willing to bring violence to Euskal Herria, just look at the pictures at Yahoo News regarding the Basque Country the last couple of years. The press in the U.S. barely talked about it, at least in Mexico there was one newspaper that printed "Spain back to Franquism" on their first page. And this is not an argument to defend Batasuna or their alleged links to ETA, this is an argument against a Government that is supposed to be a democratic government, a government that is there to ensure that violence will not engulf a society. Aznar, heir to the Francoist Regime is showing his true colors, too bad the international community has a blindfold on and will not remove it, for its own sake. From my point of view, if is not already bad to deprive 150,000 people of their right to belong to a party that expresses their political views, on top, now the Basque society has to brace itself for a new circle of violence. To see those pictures of Batasunistas going at it with Ertzaintza officers was something terrible, my worst fear came true, to have Basques fighting Basques. And to have the whole world not condemning a pseudo-democratic government for generating this kind of violence is just appalling. Should I remind everyone what was the event that triggered this last effort to outlaw Batasuna?

I have always actively supported the freedoms that make democracy possible. In 1968 I even went to court as a member of the Republican Party that I am in, in order to let an opponent political force, the American Independent Party in Idaho, present themselves for elections in our state (American Independent Party in Idaho, Inc. v. Cenarrusa, Idaho 1968). As then, I still understand that a political party is an affiliation of electors representing a political organization under a given name and its members should always have the right to present themselves for elections, no matter how erroneous the party's ideology may appear to us. In 1968 I claimed that the former statute, S.L. 1919, eh. 107, s 2, as amended by S.L. 1927, eh. 83, s 517, remained in full force and effect and so the American Independent Party in Idaho, upon which ticket there were at least three nominees for state offices, or an affiliation of not less than 1,500 electors, should run just as our party and the Democratic Party were running in elections. Thirty days before the date of the primary, the representatives filed with me, the Secretary of State, a written notice stating that they desired recognition as a political party, containing the name of the proposed party, that the subscribers thereto had affiliated with one another for the purpose of forming such party, and, finally that the subscribers to such notice intended to nominate at least three candidates for state offices whereupon such affiliation should, under the party name chosen, have all the rights of a political party whose ticket should have been on the ballot at the preceding general election. And the Idaho Supreme Court accepted my view on this matter. The Secretary of State was happy to receive the mandate of the Court, and then the political party could not be abolished without action of the people within that party.

XI. But there is more than a patent violation of a basic democratic rule behind the banning of Batasuna. Once again the political measures were directed only against Basque political organizations. Among the ballots for the March 2007 elections (and during the European elections of June 2009) in the Basque Country, there were political parties such as Falange Española Auténtica or Comunión Tradicionalista Carlista, two of the political parties included in the National Movement of manifest totalitarian ideology, ruling in the Spanish state during the forty years of Francoist dictatorship. Openly anti-democratic and with a blatant precedent of state terrorism they are still legal and present their candidates at elections.

Paper ballots for the 2009 European elections in the Spanish state. In the photograph the ballots of three openly non-democratic parties: Falange Española de las JONS (the only official political party during the Francoist dictatorship), Falange Auténtica (an excision of the last) and Frente Nacional, of openly xenophobic ideology. These political parties and others of non-democratic ideology have not been affected by the Spanish Organic Law 6/2002 of Political Parties. Source: Irujo Ametzaga archive.

Indeed, there was more behind the outlawing of Batasuna. The Basque political nationalism parties (PNV, EA, Batasuna and Aralar) represent 53.5 percent of the seats at the Basque parliament while the PP and the PSOE hardly reach the 40 percent of the seats. The left, represented by United Left (Ezker Batua, EB/IU) makes up 5.4 percent and has been historically linked to the Basque nationalist bloc. In this sense, the only way of obtaining the majority at the Basque Autonomous Community is by banning Batasuna's 10 percent.

PC. The anti-terrorist strategy of the Popular Party, backed by the Spanish Socialist Party (the banning of a political party) also led to the closure of two newspapers, which is another legal transgression of the fundamental rights of the individual.

XI. That's correct. In June 1998 examining magistrate Baltasar Garzón had "temporarily" closed *Egin*, a newspaper, under the charge of having supported ETA. Even if it was a "precautionary measure" the newspaper remains closed and no trial has been opened so far, and no one has been convicted, sentenced or even judged in relation to that case yet.

On February 20, 2003, examining magistrate Juan del Olmo ordered *Euskaldunon Egunkaria* (The Newspaper of the Basque Speakers) the main newspaper written in Basque to be closed down and ten journalists to be arrested under the Spanish anti-terror legislation (governmental detention without warrant and in complete isolation). As with Garzon's, Del Olmo's order of closing the newspaper was "temporary." Several journalists were arrested under the charge of having collaborated with ETA which supposedly controlled the newspaper. Moreover, some of the detainees declared that the Spanish police tortured them, among them the director of *Egunkaria* himself. *Egunkaria*, was founded in 1990 amd had a circulation of about 15,000 when it was shut down.

We should have expected a serious debate on human rights for such measures ordered by mere examining magistrates that violated freedom of expression, a fundamental right allegedly protected by the Spanish Constitution. The decision raised other legal problems such as if it was legal and correct to preventively determine to close a newspaper before a firm sentence of a legal judge was dictated.

Thanks to private donations raised in Basque towns and cities, only a month after Del Olmo's order, the first issue of *Berria*, a new newspaper written entirely in Basque, was published and in the streets.

PC. In the United States we are fortunate that we have the First Amendment of the U.S. Constitution which states that *the Congress shall make no law respecting an establishment of religion, or prohibiting the free exercise thereof, or abridging the freedom of speech, or the press, or of the right of the people peaceably to assemble, and to petition the government for a redress of grievances.* Without freedom of speech, of the press, religion and, the right to peaceably assemble, there is no democracy. We, in the State of Idaho and in the United States stood ready to urge and assist the Spanish government and the Basque Autonomous Community to accept the freedoms that we enjoy in the United States and in any democratic state, and once again condemned in a third Memorial passed in 2006 all violence occurring at the Basque Country and all cruel and unusual punishment by the Spanish government.

XI. Also Amnesty International alleged in a written statement on 23 February 2003 irregularities in the process against *Egunkaria*, an action that was considered clearly detrimental to the fundamental rights.[225] Similarly, on 31 May 2005, twenty-two members of the European Parliament appealed to denounce the closure of *Egunkaria* in the following terms:

> *We are in the middle of the ratification process of the "Treaty establishing a Constitution for Europe." This Treaty, in its second chapter, includes the Charter of Fundamental Rights of the European Union, Article 22 of which says:*
>
> *1. Everyone has the right to freedom of expression. This right shall include freedom to hold opinions and to receive and impart information and ideas without interference by public authority and regardless of frontiers.*
> *2. The freedom and pluralism of the media shall be respected.*
>
> *On 13 December 2004, the Government of Spain presented a Memorandum to the European Commission requesting recognition in the European Union of all the official languages of*

---

[225]   *España: debe investigarse sin demora el cierre de un periódico vasco*, Amnesty International press release, February 23, 2003. See also, http://www.egunkaria.info/default.cfm?hizkuntza=2&atala=buletinak.

Spain, including Euskera (which is, along with Spanish, the co-official language in the Basque Country) and providing a copy of the Constitutional Treaty in Euskera, while at the same time making a proposal for the official recognition in the European Union of the languages other than Spanish.

In the European context, the scrupulous respect for these principles should form part of the Community heritage, and should lead to the restoration of any right infringed in the area of freedom of expression and information. That is why, through this statement, we want to express our concern to all the European institutions, starting with the European Parliament, about the closing of the newspaper Euskaldunon Egunkaria.

On 20 February 2005 two years will have passed since the closing of the Basque-language newspaper "Euskaldunon Egunkaria", the only daily publication published in this official language in the Basque Country. It is worth remembering that the Basque language is recognized as the language of Basques in Article 6 of the law regulating the powers and institutions of the Basques, the Statute of Autonomy of Gernika. Additionally, the Basic Law on the Normalisation of the Use of the Basque Language, Article 22, "recognizes that all citizens have the right to be informed by the media both in Euskera and in Spanish."

The closing of the newspaper created a great deal of commotion, social concern and reaction, and even the Petition Commission of the European Parliament resolved to make a petition regarding it.

It must be said that Euskaldunon Egunkaria was a newspaper that also formed part of the European network MIDAS (European Organization of Daily Newspapers in Minority and Regional Languages), along with 28 other newspapers published in various regional languages, such as Dolomiten, Tageszeitung, Primorski (Republic of Italy), El Periódico de Catalunya, Avui, El Punt, Diari de Balears, Segre, Regió 7, El 9 Nou, El Correo Galego, Vilaweb (Spain), Nyan Aland, Tidningen (Aland Islands), Flensborg-avis, Serbske Nowiny (Federal Republic of Germany), Hufvudsatdbladet, Jakobstads Tidning, Vasabladet, Osterbottningen (Finland), La Quotidiana–Die Südostsweitz (Switzerland), La Voce del Popolo (Croacia), Nordschleswiger (Denmark), Lá (Republic of Ireland), HHRF (Hungarian minority of Romania, Slovakia, Serbia, Ukrania); Ujszo

(Hungarian minority, Slovakia), Szabadság (Romania). MIDAS does important work for the reinforcement of the press in the so-called minority and regional languages, forging professional and technological links among the different types of media operating in various European states.

Without detriment to the judicial steps that must be taken in this or in any other case, it is clearly noteworthy and paradoxical that the newspaper remains closed, even today, as a "precautionary measure." It is easy to see the harm caused, in a general way, to the fundamental public freedoms of expression and communication, that is, to Basque society as a whole and, with special intensity, to speakers of Euskera and, among them, the readers and subscribers of this newspaper. Also negatively affected are the newspaper's employees and collaborators, and the rights of the shareholders, and economic damage has been caused to the suppliers and creditors of the newspaper and associated companies, demonstrating that the closure affects fundamental rights.

Special mention should go to the harm caused to the persons on trial, important personalities in the world of Basque culture, who have received support and solidarity from the widest possible spectrum of political, social and institutional figures in the Basque Country.

In these times in which Europe is attempting to open new spaces for justice, prosperity, freedom and security, and in which the very text of the Treaty establishing a European Constitution emphasizes the rights of citizens in a clear way, we believe it necessary to call for the reconsideration of such closure and for the restoration of the rights of the affected Basque speakers.

European Parliament
Strasbourg, 22 February 2005.[226]

Also, a number of European newspapers created the European Association of Daily Newspapers in Minority and Regional Languages (MIDAS) that expressed its concern for the governmental manipulation of the judiciary and the violation of the freedom of speech:

---

[226]   Manifesto in Favour of Suspending the Closure of the Newspaper "Euskaldunon Egunkaria" and of Respect for the Rights of Freedom of Expression and Information of Basque-Speaking Citizens.

The European dimension opens up opportunities for cooperation between minority daily newspapers throughout the continent. National states still violate minority rights and the freedom of the press, as in the case of Egunkaria in the Basque Country. MIDAS, as a network, intervenes to avoid all kinds of violence in solving minority issues. To serve these functions properly, MIDAS provides opportunities such as study visit programs for journalists in order to develop knowledge through exchange of information and report on minority protection and cultural diversity in Europe.

Minorities must find a peaceful way to get their voices heard. The existence of quality independent journalism is a fundamental principle of our daily work. In acknowledgement of those journalists who set journalistic standards and make particular contributions to cultural diversity and the protection of minority languages, MIDAS awards the Otto von Habsburg Prize and the Midas Prize for Journalism.[227]

XI. In the end, on 12 April 2010 the Audiencia Nacional, the Spanish high court that hears these cases, acquitted under Judgment No. 27/2010 the five defendants in the Egunkaria case, seven years after the closure of the newspaper in 2003. The journalists faced from twelve to fourteen years in prison and a ban from journalism lasting up to fifteen years.

PC. Yes, I read it in the newspapers with great pleasure.[228] As reporter for the Idaho Statesman Katy Moeller wrote:

After Egunkaria had been closed five years, the group Reporters Without Borders called on Spain to drop the years-long prosecution. "The alleged links between certain members of Egunkaria's staff and ETA have never been demonstrated, despite five years of judicial investigation," the press freedom group said. "The Spanish

---

[227] Minority Dailies Association MIDAS: European Association of Daily Newspapers in Minority and Regional Languages 2001-2005, Toni Ebner and Günther Rautz (ed.), Bozen 2005, Verl.-Anst. Athesia. ISBN 88-8266-371-X. In, www.midas-press.org/NR/rdonlyres/D2FE4CEB-1205-4B08-BB30-717C7ED8D26E/0/EgunkariaEurolang1205.pdf.

[228] Moeller, Katy, "Boiseans hail acquittal of Basques," *The Idaho Statesman*, April 13, 2010.

government's fight against terrorism is legitimate, but it must be done without violating free expression." Spain's approach to that fight is an important part of the story, Woodworth and other experts said. "The background is important," Woodworth said. "An anti-terrorist strategy from Madrid... says that everything and everybody who shares any of ETA's aspirations is in reality a member of ETA - a very dangerous and undemocratic doctrine."[229]

XI. The truth is that we all kind of expected the verdict. What we did not expect was such a strong verdict coming from a Spanish judge against Del Olmo's finding.

PC. Right. I did not either.

XI. Under Judgment No. 27/2010 Judge Javier Gómez Bermúdez said that the newspaper's editorial line "allowed to reject the thesis that the paper was an instrument to commit crimes." The court presided by Judge Gómez lambasted Juan del Olmo, the judge who ordered the closure of the newspaper, saying that his decision was "difficult to fit into the Spanish legal system", adding that "the temporary suspension of a newspaper has no direct constitutional coverage" and pointing out that the measure required a reasoned judicial decision protecting the rights related to the freedom of expression and information which prohibits any kind of censorship. Judge Gómez also informed Del Olmo that the narrow and erroneous view according to which everything that has to do with the Basque language and culture must be promoted and/or controlled by ETA leads to an incorrect administration of justice. Finally, the judge also criticized private prosecutors Dignity and Justice and the Association of Victims of Terrorism for having sought to justify their thesis by saying that "what you do not see is what it is and what you do see is not what it seems," which is nothing but pure speculation.

---

[229] Moeller, Katy, "A terrorism trial on another continent is hitting close to home for some Boiseans." *The Idaho Statesman*, Boise, December 15, 2009.

Pete and Freda Cenarrusa today. Source: Cenarrusa archive.

PC. Juan del Olmo is not going to be admonished for his erroneous job and unprofessional behavior. Moreover, most probably the victims are never going to be compensated and it is unknown when the building, equipment and other seized assets are going to be returned to their owners.

XI. Right. All this is simply incredible to reporters abroad. It is tragic to find out that five journalists had paid such a heavy price in an allegedly democratic state. They were acquitted only after they were tortured, blamed, lost their jobs and their newspaper was shut down as a "precautionary measure" for almost seven years. The Spanish justice system is far from being democratic and the Spanish judges, the Spanish politicians and, in general, the Spanish citizenship is going to need at least a long century of democratic practice in order to start believing and understanding what democracy is and what the political and cultural rights of the Basques, Catalans and Galicians are. The Spanish state is a political democracy, but certainly it is not yet a social democracy: many people educated in the principles of Francoism still do not understand what democracy means.[230] People like Judge Gómez represent some hope in this regard.

PC. Del Olmo's activities have had also an impact here, in the United States. The U.S. State Department denied Berria's Director Martxelo Otamendi's application to travel as a tourist and, as a consequence, he could not attend the Jaialdi 2010 here in Boise, with us. In April, the Spanish high court acquitted Otamendi of the charges that the paper was funded by ETA. Therefore, he is not a member of ETA or a collaborationist. However, the United States Department of State Office of the Coordinator for Counter-terrorism included ETA in the list of Foreign Terrorist Organizations in accordance with section 219 of the Immigration and Nationality Act in April 2008. It is sad to have our government brought to this by the Spanish authorities. I fully agree with the editorial of The Idaho Statesman:

> *As editor of the Basque language newspaper Berria, Otamendi had hoped to travel to Boise to chronicle an event that showcases the music, dance, history and sport of the Basque people. An event that is hardly sinister and is simply celebratory - a party that turns Boise into a focal point for an estimated 30,000 Basques. But sadly, this year, one less journalist. "Our View" is the editorial position of the Idaho Statesman. It is an unsigned opinion expressing the consensus of the Statesman's editorial board.*[231]

Democracy after forty years of dictatorial repression is still deficient in Spain. The abolition of political parties and the closure of newspapers makes a mockery of democracy. The Idaho lawmakers would not accept such activities by any government. Anti-terrorism will never accomplish its goal by violating human rights in the Basque Country. The Basques once enjoyed the oldest democratic republics in Europe. The history and traditions of the Basque nation rests upon the principles of freedom from

---

230   Moeller, Katy, "Boiseans hail acquittal of Basque journalists accused of aiding terrorist group," *The Idaho Statesman*, Boise, April 12, 2010.
231   "Our View: Red tape prevents Basque journalist's trip to Boise," *The Idaho Statesman*, Boise, July 28, 2010.

oppression and rights of the citizens to life, liberty and the pursuit of happiness.

The presence of violence, the idea of killing political opponents, is certainly terrible. And the use of legal evasions and equivocations with regard to human rights to obtain political advantages is also a macabre joke. Democracy is not a game, not a political tool; this is a lesson that the still immature Spanish democracy has not learned.

On Independence. The Basque Republic

Xabier Irujo. An important point of contention among Basques, French and Spanish political parties and social groups is the definition of nation and sovereignty. The Spanish state was defined by the Spanish constitution as a "nation" and the nations within the state as "nationalities", "cultures" or "peoples" who could be organized politically into autonomous communities under certain restraints and conditions. Also, article 2 of the French constitution refers to the French state as a "nation",

> *The language of the Republic shall be French.*
> *The national emblem shall be the blue, white and red tricolor flag.*
> *The national anthem shall be La Marseillaise.*
> *The maxim of the Republic shall be "Liberty, Equality, Fraternity."*
> *The principle of the Republic shall be: government of the people, by the people and for the people.*

Pete Cenarrusa. Sabino Arana stated *Euskotarren aberria Euskadi da*, that is, the Basque Country is the motherland of the Basques. The Basque Country is a nation and thus, the Basques should have the right to become a state if the majority of the population vote for it in a referendum, that is, the Basque nation should have the right of self-determination.

Starting in the 18th century, different authors have introduced projects for the creation of an independent Basque state. Among them we may mention Manuel Larramendi's project of Vasconia (1756-58), Jean-Philippe Bela's Basque nation (1761-1766), Dominique Joseph Garat's project of New Phoenicia (1803), Agosti Xao's Basque state (1836) and Sabino Arana's Basque Republic (1893). As we mentioned, Manuel Irujo, former minister of justice of the Spanish Republic, promoted the creation of the Basque National Council, an independent provisional Basque government formally established in 11 July 1940 in London. In the summer of 1940 the British Government agreed to immediately recognize the Basque National Council as the Provisional Basque Government and to undertake to do everything in their power to secure the constitution and security of a Basque State, in the event of hostilities breaking out between the British and Spanish Governments in the context of World War Two. In 1941 Irujo proposed the Basque Republic, a constitutional project for a Basque federal state.

XI. On February 15, 1990 the Basque Parliament passed the following Resolution on the right of Self-determination of the Basque Country,

The Basque Parliament proclaims:

1.   *The Basque people have the right to self-determination. That right lies in the power of its citizens to freely and democratically decide their political, economic, social and cultural status while adhering to their own political framework or sharing, in whole or in part, sovereignty with other people.*

2.   *The exercise of the right to self-determination is aimed at nation-building in the Basque Country. In this connection, the nation-building process is a dynamic, progressive and democratic process including a various set of decisions, for instance, where appropriate, those of a plebiscite that the Basque Country will take over its history according to the internal or external conditions of its historical juncture, and the real or potential interest of the Basques.*

3.   *The Statute of Autonomy, a result of a pact endorsed freely by the Basque citizens, is a meeting point of their majority will and the legal framework that Basque society is endowed in a certain historic moment for access to self-government and to peacefully regulate coexistence, representing therefore the legitimate expression of the will of the Basque Country itself. In that sense, the statutory strategy and the deepening on self-government through the full and fair development of each and every one of the contents of the statute represent for the Basque citizens the valid framework for the gradual resolution of the problems of the Basque society, as well as to advance in a nation building process in the Basque Country.*

4.   *Being that the Basque people hold the right of self-determination, the representative institutions according to the existing political reality*

and, in particular, the Basque Parliament, are the only depository of their sovereignty, the only ones entitled to promote its exercise.

Accordingly, the legitimacy of all political ideas democratically expressed can be defended at the Parliament and (when appropriate) should be incorporated into the law. Therefore, this Parliament is entitled to decide and promote initiatives that are intended to make possible the realization of the aspirations of the Basque citizens to pose, if any, reforms of all kinds that seem appropriate, in accordance with the established procedures.

Paraphrasing the Scottish Executive, the Basque people believe that the future prosperity and development of the Basque Country is best served by becoming an independent country, a view shared in the Basque Parliament by the political parties representing the vast majority of the popular vote. Under independence the Basque Country would assume the rights and responsibilities of a normal sovereign state. This would include all decisions on economic and fiscal affairs, the constitution, foreign affairs, security and defense. The Basque Country would be recognized as a state by the international community and be part of the European Union as a full member state.

PC. It is clear that the Basques, gathered in Parliament, have requested through their democratically elected representatives to become an independent Republic and there is no force on earth that should oppose the will of the people expressed in assembly. As we once stated and still believe here, in the United States,

We hold these truths to be self-evident, that all men are created equal, that they are endowed by their Creator with certain unalienable Rights, that among these are Life, Liberty and the pursuit of Happiness. That to secure these rights, Governments are instituted among Men, deriving their just powers from the consent of the governed. That whenever any Form of Government becomes destructive of these ends, it is the Right of the People to alter or to abolish it, and to institute new Government, laying its foundation on such principles and organizing its powers in such form, as to them shall seem most likely to effect their Safety and Happiness. Prudence, indeed, will dictate that Governments long established should not be changed for light and transient causes; and accordingly all experience hath shewn that mankind are more disposed to suffer, while evils are sufferable than to right themselves by abolishing the forms to which they are accustomed. But when a long train of abuses and usurpations, pursuing invariably the same Object evinces a design to reduce them under absolute Despotism, it is their right, it is their duty, to throw off such Government, and to provide new Guards for their future security.

Banners in the streets of Lazkao, Gipuzkoa, asking for independence. 2008. Source: Irujo Ametzaga archive.

The Basque conflict is a political conflict and the only way of solving political problems in democracy is through dialogue and by accepting the will of the people expressed at assembly. The Spanish and French representatives do not understand that the majority of the Basques do not want to be Spanish nor French for they do not feel they are Spanish or French, but Basque.

In this sense, I always have felt that we must do all that we can for freedom and the opportunity for self-determination. The State of Idaho has, on three different occasions, approved memorials, or resolutions, in support of the Basques for self-determination, by the respective Legislatures. The first was in 1972, in a very strongly worded statement against the actions of General

Francisco Franco. It was passed by unanimous vote. I wrote the Memorial, which was placed in the Congressional Record by Senator Frank Church. The second one, in 2002, passed again by unanimous vote of both Houses, asked for peace, dialogue, and a referendum for self-determination in the Basque Country. The third was also passed by unanimous vote of both Houses in April of 2006, asking for peace, dialogue and meaningful autonomy. The idea behind the Idaho resolutions is not a new one. Ever since the Kennedy years a number of federated states have supported similar initiatives, aimed at attaining peace in Ireland and seeking negotiated solutions, which recognize the will of the Irish people. Much the same as the Basque sheepherders and innkeepers who migrated to America, the descendants of thousands of Irish-American settlers have not forgotten their commitment to their forefathers' and foremothers' home in Ireland.

Following our 2006 Memorial, the Senate of Chile passed a resolution on 11 October 2006 requesting the cease of all expressions of violence in the Basque Country and the respect of the political rights of the Basque citizenship, including their right to self-determination.

Since 1970 we have been arranging meetings with other Basques from Idaho and other states, in Washington DC, at the nation's Capitol, with the United States Institute for Peace, a meeting to which Lehendakari Juan Jose Ibarretxe and members of the Basque Autonomous government came some years ago. We are still working with many people, arranging for conferences, which will include meetings with the Vice President and the Speaker of the House of Representatives among other high-level members of the House and Senate committees. We will work towards freedom for the Basque Country, which, hopefully in time, will include the entire *Zazpiak Bat*, the historic Basque Country. The Basque Country, historically, has been compatible with and helpful to the United States, which the United States must honor in return. Let us not forget the historic contributions to the U.S. by the Basque Country.

XI. In *The Idaho Statesman* of November 04, 2001, we read:

On Saturday, [Spanish] Ambassador Javier Rupérez got inside what locals call the "House of the Basques." But deep differences

[391]

remain between Spain and Idaho Basques, who represent the largest population outside the homeland and who continue to press for a referendum on Basque independence. After a closed-door lunch that lasted an hour longer than planned, Sen. Larry Craig was the first to emerge from the meeting, looking a bit shell shocked. "We got into a very spirited discussion," said Craig, who had met Rupérez on a trip to Spain and arranged his visit to Idaho.

PC. Upon hearing of this Memorial by Democratic Representative Dave Bieter, the Spanish Ambassador Javier Rupérez immediately informed the Prime Minister of Spain, José María Aznar, the President of the United States and the State Department. Very soon the legislators at the State Capitol were inundated with e-mails, telephone calls and letters opposing this legislation. In spite of that, House Joint Memorial (HJM) 14 was passed in the House of Representatives unanimously and was transmitted to the Senate. The Senate Pro Tem referred the Memorial to the State Affairs committee. Chairman Sheila Sorensen was overwhelmed with messages from the office of Condoleezza Rice and several Spanish organizations. I remember someone saying that he did not know that Idaho was declaring war on Spain! We all read in The Associated Press that there are 15,000 Basques in Idaho, the biggest such community in the United States, and so Basque issues occasionally come up,

The last thing anyone in Idaho expected was an international incident. When the Idaho House took up a non-binding resolution last week urging peaceful self-determination for Spain's Basque minority, it hardly raised an eyebrow.[232]

We all thought that it was not a rational attitude. No one should be closed to letting others think, discuss and give their opinion. After almost sixty years in state government I have learned that the basic duty of a Representative is to think, speak, discuss and give an opinion. In other words, to behave as a rational person.

---

[232]   Gallagher, Dan, "From Idaho, a Political Furor that Drew the Attention of White House", *The Associated Press*, Saturday, March 16, 2002.

XI. The three Memorials adopted by the Idaho Legislature by unanimous vote focused on three major points:

1. Peace. Through three successive Joint Memorials the Idaho legislature stands with the Basques and all Idahoans in opposing all violence in the Basque Country and calling for the immediate convocation of a process to bring about a lasting peace: that peace be declared in the Basque Country. As Minister of Justice of the Basque Government, Joseba Azkarraga then advanced "this is a peace initiative not a war cry to rally troops to the Middle East or the Balkans, which the Popular Party leader seems to be so fond of doing."

2. Dialogue. To request a peace process be undertaken and a dialogue be held in order to attain permanent peace. This is a call to end violence, death and suffering.

3. Democracy and freedom. That the Basque Country be allowed to have self-determination, that is, the right to vote for independence.

By virtue of the Memorials the state of Idaho calls for an immediate cessation of all violence occurring in and near the Basque homeland, and that a peace process be immediately undertaken between the governments of Spain and France, the Basque Autonomous government, and other groups committed to peace. What is the main political intent of the Memorials?

PC. The intent of the Memorials is for the people of the United States to take affirmative action in working towards freedom and democracy for the Basque Country, such freedom as the Basques enjoyed at one time when their declaration was *Zazpiak Bat* - the seven are one. *Laurak Bat* (four are one) in Hegoalde that the Basque once enjoyed in the Southern Basque Country and *Hirurak Bat* (three are one) they once enjoyed in Iparralde or North Basque Country.

The United States understands what it means to fight for its own freedom and the engagement in the determination and realization of struggle necessary in order to achieve freedom and self government and final achievement of independence. The United Sates is well aware of what Freedom and Independence

[393]

mean, therefore, we are in an opportune position to push for freedom in the Basque Country as we did in the case of Ireland. As stated in Senate Joint Memorial 114 (SJM 114) of 2002:

> *WHEREAS, the history and traditions of this nation rest upon the principles of freedom from oppression, and rights of all citizens to life, liberty and the pursuit of happiness; and*
>
> *WHEREAS, we believe that democracy and freedom, when denied in one country, stand threatened everywhere; therefore, it is our responsibility to bring to the attention of the people of the United States, and we hope, to the people of the entire world that these freedoms of the Basque people are threatened...*

XI. The 2002 Memorial states that the Basque people are the oldest indigenous people in Western Europe and have a long history of personal accomplishment and a devotion to the preservation of their national heritage and have sought to maintain their culture, their ancient language and their self-government. Out of respect for this heritage and America's commitment to our own struggles for freedom, this Memorial expresses Idaho's support of the right of the Basques to self-determination. Is then, in your understanding, Basque self-government a constitutive element for peace in the Basque Country?

PC. Indeed, it is the prerequisite for peace. The Spanish government rejects proposals for talks with ETA's political arm. I call for a brokered peace like that engineered in Northern Ireland by George Mitchell, and for an independence referendum in the Basque territories. However it is the overall conviction of the Spanish government that there is not a political crisis within the Spanish state, and as stated by Rupérez while in Boise that any political issue should be solved mainly through the "law enforcement agencies."

XI. The 2006 Memorial enhances an *appropriate degree* of governmental autonomy for the Basque Homeland. What do you think is an appropriate measure of governmental autonomy for the Basque Homeland? In other words, what is the shape of Basque self-determination according to the Memorials? Does it refer to the Basques' right to put forth a referendum regarding the need of a peace process, or does it make reference to the right of the Basque people to gain independence?

The State of Idaho has, on three different occasions, approved memorials, or resolutions, in support of the Basques for self-determination. Source: Cenarrusa archive.

PC. The Memorials relate to the people of the Basque Country having the right to hold an election or referendum to determine among themselves whether they want independence. A yes vote from the voters would affirm independence, a no vote would defeat it. A no vote would then open a dialogue for the Basque government to collaborate with the Spanish government to attain a degree of self-government with certain rights granted to the Basque Country and certain rights granted to the Spanish government. It could be a federal system that the Spanish government would rule by certain rights in the Constitution, and all rights not enumerated in the Spanish Constitution would belong to Euskadi. Similar to the Tenth Amendment to the U.S. Constitution that provides that the powers not delegated to the United States by the Constitution, nor prohibited by it to the States, are reserved by the States respectively, or by the people (the principle of federalism). And perhaps similar to the solution described by Lehendakari Ibarretxe previously.

Idaho's Legislature believes that the Basque nation have the right and have shown the will to constitute an independent Basque Republic in Europe. The Basque people owned their own republics long before any of the surrounding states appeared in Europe. The Basques are comparable to the Swiss mountaineers; they love and honor their homeland with a devotion which one finds in a people who have lived on the same soil for centuries and who have permanent roots in it.

Francisco Letamendia, former member of the Spanish congress for Euskadiko Ezkerra and professor of Political Science at the University of the Basque Country. Photograph taken by the author in Belfast, 2008. Source: Irujo Ametzaga archive.

XI. Is peace a goal or a solution?

PC. Peace in the Basque Country is a goal, peace is a goal all over the world. However, without self-determination it is going to be difficult to achieve social peace and political rest in the Basque Country or in any other part of the world where a nation stands asking for her right of becoming independent. The Basque conflict must be resolved in a peaceful climate, and it is possible to achieve that goal. Idahoan Democratic Representative Larry LaRocco visited the Basque Country in 1993. His interest in following the current Basque situation causes him to believe that the definitive solution for resolving the problem of violence comes through "everyone's ability to talk, use the word, symbols, the press." He notes that "if I had the solution for the Basques, I'd also apply it to us" and he reiterates that "solutions come through freedom of the press, freedom of action, of expression, and as long as those routes are not restricted, through them the solutions will come." He recognizes the progress that has come about since his previous visit in 1971 although he refuses to talk of solutions.

Six years ago, following the unanimous adoption of Idaho Memorial No. 114 at the Idaho Legislature in March 2002, several representatives of the State of Idaho initiated a process by which the citizens of Idaho, through their Representatives and Senators, brought their concern for the problems of Basque society to the United States government. We believed and still do that there is an existing general vacuum of information and understanding in the United States regarding the Basque Country, its system of self-governance, and the relations between the Basque Country and the governments of Spain and France. With this in mind, Republican Senator Larry Craig, along with the United States' State Department and Colin Cleary of the United States Embassy in Madrid, and myself, serving as Secretary of State of Idaho, organized several separate meetings in September 2002. The initial letter was signed by the three organizers, the United States Senator Larry E. Craig, U.S. Ambassador to the Spanish state Mr. Colin Cleary, and myself:

The State of Idaho and the Basque provinces have significant ties reaching to the late 1800s and the appearance of the first Basque pioneer settlers in the Treasure Valley. For more than a century Idaho's economy, culture, education, and society have benefited from the Basque [population's] migration to our state. Bernardo Atxaga's 1984 "Bi letter jaso nituen oso denbora gutxian" publication depicts the transnational identity of character "old Martin" being from Vasconia and living in Boise and both being a part of his identity. Approximately 10,000 Basques living in Idaho share "old Martin's" love for their homeland. The equal devotion to their Basque homeland, heritage and ethnic identity, in addition to the

United States Constitution and the values and rights it protects, has impelled the Basque community to ask its political representatives to strengthen relations and communications with the Basque Country. Although their residence is in the United States, they share the urgent concern for the political problems between the Autonomous Communities and the Spanish State. We hope to begin a process of understanding with these initial discussions with prestigious specialists such as [yourselves].

The initial premises regarding a negotiation on the Basque political conflict were and still are the following:

1. The current situation of the Basque Country is such that there is no uniform consensus shared by the political players, nor by social organizations, to solve the society's problems.

2. The political conditions influence and predispose the definitions utilized by individuals to explain the current and future Basque society.

3. The solution to political violence emerges as an elemental and basic factor, which divides political forces and impedes the construction of a new framework of cohabitation.

4. The politics of Basque nationalism in the schema of the Spanish state continue to be an unresolved problem. The current structure of autonomy has not resolved the Basque nationalists' desires, and the relationship between the nationalists and the government of the central state continues without having found an appropriate framework. This upsets institutional stability, affects political confidence between the governments of Madrid and Gasteiz, and influences the lack of a shared evaluation between the central and autonomous institutions.

5. The reactions of the Basque political organizations have followed a path of mistrust (above all between nationalists and non-nationalists) in electoral competence and in the appraisal of the solutions to the problem that ETA poses.

6. There are no evident substantial changes foreseen on the horizon unless achieving a reduction in the influence of ETA on Basque society, a change in the framework of

cohabitation, which the Spanish State proposes today, and a reformulation of a different manner of what it means to be nationalist. This should imply the definite triumph of the strategy of implosion, which ETA is undergoing; a new mold of political framework for what is Spain and an open civil conception of Basque nationalism.

XI. And then, it seems that there are not only obvious political obstacles for achieving a solution for the Basque political conflict but there are administrative obstacles to set off a round table of political negotiation, which within a democracy is the most adequate forum for solving political problems.

PC. I have given my life as a politician, as a member of the American Republican Party. In forty years that I have been dealing with the Basque conflict, I have never had the opportunity of really discussing the Basque political conflict with a Spanish representative. They just elude any attempt to discuss the issue. In order to have a political forum of discussion the parties have to be mature enough to understand that dialogue and no other means is the only possible political tool of negotiation. On October 20 2011 ETA announced a "definitive cessation of its armed activity" but still exists, meanwhile the Spanish administration shows no will to negotiate; the vast majority of the Basque people are in between these two fronts. I like reading the comments to my opinions, because it helps me understand why there has been no solution so far. Regarding the Basque political issue, I have always been told basically the same three things from Spanish politicians, journalists or analysts:

1. That I am wrong, without telling me why.
2. That I know nothing about the Basque political conflict, while at the same time denying that such a conflict exists.
3. That an independent Basque Republic is just a Utopia.

When we passed the 2002 Memorial we received an open letter including comments on the Memorial by Spanish Ambassador Javier Rupérez,

For the benefit of clarity, I must offer the following comments to you:

1. *Spain and the Basque Country are not two separate entities. History and commonality have made us together with the other people of Spain, very much the same. The history of Spain cannot be separated from the history of the Basque Country and vice versa. The presence of Basques in all things Spanish since memory exists is good proof of that.*
2. *There is no political conflict between Spain and the Basque Country, and, as a consequence, there is no need for any political solution to a non-existing conflict. The only conflict that we have to solve is the one created by the ETA Basque terrorism. The terrorists' demands for a referendum on self-determination as a prerequisite for peace do not constitute the basis for the existence of any conflict. They only prove the irrational need for the terrorists to justify what isn't justifiable under any circumstance, i.e., the use of violence and terror. From that viewpoint, ETA's terrorists' references to self-determination are very similar to the references made by the al-Qaeda group to the situation in the Middle East.*
3. *The Spanish Constitution of 1978 has granted and guaranteed to all our citizens the benefits of the rights and freedoms of a democratic state. Among those are the recognition of regional autonomy. The Basque Region enjoys the widest degree of autonomy to be found among European and American countries, including the United States of America.*[233]

These three reasons show nothing but complete denial. Even in the event that the statements by Rupérez were true, someone still has to explain why 60% of the Basques represented at Parliament requested the right of self-determination in order to create a free Basque Republic. There must be something else about this "non-existing conflict."

Some other times I have been even "accused" of "being an American" and thus of being responsible for killing natives in Idaho... And even though I am 92 years old I have also been accused of being a member of ETA.

I have been told many things, but I have not been shown will for dialogue regarding this issue. The Spanish and French

---

[233]   Rupérez, Javier, "Spain and Basque Country share a lasting connection", *The Idaho Statesman*, Boise. In, Pete Cenarrusa's archive.

administrations feel that the best strategy for maintaining the unity of the states is by denying the right for self-determination and by slowly erasing the signs of political and cultural identity of the Basques, also destroying their will for independence. From this perspective there is no need for dialogue. Prime Minister Aznar never assented to having a dialogue. Moreover, from 2000 to 2004 he even refused to meet with Lehendakari Juan Jose Ibarretxe, president of one of the two richest communities of the state. There can never be peace and political rest without dialogue. Spain feels that they are giving in or compromising with the Basque nation. Spanish rulers would rather keep up the separatist turmoil than have peace, because attaining peace in the county is to give concessions which leads to self-determination which the Spanish rulers abhor. The closure of newspapers tells the American people that Spain does not believe in the real sense of democracy. The first amendment to the United States Constitution is freedom of the press, freedom of speech and expression, and freedom of peaceful assembly. Spain denies the Basque Country those freedoms. This tells the American people that Spain does not believe in the freedom of dissemination of information and news, and does not believe in the right of the people to freely express themselves in certain matters.

I remember that about twenty years ago I was told that it was a Utopia to believe that Lithuania, Latvia and Estonia would gain independence and freedom. And seventeen years ago the Declaration of the Restoration of Independence of the Baltic states was passed; I was told the same about Kosovo no more than five years ago, but on 17 February 2008 the Parliament of Kosovo declared independence and subsequently 85 out of 192 UN states ratified this decision. Today Kosovo is an independent state, in spite of the Spanish refusal to recognize its independence.

I am a democrat; [laughing] a small-d democrat, not a big "D" Democrat (a member of the American Democratic Party). In the way I understand democracy there is no limit for freedom but the one established by the free will of a nation expressed by a democratically elected assembly; if the Basques decide that they want to bring into being an independent Basque Republic, then it is not a Utopia, moreover, it may be Utopian to believe that the unity of a state can be ensured by closing newspapers, by banning political parties and by violating basic human rights. I am sure that the Basque Country, Catalonia and Scotland will become independent states once again.

Pete T. Cenarrusa –in the middle- as a pilot in the reserve. C. 1950. Source: Cenarrusa archive.

The tragedy of the Spanish state in this context is that in order to maintain the silence of 60% of the Basque population who vote in May and November 2011 for Basque nationalist political options in the BAC and thus defend the right of self-determination for the Basque Country, the successive Spanish governments have to violate or diminish basic humans rights such as the right of self-determination, the freedom of speech and the freedom of association. The Spanish and French states only can retain the unity and indivisibility that they proclaim in the first articles of their constitutions by seizing the right of self-determination and other freedoms from the nations that form these two states. It is tragic that a state has to be settled on mendacity.

The Basque Country has many points in their favor with regard to becoming an independent state. The growth rate and living standard in the Basque Autonomous Community (BAC) and in the Chartered Community of Navarre (CCN) are among the three highest in the Spanish state and well above the European average. Both the government of the BAC and the CCN invest about 60% of their total income in education and in the social security system (health & education), which translates into some very good social services and educational levels. To name just a few points in their favor, the CCN has the lowest unemployment rate of the Spanish state, the second highest rate of social welfare, the second highest rate of health services' efficiency, one of the three lowest levels of poverty (households whose incomes do not reach the end of the month), the highest rate of housing and household equipment and, the CCN community ranks second in the Spanish state in the index of education and disposable income per capita. The Gross Domestic Product per capita in the CCN is 123.1, which means that it is the 41st of the 254 Regional GDPs of European Union in 2007. The data in the BAC[234] match or even exceed the rates of the CCN, such as the unemployment rate (4.1% in 2006) or GDP at 130.9, which is still growing up to the point that today it is among the 10 first Euroregions of the UE-27. The BAC holds one of the highest rates of productivity per worker (130.8) of the EU-27 and the Basque population has one of the highest schooling indexes of the European Union. All this supposes a greater quality of life. In this sense, the Basque female population is one of the longest living groups in the world, only surpassed by Japanese women.[235]

The question then is, why would the Basque people *not* be able to succeed in a political scenario of non-violence and respect for the will of the majority its citizens? There should be no reason whatsoever that this success is beyond the reach of the Basques.

In this sense we may have something to learn from Scottish politics.

---

[234] See, The Basque Country in the EU-27. 27 basic indicators to understand the situation of our country within the European Union, en http://www.eustat.es/document/EUSKADIEU27_i.pdf
[235] All these are data are available at the web page of the statistical services of the BAC in three languages (Basque, English and Castilian) (Eustat: www.eustat.es), at the web page of the CCN in Castilian (Statistical Service of Navarre: http://www.cfnavarra.es/estadistica/) and at the European Union's web page in English, French and Dutch (Eustat: http://epp.eurostat.ec.europa.eu). A very accurate summary of such data (in Castilian, French and English) is summarized in the book by Zallo, Ramón, *The Basque Country Today*, Alberdania, Irun, 2006.

Pete T. Cenarrusa with President George Bush Sr. and his wife Barbara Pierce in Boise (Idaho) ca. 1985. Source: Cenarrusa archive.

XI. Yes indeed. I assisted the congress of the Scottish National Party (SNP) on 18 January 1992 where 2,500 party leaders took part in *Scotland Decides* debate, in Usher Hall, Edinburgh. I also assisted the conference of the SNP in Perth in 1995; that year SNP Roseanna Cunningham won the Perth and Kinross by-election with 40.4 percent of the vote. On the following November 30, St. Andrew's Day, the Scottish Constitutional Convention, established in 1987 to draw up a scheme for a Scottish Parliament, published *Scotland's Parliament, Scotland's Right.*[236]

However, political culture in Spain and France differs from that in England. The state nationalism or constitutional patriotism of Southern Europe, the one prevailing in the Spanish, French, Italian or Greek politics, differs notably from the one of the one prevailing in northern Europe. During one of my visits to Scotland in November 2006, *The Scotsman Newspaper* began commissioning

---

[236]   *Scotland's Parliament, Scotland's Right: presented to the people of Scotland by the Scottish Constitutional Convention on the thirtieth day of November, nineteen hundred and ninety five in the General Assembly Hall, Edinburgh*, The Convention, Edinburgh, 1995. ISBN: 1872794564.

regular monthly polls from International Creative Management (ICM) in the context of elections to the Scottish Parliament.[237] 51 percent of respondents told ICM they would favor Scottish independence, while 39 percent opposed. It was the first time in eight years that ICM recorded a majority in favor of independence. This is not extraordinary; however, the ICM poll found that, amid an upturn in Scottish support for independence, *our southern neighbors are even more enthusiastic than us about Scotland leaving the Union.* 59 percent of English voters favored Scottish independence, and 48 percent stated that they wanted England to declare its own sovereignty, separate from Scotland, Wales and Northern Ireland. The English reasons are mainly economic, some of the interviewed explained that *I pay my tax and I just want the payback that I am justified in getting. I know it's selfish, but I don't want the Scots getting all the advantages. If we were separate, then everything would be more fair.*

PC. This is something that has not happened in Spanish or French politics. British nationalism is eminently practical, far from the mystical nationalism of the southern neighbors. Also the way of understanding liberties and freedom is essentially different. We are not going to find books on politics or history telling us that "Scottish are English" but there are thousands of books written in Spanish or French endorsing the idea that Basques and Catalans are indeed Spanish or French, depending on what part of the Pyrenees they live in.

XI. One of the main efforts in getting an agreement on the political situation of the Basque Country was led by the President of the Basque Autonomous state Juan Jose Ibarretxe who initiated a forum of political discussion and debate from 2002 to 2005. The process was the following:

- September 27, 2002. At the Basque Parliament, Lehendakari Ibarretxe announced the draft of a new statute of autonomy (from then on known as the Ibarretxe Plan), setting a timetable for the process of adoption and ratification of the new text through an open and public

---

[237] This was the first regular Scottish poll since the System Three polls for the Herald petered out in 2003.

period of dialogue. The aim of the new Statute was to take a step ahead on the resolution of the Basque political conflict by establishing a new agreement for political coexistence between the Basque and the Spanish administrations.

- October 25, 2003. Presentation of the draft statute at the Basque Parliament. The Lehendakari proposed a period of twelve months to submit amendments to the proposal of the Basque government.

- December 30, 2004. Presentation, discussion and approval of the final draft at the Basque Parliament. The Draft Statute of Autonomy was passed by absolute majority at the Basque Parliament.

- February 1, 2005. Defense of the Draft Statute at the Spanish Congress and subsequent debate and vote on the proposal. After a brief discussion, the proposal was rejected by 313 votes against (90.98 percent), 29 in favor (8.4 percent) and two abstentions (0.58 percent).

PC. This result shows the situation of the conflict and the lack of mutual understanding: the petition passed by the absolute majority of the Basque people represented at the Basque parliament was rejected in Madrid by 91 percent of the Spanish people represented at the Spanish parliament. It is obvious that there is a rupture.

XI. The main point of the Draft Statute was the assertion that the Basques are a sovereign nation with its own identity in Europe. Therefore, the Basque people have the right to decide their own political future, that is, have the right of self-determination. Even though, the right to self-determination was not contemplated in the proposal by Lehendakari Ibarretxe in an effort to get Spanish approval for the text. The political formula adopted by Ibarretxe was "co-sovereignty" by virtue of which the Basque and the Spanish governments would undertake not to change the political status without a prior common agreement.

PC. Right. The Draft Statute proposed a "Status of free association" of the Basque Country with regard to the Spanish state, under which the Basque citizens could decide what type of

[406]

union or level of political autonomy they wanted to settle with the central state.

Lehendakari Juan Jose Ibarretxe and Bob Kustra, President of Boise State University, signing the agreement for the creation of the Basque Studies Program at BSU in Boise in 2006. Source: Basque Studies Program.

This is a form of political statute rooted in the Basque territories between the thirteenth and the nineteenth centuries in order to establish their links to the crowns of Castile and France, a model of coexistence that worked perfectly well until its unilateral rupture during the French Revolution (1789-1799) and the Spanish Liberal revolution (1812-1876). An essential aspect of the pact between the Basque and the Spanish administration is the fact that a new Statute of Autonomy cannot be annulled or restricted by the paralysis of the process of devolution or through the adoption of unilateral organic laws or rules by the central government of the state. Though, the practical development of the Spanish process of institutionalization from 1975 on has shown that the Basque Statute of Autonomy has been limited by the unilateral adoption of new regulations at Madrid. In order to avoid this happening again, the Draft Statute proposed by Ibarretxe included the creation of a bilateral commission at the Spanish constitutional court in charge of solving conflicts of assignment of governmental powers as well

[407]

as to ratify international treaties and agreements adopted by the Basque administration before entering into force.

XI. Yes, in this sense, the Draft Statute proposed the Basque government to have direct representation at the European Union in order to protect the community's basic rights and economic interests just as the Dutch, Belgian or German states are also guaranteed. Indeed, the text proposed a substantial increasing of the current authority of the Basque Autonomous Community. The new state would ensure exclusive jurisdiction to the BAC in public administration, social affairs, culture, sport (with the creation of a Basque national sports selection like the Scottish or Welsh), economy, education, finance, infrastructure, environment, language policy, health, public security, social security, work, transport and housing.

Another substantial point of the Draft Statute was the political recognition of Basque citizenship (as a positive legal concept) and the Basque nationality (a positive cultural concept) to all the inhabitants in the Basque Autonomous Community, enabling the enjoyment of a dual citizenship without any decreasing or increasing of the rights and duties with respect to the current Spanish universal citizenship. And, linked to the concept of Basque citizenship, the Draft Statute attempted to give a solution to the problem of the official relationship with the Chartered Community of Navarre. The Draft Statute proposed freedom of official liaison among the seven historic Basque territories on both sides of the state borders. The decisions made by citizens in each of these regions of the Basque Country would be respected by the Spanish and French governments. Navarre would have –(as it is disposed under the current Statute of Autonomy) the right to join the BAC thus generating a new Basque Autonomous Community combining all four southern Basque territories into a single administration.

PC. The proposal of Lehendakari Ibarretxe included the hot spots for the resolution of the Basque conflict. By renouncing a proposal of independence, the Basque administration was trying to create a path to solve the two basic problems that the Basque conflict is facing today: the lack of a political agreement satisfactory to both parties and violence. The logic behind this proposal is that the lack of authority of the current political autonomy of the Basque

Country feeds political violence. By adopting a new political framework for coexistence within which both parties feel comfortable enough is, no doubt, the best and probably only way to solve a conflict that remains unsolved for two long centuries now.

However, far from dialoguing, the representatives of the two main political parties of the state refused to amend the text proposed by Lehendakari Ibarretxe, moreover, they refused even to discuss the text itself. And, in a dangerous and unexpected step, the Spanish Church and the military opposed the proposal. Only few years ago, on January 2006, when the Spanish president announced that unlike in the Basque case, the renewal of the Catalan Statute of Autonomy was possible, General José Mena Aguado, member of the General Staff of the Spanish army, stated that in the case the new Statute was passed, the army would have to intervene to guarantee the unity of the Spanish state. The international impact was obviously huge:

It is a basic principle of democracy that army officers do not publicly challenge the legitimacy of elected governments or talk about marching their troops into the capital to overturn decisions of Parliament. Yet that is just what has happened twice this month in Spain, a country whose 20th-century history compels it to take such threats seriously, even when the chances of insubordinate words leading to insubordinate actions seems quite unlikely. The response of the center-left government of Prime Minister José Luis Rodríguez Zapatero has been appropriately firm, including the dismissal and arrest of one of the culprits, a senior army general. Regrettably, the center-right Popular Party, the main opposition group, seems more interested in making excuses for the officers than in defending the democratic order in which it has a vital stake. Spain's swift and smooth passage to modern democracy after the death of Francisco Franco in 1975 makes it easy to forget the horrors of the civil war and the brutal dictatorship that preceded it. Those nightmares began when right-wing army officers rebelled against an elected left-wing government they considered to be illegitimate and too deferential to regional separatists. Spanish society, Spanish politicians and, for the most part, Spanish military officers have come a long way from that era, moderating their views and deepening their commitment to democratic give-and-take. But the Popular Party has had a hard time getting over its electoral defeat nearly two years ago, days after the terrorist bombings of commuter trains in Madrid. It has never really accepted the democratic legitimacy of that vote. It is time for the Popular Party to move ahead. Spanish democracy needs and deserves vigorous bipartisan support.[238]

And, far from retracting, General Mena has recently published a book entitled *Militares: los límites del silencio*,[239] in which he suggests measures to be adopted seeking a "regeneration of democracy" and ensures that his opinion expressed on TV on January 2006 was and still is endorsed by most of his subordinates for, as a member of the General Staff, few more than the King himself were above him within the hierarchy of the Spanish army.

XI. However, the process that is currently taking place in Scotland represents a good example of how to manage a political process of dialogue concerning the celebration of a referendum on the constitutional future of a nation.

The Scottish National Party, as well the Basque nationalist political forces support independence. As explained by Alex Salmond, current First Minister of Scotland, independence is not a matter of politics only, but a matter of better serving the interest of the citizens:

The Scottish Government believes that Scotland's future interests would be best served by it assuming all of the responsibilities and rights of a normal European state. Independence would give the Scottish Parliament and Government full responsibility for those matters currently reserved to the United Kingdom Parliament and Government, including key economic and political powers and the right of representation for Scotland in the European Union. Other aspects of an independent Scotland would remain the same. Her Majesty The Queen would remain as Head of State and the social union with the remainder of the UK would be maintained, with the nations continuing to co-operate on a range of matters.[240]

---

[238] "Army Troglodytes in Spain", *New York Times*, Editorial, January 24, 2006.

[239] Published in Spanish in February 2008. ISBN: 9788495461315.

[240] *Scotland's Future: Draft Referendum (Scotland) Bill Consultation Paper*, The Scottish Government – Riahaltas na h-Alba, 2010. P. 5.

The Treaty of Union between the independent kingdoms of Scotland and England came into force on 1 May 1707. The Treaty unified the Crowns of Scotland and England and formed the Parliament of Great Britain which, in the practice meant the elimination of the Scottish parliament, the end of Scottish independence and the creation of a new state, the United Kingdom of Great Britain under complete English control. After two centuries of claim for devolution, Scottish Home Rule returned as a key issue in the twentieth century with the creation of the Scottish National Party (SNP) in 1934 from the National Party of Scotland and the Scottish Party. Winifred 'Winnie' Ewing's victory in the Hamilton by-election of 1967 helped reinstating the SNP and brought the issue of devolution and independence to Scottish politics. Indeed, a year later, Conservative leader Edward Heath expressed the need for supporting some form of devolution and, in 1970 the Scottish Constitutional Committee of the Conservative government published *Scotland's Government*, which recommended the creation of a Scottish assembly.

Almost two decades later, in July 1997, the government published the white paper *Scotland's Parliament* which was the basis for the pre-legislative referendum which was held on September 11, 1997. Over 74 percent of the Scottish people voted in favor of the creation of a Scottish parliament in that referendum. The Scotland Act 1998 was subsequently passed to provide for the establishment of a Scottish Parliament, named the Holyrood, and a Scottish Administration. The Act devolved to a Scottish Parliament and Scottish Government all matters not reserved specifically to the British government, in practice domestic matters administered previously by the Scottish Office. On 1 July 1999 the Scottish Parliament was formally vested with its full responsibilities.

The Scottish National Party (SNP) has gradually gained votes in the Scottish elections from 672,757 constituency votes (28.74 percent) in 1999 to 902,915 votes (45.4 percent) in 2011. The SNP got thirty-five seats at the Holyrood in 1999 and, as a result of May 2007 elections, for the first time became the largest party in the Holyrood. With forty-seven seats at the Holyrood (32.9 percent), the SNP formed a minority administration in the Scottish executive and committed to hold a referendum for the political future of Scotland. In May 2011, Alex Salmond led the SNP to a historic victory over Labour and Liberal Democrats, resulting in a majority in the Scottish parliament. The SNP got 65 of the 129 seats at the Holyrood (50.4 percent). No party had previously held an overall majority in the Holyrood and the Labour Party endured its worst election in Scotland for eighty years.

After elections Salmond declared that the SNP would first demand much greater economic freedom for the Scottish parliament and, that the SNP would bring forward a referendum and trust the people on Scotland's own constitutional future: "Just as the Scottish people have restored trust in us, we must trust the people as well." David Cameron, British Premier, congratulated Salmond, but warned him that he would oppose any move towards independence for Scotland "with every single fiber I have."[241]

On 14 August 2007 the Scottish Government published a book under the title *Your Scotland, Your Voice: A National Conversation*.[242] The National Conversation prompted extensive debate across Scotland on the options for the constitutional future of the country. It was basically an inclusive debate intended to inspire ideas and opinions around the options regarding Scotland's institutional architecture that became to be three. The Scottish Government's white paper *Choosing Scotland's Future*, published in August 2007, identified these three principal options as follows:

1. *The current devolution scheme, with the possibility of further devolution on individual matters as occasions arise.*

2. *A package of specific extensions to devolved responsibilities, including fiscal autonomy, but short of independence. Such a package might need, or benefit from, the consent of the Scottish people in a referendum.*

3. *Independence: Scotland would assume all the responsibilities and rights of a normal European state, including membership of the European Union and other international bodies, the ability to determine economic policy, including the currency, and full responsibility for defence and security.*[243]

---

[241]   "SNP wins majority rule over Scottish Parliament," Herald Scotland, May 6, 2011.

[242]   *Your Scotland, Your Voice: A National Conversation*, The Scottish Government – Riahaltas na h-Alba, Edinburgh, 2009. ISBN: 978-0-7559-8114-4. Also accessible online.

[243]   *Choosing Scotland's Future: A National Conversation*, The Scottish

PC. The first two options are very similar.

XI. Yes. Indeed, the final draft of the draft bill for public consultation contemplates only two options: devolution and independence.

As part of the National Conversation effort, the Labour Party, the main political party of the opposition, proposed the creation of an independently chaired commission to review devolution in Scotland. The proposal was opposed by the governing Scottish National Party but, following the debate in the Scottish Parliament on 6 December 2007, the Holyrood resolved with the votes of Labourites, Conservatives and Liberal Democrats to support the establishment of the Commission on Scottish Devolution, also called Calman Commission or Calman Review, to review the provisions of the Scotland Act 1998 in the light of experience and to recommend changes to the present constitutional arrangements that would enable the Scottish Parliament to serve the people of Scotland better, improve the financial accountability of the Scottish Parliament, and continue to secure the position of Scotland within the United Kingdom.[244]

In a written Ministerial Statement on 25 March 2008, the Secretary of State for Scotland expressed the will of the British Government to work with the Scottish Parliament to provide support for the Commission. The appointment of Sir Kenneth Calman to chair the Commission was announced on the same day, and the rest of the members were confirmed on 28 April.

The Calman Commission met for the first time in the Scottish Parliament on 28 April 2008 and issued its final report on 15 June 2009. The report, under the title *Serving Scotland Better: Scotland and the United Kingdom in the 21st Century*, made sixty-three recommendations excluding independence.[245] The Scottish

---

Government – Riahaltas na h-Alba, Edinburgh, 2007. ISBN: 978-0-7559-5493-3. Also accessible online.

244   HC Deb 25 March 2008, cc7-8WS. Back.

245   *Serving Scotland Better: Scotland and the United Kingdom in the 21st Century*, *Presented to the Presiding Officer of the Scottish Parliament and to the Secretary of State for Scotland, on behalf of Her Majesty's Government*, June 2009. At, www.commissiononscottishdevolution.org.uk

Parliament debated and supported the Commission's final report on 25 June with the support of the main opposition parties. The Scottish government announced the celebration of a referendum on the independence of Scotland in September 2009. However, the Scottish National Party with 47 seats at the Holyrood had the only support of the two members of the Scottish Green Party, totaling 49 seats or 37.98 percent. The SNP faced the opposition of the Labour Party (46 seats), the Conservative Party (16) and Liberal Democrats (16), a majority of 78 seats or 60.46 percent of the votes at parliament to pass the Referendum Bill.

The Scottish Government then published a formal response to the Commission's recommendations on 9 November 2009, on Scottish independence. And, on November 25, 2009 the British Labour Government published a white paper on a proposed Scotland Bill based on the final report of the Calman Commission that was criticized by Alex Salmond who announced the Scottish Government's white paper *Your Scotland, Your Voice: A National Conversation*, issued five days later, on St. Andrew's Day, November 30, 2009. It is a comprehensive examination of the options for Scotland's future, namely, devolution and independence, the culmination to the National Conversation.[246]

The Scottish government issued the booklet titled *Scotland's Future: Draft Referendum (Scotland) Bill Consultation Paper* on 25 February 2010 containing a draft version of the bill and providing information on the framework for the conduct of a multi-option referendum.[247] While believing that the future prosperity and development of Scotland is best served by becoming an independent country, the Scottish Government recognized that several sectors of Scottish citizenship support other more limited ways for extending the powers of the Scottish Parliament. Thus, the draft Bill provided the people of Scotland with the opportunity to vote on two questions: the first about an extension of the powers and responsibilities of the Scottish Parliament, short of independence; the second about whether the Scottish Parliament

---

[246] *Your Scotland, Your Voice: A National Conversation*, The Scottish Government – Riaghaltas na h-Alba, 2009. ISBN: 978-0-7559-8114-4. Accessible online.

[247] *Scotland's Future: Draft Referendum (Scotland) Bill Consultation Paper*, The Scottish Government – Riaghaltas na h-Alba, 2010. ISBN: 978-0-7559-8244-8. Accessible online.

should also have its powers extended to enable independence to be achieved.[248]

The coalition of Conservative and Liberal Democrats got 340 of the 363 seats at the British parliament in the the elections of May 2010 but, with only 12 of them from Scotland, the new government's mandate in Scotland was not solid. The new British coalition government committed itself to maintaining the Union and to show that it respected Scottish differences and that the historic Scottish rights could be accommodated within a decentralized United Kingdom by implementing the recommendations of the Calman Commission. As a result, few days after the elections, the Scottish Liberal Democrats invited the SNP to study the implementation of a 'Calman Plus' package, similar to the 'devolution max' proposal included in the draft referendum bill issued by the Scottish government in February 2010. The SNP refused to participate and, after the overwhelming electoral victory of May 2011, the Scottish government announced a referendum on the constitutional future of Scotland for 2014 or 2015. Since the Scottish Government does not have the power to declare independence from Great Britain, the referendum is a consultative initiative. However, whether the Scottish voters opt for devolution or for independence, the British and Scottish parliaments will have to act on the expressed will of the Scottish people and, the British and Scottish governments would have to start a process of political negotiation.

In sum, the steps taken towards the celebration of the referendum for Scotland's constitutional future have been the following:

1. National Conversation from 2007 to 2009. A debate concerning the two main options for Scotland's constitutional future. Devolution is the alternative encouraged by the Labour party, the Conservative party and the Liberal democrats while the creation of an independent Scottish state is the option defended from the Scottish National Party and the Scottish Green Party.

---

[248] *Scotland's Future: Draft Referendum (Scotland) Bill Consultation Paper,* The Scottish Government – Riahaltas na h-Alba, 2010. P. 5.

2. After two years of national conversation, debate and exchange of ideas, the Calman Commission issued its final report on devolution on 15 June 2009 and, the Scottish government published the white paper for the Referendum Bill, setting out the different options for the constitutional future of Scotland on 30 November 2009.
3. The Scottish government made public the draft version of the bill and providing information on the framework for the conduct of a multi-option referendum on 25 February 2010.
4. After a further debate, a bill will be passed at the Scottish parliament to set out the arrangements for the referendum.
5. An advisory referendum of the Scottish electorate on extending the powers of the Scottish Parliament (devolution or independence from the United Kingdom) shall be held in either 2014 or 2015.

Although difficulties had arisen and the political dialogue had been occasionally thorny and even strenuous, the whole process has been marked by responsibility, maturity and capacity of dialogue. All parts have discussed, listened to each other and agreed on giving the people of Scotland the power of decision. A unique exercise in participative democracy.

The referendum is consultative but the British government has allowed it and has not tried to legislate against the celebration of such a referendum. Moreover, far from try to block the process, the Westminster government supported the Calman Review's recommendations on further devolution for Scotland and thus was involved in the National Conversation.

PC. In unison to the cease of violence and in the context of a post-conflict environment, the Basque people will have to address the political conflict and decide with regard to the institutional architecture of the Basque Country in very similar terms.

XI. Right. As in Scotland, the alternatives for the constitutional future of the Basque Country are three: 1) continuing with the current situation (status quo); 2) extending the responsibilities of the Basque Legislative, Executive and Judiciary (partial or total devolution); 3) independence for the Basque Country.

Sign in the road from Gernika to Lekeitio, in Bizkaia, asking for independence. 2008. Source: Irujo Ametzaga archive.

If we analyze the processes that have led to the referendum on the constitutional future of Quebec (20 May 1980 and 30 October 1995), Montenegro (21 May 2006) or Scotland (to be celebrated in 2014 or 2015), we observe that there are aspects that favor the successful celebration of a referendum in the Basque Country to bring the Basque political conflict to an end.

Among the pros for the celebration of a referendum on the independence of the Basque Country we should mention, firstly, that as in Scotland there is a will and, where there is a will there is a way. The support of nationalist political parties in the Basque Autonomous Community is bigger than in Scotland. As we have mentioned the Scottish national Party won overall majority at Holyrood on 5 May 2011 and took 45.4 percent of the constituency vote and 44.7 percent of the regional vote. The Basque nationalist forces took 61.14 percent of the regional votes and 59.65 percent of the municipal votes in the elections celebrated on 22 May 2011 in the Basque Autonomous Community (BAC), while the constitutionalist bloc (PSOE and PP) achieved 31.8 percent of the vote. The presence of Basque nationalism in the Chartered Community of Navarre (CCN) is lower though. The Basque nationalist bloc got 28.44 percent of the votes, while the regionalist and constitutionalist bloc got 57.6 percent of the Navarrese votes (34.5 percent for the regionalists and 23.1 percent for the constitutionalists) on 22 May 2011. In the Northern Basque Country (Iparralde) the support for the Basque nationalist political options reached about 18 percent in the regional elections held in March 2010, in coalition with the strong political force Europe Écologie.

However, there are also several serious problems to face. The first and most relevant problem is the existence of terrorist activity. It seems that in 2011 we have assisted to the beginning of a new era of peace in the Basque Country that, although the many hindrances, setbacks and even eventual crisis of the current peace process, seems to be a path of no return.

PC. In a scenario of peace and social democracy, every political option is open to discussion.

XI. Right. However, the Basque political conflict has to face some other serious problems. Unlike Scotland the Basque Country is a nation divided into two states. The northern Basque Country is currently included in the French republic and the Southern Basque Country in the Spanish monarchy. That makes of the Basque conflict a more complex one, involving three administrations, the French, the Spanish and the Basque. Moreover, the Basque Country has been from 1200 to 1876 a nation divided into six (seven after 1521) separated and independent states and each one of them lost independence in different times and through diverse agreements and protocols.

The Treaty of Union that was agreed on 22 July 1706 and ratified a year later by the English and Scottish parliaments is now more than 300 years old. This is what the current process of constitutional debate has to settle in Scotland. The reality in the Basque Country is more complicated. The northern Basque states lost their independence in the course of the events following the French Revolution in 1789 and the riot of 1794, more than 200 years ago. As a consequence, the Northern Kingdom of Navarre, the Country of Lapurdi and, the Country of Zuberoa, became parts of the French Republic. Basque citizens of these territories (representing 6.32 percent of the Basque population) have to settle an agreement with the French government. The alternatives for the constitutional future of this part of the Basque Country are three: 1) continuing with the current situation (status quo); 2) extending the responsibilities of these territories, including the formation of a Basque department (*départment basque*) within the French Republic (partial or total devolution); 3) independence as part of a Basque Republic or as independent states.

The Pact of Union between the governments of the Kingdom of the Southern Navarre and the newborn Spanish state was signed in 1841 as the culmination of a long political and military process starting in 1839. However, the process of constitutional and institutional casting of the southern Basque states concluded thirty-seven years later, in 1878, at the end of the Second Carlist War (1872-1876). The law of 21 July 1876 terminated the constitutions of the states of Araba, Bizkaia, and Gizpuzkoa and, reinforced the Pact of Union of 1841 in Navarre. Thus, Navarre was an independent kingdom from 824 to 1841/76 when the Treaty of Union between the Spanish and Navarrese kingdoms came into force, 135 years ago. One thousand years of independent government obviously gives the Navarrese (representing 20.42 percent of the Basque population) the right to decide their own constitutional future as part of the Spanish state (status quo or partial devolution), as a Navarrese independent state (total devolution) or, as part of an independent Basque Republic.

The alternative for the Basque citizens of Araba, Bizkaia and Gipuzkoa (representing 73.25 percent of the Basque population) are also three: 1) continuing with the current situation (status quo); 2) extending the responsibilities of these territories within the Spanish state (devolution); 3) independence as part of a Basque Republic.

We may conclude that regarding the constitutional future of the Basque Country today and, in view of the electoral results in the last decade, the alternative of independence is the strongest option in the Basque Autonomous Community where Bildu and EAJ-PNV endorse it, representing 61 percent of the popular vote. In Navarre, devolution may be the strongest position, favored by both the regionalists but also the Basque nationalist. Status quo may be the most popular option in Iparralde, although the *Revendication d'un département basque* has also a long tradition in the Northern Basque Country.

PC. As we have already mentioned, the Spanish and French political cultures have also been an obstacle for the resolution of the conflict in the past. Like the Scottish, the Basques went through a process of political debate from 2002 to 2005 when President Juan Jose Ibarretxe presented the draft proposal of political statute for the Basque Country but, unlike the Scottish process, the Basque process was marked by the naked application of political muscle. Vetoes followed threats of vetoes and, on 23 December 2003 the Spanish Criminal Code was amended prohibiting the celebration of referendums under penalty of three to five years of imprisonment. The main political parties of the Spanish arena, PSOE and PP, opposed the process of dialogue and avoided taking part in the negotiations. The Basque Parliament's plenary approved the proposal of political statute for the Basque Country by absolute majority after a long debate on 30 December 2004 while the Spanish parliament rejected it after a short discussion by 313 votes against (90.98 percent) and 29 in favor (8.4 percent) on 1 February 2005. Moreover, Basque president Ibarretxe was taken to court in 2007 for meeting with members of Batasuna in order to foster the trust and sharing that is essential in a peace process.

XI. A referendum on the political options for future would give the people the chance to express themselves and exert their right of decision. A referendum is an exercise of democracy. No matter the result of the referendum, the celebration of a popular consultation helps to redirect efforts, channels a process of political dialogue and, finally, helps to solve a political conflict. On 15 October 2009, Alex Salmond declared: "Do parties in Scotland really believe that the people of Scotland will give them their votes if they refuse to give the people of Scotland a vote on the constitutional future of the country?" Basque people think similarly.

Ensuring the public can participate in the democratic process is a central tenet of modern societies and democracy. In the Basque Country we should reaffirm an ancient political tradition which asserts that it is the people in an open assembly who are sovereign.

PC. Right.

XI. We may well finish this dialogue by posing a number of general questions for anyone trying to find a solution or part of the solution to the Basque conflict or to any other given policital conflict around the world. I have taken them from the questions that my students at UNR, BSU and UCSB have asked me in class:

1. Is there a Basque political conflict? Or is the conflict cultural in nature and origin? Are all political conflicts cultural conflicts in origin?
2. If the solution to any conflict should be based on a previous diagnosis, peace building should be built on understanding. Then, which is the origin, nature and scope of the Basque political conflict?
3. Political violence is the product of the political conflict, or the origin of it? What is the scope and meaning of violence in the Basque Country?
4. In this sense, what is peace, a goal or a solution?
5. Which have been the main causes bringing Batasuna to ask from ETA a farewell to arms?
6. How much faith should we have in ETA's peace declaration?
7. What does ETA's declaration mean for the Basque Country?
8. Why has ETA made this decision? Which have been the main elements bringing ETA to an end?
9. With an upcoming victory by the Popular Party in Spain, could ETA's declaration be jeopardized?
10. Who are the victims of the conflict?
11. Has the Basque society been a victim of terrorism also?
12. What can be done to help the victims?
13. How should we understand the concept of justice in the current post-violent stage of the peace process?
14. Should the Spanish government now send ETA prisoners closer to home?
15. Should the anti-terror legislation be adjusted? Should the Criminal Code be modified?
16. What is the biggest obstacle for a solution to the Basque political conflict today?

17. Is dialogue a key to solving the Basque political conflict and, if so, which are the main obstacles for setting a round table of negotiation?
18. Once a table of negotiation is settled, which are the main obstacles its members have to face?
19. What measures should be taken for ETA to disappear after its farewell to arms?
20. What can you comment on the responsibility of the political representatives and media in the context of a peace building process?
21. What role do you believe the political and social organizations in the Basque Country should play in the current post-violent stage of the peace process?
22. What role do the Spanish and the French governments play in this peace-building process? And what role should they play?
23. Is the Basque Government promoting peace? Is the Navarrese government involved in the process?
24. Is the Basque Government promoting solutions for the constitutional future of the Basque Country?
25. How should we interpret the results of the May 2011 elections (61 percent Basque nationalist vote at the BAC) regarding the peace process?
26. Should a referendum on the constitutional future of the Basque Country be held? Why?
27. What should a referendum on the political future of the Basque Country ask the citizens?
28. Is self-determination a basic human right? Is it universal? Should it be a universally recognized right?
29. Is self-determination one of the keys to solve the Basque political conflict? Is the recognition of the right of self-determination the key for solving political conflicts?

Basque nationalism and Europeism

Pete Cenarrusa. All Basque nationalist political forces are in essence pro-European movements supporting the project of Herrien Europa, the Europe of the Peoples.

Xabier Irujo. Yes. Herrien Europa (Europe of the Peoples) is the political and social project defended by various European political parties, especially of those forces that form part of the European Free Alliance (EFA), an electoral coalition formed in 1981 to take part in the elections to the European Parliament. By virtue of its constituent declaration, adopted at its first general assembly in Brussels in 1981, the EFA is a pan-European political force that consists of various political parties promoting the creation of a European union of free nations based on the principle of subsidiarity and the application of the right of self-determination. The declaration issued at the Brussels Convention in 1981 emphasized that *the EFA's political credo was based on fruitful interaction between individual identity and the identity of peoples and found practical expression in the federal model, with decisions being taken at the lowest possible level.*[249] The EFA was thus ten years ahead of its time in placing the debate on subsidiarity at the heart of its political discourse.

EFA members are mostly nationalist and progressive parties, although the alliance is open to conservative or Christian democratic forces such as the South Tyrolean Freedom (STF, Süd-Tiroler Freiheit), the Bavaria Party (BP, Bayernpartei), the New-Flemish Alliance (NVA, Nieuw-Vlaamse Alliantie) or the Venetian Republic League (LVR, Liga Vèneta Republica). The coalition has been historically headed in the Basque Country by Basque Solidarity (EA, Eusko Alkartasuna) but comprises nearly forty other European nationalist political parties from most of the stateless nations in Europe such as Andalusia, Aragon, Brittany

---

249   European Free Alliance (EFA), *The European Political Parties: The Regionalists*, Brussels, October 1995.

Catalonia, Cornwall, Corsica, Flanders, Friesland, Galicia, Occitania, Scotland, Tyrol, Wales…[250]

In the first 1979 European Parliament election the Scottish National Party (SNP), the Flemish People's Union (VU, Volksunie),[251] the Waloon Democratic Front of Francophones (FDF, Front Démocratique des Francophones) and the South Tyrolean People's Party (SVP, Südtiroler Volkspartei)[252] got representatives at the European parliament but they did not join in a single political group or party. In view of this situation, in 1981 several European nationalist and progressive parties joined together to form a pan-European political force known as the European Free Alliance (EFA) during the assembly held in Brussels.

PC. The first elections to the European Parliament by direct universal suffrage in 1979 made access to the European Parliament possible and, as a consequence, also brought access to the European institutions, to several persons belonging to nationalist parties. Maurits Coppieters from the Flemish People's Union (VU, Volksunie) and Neil Blaney from the Independent Fianna Fail Republican Party of Ireland joined the Group for the Technical

---

[250] The member parties of the EFA are: Alands Framtid, Bayernpartei, Bloque Nacionalista Galego, Chunta Aragonesista, Die Friesen, Enotna Lista, Esquerra Republicana de Catalunya, Eusko Alkartasuna, Fryske Nasjonale Partij, Libertà Emiliana-Nazione Emilia, Liga Repubblica Veneto, Ligue Savoisienne, Lithuanian Polish People's Party, Mebyon Kernow, Moravana, Mouvement Région Savoie, Omo Ilinden Pirin, Partei der Deutschsprachigen Belgier, Partido Andalucista, Partit Occitan, Partit Socialista de Mallorca i Menorca-Entesa Nacionalista, Partito Sardo d'Azione, Partitu di a Nazione Corsa, Plaid Cymru-the Party of Wales, Rainbow-Vinozhito, Scottish National Party, Silesian Autonomy Movement, Slovenska Skupnost, Sociaal Liberale Partij, Strana regionov Slovenska, Süd Tiroler Freiheit, Union Démocratique Bretonne, Union du Peuple Alsacien and Unitat Catalana. And the observer parties are: Lista Per Fiume, Movimento per l'Indipendenza della Sicilia, Hungarian Roma Party, ProDG, Renouveau Valdotaine, Südschleswigscher Wählerverband and Wendische Volkspartei.

[251] Maurits Coppieters was elected MP and Jaak Vandemeulebroucke worked as his assistant.

[252] Currently the SVP is a member of the European People's Party (EPP).

Coordination and Defence of Independent Groups and Members (CDI), a mixed political group formed by eleven MPs.[253]

The Greens / European Free Alliance (EFA) Coalition logo, 2011. Source: EFA.

XI. Yes, it was the first attempt to create a common organization for nationalist parties at European level. And the European Free Alliance was created soon after. Among the political parties that joined EFA between 1981 and 1990 there were the Union of the Corsican People (UPC, Unione di u Populu Corsu)[254] in 1981, the Frisian National Party (FNP, Frysk Nasjonale Partij) in 1981, People's Union (VU, Volksunie) in 1983, Plaid Cymru (Plaid, The Party of Wales) in 1983, the Sardinian Action Party (PSd'Az, Partito Sardo d'Azione) in 1984, Basque Solidarity (EA, Eusko Alkartasuna) in 1986, the Occitan Party (PO, Partit Occitan) in 1987, the Breton Democratic Union (UDB, Unvaniezh Demokratel

---

253   European Free Alliance (EFA), *The European Political Parties: The Regionalists*, Brussels, October 1995. P. 1.
254   In 2002 this political force merged together with A Scelta Nova and A Mossa Naziunale into the Party of the Corsican Nation (PCN, U Partitu di a Nazione Corsa).

Breizh/Union Démocratique Bretonne) in 1987, the Scottish National Party (SNP) in 1989, Republican Left of Catalonia (ERC, Esquerra Republicana de Catalunya) in 1989.

According to the new statutes of the EFA passed at the general assembly held in Cardiff, the member parties gave the green light for the transformation of the EFA into a federation of political parties. The new Article 1 of the EFA's statutes states that, "the European Free Alliance is a federation of political parties" which subscribes "the principle of the self-determination of peoples" and "the principles of parliamentary democracy and human rights." Article 2 of the statutes lists the party's objectives, which include "providing nationalism and democratic regionalism with a political structure which clears the way for the development of practical initiatives" at the European level and "facilitating participation in European politics for parties which, by virtue of their own size or the size of the territory they represent, would inevitably be excluded from that process."[255]

In 1984 Jaak Vandemeulebroucke, Willy Kuijpers, Michele Columbu and Carlos Garaikoetxea (main leaders of the EFA at the time) prompted a coalition with the Green Party and other progressive political forces under the name of the Rainbow Group that got twenty seats (4.6% of the total) at the European parliament, although only three of them were members of the EFA, Jaak Vandemeulebroucke and Willy Kuijpers representatives of the Flemish People's Union (VU, Volksunie) and Michele Columbu representative of the coalition formed by the Sardinian Action Party (PSdA, Partito Sardo d'Azione) and the alliance Federalism Europe of the Peoples (FED, Federalismo Europa dei Popoli) organized by the Valdotanian Union (UV, Union Valdôtaine) and independents. In 1984 the Scottish National Party (SNP) also got one seat at the European parliament but did not join the EFA, they joined the Group of the European Democratic Alliance (EDA) instead.[256]

In 1989 the Rainbow Group was reduced to thirteen representatives (2.5%), due to the fact that the Greens formed their

---

[255] European Free Alliance (EFA), *The European Political Parties: The Regionalists*, Brussels, October 1995. P. 9.

[256] In French, Groupe du Rassemblement des Démocrates Européens (RDE)

own Green Group at the European parliament. However, the number of seats won by the EFA increased from three representatives in 1984 to seven in 1989: Jaak Vandemeulebroucke representative of the Flemish People's Union (VU, Volksunie), Mario Melis of the Federalism Europe of the Peoples (FED, Federalismo Europa dei Popoli),[257] Francesco Enrico Speroni and Luigi Moretti of the Lombard League (LL, Lega Lombarda), Winifred Margaret 'Winnie' Ewing for the Scottish National Party (SNP), Pedro Pacheco of the Andalusian Party (PA, Partido Andalucista) and Carlos Garaikoetxea as the representative of Basque Solidarity (EA, Eusko Alkartasuna).[258]

In the 1994 European Parliament election the elected members of the EFA ranged from seven to eleven although in that year only five EFA parties got seats: Marilena Marin, Raimondo Fassa, Luigi Moretti, Gipo Farassino, Marco Formentini and Umberto Bossi of the Northern League (LN, Lega Nord), Winnie Ewing and Allan Macartney for the Scottish National Party (SNP), Jaak Vandemeulebroucke of the Flemish People's Union (VU, Volksunie), Josu Jon Imaz of the Basque Nationalist Party (EAJ-PNV) and Isidoro Sánchez of Canarian Coalition (CC, Coalición Canaria). However, after the elections the member of the Basque Nationalist Party (EAJ-PNV) joined the European People's Party and the Northern League (LN, Lega Nord) was expelled from the EFA and, as a consequence from the ERA, for entering into a coalition government in Italy with the post-fascist National Alliance (AN, Aleanza Nationale). The three remaining members of the EFA (SNP, VU and CC) entered with the Left Radical Party

---

[257] In 1989 the alliance Federalismo Europa dei Popoli (FED) was renewed and included the following political forces: Sardinian Action Party (PSdA, Partito Sardo d'Azione), Valdotanian Union (UV, Union Valdôtaine), Occitan Autonomist Mouvement (MAO, Movimento Autonomista Occitano), Friulian Movement (MF, Movimento Friuli/Moviment Friûl), Southern Movement (MM, Movimento Meridionale), Slovene Union (SS, Slovenska Skupnost/Unione Slovena), Union for South Tyrol (UfS, Union für Südtirol) and Union of the Venetian People (UPV, Union del Popolo Veneto). As a consequence, Mario Melis of the PSdA was elected MP.

[258] Following the first European Parliament elections held in the Spanish state in 1987.

(ER, Energie Radicale) into the European Radical Alliance that got 19 MPs after the exclusion of the six members of the Lega Nord.

Following the 1999 European Parliament election the EFA increased its representation at the European parliament and formed a common European parliamentary group with the European Green Party called The Greens-European Free Alliance that got forty eight seats at the Europarliament, 7.7% of the total. In total the parties at the EFA got ten seats at the European parliament in 1999, the best results ever obtained: Ian Stewart Hudghton and Sir (Donald) Neil MacCormick from the Scottish National Party (SNP), Jill Evans and Eurig Wyn of the Welsh Plaid Cymru, Bart Staes and Nelly Maes of the Flemish People's Union (VU, Volksunie),[259] Josu Ortuondo of the Basque Nationalist Party (EAJ-PNV), Gorka Knörr for Basque Solidarity (EA, Eusko Alkartasuna), Isidoro Sánchez of the Andalusian Party (PA, Partido Andalucista) and Camilo Nogueira of the Galician Nationalist Bloc (BNG, Bloque Nacionalista Galego).

In 2004 the EFA became a European political party but at the European Parliament election the EFA was reduced to four MEPs, Ian Hudghton and Alyn Smith of the Scottish National Party (SNP), Jill Evans of the Welsh Plaid Cymru and Bernat Joan i Mari of the Republican Left of Catalonia (ERC, Esquerra Republicana de Catalunya), replaced at the mid-term by Mikel Irujo of Basque Solidarity (EA, Eusko Alkartasuna).[260] As in 1999, in coalition with the Greens, The Greens-European Free Alliance Group took 42 seats at the European parliament, 5.7% of the total.

---

[259]   In coalition with ID21.

[260]   From the coalition Europe of the Peoples-The Greens formed by the following parties: Republican Left of Catalonia (ERC, Esquerra Republicana de Catalunya), Basque Solidarity (EA, Eusko Alkartasuna), Aragonese Council (CHA, Chunta Aragonesista), Socialist Party of Andalusia (PSA, Partido Socialista de Andalucía), Andecha Astur (AA), Cantabrian Nationalist Council (CNC, Conceju Nacionaliegu Cántabru), Citizen Initiative of La Rioja (ICLR, Iniciativa Ciudadana de la Rioja) and Canarian People's Alternative (APC, Alternativa Popular Canaria).

Year	1984	1989	1994	1999	2004	2009
Party MPs	2 VU 1 FED	1 VU 1 FED 2 LL 1 SNP 1 PA 1 EA	1 VU 2 SNP	2 VU 2 SNP 2 Plaid 1 EA 1 PA 1 EAJ-PNV 1 BNG	2 SNP 1 Plaid 1 EFA/ Greens	2 SNP 1 Plaid 1 N-VA 1 PNC 1 EFA/ Greens 1 FHRUL
Total MPs	3	7	3	10	4	7

Parties and number of MPs of EFA from 1984 to 2009.

In the last elections of 2009 to the European Parliament (375 million eligible voters) the EFA increased again to seven MEPs elected: Ian Hudghton and Alyn Smith of the Scottish National Party (SNP), Jill Evans of The Party of Wales (Plaid Cymru), François Alfonsi of the Party of the Corsican Nation (PNC, U Partitu di a Nazione Corsa), Oriol Junqueras of the coalition Europe of the Peoples-The Greens (EFA-Greens, Europa de los Pueblos–Los Verdes),[261] Tatjana Ždanoka, individual member of the EFA in Latvia (leader of For Human Rights in a United Latvia, FHRUL) and Frieda Brepoels representative of the New-Flemish Alliance (N-VA, Nieuw-Vlaamse Alliantie). In coalition with the Greens, the Greens-EFA Group currently has 55 representatives at the European Parliament, 7.5% of a total of 736 and the EFA member political parties have representation in seventeen member states of the European Union.

---

[261] The coalition Europe of the Peoples-The Greens is formed by the following political forces: the Republican Left of Catalonia (ERC, Esquerra Republicana de Catalunya), Basque Solidarity (EA, Eusko Alkartasuna) and Aralar from the Basque Country, the Galician Nationalist Bloc (BNG, Bloque Nacionalista Galego), Aragonese Council (CHA, Chunta Aragonesista), Majorcan Socialist Party–Nationalist Agreement (PSM-EN, Partit Socialista de Mallorca – Entesa Nacionalista), Agreement for Majorca (EM, Entesa per Mallorca), The Greens (Els Verds), Confederation of the Greens (Confederación de los Verdes), New Canarias (Nueva Canarias) and Unidá.

[429]

Political Parties	BAC			CCN		
EAJ-PNV (CEU)	207,040	28.76%	50.46%	3.601	1.80%	20.24%
Batasuna (II)	152,911	16.01%		22,985	11.46%	
EA/Aralar	40.963	5.69%		13,992	6.98%	
IU	13,121	1.82%	1.82%	6,719	3.35%	3.35%
PSE	200,249	27.81%	45.40%	62,738	31.29%	71.32%
PP	115,911	16.10%		75,989	37.9%	
UPyD	10,818	1.49%		4,280	2.13%	
Total			97.68%			94.91%

Results of the European parliament elections of 2009 in the Basque Country.

PC. Starting in 1981, the EFA has worked long and hard to develop its political doctrine, namely, full political independence or some form of devolution for their nations. At its forty annual general assemblies held in different European cities (Brussels, Cardiff, Bilbao, Barcelona, Bastia, Eupen, Cagliari, Strasbourg, Ostend...) the EFA member parties have organized seminars on the various aspects of European politics. The new statutes of the EFA were approved at the meeting of the General Assembly of the organization held in Brussels in November 2004 and reviewed at the General Assemblies held in Rennes in May 2005 and Brussels in May 2006. According to Article 3 the EFA has a common program with the following goals:

- *European unity and the creation of a European union of free peoples based on the principle of subsidiarity who believe in solidarity with each other and other peoples of the world;*
- *The defense of human rights and the rights of peoples, in particular the right to self-determination;*
- *Protection of the environment and sustainable development;*
- *The creation of a fair society based on solidarity, with policies which favor progress, social cohesion and equal opportunities for all citizens;*
- *Acceptance of the principles of the parliamentary democracy;*
- *Agreement to strive for and promote more close and continuing co-operation between its members with the realization of its goals as the main focus;*

- o *Taking an active part in the promotion of a free and pluralistic democracy;*
- o *Promoting European integration based on the diversity of peoples, cultures, languages and regions;*
- o *Integrating all these goals in a coherent and common political program.*

XI. The program is based on two main principles of European integration: diversity and cooperation. EFA is a pro-European party seeking for a more democratic and decentralized European Union. Currently the only European institution directly elected by the peoples is the European Parliament. The Council of the European Union, which represents the individual member states, and the European Commission, which seeks to uphold the interests of the Union as a whole, are formed by elected representatives of the European states.

PC. The goal is thus to create a European federation of nations and peoples that protects cultural diversity while taking advantage of what a stronger union has to offer in economic, social and political terms.

XI. Exactly. And the political tool to achieve this is subsidiarity, a political principle first shaped in 1936 according to which decision-making has to be brought closer to the citizens. The idea is that the administration of political institutions is more effective when decisions devolve to the lowest practical level rather than providing powers to a dominant central organization.

PC. In the context of a reform of the European Union's institutions, the European Parliament resolution of 26 October 2000 on better lawmaking, underlined that the European nations should have political and legislative powers in their executive, legislative and judicial relations with the current EU institutions. In this regard, member parties of the EFA emphasize the necessary development and democratization of the European Parliament to create greater openness and transparency in decision making with legislative power vested in two chambers. According to the EFA *Declaration of Brussels*, of 9 November 2000, the Committee of the Regions should be reinforced and turned into a European Senate for the representation of all European nations or cultures. Democratization of the European decision-making process requires a radical reform consistent with sustaining the essentially confederal character of the European Union. A necessary first step towards a federation of European nations is the reform of the European electoral map to match the territorial framework of the nations that should constitute separate electoral constituencies with their own elected MPs.

European MP Mikel Irujo during a session held in Bilbao in June 2008 with Lhamo Sualto and Gyaltsen Drolkar, an exiled Tibetan nun who was interned by the Chinese authorities at the Drapchi prison. Source: Irujo Ametzaga archive.

XI. Right. EFA expressed concern in the Ljouwert resolution of 14 February 1987 that the Single Act had strengthened the European Community's mercantilist approach (confining itself to speeding up the completion of the internal common market) but failed to advance towards the democratization of the Union by allocating more substantial legislative powers to the Parliament against the Council of Ministers. In the wording of the *Declaration* of 1996 on the European political parties, the EFA took the view that the changes made by the Single European Act fell well short of establishing the federal Europe advocated by the Alliance. In that connection, it proposed the establishment of a two-chamber Parliament as a practical counterweight to the current Council of Ministers and its powers: a Parliament elected by direct universal suffrage and a senate comprising equal-sized delegations from the regions of Europe.

PC. The EFA member parties seek to enhance the participation of the citizens through a direct election of the President of the Commission. According to the *Declaration* of 1996 on the European political parties, the EFA member parties acknowledged that the Maastricht Treaty contained a number of positive features, such as the moves towards political and monetary union and the establishment of the basis for a new Cohesion Fund. However, in 1996 the EFA previewed basic needs in several significant institutional levels such as:

- *The need for a social and employment union to accompany Economic and Monetary Union;*
- *The establishment of a more effective and coherent foreign policy, which should no longer be based on simple intergovernmental cooperation and should provide for a partial and gradual transfer of diplomatic and military powers to the Union;*
- *The need for the objective of sustainable development to be more firmly enshrined in the Treaty; the unilateral choice made by the European Union in favor of nuclear energy should be abandoned and priority given to the development of renewable energy sources and the rational use of energy;*
- *The organization of the European continent on the basis of concentric circles or levels of solidarity, with a more closely integrated federal core. The federal model advocated by the DPPE-EFA was not a centralizing European State based on the French Jacobin model or a federation of nation states. In institutional terms, the Union should have two law-making chambers (a European Parliament and a 'Senate of the peoples and regions' combining features of the Council and the Committee of the Regions), with a government elected by those assemblies; the national and regional parliaments should continue to play an important role by ensuring democratic scrutiny of any breaches of the Union's powers;*
- *The launch of an in-depth debate on the division of powers;*

- *An enhanced role for the Committee of the Regions, which should be a fully independent institution;*
- *Acknowledgement of the equal status of all the languages spoken in the territory of the Union; any language with official status in its own territory should be recognized at Union level on the basis of an enhanced version of the status which the European Parliament's report of 11 December 1990 had granted Catalan;*
- *Clear provision should be made for Member States to leave the Union, highlighting the democratic and voluntary nature of that link.*[262]

XI. These principles link to the concept of 'shared sovereignty' or co-operative bilateral relations between the European Union and self-governing states and entities. Not all European states are 'nations'; quite the opposite, most of them are complex entities made up of several nations called 'stateless nations' or also nationalities, autonomous communities, länders or regions. In the words of the authors of the EFA manifesto for the June 2009 European elections entitled *Vision for a People's Europe,*

> *A new category of political entities is emerging in the EU: the Emerging States. As political and juridical rights in the EU are linked to "statality," the historical nations co-existing within the framework of the present Member States are blowing fresh air in the direction of full recognition. Some of these nations try to get recognition of their collective rights by creating their own states. Demands for public and democratic consultation in Scotland, Wales, the Basque Country and Catalonia are a first step in this direction.*[263]

PC. In recent years, we have seen Montenegro (2006) and Kosovo (2008) become independent states. Flanders, Scotland, Wales, Catalunya and the Basque Country are also on their path to national self-determination and a full voice at the European institutions.

---

[262]   European Free Alliance (EFA), *The European Political Parties: The Regionalists*, Brussels, 1996.
[263]   European Free Alliance (EFA), *Manifesto for the June 2009 European elections "Vision for a People's Europe,"* Barcelona, March 2009.

XI. As expressed in the *Declaration of Brussels* of 2000, this is the expression of a very specific form of nationalism shared by the EFA member parties that has several essential characteristics: 1) It is pro-European, democratic and constitutionalist, even if constitutional or political arrangements in most of the European and non-European states directly affect the survival of native cultures and languages and, in some cases, also destabilize the social and economic welfare of these nations; 2) It is committed to social justice and the respect for equality and for human rights and the rights of minorities and it is resolutely opposed to racism and xenophobia of any kind; 3) It is universalistic in asserting the right to self-determination to all peoples, nations and cultures; 4) It is civic and inclusive in seeking to identify the relevant national communities around common civil institutions rather than supposed ethnicity or blood ties; 5) It is committed to sustainable development and respect for cultural and ecological diversity; 6) It is committed exclusively to peaceful means in the pursuit of political objectives.[264]

PC. Indeed, the preservation of ecodiversity lies at the very basis of the political program of the EFA member parties and the defense and protection of the cultural and language rights of the European and non- European nations is the main reason for demanding political independence or statehood. The right to self-determination is demanded on the ground of cultural self-preservation.

XI. The EU currently has twenty-seven member states and twenty-three official or communitarian languages. But there are many more languages in Europe; there are at least seventy-five languages grouped in five main language families (Indo-European, Finno-Ugric, Turkic, Semitic and Basque). And some authors consider the North and South Caucasian languages to be also European. As of 2009, Basque −(an isolated language related to the ancient Proto-Basque), Catalan, Galician, Welsh and Scottish Gaelic are also used at the EU institutions, but do not have full official status.

---

264   European Free Alliance (EFA), *Declaration of Brussels*, Brussels, 9 November 2000.

[435]

The six EFA members at the European Parliament in 2009. Source: Irujo Ametzaga archive.

PC. According to the UNESCO, by the end of this century half of the 6,700 existing languages are endangered and likely to disappear. Moreover, according to a 2003 report of a committee of experts of the UNESCO the world loses 20-30 languages a year. It is essential to notice that more than 90% of the endangered languages are not official languages, that is, most of them have not been given official status and, as a consequence, parents cannot (for instance) take their children to school to be taught in their own mother language. This is the case of the Basque language at the fiercely centralized French republic (where only one of the nearly thirty languages and linguistic varieties is official) or the case of our native languages in the USA. It is clear that this process that can only be slowed if resolute and persistent political action is taken by governments.

XI. The EFA member parties consider that the EU has to officially recognize all these languages and provide to all of them the same official status, for only by doing so will the European Union promote a true linguistic diversity based on respect for the linguistic rights of the European peoples. For this reason, considering Article 14 of the Council of Europe's Convention for the Protection of Human Rights and Fundamental Freedoms, of 4

November 1950, the EFA has called, since its creation in 1981, for a UN Declaration of Linguistic Rights. The Declaration in the Rights of Persons Belonging to National or Ethnic, Religious and Linguistic Minorities was finally adopted by the UN Commission on Human Rights in its resolution 1992/16, 21 February 1992 and by the General Assembly in its resolution 47/135 on 18 December 1992. This prompted the approval of the European Charter for Regional or Minority Languages of 29 June 1992 and the subsequent Declaration on National Minorities made by the Summit Meeting of the Council of Europe on 9 October 1993; and the Framework Convention for the Protection of National Minorities of November 1994.

PC. However, as we have already noted, several European governments such as the French, have refused to sign some of the articles of the European Charter for Regional or Minority Languages and, therefore, Basque, Catalan, Breton, Corsican or Occitan are not official languages in the République Française; in general terms we may affirm that nearly two thirds of the languages spoken in Europe have not gained official status.

XI. Right. The 2003 Convention for the Safeguarding of Intangible Cultural Heritage, and in particular, Article 1-3.3 of the draft constitutional text called for support for linguistic diversity as a preeminent objective in its Constitution, to which end the EU will "respect its rich cultural and linguistic diversity, and shall ensure that Europe's cultural heritage is safeguarded and enhanced." After the approval of that draft of the text, EFA urged the Union to include all references to cultural and linguistic diversity in the project for a European Constitution, "as an absolute minimum" and called upon all member states to sign and ratify the Council of Europe's Charter for Regional or Minority Languages. They also called upon the member states to sign and ratify the Framework Convention for the Protection of National Minorities. Furthermore and considering the issue of worldwide language endangerment, the EFA called upon the European Parliament and all EU member states to sign the UNESCO Convention for the Protection of Intangible Cultural Heritage.[265]

---

265   European Free Alliance (EFA), *Joint Eurolang - EFA Call for*

PC. After the adoption of the EU Regulation allowing the creation of European foundations affiliated to Euro-parties, in September 2007, the EFA established the Centre Maurits Coppieters (CMC), which has organized several conferences on cultural diversity. The Centre Maurits Coppieters organized "The crisis and the future of Europe: Outlook of the Peoples," a series of debates reflecting on economic policy options for sub-central governments and, invited Dr. Daniel Turp, professor of Constitutional Law at the University of Montreal and Vice president of the Québec Nationalist Party (PQ, Parti Québécois), to discuss "Collective rights: Lessons from Quebec." On 4th March 2010, The European Free alliance organized the conference *Language Diversity: A Challenge for Europe* on cultural diversity at European institutions.

XI. A long road to hoe yet.

Documental Appendix

Pete Cenarrusa raising his hammer *against Franco*. Source: Cenarrusa archive.

House Joint Memorial No. 115

Boise, April 6, 1972

A joint memorial to the President of the United States, the Secretary of State of the United States, the President of the Senate and the Speaker of the House of Representatives of the United States in Congress Assembled, the Senators and Representatives representing this State in Congress, the Governors of the fifty States, and the Basque Government in exile in France.

We, your Memorialists, the Senate and the House of Representatives of the state of Idaho assembled in the Second Regular Session of the Forty-first Legislature, do hereby respectfully represent that:

WHEREAS, the history and traditions of this nation rest upon the principle of freedom from oppression and the rights of all citizens to life, liberty and the pursuit of happiness; and

WHEREAS, we believe that democracy and freedom, when denied in one country stand threatened everywhere; therefore, it is our responsibility to bring to the attention of the people of the United States, and, we hope to the people of the entire world that these very freedoms of the Basque people are threatened under the Franco regime in Spain today; and

WHEREAS, the Basque people have a long and glorious history of personal accomplishment and a devotion to the preservation of their national heritage; and

WHEREAS, the sole aim of the Basques, since human time began, has been to bar the world's wars, tribal, racial, religious, imperialistic or civil, from the tiny green mountain land which was their own before history began; and

WHEREAS, no other country in the world holds the traditions of its forefathers so sacred as Euzkadi, as the Basques call their homeland; and

WHEREAS, the Basques have been denied the right to learn their own language, have been jailed, and have been denied human rights by the Franco regime and are virtually threatened in their continued existence; and

WHEREAS, the stare state of Idaho is known as the North American center of the Basque population, and

WHEREAS, the Basques of North America have carried the traditions of their forefathers as honest and self-reliant peoples, possessing the basic elements of democracy, humanity, charity and mercy; and

WHEREAS, the Basques of North America feel first that they are Americans, and as such they feel for America as the Basques of Euzkadi felt for their country, which is:

Gu Amerikarentzat eta America, Jaungoikoarentzat.
which means
We are for America, and America is for God.

WHEREAS, in World War II thousands of American lives were lost in a war which was precipitated from the Spanish Civil War, a war of genocide of the Basques, by the three dictators, Franco, Mussolini, and Hitler; and

WHEREAS, the Basques, who once enjoyed the oldest democratic republic in Europe, fought for the Allies in World War II and

WHEREAS, over 2.4 billion dollars in aid has been given to Franco's Spain for economic and military assistance since 1946 by the government of the United States.

NOW, THEREFORE, BE IT RESOLVED by the Legislature of the state of Idaho that we voice our strong belief that as a nation we should reward our friends and not our enemies, and we deplore any free and democratic nation providing assistance to a ruthless, totalitarian government, directly or indirectly.

BE IT FURTHER RESOLVED that we urge all steps be taken to cause the Spanish government to cease and desist the denial of the Universal Declaration of Human Rights of Man and insist that general amnesty for all Basques and Spaniards now imprisoned or exiled for their political and social activities be extended by the Franco government.

BE IT FURTHER RESOLVED that if such steps are not carried out, the President of the United States, the Secretary of State, and Congress of the United States take all necessary steps to withdraw all foreign aid or benefits to the Spanish dictatorship.

BE IT FURTHER RESOLVED that the Secretary of the Senate be, and he is hereby authorized and directed to forward copies of this Memorial to the President of the United States, the Secretary of State of the United States, the President of the Senate and the Speaker of the House of Representatives of Congress, the Senators and Representatives representing the state of Idaho in the Congress of the United States, the Governors of the fifty states of the United States and to the Basque government in exile in France.

House Joint Memorial No. 14
Boise, March 13, 2002

A Joint Memorial to the President of the United States, the Secretary of State of the United States, the Senate and House of Representatives of the United States in Congress assembled, the Congressional Delegation representing the State of Idaho in the Congress of the United States, the President of the Basque Autonomous Government, the French Prime Minister, the Spanish Prime Minister and the King of Spain.

We, your Memorialists, the House of Representatives and the Senate of the State of Idaho assembled in the Second Regular Session of the Fifty-sixth Idaho Legislature, do hereby respectfully represent that:

WHEREAS, during the early part of the twentieth century, a wave of Basque immigrants left a stretch of coastline along the Bay of Biscay destined for the state of Idaho where many initially found work as sheepherders in the ranges and pastureland of Idaho; and,
WHEREAS, the state of Idaho has long since been known as the North American center of the Basque population and many citizens of the state have kept close ties to the homeland of their forefathers; and,
WHEREAS, in the year 1972, the Senate and House of Representatives of the State of Idaho assembled in the Second Regular Session of the Forty-first Idaho Legislature passed Senate Joint Memorial No. 115 condemning the totalitarian dictatorship of Franco and insisting on total general amnesty for all Basques and Spaniards imprisoned or exiled for their political and social activities; and,
WHEREAS, the Basque people are the oldest indigenous people in western Europe and have a long history of personal accomplishment and a devotion to the preservation of their national heritage; and,

WHEREAS, the Basque homeland was claimed in the mid-seventeenth century by the emerging nation states of Spain and France and is now divided into seven provinces, four of which are located in Spain and three of which are located in France; and,
WHEREAS, notwithstanding this division, the Basque people have sought to maintain their autonomous culture, their ancient language and their self-government; and,
WHEREAS, despite conflicts associated with the configuration of the Basque Country and its relationship with the Spanish and French states, all but a marginalized fraction of Basques oppose all incidents of violence.

NOW, THEREFORE, BE IT RESOLVED by the members of the Second Regular Session of the Fifty-sixth Idaho Legislature, the House of Representatives and the Senate concurring therein, that the state of Idaho calls for an immediate cessation of all violence occurring in and near the Basque homeland, and that a peace process be immediately undertaken between the governments of Spain and France, the Basque Autonomous Government, and other groups committed to peace.

The state of Idaho further supports the right of the Basques to self-determination.

2

BE IT FURTHER RESOLVED that the Chief Clerk of the House of Representatives be, and she is hereby authorized and directed to forward a copy of this Memorial to the President of the United States, the Secretary of State of the United States, the President of the Senate and the Speaker of the House of Representatives of Congress, the congressional delegation representing the State of Idaho in the Congress of the United States, the President of the Basque Autonomous Government, the French Prime Minister, the Spanish Prime Minister and the King of Spain.

House Joint Memorial No. 26

Boise, April 12, 2006

In the House of Representatives
House Joint Memorial No. 26
By Ways and Means Committee

A Joint Memorial to the Senate and House of Representatives of the United States in Congress assembled, and to the Congressional Delegation representing the State of Idaho in the Congress of the United States, the President of the Government of the Basque Autonomous Region of Spain, the Prime Minister of Spain, and the Prime Minister of France.

We, your Memorialists, the House of Representatives and the Senate of the State of Idaho assembled in the Second Regular Session of the Fifty-eighth Idaho Legislature, do hereby respectfully represent that:

WHEREAS, during the early part of the twentieth century, a wave of Basque immigrants left the Basque region of northern Spain and southern France to come to Idaho and other states of the American West; and
WHEREAS, the state of Idaho has long been known as the North American center of the Basque population and many citizens of this state have kept close ties to the homeland of their forefathers in the Basque region of Spain and France; and
WHEREAS, from the time of the government of Francisco Franco of Spain until the present, the Basque Homeland has experienced decades of terror and violence in large part due to a group organized under the name of Euskadi ta Askatasuna (ETA); and
WHEREAS, in the year 1972, the Second Regular Session of the Forty-first Idaho Legislature adopted Senate Joint Memorial No. 115, condemning the government of Francisco Franco of Spain and urging peace and democracy in the Basque Homeland of Spain; and

WHEREAS, in the year 2002, the Second Regular Session of the Fifty-sixth Idaho Legislature adopted Senate Joint Memorial No. 114, which condemned ETA and all other terrorist organizations operating in the world and expressed strong support for an immediate end to violence in the Basque Homeland and for the establishment of peace through all lawful means; and

WHEREAS, Senate Joint Memorial No. 114, 2002, condemned all acts of terrorism and violence committed by any and all organizations and individuals within the Basque Homeland and throughout the world, such as ETA; and

WHEREAS, on March 22, 2006, ETA announced that it is permanently ending its campaign of violence and laying down its arms; and

WHEREAS, the governments of the Basque Autonomous Region and Spain have vigorously and endlessly opposed violence in the Basque Homeland and have engaged in an active effort to end the violence and establish a lasting peace.

NOW, THEREFORE, BE IT RESOLVED by the members of the Second Regular Session of the Fifty-eighth Idaho Legislature, the House of Representatives and the Senate concurring therein, that the state of Idaho recognizes ETA's decision to lay down its arms and commends and congratulates the governments of the Basque Autonomous Region and of Spain and all other parties in Spain and France for their actions to promote the cessation of violence and to achieve a lasting peace in the Basque Homeland and all of Europe.

2

BE IT FURTHER RESOLVED that the state of Idaho extends its encouragement and support to these governments in their ongoing efforts to establish a process to bring a lasting peace in accordance with the democratic voting process, as well as enhance an appropriate degree of governmental autonomy for the Basque Homeland of Spain.

BE IT FURTHER RESOLVED that the Chief Clerk of the House of Representatives be, and she is hereby authorized and directed to forward a copy of this Memorial to the President of the Senate and the Speaker of the House of Representatives of Congress, and the congressional delegation representing the State of Idaho in the Congress of the United States, the President of the Government of the Basque Autonomous Region of Spain, the Prime Minister of Spain, and the Prime Minister of France.

Senate Joint Memorial No. 14

Boise, March 26, 2012

In the House of Representatives
Senate Joint Memorial No. 14
By State Affairs Committee

A Joint Memorial to the President and Secretary of State of the United States, to the Senate and House of Representatives of the United States, to the Congressional Delegation representing the State of Idaho in the United States, the Prime Minister of Spain, the President of France, the President of the Government of the Basque Autonomous Community, and the President of the Foral Government of Navarre.

We, your Memorialists, the Senate and House of Representatives of the State of Idaho assembled in the Second Regular Session of the Sixty-first Idaho Legislature, do hereby respectfully represent that:

WHEREAS, the state of Idaho is a North American center of the Basque population and many of those citizens of this state have kept close ties to the homeland of their forefathers; and

WHEREAS, from the time of the government of the last dictatorship in Spain until the present, the Basque Country has experienced decades of terrorism and violence; and

WHEREAS, in 1972, the Second Regular Session of the Forty-first Idaho Legislature adopted Senate Joint Memorial No. 115, condemning the government of the last dictatorship in Spain and urging peace and democracy in the Basque Country; and

WHEREAS, in 2002, the Second Regular Session of the Fifty-sixth Idaho Legislature unanimously adopted Senate Joint Memorial No. 114, which condemned all terrorist organizations operating in the world and specifically the terrorist organization Euskadi 'ta

Askatasuna (ETA) in Spain and expressed strong support for an immediate end of all violence in the Basque Country for the establishment of peace and freedom through all democratic and lawful means as well as the recognition of the right to self-determination;

WHEREAS, in 2006 the Second Regular Session of the 58th Legislature adopted Senate Joint Memorial No. 26, which condemned all acts of terrorism and violence by all organizations and individuals within the Basque Country and throughout the world; and

NOW THEREFORE BE IT RESOLVED by the members of the Second Regular Session of the Sixty-first Idaho Legislature, the Senate and House of Representatives concurring therein, that the state of Idaho recognizes and commends ETA's statements of a definitive cessation of its armed activity and end to terrorism, and further commends the governments of Spain, France, the Basque Autonomous Community and Navarre for their actions to promote dialogue on the future of the Basque territories and achieving a lasting peace.

BE IT FURTHER RESOLVED that the state of Idaho extends its encouragement and support to their democratic governments in their ongoing efforts to establish a negotiation process to create a lasting peace, to recognize all victims of terrorism, and to consider all democratic forms of referenda on the constitutional future of the Basque territories.

BE IT FURTHER RESOLVED that the Chief Clerk of the House of Representatives be, and she is hereby authorized and directed to forward a copy of this Memorial to the President and Secretary of State of the United States, to the President of the Senate and the Speaker of the House of Representatives of Congress, to the congressional delegation representing the State of Idaho in the Congress of the United States, the Prime Minister of Spain, the President of France, the President of the European Parliament, the President of the Basque Autonomous Community, and the President of Navarre.

Answer by 180 scholars to the article written by Keith Johnson in the Wall Street Journal in November 2007

Sunday, November 18, 2007

Dear friends from the Wall Street Journal,

Please accept this article written, approved and signed by 180 individuals, representing twenty different institutions, media, and universities in eight countries. We are scholars, researchers, writers, librarians and professionals whose paramount objective is to correct the misinformation and inaccuracies of the Keith Johnson article regarding the Basque language. Among us, there are specialists in linguistic legislation, sociolinguistics, minority languages and endangered languages. We also represent different aspects of science, from nuclear physics to cellular biology and we conduct our investigations and publish our research in Basque among other languages. One eminent politician is included in the list, Pete T. Cenarrusa, former Secretary of State of Idaho (1967-2003) for the Republican Party. Mr. Johnson's piece has ignited an international network of specialists who believe a resolute and official retraction is appropriate and required from the Wall Street Journal out of respect to its readers and minority peoples around the world.

We would suggest a supplementary follow-up article, based on facts and data which we would be more than happy to facilitate from the European Union, the EBLUL, the United Nations, the EUSTAT and numerous scholarly research projects conducted in the Basque territories and those with minority language users around the world. Our attached statement gives an indication of the gross errors introduced into the minds of your readers when

Mr. Johnson's article was given front page status. The corrections and amplifications of November 7, 8 and 15 included in the online version of the WSJ are not sufficient; nor the article "Euskera, the Very Ancient Basque Language, Struggles for Respect", published on November 16. Indeed, the readers are the ones who deserve respect. We would hope that our statement or another article be published also on the front page, demonstrating that corrections are given equal importance to previously published erroneous and misrepresentative stories. The WSJ must maintain its reputation of international excellence and serve as an example of responsibility, dependability and accuracy in journalism.

We are making a public request to you. This letter and your response to it will be published in several American and international academic journals, in the Basque, Catalan and other presses, and for many years to come in the future research conducted in sociolinguistics and endangered group identity issues. We are certain the WSJ will accept the obligation to correct itself and we look forward to collaborating and being a part of a solution by writing a new guest article for you, or assisting Mr. Johnson in writing a follow-up piece.

We look forward to your response and a discussion of possibilities for a positive outcome.

Sincerely,

****

The Basque Language among other worldwide endangered languages

Having read the article entitled "Basque Inquisition: How Do You Say Sheepherd in Euskera? Through Fiat, Separatists Bring Old Tongue to Life..." published on November 6, we enclose an answer based on the facts and the laws of the Basque Country, since it seems that the author of the article has based it on only one biased testimony without any further research and without a minimum knowledge of the facts.

Let's start with the map; the article includes a really "original" map of the Basque Country according to which the Basque Country is about 550 miles (880 kilometers) wide. Without looking any further than Google, you will find out that the Basque Country is not even 100 miles wide.

Now to focus on the main idea of the article: Mrs. Esquivias, a math teacher at a school in the Basque Country, is going to be dismissed from her job if she does not learn Basque.

This is simply false.

The Spanish constitution states in its preamble that it will *protect all Spaniards and peoples of Spain in the exercise of human rights, of their culture and traditions, languages and institutions.* Article 3 states as well that:

1. *Castilian is the official Spanish language of the State. All Spaniards have the duty to know it and the right to use it.*
2. *The other Spanish languages shall also be official in the respective Self-governing Communities in accordance with their Statutes.*
3. *The richness of the different linguistic modalities of Spain is a cultural heritage which shall be specially respected and protected.*

According to Spanish law, every Spanish citizen has the right and the duty to know Spanish and only the right to know Basque, Catalan or other official languages of the Spanish state.

By virtue of this constitutional rule and according to the Law 10/1982 of November 24, on the normalization of the Basque language (article 14.2), *the authorities will determine the places for which it is prescriptive to know both languages* (Spanish and Basque). That is to say, there are certain positions for which it would be compulsory to know "both languages" (Basque and Spanish). An example of these positions is "Basque language teacher," for which, as everyone will understand, it is compulsory to know Basque. The law 10/1982 was reviewed and approved by the Spanish Constitutional Court, the institution in charge of examining the adaptation of the laws to the Constitution. (Anyone can search the resolution 82/1986, on June 26, by the constitutional court on the internet, available only in Spanish).

The law that determines the use of both languages (Spanish and Basque) at any public job in the Basque Autonomous Community (BAC) is the *Basque Civil Service Law, la Ley de Función Pública Vasca* 6/1989, of June 6, according to which each one of the positions in the Basque administration will have a "Linguistic Profile" (LP). Based on the requirements of the job, it will be necessary or not for the person applying for the position to know Basque, but it will always be compulsory to know Spanish, for it is a constitutional requirement (article 3.1). By virtue of the requirements for each job, there are four different LPs: LP1, LP2, LP3 and LP4 (LP1 being "no knowledge of Basque" and LP4 being "full knowledge of Basque"). Each public job at the BAC has been assigned an LP. It could happen that according to the requirements of the job, the requisite linguistic profile may change from LP1 to LP2. in In such a case the public officer may either increase their [his/ her] proficiency in Basque or be transferred to another position in which he/she maintains his/her LP. However, he/she would never lose his/her job. Another serious error in Johnson's article.

There are two fields of the BAC administration that are out of the LP system: health care and law enforcement (police). In neither case is it required to know Basque or to have a basic LP in Basque.

In the specific case of Mrs. Esquivias (education) there are only two existing LPs: LP1 (only Spanish is required) and LP2 (Spanish and Basque are required). In this specific case LP2 is required when the class has to be taught in Basque (Basque language or any other subject to be taught in Basque). The law that regulates the LPs in education is the Decree 47/1993, of March 9, and anyone can find it in the internet (http://www.euskadi.net/cgiin_k54/ver_c?CMD=VERDOC&BASE=B03J&DOCN=000009334&CONF=/config/k54/bopv_c.cnf).

The problem Mrs. Esquivias has is not that she is going to be removed from her job if she does not learn Basque (This is as false as it is illegal), but that she is running out of students. Most of the students are taking math in Basque. In other words, more and more students are electing to have math taught in Basque and not in Spanish, so there is a need for Basque-speaking math teachers. However, according to the law, Mrs. Esquivias cannot be removed from her job for not learning Basque.

Indeed, she has the opportunity to take a two year sabbatical, with full salary, in order to learn Basque. She has elected to do so, not because it has been imposed to her (which would be illegal under Spanish law), but because she has elected to do so. To suggest otherwise should be considered an exaggeration or a plain lie.

Moreover, the author should have added that the Basque language is completely banned in public administration (including, naturally education) in the southern part of the Chartered Community of Navarre (CCN), more precisely in the area named the "non-Basque speaking zone." The author should have mentioned that in the Basque territories of the French state (*Pays basque*) the Basque language is not official at all.

However, apart from the main point of the article, which is that "Basque inquisitors are abolishing the right of citizenship to speak Spanish," which, in our opinion, can only be said from a complete ignorance of the rule of law or with a clear political bias, the article makes comments on several linguistic or sociolinguistic principles that have to be clarified.

The author of the article states that only 630,000 people speak Basque while 450 million speak Spanish. We can be certain that the author does not mean by that that it is not worth it to speak or to learn Basque... For, according to that line of reasoning, we all should be speaking Chinese or Portuguese, or maybe English. However, again, the data are quite inexact perhaps because, even if the author does not cite the source of information being used, data as old as that of 1996 has been used to write the article. In any case, in 1996, the Basque Country had nearly 3,000,000 inhabitants (accurately 2,098,055 of them living at the BAC) and according to the official statistics in 1996, 60% of the population in the BAC had an average or good mastery of Basque (far from the 30%

expressed in the article). The statistics by Eustat and other agencies are available on the internet. No further research was necessary in order to have accurate data for 2007: http://www.eustat.es/indice.asp?idioma=i and almost everything is available in English. There is no excuse not to know. Statements such as "Euskera just isn't used in real life" are quite an exaggeration or simply a lack of knowledge of contemporary reality.

From the point of view of the history of language (concretely history of semantics) the statement expressing that words such as "Airport, science, Renaissance, democracy, government, and independence," are all newly minted words with no roots in traditional Basque, is certainly curious. Clearly, the author does not know Basque, for he does not know that "Renaissance" is "Berpizkunde" in Basque, or "govern" is "jaurlaritza" or "independence" is "askatasuna." As for the rest of his examples, it is noteworthy that "airport" is "aeropuerto" in Spanish, "aéroport" in French, "aeroporto" in Italian, "aeroporto" in Portuguese... and so on. "Democracy" is "democracia" in Spanish, "démocratie" in French, "demokratie" in German, "democrazia" in Italian, "democracia" in Portuguese... and so on. But, is not that the beauty of language? Is not it delightful to have words like "democracy" or "telephone" or "penicillin" constructed with ancient Latin and Greek roots? Over the centuries, languages have given words to each others and the author may not know that Spanish words such as "bizarro" (bizarre in English), "izquierda" (left), "chalupa" (boat), "escarcha" (frost), "landa" (field), "mozo" (guy), "sidra" (cider), "silueta" (silhouette) or "zoquete" (silly), among some 200 others, are of Basque origin. Should not communication among languages and cultures be celebrated? Should not human civilization promote the exchange of knowledge instead of defending isolationism? We are sure that more than one specialist in semantics would answer affirmatively.

It is simply sad to hear Basque referred to as "an ancient language little suited to contemporary life...." We lament knowing that there are still people defending the idea that there are classes among languages; that some languages are fossils that no longer evolve. Everything evolves in life; we are sure that all Basque people who work in schools, Basque writers who have had their original Basque novels translated into more than 30 languages (Atxaga...), Basque engineers working at technology industries (Mondragon, CAF...), people working at the edge of technology in the Aeronautic industry (Aernnova, ITP, Sener, MTorres...) or even developing revolutionary scientific theories in Basque (Etxenike...) would take issue with Mr. Johnson's statement. Moreover, people living in Basque every single day of their lives may think it erroneous to state that to say "I love you" in ancient Basque is no longer "suitable." But we all know who Leopoldo Barreda is (not Barrera as it appears in the article, another error) and what political party he works for.

We hope that the author of the article has read, one by one, Basque textbooks before formulating the accusation that "Basque-language textbooks used in schools never tell students that the Basque Country is part of Spain." And, if he has, we suggest he should do it again. He may find himself quite wrong.

Also, the author should review a few books and archives on Basque history, as the statement "Basque separatists have been waging a struggle for independence from Spain for 39 years..." appears to be some 200 years off. In fact, the government of Gipuzkoa asked for independence in 1793, almost 214 years ago, more accurately the claim for independence in the Basque country is as old as the Spanish and the French states. Just another error.

We are sure that the *Wall Street Journal* demands accuracy, seriousness and responsibility from its collaborators because the *raison d'être* of an article is to inform and to provide precise, correct and exact data. We hope that the errors of this politically biased article will be corrected.

Following 180 Signatures

Selected readings (in English)

Aguirre Lecube, Jose Antonio, *Escape via Berlin: Eluding Franco in Hitler's Europe*, University of Nevada Press, Reno, 1991.

Aguirre Lecube, Jose Antonio, *Freedom Was Flesh and Blood*, Victor Gollancz, London, 1945.

Ahedo Gurrutxaga, Igor, *The Transformation of National Identity in the Basque Country of France, 1789-2006*, Center for Basque Studies, Reno, 2008.

Aldecoa, Francisco, Keating, Michael, *Paradiplomacy in Action: The Foreign Relations of Subnational Governments*, F. Cass, London and Portland, 1999.

Alexander, Yonah; Swetnam, Michael S.; Levine, Herbert M., *ETA: Profile of a Terrorist Group*, Transnational Publishers, Ardsley (NY), 2001.

Alonso, Andoni; Oiarzabal, Pedro J. (Eds.), *Diasporas in the New Media Age: Identity, Politics, and Community*, University of Nevada Press, Reno, 2010.

Anderson, Wayne, *The ETA: Spain's Basque Terrorists*, Rosen Pububllications Group, New York, 2003.

Arenillas, José María, *The Basque Country: The National Question and the Socialist Revolution*, I.L.P. Square One Publications, Leeds, 1973.

Aretxaga, Begoña et al., *Empire & Terror: Nationalism/Postnationalism in the New Millennium*, Center for Basque Studies, University of Nevada, Reno, 2005.

Aretxaga, Begoña, *States of Terror: Begoña Aretxaga's Essays*, Center for Basque Studies, University of Nevada, Reno, 2005.

Atwater, Kevin, *Ethnic Identity in a Divided Territory: The Geography of Basque Nationalism*, Master's thesis, Maxwell Graduate School of Citizenship and Public Affairs, Unpublished, 1988.

Azpilikoeta; Casañas, Luis; Sobrino, Pedro, *The Basque Problem, as Seen by Cardinal Goma and President Aguirre*, Basque Archives, New York, 1939.

Bacon, John F., *Six Years in Biscay, Comprising a Personal Narrative of the Sieges of Bilbao in June 1835, and Oct. to Dec. 1836 and of the Principal Events which Occurred in that City and the Basque Provinces*, Smith Elder and Co., London, 1838.

Balfour, Sebastian; Quiroga, Alejandro, *The Reinvention of Spain: Nation and Identity since Democracy*, Oxford University Press, Oxford and New York, 2007.

Balfour, Sebastian (Ed.), *The Politics of Contemporary Spain*, Routledge, London and New York, 2005.

Barahona, Renato, *Vizcaya on the Eve of Carlism: Politics and Society, 1800-1833*, University of Nevada Press, Reno, 1989.

Bard, Rachel, *Navarra, the Durable Kingdom*, University of Nevada Press, Reno, 1982.

Bell, Adrian, *Only for Three Months: The Basque Children in Exile*, Mousehold Press, Norwich, 1996.

Berberoglu, Berch, *The National Question: Nationalism, Ethnic Conflict, and Self-determination in the 20th Century*, Temple University Press, Philadelphia, 1995.

Bew, John; Frampton, Martyn; Gurruchaga, Íñigo, *Talking to Terrorists: Making Peace in Northern Ireland and the Basque Country*, Columbia University Press, New York, 2009.

Bilbao, Jon, *Basque Nationalism in Present-Day Spain*, Basque Studies Program, Reno, 1974.

Blinkhorn, Martin, *Carlism and Crisis in Spain, 1931-1939*, Cambridge University Press, Cambridge and New York, 1975.

Bourne, Angela K., *The European Union and the Accommodation of Basque Difference in Spain*, Manchester University Press, Manchester and New York, 2008.

Bowers, Claude G. *My Mission to Spain: Watching the Rehearsal for World War II*, Simon and Schuster, New York, 1952.

Bray, Zoë, *Living Boundaries: Frontiers and Identity in the Basque Country*, P.I.E.-P. Lang, Brussels, 2004.

Broin, Eoin Ó, *Matxinada: Basque Nationalism & Radical Basque Youth Movements*, Left Republican Books, Belfast, 2003.

Büttner, Wolfgang, *Corsica and the Basque Country: A Comparative Conflict Analysis*, Ibidem-Verlag, Stuttgart, 2001.

Carnarvon, Henry J. G. Herbert Earl of, *Review of the Social and Political State of the Basque Provinces: With a Few Remarks on Recent Events in Spain*, J. Murray, London, 1836.

Chaffee, Lyman G., *Political Protest and Street Art: Popular Tools for Democratization in Hispanic Countries*, Greenwood Press, Westport, 1993.

Chapman, Sandra, *Report on the Basque Conflict. Keys to Understanding ETA's permanent ceasefire* [electronic resource],[266] Lokarri. Citizen Network for Agreement and Consultation, 2006.

Clark, Robert P., *Negotiating with ETA: Obstacles to Peace in the Basque Country, 1975-1988*, University of Nevada Press, Reno, 1990.

Clark, Robert P., *The Basque Insurgents; ETA, 1952-1980*, University of Wisconsin Press, Madison, 1984.

Clark, Robert P., *The Basques: The Franco Years and Beyond*, University of Nevada Press, Reno, 1979.

Conversi, Daniele, *The Basques, the Catalans, and Spain: Alternative Routes to Nationalist Mobilization*, University of Nevada Press, Reno, 1997.

Corcuera Atienza, Javier, *The Origins, Ideology, and Organization of Basque Nationalism, 1876-1903*, Center for Basque Studies, University of Nevada, Reno, 2006.

Coverdale, John F., *The Basque Phase of Spain's First Carlist War*, Princeton University Press, Princeton, 1984.

Da Silva, Milton, "Modernization and Ethnic Conflict: The Case of the Basques", *Comparative Politics*, Vol. 7, No. 2 (Jan., 1975), pp. 227-251.

Da Silva, Milton, *The Basque Nationalist Movement: A Case Study in Modernization and Ethnic Conflict*, Ph.D. thesis, University of Massachusetts, Unpublished, 1972.

Darby, John P.; Mac Ginty, Roger, *The Management of Peace Processes*, Palgrave, New York, 2000.

Díez Medrano, Juan, *Divided Nations: Class, Politics, and Nationalism in the Basque Country and Catalonia*, Cornell University Press, Ithaca, 1995.

Douglass, William A., *Global Vasconia: Essays on The Basque Diaspora*, Center for Basque Studies, University of Nevada, Reno, 2006.

Douglass, William A. (ed.), *Basque Politics and Nationalism on the Eve of the Millennium*, Basque Studies Program, University of Nevada, Reno, 1999.

---

266   Available at: www.lokarri.org/files/File/PDF/Inform.pdf?

Douglass, William A. (ed.), *Essays in Basque Social Anthropology and History*, Basque Studies Program, University of Nevada, Reno, 1989.

Douglass, William A. (ed.), *Basque Politics: A Case Study in Ethnic Nationalism*, Basque Studies Program, University of Nevada, Reno, 1985.

Douglass, William A., Da Silva, Milton, *Basque Nationalism*, Basque Studies Program, University of Nevada, Reno, 1971.

Eiguren, Joseph, *The Basque History: Past and Present*, J. Eiguren, Nampa (ID), 1973.

Eriksson, Johan, *Partition and Redemption: A Machiavellian Analysis of Sami and Basque Patriotism*, Umeå University, Dept. of Political Science, Umeå, 1997.

Espiau Idoiaga, Gorka, *The Basque Conflict: New Ideas and Prospects for Peace* [electronic resource],[267] U.S. Institute of Peace, Washington, 2006.

Fereday, Lynne, *The Basques: Preservation of a Culture: A Study of Basque Language and Culture Preservation during the Romanization of the Iberian Peninsula (218 B.C. to 476 A.D.)*, Lynne Fereday Scholarship Memorial, Boise, 1971.

Flynn, M. K., *Ideology, Mobilization and the Nation: The Rise of Irish, Basque, and Carlist Nationalist Movements in the Nineteenth and Early Twentieth Centuries*, Macmillan Press, New York, 2000.

Foster, Charles, *Nations without a State: Ethnic Minorities in Western Europe*, Praeger, New York, 1980.

Gallop, Rodney, *A Book of the Basques*, Macmillan and co. Limited, London, 1930.

Guibernau i Berdún, Montserrat, *Nations without States: Political Communities in a Global Age*, Blackwell Publishers, Cambridge, Oxford and Malden, 1999.

Gunther, Richard, *Politics, Society and Democracy: The Case of Spain*, Westview Press, Boulder, San Francisco, Oxford, 1993.

Gunther, R.; Diamandouros, P. N.; Puhle, H. J. (Eds.), *The Politics of Democratic Consolidation: Southern Europe in Comparative Perspective*, The Johns Hopkins University Press, Baltimore, 1995.

---

[267]   Available at the USIP web site.

Hamilton, Carrie, *Women and ETA: The Gender Politics of Radical Basque Nationalism*, Manchester University Press, Manchester, 2007.

Hannum, Hurst, *Autonomy, Sovereignty, and Self-determination: The Accommodation of Conflicting Rights*, University of Pennsylvania Press, Philadelphia, 1996.

Hayes, Carlton, *The United States and Spain: An Interpretation*, Sheed & Ward, New York, 1951.

Hayes, Carlton, *Wartime Mission in Spain, 1942–1945*, Macmillan, New York, 1945.

Heiberg, Marianne, *The Making of the Basque Nation*, Cambridge University Press, New York, 1989.

Heiberg, Marianne, *Insiders/outsiders, Basque Nationalism*, Plon, Paris, 1975.

Henningsen, Charles F., *The Most Striking Events of a Twelvemonth's Campaign with Zumalacarregui in Navarre and the Basque Provinces*, J. Murray, London, 1836.

Heywood, Paul, *Special Issue on Politics and Policy in Democratic Spain: No Longer Different?*, Frank Cass, Essex, 1998.

Hiriartia, J., *The Case of the Basque Catholics*, Basque Archives, New York, 1939.

Honan, Michael, *The Court and Camp of Don Carlos: Being the Results of a Late Tour in the Basque Provinces, and Parts of Catalonia, Aragon, Castile, and Estramadura*, John Macrone, London, 1836.

Ibarra, Pedro; Irujo, Xabier (Eds.), *Basque Legal Systems*, Center for Basque Studies, University of Nevada, Reno, 2011.

Ibarra, Pedro, *Relational Democracy*, Center for Basque Studies, University of Nevada, Reno, 2008.

Ibarretxe, Juan Jose, *The Future Is Ours*, Center for Basque Studies, University of Nevada, Reno, 2011.

Ibarretxe, Juan Jose, *The Peace Process in Euskadi: President Juan José Ibarretxe Markuartu's Talk at the United States Institute of Peace (USIP)*, Eusko Jaurlaritzaren Argitalpen Zerbitzu Nagusia, Gasteiz/Vitoria, 2007.

Ibarretxe, Juan Jose, *A Political Initiative Aimed at Resolving the Basque Conflict: Peace Proposal Included in the Lehendakari's Address to the Basque Parliament*, 28 September 2007, Eusko Jaurlaritzaren Argitalpen Zerbitzu Nagusia, Gasteiz/Vitoria, 2007.

Intxausti, Joseba, *Euskal Herria: The Country of the Basque Language*, Basque Government's Publication Service, Gasteiz/Vitoria, 1992.

Irujo, Xabier, *Expelled from Motherland: The Government of President Jose Antonio Agirre in Exile (1937-1960)*, Center for Basque Studies, University of Nevada, Reno, 2011.

Irujo, Xabier, Iñigo Urrutia, *A Legal History of the Basque Language (1789-2009)*, Eusko Ikaskuntza / Society for Basque Studies – Stanford University, Donostia/San Sebastián, 2009.

Irvin, Cynthia L., *Militant Nationalism: Between Movement and Party in Ireland and the Basque Country*, University of Minnesota Press, Minneapolis, 1999.

Jacob, James E., *Hills of Conflict: Basque Nationalism in France*, University of Nevada Press, Reno, 1994.

Janke, Peter, *Spanish Separatism: ETA's Threat to Basque Democracy*, Institute for the Study of Conflict, London, 1980.

Jauregui, Gurutz, "National Identity and Political Violence in the Basque Country", *European Journal of Political Research*, 14, 5-6, 11, 1986, pp. 587-605.

Kasmir, Sharryn, *The Myth of Mondragón: Cooperatives, Politics, and Working-class Life in a Basque Town*, State University of New York Press, Albany, 1996.

Kenyon, Quane; with Pete T. Cenarrusa, *Bizkaia to Boise: The Memoirs of Pete T. Cenarrusa*, Center for Basque Studies, University of Nevada, Reno, 2009.

Kimball, James, *Violence and Regionalism in the Basque and Catalan Regions of Spain: No Exit?*, Honors degree thesis, University of Utah, Dept. of Political Science, Unpublished, 1985.

Knippenberg, Hans; Markusse, Jan (Eds.), *Nationalising and Denationalising European Border Regions, 1800-2000: Views from Geography and History*, Kluwer Academic, Boston, 1999.

Kockel, Ullrich, *Regions, Borders and European Integration: Ethnic Nationalism in Euskadi, Schleswig and Ulster*, University of Liverpool Institute of Irish Studies, Liverpool, 1991.

Kurlansky, Mark, *The Basque History of the World*, Walker and Co., New York, 1999.

Larrea, Maria A., Mieza, Rafael, *Introduction to the History of the Basque Country*, Basque American Foundation, Bilbao, 1985.

Selected readings

Laxalt, Paul, *Nevada's Paul Laxalt: A Memoir*, Jack Bacon & Co., Reno, 2000.

Lecours, André; Moreno, Luis (Eds.), *Nationalism and Democracy: Dichotomies, Complementarities, Oppositions*, Routledge, London & New York, 2010.

Lecours, André, *Basque Nationalism and the Spanish State*, University of Nevada Press, Reno, 2007.

Legarreta, Dorothy, *The Guernica Generation: Basque Refugee Children of the Spanish Civil War*, University of Nevada Press, Reno, 1984.

Leoné, Santiago; MacClancy, Jeremy, *Imaging the Basques: Foreign Views on the Basque Country*, Eusko Ikaskuntza / Society for Basque Studies, Donostia, 2008.

Light, Daniel, *The Emergence and Transformation of Basque Nationalism, 1875-1975*, Master's thesis, Carleton University, Unpublished, 1988.

MacClancy, Jeremy, *The Decline of Carlism*, University of Nevada Press, Reno, 2000.

Madariaga, Juan, *Anthology of Apologists and Detractors of the Basque Language*, Center for Basque Studies, University of Nevada, Reno, 2006.

Mansvelt-Beck, Jan, *Territory and Terror: Conflicting Nationalisms in the Basque Country*, Routledge, London and New York, 2005.

Mar-Molinero, Clare; Smith, Angel, *Nationalism and the Nation in the Iberian Peninsula: Competing and Conflicting Identities*, Berg, Oxford and Washington, 1996.

Marcaida, Miren, *Basque National Liberation and the Spanish Regime: Ethnic Separatist Terrorism and the Responses of a Traditional Polity*, Ph.D. thesis, University of Texas, El Paso, Unpublished, 1989.

Mastrovito, Frank, *Basque and Catalan Nationalism: A Comparison*, Master's thesis, Indiana University, Bloomington, Unpublished, 1993.

Mata, José, *Nationalism and Political Parties in the Autonomous Community of the Basque Country: Strategies and Tensions*, Institut de Ciéncies Politiques i Socials, Barcelona, 1998.

Mayo, Patricia, *The Roots of Identity: Three National Movements in Contemporary European Politics*, Allen Lane, London, 1974.

Medhurst, Kenneth, *The Basques and Catalans*, Minority Rights Group, London, 1987.

Mees, Ludger, *Nationalism, Violence and Democracy: The Basque Clash of Identities*, Palgrave Macmillan, New York, 2003.

Mestellan, Jacques, *The Basque Country*, Editions Euskal Herria, Baiona, 1945.

Merry del Val, Alfonso, *Spanish Basques and Separatism*, Burns Oates, London, 1939.

Monreal Zia, Gregorio, *The Old Law of Bizkaia*, Center for Basque Studies/University of Nevada, 2005.

Moreno, Luis, *The Federalization of Spain*, F. Cass, London and Portland, 2001.

Morlino L., *Democracy Between Consolidation and Crisis: Parties, Groups, and Citizens in Southern Europe*, Oxford University Press, New York, 1998.

Moxon-Browne, Edward, *Spain and the ETA: The Bid for Basque Autonomy*, Centre for Security and Conflict Studies, London, 1987.

Muro, Diego, *Ethnicity and Violence: The Case of Radical Basque Nationalism*, Routledge, New York, 2008.

Niño-Murcia, Mercedes, *Bilingualism and Identity: Spanish at the Crossroads with Other Languages*, John Benjamins, Amsterdam, Philadelphia, 2008.

Nolan, John, *Life in the Land of the Basques: A Proud People of Unknown Origin Clings to its Unique Language and Traditional Way of Life in the Western Pyrenees*, Washington D.C., 1945.

Nordberg, Ilkka, *Regionalism, Capitalism and Populism: The Basque Nationalist Party, the PNV, and Politico-economic Power in the Basque Country of Spain 1980-1998*, Finnish Academy of Science and Letters, Helsinki, 2007.

Nuñez Astrain, Luis, *The Basques: Their Struggle for Independence*, Welsh Academic Press, Cardiff, 1997.

O'Broin, Eoin, *Matxinada: Basque Nationalism & Radical Basque Youth Movements*, Left Republican Books, Belfast, 2003.

O'Donnell, Schmitter: Whitehead, *Transitions from Authoritarian Rule: Prospects for Democracy*, Johns Hopkins University Press, Baltimore, 1986.

Ott, Sandra, *War, Judgement, and Memory in the Basque Borderlands, 1914-1945*, University of Nevada Press, Reno, 2008.

Pasture, Patrick; Verberckmoes, Johan, *Working-class Internationalism and the Appeal of National Identity: Historical Debates and Current Perspectives*, Berg, Oxford and New York, 1998.

Payne, Stanley (Ed.), *The Politics of Democratic Spain*, The Chicago Council of Foreing Relations, Chicago, 1986.

Payne, Stanley G., *Basque Nationalism*, University of Nevada Press, Reno, 1975.

Pérez-Agote, Alfonso, *The Social Roots of Basque Nationalism*, University of Nevada Press, Reno, 2006.

Pontvieux, Delphine, *ETA: Estimated Time of Arrest*, Miss Nyet Publishing, Chicago, 2009.

Raushenbush, Richard Walter, *Ethnic Separatism and the Strategy of Terror: A Study of the Basques*, Honors degree thesis, Harvard University, Unpublished, 1981.

Roach, Steven C., *Cultural Autonomy, Minority Rights, and Globalization*, Burlington, Aldershot and Hampshire, Ashgate Publishing Inc., 2005.

Rowe, Vivian, *The Basque Country*, Putnam, London, 1955.

Ruane, Joseph; Todd, Jennifer; Mandeville, Anne, *Europe's Old States in The New World Order: The Politics of Transition in Britain, France and Spain*, University College Dublin Press, Dublin, 2003.

Sabanadze, Natalie, *Globalization and Nationalism: The Cases of Georgia and the Basque Country*, Central European University Press, Budapest and New York, 2010.

Schuster, Katherine; Witkosky, David (Eds.), *Language of the Land: Policy, Politics, Identity*, Information Age Publications, Charlotte, 2007.

Shafir, Gershon, *Immigrants and Nationalists: Ethnic Conflict and Accommodation in Catalonia, the Basque Country, Latvia, and Estonia*, State University of New York, Albany, 1995.

Shain, Yossi (Ed.), *Governments in Exile in the Contemporary World of Politics*, Chapman and Hall, London, 1991.

Southern, Henry, *The Policy of England towards Spain: Considered Chiefly with Reference to "A Review of the Social and Political State of the Basque Provinces, and a Few Remarks on Recent Events in Spain"* [by Carnarvon], James Ridgway and Sons, London, 1837.

Southworth, Herbert R., *Guernica, Guernica! A Study of Journalism, Diplomacy, Propaganda and History*, University of California Press, Berkeley, Los Angeles, 1977.

Steer, George L., *The Tree of Gernika: A Field Study of Modern War*, London: Faber & Faber, 2009.

Steer, George L., *The Tree of Guernica*, Hodder and Stoughton, London, 1938.

Stephens, Edward, *The Basque Provinces: Their Political State, Scenery, and Inhabitants with Adventures among the Carlists and Christinos*, Whittaker & Co., London, 1837.

Sullivan, John, *ETA and Basque Nationalism: The Fight for Euskadi, 1890-1986*, Routledge, London and New York, 1988.

Tangen Page, Michael von, *Prisons, Peace, and Terrorism: Penal Policy in the Reduction of Political Violence in Northern Ireland, Italy, and the Spanish Basque Country, 1968-97*, St. Martin's Press, New York, 1998.

Totoricagüena, Gloria; Urrutia, Iñigo (Eds.), *The Legal Status of the Basque Language Today: One Language, Three Administrations, Seven Different Geographies and a Diaspora*, Eusko Ikaskuntza/Society for Basque Studies, Donostia, 2008.

Totoricagüena, Gloria, *Opportunity Structures in Diaspora Relations: Comparisons in Contemporary Multilevel Politics of Diaspora and Transnational Identity*, Center for Basque Studies, University of Nevada, Reno, 2007.

Totoricagüena, Gloria (Ed.), *Identity, Culture, and Politics in the Basque Diaspora*, University of Nevada Press, Reno, 2004.

Totoricagüena, Gloria, *The Basques of New York: A Cosmopolitan Experience*, Center for Basque Studies, University of Nevada, Reno, 2004.

Totoricagüena, Gloria, *Boise Basques: Dreamers and Doers*, Eusko Jaurlaritzaren Argitalpen Zerbitzu Nagusia, Gasteiz, 2002.

Urla, Jacqueline, *Being Basque, Speaking Basque: The Politics of Language and Identity in the Basque Country*, Ph.D. thesis, University of California, Berkeley, Unpublished, 1987.

Vazquez, Roland, *Politics, Culture, and Sociability in the Basque Nationalist Party*, University of Nevada Press, Reno, 2010.

Vennemann, Theo, *Europa Vasconica, Europa Semitica*, Mouton de Gruyter, Berlin, New York, 2003.

Waisman, Carlos H.; Rein, Raanan (Eds.), *Spanish and Latin American Transitions to Democracy*, Sussex Academic Press, Portland, 2005.

Walton, John, *Doing Comparative Social History: North-West England and the Basque Country from the 1830s to the 1930s: An Inaugural Lecture Delivered at the University of Lancaster on 12 June, 1996*, Leicester University Press, Leicester, 1996.

Selected readings

Watson, Cameron, *Basque Nationalism and Political Violence: The Ideological and Intellectual Origins of ETA*, Center for Basque Studies, University of Nevada, Reno, 2007.

Watson, Cameron, *Basque Nationalism during the Dictatorship of Primo de Rivera, 1923-1930*, Ph.D. thesis, University of Michigan, Unpublished, 1992.

Weaver, Michael T., *Protest, Radicalism and Militancy in Spain's Basque Country: The Basque Nationalist Movement and the Persistent Struggle of ETA*, [electronic resource],[268] Honors degree thesis, College of St. Benedict/St. John's University, 2002.

Woodworth, Paddy, *Dirty War, Clean Hands: ETA, the GAL and Spanish Democracy*, Cork University Press, Cork, 2001.

Zirakzadeh, Cyrus E., *A Rebellious People; Basques, Protests, and Politics*, University of Nevada Press, Reno, 1991.

Zulaika, Joseba, *Terrorism: The Self-fulfilling Prophecy*, University of Chicago Press, Chicago, 2009.

Zulaika, Joseba, *Basque Violence: Metaphor and Sacrament*, University of Nevada Press, Reno, 1988.

---

[268] http://www.csbsju.edu/Documents/Libraries/thesis_1.pdf

Made in the USA
San Bernardino, CA
17 March 2014